The Healing of a Nation

And I John saw the New Jerusalem. . . .
And he showed me a pure river . . . on
either side of the river was there
the tree of life . . . and the leaves
of the tree were for the healing
of the nations.   REVELATION

The
Healing

of a Nation

BY DAVID LOYE

W · W · NORTON & COMPANY · INC · NEW YORK

Dedicated to the memory of
Kurt Lewin and W. E. B. Du Bois

CONTENTS

PART TWO

HEALING THE NATION

PART ONE

The Years
of Sickness
and the Search
for Therapies

CHAPTER 1

Of Sickness and Health:
An Introduction

The year is 1976. The dome of the capitol nearby, and, in the distance, the Washington Monument gleam unbelievably white under the rare blue brilliance of the sky and the heat of the sun. The crowd strains to see the speaker. He is only a head among the far-off ribbons, rosettes, and fluttering banners of red, white, and blue. A loudspeaker squeals. There is a flurry of technicians, the low sound of laughter; from somewhere in the crowd a child cries out; a jet passes overhead. Then the telltale blip of a switch signals

11

a live microphone. A moment of silence, and the small form in the distance begins to speak.

"My fellow Americans. We have arrived at a rare time in our life as a nation. We must pause now, history tells us, to celebrate, for the birthdays of nations come only once every one hundred years. At our beginning it was 1776. One hundred years passed and it was 1876. And now it is 1976. We shall celebrate, yes; throughout our nation, and in a multitude of ways. But celebrations, however jubilant, are short-lived. We must use this occasion for a larger, longer purpose: We must pause to take stock. We must ask of the past where we came from, who we are, what we have aspired to—and what commitments we have made, and how well we have kept them. Two hundred years ago, upon this very ground . . ."

And so the past is sounded. And there are two kinds of questions, and they produce different answers. One kind of question is what can we learn from the past; the answer gives us that ancient but vital and undervalued wisdom known as the "lessons of history." The other kind of question is an increasingly crucial one: We must ask not only what may history teach us, but how may we transcend or transform our history. It was to answer a question of this type, for example, that the nation itself was founded. History showed us that men were ruled by kings and that colonies paid tribute, but our question was: Is this social arrangement right? Our answer was the American Revolution. This response was partly based on past human experience, but it was also partly a bold leap into the unknown, based on the first gleam of modern social science in the minds and words of Baruch Spinoza, John Locke, and Jean-Jacques Rousseau.

Of all the questions of both types we may ask in this age, few are more urgent than those centering upon one old and basic American aspiration that is still unfulfilled: justice for the black man—or, to put it within the much broader context of our guiding metaphor of a search for healing, the question of how we may cure the black and white sickness in America. For amid the clinking of glasses at the nation's bicentennial birthday celebration a specter will be at every elbow—the knowledge that behind the bright faces and the show of friendship there still works among us this insidious, tentacled, destroying thing that after 350 years blacks still experience intensely, and that still feeds steadily upon whites.

History is the casebook of this old disease, but not, of course, the blind white American history that most of us, black and white, have been taught. The casebook of this sickness is only now being written in a new *black* and white history—an outpouring of recent years that has been an eye-opener for whites and blacks alike. But to thrill to its heroes and horrors is not enough. Years ago Santayana noted that those who cannot remember the past are doomed to repeat it. Seldom has this worn truth been thrust home with such vengeance as in the case of black and white in America. For no matter where you dip into the wriggling, bloody body of this history you will generally find some pustulent eruption of the sickness that was decried and fought over and thought ended for all time still at work upon us today.

The abolitionists thought the insane colonization scheme to send the blacks back where they came from was ended with the blood and death of over 622,000 men during the Civil War. Yet a century later the original "ship 'em back to Africa" solution and its separatist variants are still being proposed by rightist whites, by militant blacks, and even by the outgoing president of the American Sociological Association in 1967! [1]

The idea of an innate, genetic black-white difference in IQ was cherished by experts at the dawn of modern social science, for such a theory not only easily accounted for a vast social gap but also justified doing little to close it. Despite the great advance of knowledge over seventy years discrediting this view, and an overwhelming preponderance of expert opinion against it today, this poison was again being injected into the public mind in the late sixties and early seventies by a Nobel prize winning physicist, William Shockley, and a well-known psychologist, Arthur Jensen. [2]

Our bicentennial year itself, 1976, not only evokes the glory of the nation, but also the virus at its worst. For it must remind us of the rounding of our first century, 1876, which brought the end of Reconstruction, the Hayes sellout of 1877, and what only now can be seen quite clearly as the greatest across-the-board failure of leadership in American history. And yet in 1970, amid other danger signals, an American President could nominate and passionately fight for a racist candidate for the Supreme Court and relentlessly pursue a "Southern strategy" to gain the support of demagogues. [3]

And as if this weren't bad enough, still everywhere embracing

us, like a mythic mother's arms, is the comforting and abiding
American belief in a problem-solving process that will automatically find solutions for every deficiency. This mystic process can
neither be hampered nor hurried by the individual, many of us feel,
so even though we may "feel bad about the Negro problem," we
go our way, knowing that it will all work out for the best somehow,
sometime.

Known as Social Darwinism in the late 1800s, and generally
coupled then with the assumption that blacks were members of an
inferior race, this view of a "natural," benign, white-dominant
order to society was thought to be thoroughly discredited by the
turn of the century. Yet this voice of the "dead" still speaks loudly
throughout our land. And even when one turns to the alternative
to Social Darwinism—to the activist vision of society as something
to be changed to fit the needs of man, with the individual as the
key change-agent, a view that lies at the heart of the American
Revolution itself—we find the dismal results of an eternally recurring naïveté. Activism is not new, yet we treat it so. Generally
lacking knowledge of America beyond the narrow periphery of our
own class and time—or any really deep knowledge of ourselves as
human beings—many of us who pride ourselves on being daring
and liberal still see the "Negro problem" as something new in history. And so we agree with the conservative that it must be ap-
roached with cautious baby steps, as though there were nothing to
be learned from our 350-year struggle to free ourselves from the
grip of this awesome social cancer.

Again and again, right down to our own supposedly enlightened
time, through the agony and at times the death of hundreds of
thousands of us, we have learned how to remedy this sickness only
to turn our backs on what we have learned, leaving succeeding
generations to flounder through the same old tracks. Ignorance and
neglect are excusable if there is no alternative. But for almost as
long as the sickness has existed there *has* been an alternative.
Modern social science, weak at first, but since the turn of the century increasingly powerful, has offered us a means both to preserve this knowledge and to apply it to the search for cures.
History, as a bridge between art and social science, has offered us
the potential storehouse, and the fields of psychology, sociology,
anthropology, economics, and political science have offered us

potential mechanisms for converting past wisdom into present therapy.

The vision of social science as not only the discoverer of social truth but the guide to its use in therapy as well, is an old one. It dates back at least to the late 1700s and the incredible Henri de Rouvroy, comte de Saint-Simon. The American historian knows him as one of the French generals who came to our aid during the American Revolution. The social scientist, however, knows Saint-Simon as being more the true "father" of sociology than his disciple, Auguste Comte. And the social philosopher knows him in still another role: as the proponent of the idea that knowledgeable men might make healing interventions not merely into the lives of the troubled individual, but into the troubled lives of societies.[4]

For some time, the "Negro problem" has been of interest to the modern descendants of Saint-Simon and others in the social sciences. But all too often it has been seen only as a "problem," with all the denaturing, abstracting, and depersonalizing that the word connotes. At its worst, this attitude has led in our time to the abuse of social science as a way of defusing and shelving social issues. Horrible as it is, much of the advanced schooling in the social sciences has been directed to the training of workers who are clever in the means of their science, but who lack either the sense of, or the courage or the means to choose, its proper ends. Once they are funded by the agents of the status quo, these well-intentioned workers dutifully insinuate their way into the arena, chloroform the issue and its participants, and then after freeze-drying and pulverizing their captives for analysis, issue a report that is guaranteed to reduce horror to a pallid formula and put alarm to sleep.

But this is only one aspect of the problem. Something larger and more basic works against realizing the social scientific potential for liberating the black and ending the sickness: The overwhelming majority of modern social scientists have been, and are, white; and for all our protestations that this makes no difference, it just isn't so. One has to be there, go there, somehow find the entry point, to realize at last that it is, indeed, easier for a camel to pass through the needle's eye than it is for the white scientist to see through the eyes and feel through the skin of the black man. A few have managed some remarkable empathizing, but this experiential constraint reduces the effectiveness of the white in innumerable ways.

Despite these limitations, modern social science has actually made a tremendous contribution to the ending of the sickness. But because this contribution has seldom been spelled out—the connections made across fields, theory related to practice, the concepts integrated—much of it has gone unnoticed. And the deplorable social consequence has been that far too little of it has been put to use. For the main purpose of social science has been not to bury itself in the particulars of a problem—like racism—but to seek in and out of particulars the general laws that may govern the behavior of men everywhere. And it is out of this central tradition that the basic tools for social therapy have come. In their own way, many of these discoveries are as fascinating as the findings of the new black history. And all too often, they are as generally unknown. Particularly obscure are the workings of experimental psychology, an approach that tries to go beyond personal observation to demonstrate objectively exactly how and why things human happen—and how they may be changed for the better.[5] Broadly interpreted, this approach offers a method for the transcending of history, as we hope the chapters on the life and works of Kurt Lewin will suggest.

But for all our hopes, it would be foolish to think that knowledge alone, whether of history or of social science, will "cure" the black and white sickness. Knowledge can only serve to equip caring, and caring comes from something else. Those who through history have cared about gaining health out of this sickness form a unique body of American leadership. They are that brighter, morally better white and black minority, many of them young but of all ages and classes, who have taken our national purpose seriously and have insisted that others do so, too. It is mainly for them that this book was written. For it is possible that the sickness *can* be ended, and that health *can* be ours, if two very important kinds of knowledge become the intellectual property of this leadership and those it can influence.

One kind of knowledge will come from experiencing our true history as a people, black and white, trying to live together in a new land. As the neurotic seeks release from the bias, the distortion, the hypocrisy, the "not me" of his past through therapy, so we as a people must dredge up the horror of our national past and exorcise it through understanding. However painful the process is, we must work through old repressed events that still vibrate powerfully within our social system and within every one of us living today, and thereby achieve the catharsis, the cleansing, the insight needed to free ourselves from the sickness of "Nigger" and "Whitey," and become simply mutually respectful Americans of a refreshingly different color.

The other kind of knowledge we must possess is of the liberating potential of modern social science. A glamorous and well-publicized physical science has made it possible for us to fly and to eat well and to control birth and to gain the moon. An obscure social science has given us many of the tools we need to reclaim two troubled races and a deeply troubled nation, but few Americans know it. Somehow what is known to a handful of experts—and to most of them only in small pieces bounded by their specialities—must reach out to fire a more general understanding.

One way to do this is to try to bring the two strains together—history and the relevant social science—and that is the plan of this book. Alternating chapters will present a sketch of a particular time in history followed by a look at some basic work in social science that might help us understand what happened during that time. Part I deals mainly with the symptoms, causes, and workings of the sickness, with here and there a glimpse at, or a foreshadowing of, cures. Part II deals specifically with cures—and not merely speculative remedies, but cures that in the main are proven by historical experience or backed up with social scientific theory and rigorous research.

The book is meant for both the general reader and the specialist. The general reader should, by all means, begin with Part I, as it will give him both the historical and the social scientific pilings upon which the last part rests. The specialist, or the activist in a hurry, may want to read the last part first, as it deals directly with matters of great current concern.

As for the terms "cause" and "cure," about which formal social science must be extremely sensitive, we should add this clarification. Our use partly derives from our guiding metaphor, of a search for the means—the therapies, remedies, prescriptions—which may be used to heal this troubled nation. But also it derives from hope —a simple, nontechnical hope that if one can know the causes, one may find the cures.[6]

CHAPTER 2

Some Beginnings

You are a young man out for a stroll with your wife and new baby. The sun is high and hot overhead, but a breeze moves up over the green meadow from the river. It is good to feel the caress of hot sun and cool breeze, you think, as you take a deep breath. And it is good to look upon your wife and child (she smiles now, her eyes large, liquid, intimate, responding to your gaze, the child's head upon her shoulder, his eyes closed, his beautiful small mouth open as he nods, unaware). It is good to feel the solidity of the earth beneath your feet, the openness of the air about you—to sense moving out from you unimpeded the great ranging of self that is your freedom. A grasshopper leaps upon your arm. Instead of trying to squash him or brush him off, you let him remain there, bearing him with some small delight as a jewel of sorts upon your arm, a small, green, jeweled omen of good feeling, good luck, respect for life, who knows?

And then, as you enter the trees, they leap upon you. Their robes are bright, but they stink, these rival tribesmen. You see the white men with them. Your wife screams. Your baby screams. You curse. You struggle. But now your mouth is shattered by a blow, the ropes bite into your wrists. The 300-year nightmare has begun.[1]

They think of you now (and will for years to come) as a dumb beast; but you are to learn far more quickly than they suspect. Already the great historical lesson for blacks about whites is beginning as their workers drag you through the jungle, your neck bound to a long lead rope to which your wife is also attached by the neck, her hands free to carry the baby. The whip flicks as you stumble, and you experience the first surge of a new kind of fear and hatred. Like black beads being strung to form a necklace, more and more victims are added to the rope as the whites and their black helpers work toward the coast. Sometimes the beads go slack on the string and a black body is cut loose to fall to the ground. (Years later men will note an abundance of skeletons along this caravan route.)

A great wailing bursts from you when you see the ocean. The whips cut among you, but all wail, for you have all heard of the magic vessels that bring the white people who give gold for black people. And now you and your wife are stripped naked before a small knot of these white men. They eye you briefly, speaking in a strange tongue; one gestures toward the pair of you; another jerks you from the line; and then, together, the cries tear out of you and you lunge and reel as the glowing iron sears a small, red pattern upon your black flesh.

Why do they do this, you wonder when the pain subsides and you are glad merely to be still alive. Why do they want us, you ask as you are herded aboard the strange great boat and the terrible sea voyage begins. Will they torture us again and then eat us? Will they feed us to some white sea god?

But this speculation is short-lived. By the neck and by the legs you are chained into a small box of wood and flesh—you are pressed, top and bottom, by the wood of shallow decks that are separated by only eighteen inches and you are pressed in from the sides by other chained blacks. You eat what little you can, vomit as the ship heaves, defecate and lie in it, and as your own and the body heat and the stench of the waste of a hundred other blacks presses in upon you, you cease to think, only to exist. Night after night you hear about you the raving and the gasping and the dying. One incredibly hot, becalmed night your child dies. You hear the splash as, like garbage, the small body is flung overside, and your only emotion is a dull sense of relief. You see your wife raped by three white sailors. You try to rage like a man but you can only vomit and look away.

The voyage is not what comfortable modern folk, accustomed to thinking that learning is something confined to schools, would call an "educational experience." Yet it is, and as we shall see very shortly, it was a method of teaching that made use of the most fundamental, thorough, and persistent type of learning known to man. By the time you are dumped ashore in the new America, half-alive, practically everything that was of anchoring value or meaning in your old life has been taken from you, and into your pulp has been beaten one simple and permanent lesson of submission—you must fear and obey the white or die. But also, because you are a man and even in chains you will again breathe clean air and because you are more clever than they think, you have learned another, deeper lesson. You will soon learn to exhibit fear and submission in ways ranging from kneeling and begging to dancing jigs and playing the banjo. But beneath this outward show, you will nurse a deep and abiding hatred of the white, and a deep, abiding, lifelong desire for freedom.

And so, in 1685 (for a suitable year and place), you were hauled into the largest slave market in the middle colonies, Perth Amboy, New Jersey, and you and your wife were sold for the second time to a new white broker with a good eye for bargains in black flesh.

Of course you do not think of yourself as a slavebroker. You do buy and sell a few negroes when other things are slow, but mainly you try to deal in land, and also sometimes whiskey and fine imported linens. You have also farmed a little, growing whatever was scarce and bringing a good price. Once you even advertised a commercial school offering instruction in language and basic skills to immigrants and freed slaves, and served as both promoter and schoolmaster to six pupils. But there proved to be too little profit and you abandoned the venture.

You are, in short, a respectable and—in your own loquacious, persistent, protean way—a fascinating small-time colonial entrepreneur.[2] Not a gentleman, of course. The colonial gentleman with family money has no need to grub for a living. But you, with no background or estate, must win both for yourself by whatever means are within the law (or close to it); and you have learned that if one is to make a pretty penny, or any penny, in this new land, one can't afford to be delicate about the means.

As for buying and selling blacks, you did feel uneasy about it at first. You felt sorry for them, but fortunately you soon realized this was a very green, very poor attitude. You couldn't be a farmer if you winced at branding cattle or castrating pigs, and the principle was the same here. You must learn to see them for what they are, you would say. You must see them not as black men who live like animals, but as black animals who look like men.

You had told yourself and others this so often that at last, praise be, you had succeeded in believing it. Soon, also, you discovered that the view was most effective in sales, and you honed it into an ingenious rationale that had, you didn't mind saying, put many a black into the hands of a previously nervous or uncertain buyer. Once you have learned to look at them as animals, you often explained, the bounteous wisdom of God became apparent. One had to see it this way: The colonial had been given a beautiful and unbelievably fertile new land, lacking only some beast more versatile than the horse to work it and turn it to a profit. A horse had it for strength over most anything but an elephant, but a horse could not chop a tree, or plant seed, or reap crops. So obviously what was needed was something with arms, hands, fingers, and legs, something much like a man, with just enough brain so that you could show it what to do and it would then go on doing it—like turning around at the end of the row and working back on its own, for example. Indians had been tried, but they sickened and died.

Indentured Scotch had been tried, but because they were white they thought they were as good as the master and soon gained their freedom.

What was needed was some form of savage other than the Indian that would be tremendously healthy, and that could be hauled in from some place so far away that he would have no sense of the land being his. Ideally, he would be a savage, strong and ignorant, but so poor where he was that he would look upon the opportunity to work for you all his life as a great boon. And it would be excellent were there a large supply of these creatures, so that as men prospered in this new land there would be no danger of the supply running short. And last (and here your eye would roll toward your prospective buyer and the corner of your mouth would twist with a practiced drollery), it would be nice were they good breeders. It would be a pretty bonus if a man might multiply an investment in only two of them, male and female, into a herd of sorts that could be used or sold, as one wished. This (you would say in closing, clapping the prospect on the back) is why you counseled good gentlemen to buy negroes, God's answer to the colonial's need.

And so you, too, coming to the black and white experience as a young white man, also with a wife and child, had learned your part well. You had learned the use of the frown, the shout, the whip, even hanging if need be, to maintain the lesson of fear taught the black on the slave ship. (You had also learned the immeasurably more powerful and useful knack of looking at a black and seeing only an animal or a subhuman, a means whereby you were to undermine and destroy his aspirations more effectively than with the most brutal of repressions. After 280 years, learned men would give this crushing tool of repression the mild name *expectancy*.)

But you, too, along with the black man you bought for resale, had learned something subterranean. In his singing, in his laughter, in his quickness in certain ways, you were touched by the recognition of a common humanity when your guard was down. And far within you something very small recognized and resonated to the poor black's desire for freedom. And much larger and nearer the surface loomed your fear of him, your fear of retaliation for what you had done to him. And this unsettlement made you savage with him whenever he expressed his hatred or his aspiration, for his voice spoke so dangerously to your own.

Thus began the life of black and white together. Sometimes the scholar, in seeking causes of the black and white sickness, will offer complexities that make it seem that no one can ever hope to solve this great social mystery. But if one goes back to the beginning of the disease one finds something rather obvious and commonplace. It is apparent that at one time there were reasonably healthy whites living lives uninvolved with black slaves, and there were reasonably healthy blacks living lives uninvolved with white masters. And the sickness began when one seized the other and attempted to make a *thing* of him.[3]

There is considerable evidence that the color difference also played an important part. From the very beginning, his blackness in a dominantly white society marked the black man as different, strange and apart to an all-powerful white eye. This was at a glance, consciously. And at a deeper level—within the unconscious, the symbolic layer of the white mind—the association of blackness with evil, lust, and animality, and these associations' triggering of deep fears, also worked against acceptance of the black as a legitimate equal.[4] Many volumes could be expended applying psychology to the historical and present-day meanings and impacts of this fundamental black-white color difference, but this sort of effort always risks obscuring a much more fundamental, much more important fact. The deepest cause, then as now, is situational and obvious: Men hate those who misuse and oppress them, and oppressors fear those whom they have misused. The situation of exploitation, a primary cause, leads to fear and hatred on both sides, and this becomes the loom, the strings, and the shuttle to which the yarn of a basic black and white difference is applied. Thus there is woven through history the strange fabric of symptomatic attitudes that lie behind the increasingly strange symptomatic actions of the victims of the black and white disease.

Starting in 1619, ship after ship hauled in these ideal black people to the colonies. There was, of course, a tremendous job of development at hand, a tremendous need for them. To help meet this need the good queen of England, ever mindful of profit and her colonies, thoughtfully chartered the Royal African Company in 1702 to increase the flow. The slaves then dutifully bred and helped swell the black population to more than three-quarters of a million by 1790.[5]

As the slaves increased in this new land, so grew the need for more sure means of controlling them. After the initial breaking and humbling of the black man in accordance with the uses of terror, another ancient, highly effective social mechanism was put to use: the binding and shaping relation of master to slave. As tiny infants blacks and whites might play together as equals, but through diligence their parents taught each the *role expectations* of inequality —taught one the peremptory or patronizing gestures and other signals considered proper to masters, and taught the other the shuffling, submissive responses considered proper for the slave.

But though the matter might have appeared settled on the surface, beneath the façade of master and of slave old needs and old fears boiled. The underlying black hatred and aspiration erupted into action at least 250 times during this era, although most of these "revolts" were only bubbles of protest that quickly burst when confronted with the might and the increasingly savage repression of the whites.[6] The whites of the time, of course, saw brutal measures as cures for these social eruptions, much as they believed in blood-letting to cure physical ills. Of several bloody years, 1741 is the most instructive for our time. After an especially cold winter marked by strikes and other unrest, two Negroes in Hackensack, New Jersey, "perhaps exhilarated by the returning warmth of spring," burned down several barns.[7] They were caught and burnt at stake—burning at stake being then by law in New Jersey a punishment that could be given for offenses ranging downward from murder and rape to the stealing of as little as five pounds by a slave.[8] Shortly thereafter, with the setting of fires in public places in New York City, an upheaval began that ended with the burning of thirteen blacks, the hanging of eighteen, the hanging of four whites, and the shipping of seventy blacks out of the colony. "The grip of hysteria weakened as the exceptionally hot summer wore on and the jails became insupportably packed with frightened Negroes," noted one commentator.[9]

A milder form of repression, but a more revealing symptom of the workings of the black and white sickness in its early years, was the quiet but pervasive network of repression represented by the law and custom of the time. For example, in 1751 the New Jersey colonial legislature passed an ingenious "Act to Restrain Tavern Keepers from selling strong Liquors to Servants, Negroes and Molatto [sic] Slaves, and to Prevent Negroes and Molatto Slaves from meeting in large Companies, and from running about at Night." This was a "cure" of some sophistication in that it provided for varying strengths of the medicine and for a variety of conditions for its application. To restrain the white tavern keeper it provided for a small fine—and for the black, twenty lashes. He was also to be lashed if he was among more than five slaves found assembled together anywhere. He was also to be lashed if he was caught out on the streets or gone from the slave quarters after nine o'clock at night. To be sure, the Act did exclude the church from its provisions, allowing the slave this form of congregating without punishment. And it would be comforting to think that some touch of humanity accounted for this provision; however, it is doubtful if the usefulness of the church as the promoter of submission had been overlooked by these careful social physicians. The Act also allowed the blacks to congregate to bury their dead without penalty—but only "with their Masters or Mistresses Consent." [10]

It seems a horrible age today, but its brutalities were those of children compared to the sophisticated beastliness that lay ahead in the south—and at least the land in that age was relatively untouched. It was a beautiful land, green-grassed, green-forested. The streams were clear, and beneath a clean sky the rivers ran blue and clean down through the fields, through the new towns and woods, and out into the gull cries, and wings, and the choppy, salty, clean white and blue water of the bays. Mornings might bring the sight of a moose stepping up stilt-legged from the lake. Noon could bring the roar and the darkening of the skies with passenger pigeons. The valleys were days-long adventures by foot and many hours by horse, and there were blue mountains in the distance that would, in time, lure many westward.

It was, like much of the earth even yet, a garden of plenty for all men, could they see beyond the sweep of their own eyeballs, or feel beyond the sweating periphery of their own skins. But rather than see it as a gift to be shared, the colonials were forced by their situation, tradition, their time in history—and by, too, the fundamental zest for conquest and practical creativity—to see the new land as a prize to be won. The strongest would, of course, win the most. The strength that mattered was measured by the number of working bodies—men and animals—one could field in the attack upon the land. So the need grew rapidly for more and more slaves with which one might attack the land and expand one's personal domain. And so grew the need for repression.

To a far greater degree than we care to admit, the individual is shaped by his society. And by such means as this, at the outset, the white taught himself to be a brute, and the black was carefully, steadily, diligently taught to be a dutiful, amiable, harmless, dependably good child, who must never dare dream of growing up to be a man.

CHAPTER 3

Fear Conditioning and Role Imprisonment

It is a long way from colonial America to czarist Russia, but the journey can be enlightening. For at its end stands a man who gave mankind one of its most useful tools for understanding the physiological underpinnings of practically everything we think or do.

This Russian psychological pioneer, Ivan Pavlov, looked somewhat like a more stolid, peasant version of George Bernard Shaw—both sported much the same type of majestic and self-assertive white beard. When Pavlov began his work, Russia was still under

Czarist rule and he was a member of one of the most unusual intellectual communities in history. Up from the ranks of the peasants there had surfaced a number of brilliant young men. They were supported in their work because the need for intellect, wherever it might come from, was recognized. But they were a lonely group, separated by achievement from their people and separated by class and background from the ruling aristocracy. As a group, these young Russian peasants became one of the most exceptionally learned in our time, and it has been speculated that their social loneliness—they had only this self-created intellectual community to call their own, which curiously parallels the situation of today's black collegians—may have accounted for the phenomenal range and intensity of their intellectualizing.

Certainly Ivan Petrovich Pavlov, from the village of Ryazan, was one of their prime exhibits.[1] He was a Nobel Prize winner in 1906. In the memories of most of us he is generally linked with a rather ordinary looking dog in a peculiar harness. But between the two of them, man and dog, an insight into learning was established that is of great relevance to the black situation in America. Pavlov's exceptionally important discovery was the phenomenon now known as the *conditioned reflex*.

The sequence is well known: how he noticed the dog would salivate when shown food; how he rang a bell along with the food; how the dog then salivated to the bell without the food. Like many great discoveries it all seems simple now—and most deceptively so, for Pavlov spent thirty-four years, from 1902 to 1936, exploring the ramifications of this happenstance entering of a fundamental unit of human behavior. It was eventually, for psychology, almost as significant as getting inside the human cell would be for biology. For the linking of stimulus with response to form the S-R unit opened the way into a world of incredibly delicate and meaningful variations, where the slightest of changes in the timing and sequencing of stimuli produces vast differences in behavioral response. Beneath all the repellent experimental paraphernalia existed an almost musical world of theme and variation, to which Edward Thorndike's study of the effect of reinforcement, or reward, added some mighty bass notes.

Of relevance to our search for the causes of the black and white sickness is the early branching of this investigation in two very different directions. One "school" set out to explore the effects of pleasurable rewards, such as food and love and praise—a direction best expressed by the work and views of B. F. Skinner, which he has related to our everyday lives in programmed learning and in his social utopian novel *Walden Two*. This direction might hold something of value for the black and white future, but in regard to the past the other direction that conditioning research took is more revealing. This was the exploration of the dark region of pain and fear conditioning.

Though the name of Pavlov is known to everyone, only graduate students and Russians know about his more colorful professional rival, Vladimir M. Bechterev. This dashing figure introduced the darker side of conditioning experimentation with what is known as the "finger flex" experiment. Using a mild electric shock applied to the forefinger of a hapless student while a bell was being rung, Bechterev conditioned men to flex their finger to the bell rather than the shock. This method became known as aversive or *fear conditioning,* and in extending it through other studies Bechterev became an important early social psychologist and the "father" of modern Soviet psychotherapy.

But the America of Wilbur Wright and Henry Ford was not to be outdone by the Russians in the matter of finding the mechanism in man. Following the parallel pioneering of conditioning studies by Thorndike, and inspired by the first accounts of the Russian work, the flamboyant "father" of American behaviorism, John B. Watson, was soon busy expanding our understanding of what was going on here.[2] In the most startling early demonstration of the power of fear conditioning he placed an eleven-month-old boy named Albert in a pen with a gentle white rat, and then struck a steel bar with a hammer near the boy. As one might expect, Albert was startled by the noise and cried. And after a number of repetitions of this pairing of white rat and banging steel Albert would cry and crawl away at the sight of the rat without the noise. But the truly important Watsonian demonstration was this: Albert would cry at the sight of *anything white and furry,* a rabbit, a white fur muff, even a Santa Claus mask. By such means, Watson had showed how conditioning can generalize to attach a fear to things remote in actuality from the originating fear but associated with it through a similarity of look or sound or feeling.

The Pavlov-Watson-Bechterev approach was later the basis of some ingenious work with rats by experimental psychologist Neal

Miller, and also the basis of a new psychotherapy developed by
Miller, John Dollard and others[3]—an approach based on understanding fear conditioning as the prelude to removing or *decondi-
tioning* fears. Again, two findings by Miller using rats supported
Watson's findings with young Albert earlier: one, that a slight cue
can evoke a mighty fear; and two, that some behavior can be very
baffling if one is not aware of how the fear that lies behind the behavior was originally established. Also, Miller and many others
showed that fear conditioning can establish remarkably persistent
behavior.

The relation to what happened to the black man in colonial
America is straightforward and fundamental. It is evident that
seizure, the horror of the Middle Passage, the branding, beating,
burning at stake, and all the other brutal measures of the time
served much as the electric shock for Bechterev and Miller and
the banging of the steel bar for Watson. They established a massive fear that could then be evoked at will by even the slightest cue
of white displeasure. Why weren't there more slave revolts, some
whites have asked, assuming that they never would have submitted had the roles been reversed. Only by observing—or better
still, experiencing—actual conditioning experiments can one begin
to appreciate the incredible power of the processes involved here.
Perhaps, also, the reminder that conditioning principles were used
in the dramatically effective brainwashing of prisoners by the North
Koreans and the North Vietnamese will serve to make the point.

In the *continuing* suppression of the blacks, generation after
generation, many other mechanisms came into play; but to this
day the effects of fear conditioning can be seen. It is something of
what lies behind the black fear of "police brutality" and the black
sensitivity to the Southern lynching tradition.

We have come a long way from the methods of the slave's
America, but their strength is still discernible in old scar tissue as
well as fresher wounds.

Of Roles and Role Imprisonment: James, Cooley, and Mead

> No more fiendish punishment could be devised, were such a thing
> physically possible, than that one should be turned loose in so-
> ciety and remain absolutely unnoticed by all the members thereof.

> If no one turned around when we entered, answered when we spoke, or minded what we did, but if every person we met "cut us dead," and acted as if we were nonexisting things, a kind of rage and impotent despair would ere long well up in us, from which the cruellest bodily tortures would be a relief; for these would make us feel that, however bad might be our plight, we had not sunk to such a depth as to be unworthy of attention at all.[4]

Perhaps no other passage in all of psychology contains so much insight in such a small handful of words. The writer was William James. It is a recurring wonder how little that has happened in this field since his time can't be found tucked away somewhere in the speculations of the great pragmatist. He speaks here of a feeling eloquent black writers articulate; it is found repeatedly in the works of W. E. B. Du Bois, Ralph Ellison, and James Baldwin. He anticipates the dramatic work of the Canadian psychologist Donald Hebb in what is known as *stimulus deprivation,* of social psychologist Robert Rosenthal in *expectation,* and—in his remarkable torture-seeking insight—the work of countless clinicians from Freud through Erik Erikson. But directly to our purpose at this point, he is stating the basis for the power of the concept of *role,* and *role pairings.*[5]

Originally suggested by James, role theory is now identified with its first developers, Charles Cooley, a shaper of American sociology, and George Herbert Mead, often called the father of American social psychology. The basic idea is familiar to most of us, but its elaboration and phenomenal interpretive power are not. A useful approach to the concept is developmental—that is, to see it as it first comes into and then grows with our lives. So we are born and first learn to play the role of Baby. A face hovers above the crib. It will smile if we coo. It will pick us up or bring food if we scream. And so cooing and screaming become part of the familiar role of Baby, which powerfully determines our actions. But, depending on conditions, this power can be quite transitory. For all their strength, roles are also inherently flexible and disembodied— part of us, yet not a part, like clothes that can be discarded or exchanged as we move and change and grow. Leaving Baby behind, we learn the role of Boy, or Girl. Later still, of Man, or Woman. And along the way we become involved in many other roles—Mother, Father, Doctor, Lawyer, even Rich Man, Poor Man, Beggarman, Thief.

For each of these roles there are certain social expectations. For example, Father does not cry when upset, but Mother does; the Banker does not go to work in overalls, but the Carpenter does; the Beggarman cannot kiss pretty mothers and babies, but the Politician can. Another curious fact about roles is that they often operate in terms of *role pairs*. That is, a Mother is only a Mother in relation to a Son or Daughter. For every Buyer, there must be a Seller; for every Doctor, a Patient; and other familiar pairs include Lawyer-Client, Teacher-Student, Parent-Child, and so on.

One of the most useful things about the concept is that while roles operate so evidently on the individual level, shaping the behavior of each of us, they also tie beautifully into the social system. Role is, in fact, the central linking concept between psychology and sociology for many social theorists. Roles on the individual level are linked to customs, to norms, to mores on the cultural and social levels. In general, these all act as forms of social *expectation* that dictate what one must do to play his roles acceptably in the unavoidably real drama of life. And the important point in this context is the phenomenal strength of these role expectations, which literally draw power from all levels of our existence as human beings. Numerous experiments have demonstrated this power. Indeed, so great is the influence of role expectations on human behavior that *role playing* is used as a method of therapy and attitude change. A timid man who cannot speak up to his boss or talk back to his wife, for example, will be given roles of some ferocity to play to fortify him for handling his troubled areas.

What happens seems to operate like this: We are all somewhat like actors playing to an audience, and we base our idea of our own identity and our self-esteem upon the expectations of an audience of "significant others." This audience, in turn, expects of us certain behavior appropriate to our age, sex, race, class, occupation, and so on, and these expectations are not helter-skelter but are rounded and tied together by the idea of the roles one plays. Notably, then, roles shape not only the action but the actor. As we repeatedly do what is expected of us, over a period of time we tend to become the expectation. The uncertain young soldier becomes the bold veteran, the fumbling intern becomes the skillful surgeon, the legal tyro becomes the clever trial lawyer—and the Negro becomes whatever his role may call for.

Through most of American history the role of Negro has called for one to be submissive, servile, and to accept ignorance and inferiority. A moving demonstration of this in the research setting has been work based on the classic doll-play study of the best-known black psychologist, Kenneth Clark, and his wife, Mamie.[6] The Clarks observed black and white children playing with black and white dolls to see what happened. Out of this type of experiment has come repeated evidence that awareness of racial differences begins around age three and sharpens thereafter, and that both whites and blacks quickly learn to assign to whites the superior and to blacks the inferior roles. This was evidenced by a preference of black children for white dolls, a reluctance among black children to admit even to themselves that they were Negro, and the speed with which both black and white children assigned the poorer houses and the garbageman and servant roles to the Negro dolls.

This is the basis for the debilitating impact of the Master-Slave role pairing on the early white and black Americans. Contrary to the opinion of those who then saw (and still see) this as a natural fact of life—the whites being born naturally to rule and blacks naturally to serve—the roles had to be carefully taught to both parties. No doubt, it was not easy at first, but after a few generations both races settled into the roles with what then began to appear to be natural propensities. This relation also became one of the most characteristic symptoms of the sickness—the peremptory Master gestures, the shuffling Slave responses. And if there should emerge, on either side, a simple impulse to relate to the other as a human being, always the social expectation of role must quickly intrude and cut off any possibility for communication.

Thus, white and black alike were imprisoned by a role, the Master in one world, and the Slave in another, and the gulf between the two worlds deepened and widened.

CHAPTER 4

Freedom?

As we saw in Chapter 2, the white needs of colonial America dictated that the black man must be repressed. His developmental ceiling must be fixed at the level of child or animal. This policy of the Repressor, however, early began to encounter the exasperating activities of that tactless gadfly and social irritant, the colonial Uplifter. Generally backed by the law, the Crown, and the spirit of colonial commerce, the Repressor had good reason for confidence in the belief that his brand of common sense and higher logic would prevail. Still, it was disconcerting to be confronted by these men, mainly economic parasites like ministers and schoolmen, who, by some woolly-headed reasoning, claimed that the black should not be a slave, but free.

The most remarkable of these voices was that of John Woolman of Mt. Holley, New Jersey.[1] A tailor by trade, a clerk and a shopkeeper, Woolman was anything but an impressive figure to an unkind eye. He was small, his bony face had the look and charm of some blunt kitchen instrument, his clothes were of most unfashionable plain homespun, and he sometimes broke down and cried when audiences proved hostile or indifferent to his feelings against slavery. Yet this odd, mild man became the most influential Quaker of his time and America's first bona fide saint.

His impact came from several rare qualities. He was, first, a man of such evident honesty, sincerity, integrity, and consideration for others that few could resist the appeal of such a novelty for the times. But to this almost inconceivable goodness and wholesomeness was added a seer's clarity of vision and passion, and a savant's feeling for logic and style. Within his own time he was chiefly responsible for persuading the Quakers to become the first white group in America officially to renounce slavery. His method was not strident. He was simply quietly (and sometimes tearfully) insistent over a number of years; and he was so skillful in keeping the ear of Quakerdom, and so obviously right, that they finally gave in and let him have it his way.

But the most remarkable thing about Woolman was not his influence on his own time, which was actually quite small, but the timelessness of his appeal. During the early years of the black and white sickness, he saw the problem with a wholeness of vision that few have equalled since. He diagnosed the causes of the disease, carefully noted symptoms and workings, prescribed cures, and even predicted the social disaster that would result if white America did not act decisively in his time to stop the spread of the disease. (His spiritual descendent, the Quaker poet and abolitionist, John Greenleaf Whittier, was convinced that Woolman had predicted the Civil War.) His most characteristic insights were expressed in "Some Considerations on the Keeping of Negroes," a first essay written in 1746 but not published until 1753 (more of this later), and a second essay published in 1762.

For all his famous "simplicity," Woolman is not easy for the modern reader to follow, and his psychological insight is easily overlooked while one struggles with the style. Yet no paraphrase alone does justice to the man. This is what Woolman said in 1746:

> When a people dwell under the liberal distribution of favours from heaven, it behoves them carefully to inspect their ways, and consider the purposes for which those favours were bestowed lest, through forgetfulness of God, and misusing his gifts, they incur his heavy displeasure whose judgments are just and equal, who exalteth and humbleth to the dust as he seeth meet.
>
> Suppose then, that our ancestors and we had been exposed to constant servitude, in the more servile and inferior employments of life; that we had been destitute of the help of reading and good company; that amongst ourselves we had had few wise and pious instructors; that the religious amongst our superiors seldom took notice of us; that while others, in ease, have plentifully heaped up the fruit of our labour, we had receiv'd barely enough to relieve nature, and being wholly at the command of others, had generally been treated as a contemptible, ignorant part of mankind: should we, in that case, be less abject than they now are? Again, if oppression be so hard to bear, that a wise man be made mad by it, Eccl. vii. 7, then a series of those things, altering the behavior and manners of a people, is what may reasonably be expected. . . . These and other circumstances, rightly considered, will lessen that too great disparity which some make between us and them.[2]

Seldom in all the history of this illness has so much been said in so few words. Nor have such observations remained so dismally unchanging. But for the shift in verbal fashions, Woolman's admonition to the affluent whites of his time is remarkably like what the Kerner Riot Commission Report, and John Gardner, Robert Kennedy, and others were saying to the affluent whites of 1967 and 1968.[3] He warns of the social disaster that can attend misuse of their advantages by the socially privileged. Then he proceeds to make the environmentalist case for the degradation of the black— that we are more the product of our status and our surroundings than our protoplasm. This view, it should be noted, has been stated for some time by modern anthropologists, but was extensively explored by research psychologists only relatively recently. Woolman refers to the effect of the Master-Slave role pairing, which we have examined. And then he notes the relevance of other matters affecting blacks that, again, were only recently studied by American social scientists in the context of the needs of the blacks: Cognition, modeling, expectancy—all to be examined during the course of these pages.[4]

Perhaps most remarkable, however, is Woolman's suggestion of how, through conditioning, "the behavior and manners of a people" are gradually changed over time by a series of steps. This not only faintly anticipates an element of Darwin's view of evolution and the Hegelian dialectic, but it is also the basis for the Skinnerian approach to learning, again a relatively recent development. (Known as *operant* conditioning, this Skinnerian advance over "classical" conditioning views learning as the cumulative shaping of an organism by rewarding or not rewarding tiny bits of behavior over extended periods of time.[5])

It would seem that all this would certify that Woolman was not only a prophet, but quite a remarkable one at that. However, he had even more to say of direct relevance to the modern sufferer from this old disease.

"When self-love presides in our minds," he ventures, "our opinions are biased in our favor. In this condition, being concerned with a people so situated that they have no voice to plead their own cause, there's danger of [accustoming] ourselves to an undisturbed partiality, till, by long custom, the mind becomes reconciled with it, and the judgment itself infected." He speaks here of the ethnocentric base for prejudice, not explored thoroughly until the late 1940s and the well-known *authoritarian personality* study by T. W. Adorno and associates. And the final passage, linking self-esteem to the perceptual walling in of oneself, the walling out of others, and the undermining of judgment, embraces a considerable sweep of modern cognitive research and theory, which we will be examining.

Consider the recency of our school desegregation efforts, the infancy of Head Start programs, and, by 1970, the mounting talk of the need for more research into early learning. And in 1754 John Woolman wrote, "And if children are not only educated in the way of so great temptation, but have also the opportunity of lording it over their fellow creatures, and being masters of men in their childhood, how can we hope otherwise than that their tender minds will be possessed with thoughts too high for them?"

By 1970 the notion was again prevalent that if whites might somehow just ignore the "black problem" it would go away. But Woolman's vision was factual and unrelenting. "For while the life of one is made grievous of the rigour of another, it entails misery on both."

Over the course of these pages we will examine the historical evidence of *expectancy,* and of what has become known only within our time of the workings of this powerful social-psychological mechanism. And Woolman said in 1762, "Placing on men the ignominious title, slave, dressing them in uncomely garments, keeping them in servile labours, in which they are often dirty, tends gradually to fix a notion in the mind, that they are a sort of people below us in nature, and leads us to consider them as such in all our conclusions about them."

Also, when the question arises as to why blacks emerged with such difficulty from slavery, while the white slavery of colonial times soon disappeared—or why Scotch, Irish, Jewish, German, Polish, or any other white emigrant groups were able to blend so quickly into mainstream America, in contrast to the "backward Negro"—it is well to be aware of something else Woolman said in 1762. Anticipating a good bit of psychoanalytic insight and neo-Pavlovian research, he observed, "This is owning chiefly to the idea of slavery being connected with Black color, and liberty with White: and where false ideas are twisted into our minds, it is with difficulty we get them fairly disentangled."

It is said that the porpoise has the highest intellect of any living creature other than man, but because he does not have hands he is unable to create social diversity and so must remain a hauntingly lonely intelligence imprisoned within the vastness of the sea. So Woolman seems, over the years, a voice trying to reach an age with knowledge that even in our time is only beginning to be substantiated—and is still not heeded. No wonder he wept. But his tears were not wasted. Within the movement of our history he remains the most striking early appearance of one of the most crucial elements of therapy: bold moral leadership

Another Quaker—Anthony Benezet, a Huguenot who lived in

Philadelphia—was one of the first great figures behind two other major aspects of an emerging therapy. A close friend of Woolman's and a teacher, Benezet founded one of the earliest schools for black children, thus helping establish the therapy of education, so important throughout our history. But Benezet's greater talent was as a publicist.[6] Much as Tom Paine and Samuel Adams were later to play crucial roles in promoting the American Revolution, Anthony Benezet steadily worked upon the Quakers and others with moving and alarming antislavery publications.

The operations are larger today, but the methods and basic approach for this seldom-remarked therapy remain much the same. Benezet simply noted and clipped and built huge files of every scrap of antislavery news or comment he came on over a number of years. Out of this file he then assembled, printed, and widely distributed a fairly steady stream of antislavery booklets and broadsides. And the effect of these little booklets was to arm antislavery advocates with ammunition, and to work upon the conscience of the hapless slaveholding Quakers whom Benezet set out to unsettle.

Something mightier than the antislavery voices, however, was boiling up from the depths to dismay the Repressor. The great white American liberation was stirring. The shots were fired at Lexington, the Declaration of Independence was signed, George Washington took command, the battles were won, and the great, moving, meaningful white history we generally know a little about began to take shape out of the chaos of revolution. Considerably less well known, however, is the extent to which a special feeling for the black was developing among some Presbyterians and Baptists as well as among the Quakers, and how this—and the basic black aspiration itself—became a force of importance in the gaining of American independence.[7] To many the causes were viewed as one, freedom for the white American from British repression being equated with freedom for *all* Americans, black as well as white. As though providence wanted to make the point quite clear, in 1776, as our War of Independence got underway, the Quakers also met in Philadelphia to abolish slavery throughout the entire denomination.

The blending of black and white aspirations in the common cause of freedom is seemingly further emphasized by a far more

famous event in 1776. On Christmas Eve, as George Washington
set out on his well-known trip across the ice floes of the Delaware,
there were two blacks with him—Prince Whipple and Oliver
Cromwell; one can even be found close to him in the famous
painting of the event. Within the next few days, Washington and
his tiny force of 2,400 Americans were to fall upon the British and
the Hessians at Trenton and at Princeton, and with him during
these two crucial battles, so legend has it, were his two faithful
black cohorts.

Behind this comforting vision, however, the old repressions
were at work even in the aspiring nation's finest hours. Sad to say,
the only reason that Prince Whipple and Oliver Cromwell were
with General Washington on that historic Christmas Eve was because Washington had been forced to include them. At the start
of the war in 1775 there had gone out an order over his signature
excluding blacks from service in the new American Army. But the
British, with long practice in the art of manipulating the motivations of suppressed peoples, had seized the opportunity to offer to
free any black slave who would join the British Army. To meet
their threat Washington was forced to countermand his original
order and encourage black enlistment in this first American army.
As a result, out of a total of 300,000 Americans who served in
our War of Independence, 5,000 were black, and they saw action
in every major battle of the war.[8]

Washington's discrimination was, of course, in part a function
of his place and time in history. However, there is more to it than
this, and just as Woolman's feeling for black advancement transcends his place and time, so does the racism of the "father" and
other founders of our nation have aspects that persist to our day.
Washington's personal situation is well known. Before he became
General and President Washington, he was a wealthy slaveholding
Southern plantation owner (and remained so to his death). But his
racism was neither simple nor common, in the terms of today.
While subject to the attitudes of his place and occupation, like
many other whites of good sense and character, he could transcend
the times in being troubled by the practical and moral aspects of
slavery. As a businessman he found its long-range economics questionable, and as a citizen he foresaw nothing but trouble for the
country from this practice, so in conflict with the avowed purpose

of the nation. Thus, Washington as a person was potentially free of racism; if he had been born in a later time and in a different country, he might have avoided it.

But two other aspects of his racism were not so arbitrary. They were, in fact, linked to what are known as *structural* aspects of society because they bind together and support the society. And the relation of Washington and our other founders to these two structural aspects of American racism is of interest because the founders were both shaped by them and incorporated them into the structure of the new nation.

One of these aspects was the basic, white-valuing ethnocentricism that was injected into America by history. By Washington's time the conquest of the Indian that began with the Spanish conquistadors, and the seizure and transport of the blacks as slaves to America, had laid down a firm basis in historical and everyday reality for believing the dominance of the white and the subjugation of the nonwhite to be a natural fact of life. Thus, for the whites of Washington's time, it was literally impossible to be born in America without immediately inheriting this built-in racial bias. It permeated every aspect of the old society and, with very little modification, the new as well. It would have been easier to fly to Mars than to erase immediately this bias from the attitudes, norms, customs, mores, and laws of the new nation; and the grip of this historical fact persists to this day.

The other aspect was political, and it derives from the most passionate conviction of Washington and the other founders. It was the holy cause to which they were willing to sacrifice their lives and often considerable belongings; government not by the fiat of the "enlightened," but with the consent of those governed. The government they created was thus built upon the principles of consensus, of taking action according to the will of the majority, and its social product was to be the result of a compromise of many forces, many interests, many powers. This meant that the fate of the black must be determined by neither the "enlightened" nor the "unenlightened," but by whatever compromise the two might effect according to the new political rules.

The effects of this new arrangement were soon evident. Benjamin Franklin and Alexander Hamilton had founded two of the earliest abolitionist societies, and Franklin was the printer of Wool-

man's great antislavery essays.[9] However, beyond their feelings
and actions as individuals they were public figures subject to the
pressures of compromise that were then, and are today, a fundamental fact of American political life. Thus, they worked diligently
and passionately to help shape and gain ratification of a Constitution that in the end not only failed to end slavery, but even
sanctioned it.

Of these early figures, however, Thomas Jefferson best illustrates
the plight of the leader of intelligence and morality caught in the
sticky web of political and social compromise. Jefferson the humanist wrote a strong condemnation of the slave trade in the first
draft of the Declaration of Independence. But then Jefferson the
public figure was forced to strike it out in order to gain Southern
signatures. In his *Notes on Virginia* this most brilliant of the
American founders at times seems to rival Woolman in his analysis
of the black and white sickness, and even in an apparent sympathy
with black advancement. But for every coin Jefferson the humanist
and moralist had to deposit to the black's credit, Jefferson the
social man took away three. Comparing blacks to whites, he said
of the blacks, "They are at least as brave, and more adventure-
some," but then added, "this may perhaps proceed from a want
of forethought, which prevents their seeing a danger till it be
present. When present, they do not go through it with more cool-
ness or steadiness than whites." [10]

Or again, "It appears to me that in memory they are equal to
the whites." But then he added, "in reason [they are] much inferior, as I think one could scarcely be found capable of tracing
and comprehending the investigations of Euclid: and that in imagination they are dull, tasteless, and anomalous."

The range of Jefferson's mind in appreciating, along with Woolman, the cultural and sociological impact that accounted for
black-white differences is clearly reflected by: "It will be right to
make great allowances for the difference of condition, of education, of conversation, of the sphere in which they move." But then
again he takes it all away: "Yet many have been so situated that
they might have availed themselves of the conversation of their
masters. . . . Some have been liberally educated, and all have lived
in countries where the arts and sciences are cultivated to a considerable degree. . . . The Indians, with no advantages of this kind,

will often carve figures on their pipes not destitute of design and merit. . . . But never yet could I find that a black had uttered a thought above the level of plain narration; never see even an elementary trait of painting or sculpture."

It was in 1787, however, during the forging of our revered central body of law, the U.S. Constitution, that perhaps the one most revealing commentary on the miserable business of reconciling repression with liberative ideals came to be. The question was how representation was to be determined. The delegates from the North, which supposedly was the most humanistic region because it had fewer slaves, wanted to keep down Southern representation. So they insisted that slaves did not count as people; they were merely property. Confronted with the possible loss of voting strength, the Southern delegates then advanced the fervent claim that these black slaves—whom for all other purposes they classified as animals—were indeed people who deserved representation.

The result was the incredible decision to count each slave as three-fifths of a man.[11] It went into print in the body of the Constitution and can still be seen there today (though generally bracketed to indicate a later change by Amendment): The official branding of the black as three-fifths of a man. Even so, hope remained high among the blacks and their supporters that the new freedom was still close at hand. And for a short time following the War for Independence these hopes appeared justified. But the constitutional compromise—and in 1793, the invention of the cotton gin—foreshadowed a crippled hope and a fractional man.

CHAPTER 5

Altruism, Dissonance, and Compromise

How does one account for men like Woolman? For some time in this country it has not been easy because it has been so unfashionable to be good. To the sophisticate, goodness has generally meant the lower-class Salvation Army lass, the upper-class eccentric "do gooder," or the stuffy and suspect middle-class Rotarian. Our one "good" folk hero, Johnny Appleseed, lumbers through history with a foolish smile and an outlandish pot on his head. In our literature Lewis's Elmer Gantry is a slippery con man and

Melville's Billy Budd must stutter and not be very bright. And perhaps it is also worth noting that while most people have a reasonably firm sense of this century's two leading devils, Hitler and Stalin, few know much about its one saint, Mahatma Gandhi.

One reason for the drop in the market value of goodness may be that we have begun to base our attitudes on social science, but the only forceful social science most of us are aware of are the dark cartoons that have been made of the giants Freud, Marx, and Pavlov. And these cartoons are now more than a half-century old. For the cartoon Marx and Pavlov, goodness was something that was stamped into an inherently dumb, passive, or devious organism by the devices of more enlightened souls—into man by a new society and into the dog by conditioning. For the cartoon Freud, goodness was what one did to escape the wrath of a vengeful super ego. It was the thin veneer of culture covering the great, greedy, totally amoral drive of the id. Goodness, along with rationality, was seen as the uneasy work of an ego engaged in a shaky holding action against the onslaught of the id, or as an oily disguise for darker motives.

These dark views were and still are useful assessments of the workings of simple mechanisms and of pathology. But over the past forty years the importance of more complex mechanisms—and the importance of basing psychological theory on health rather than on sickness—has become increasingly apparent. An older, mellower Freud began to move in this direction with his articulation of an aspirational side to man, the ego ideal.[1] Followers such as Erich Fromm and Erik Erikson took off from this point to explore the implications of love and growth into psychological maturity.[2] In sociology, the voices of Prince Kropotkin and, later, of Pitrim Sorokin insisted that man was also motivated by altruism, and there were many other important influences. But perhaps the greatest thrust to this general "exploration-of-goodness" movement has come from a loose gathering of psychologists of many backgrounds into what has been called the "Third Force" view. (Freud being viewed as the first force, Pavlov as the second, and this new trend, the third.) At the core of the movement are a number of very warm, personable, large-souled existentialist psychotherapists like Rollo May and Carl Rogers. A key tenet of their views is that man is not merely a simple product or captive of his back-

46	THE HEALING OF A NATION

ground, but that he is potentially more good than neutral or evil, and that he has been given special equipment to shape himself and his destiny to good ends.[3]

So in a roundabout way, social science has begun to catch up with John Woolman. There are some, of course, who maintain that the Third Force view is unscientific and unproven, but a few experimentalists have abandoned more popular professional pursuits to work in this area. One of the main "goodness" processes they are studying is *modeling*. The basic idea is Freudian—that we pattern our behavior after models that impress us in early childhood, that our personalities and consciences are shaped by parents and other adult figures whom we observe, imitate, and identify with. Using a variety of odd laboratory devices, psychologist David Rosenhan has studied many aspects of modeling. One experiment, for example, makes use of what appears to be a miniature bowling alley in which children bowl and win and then are given a chance to donate their winnings to a fictitious charity. Significantly more children donated their winnings after observing an adult model donate his winnings than those who had no model to observe.[4]

While laboratory research can be neat and forceful, it is best to double-check it with experiments in real-life settings. A co-worker of Rosenhan's, James Bryan, extended this child-lab work to adult-field studies. One of the most dramatic was his "flat tire" experiment. An apparently helpless woman is stranded along a highway beside a car with a flat tire. Unknown to those who pass her by, two situations have been arranged for an ingenious comparison. In Situation One the passing motorist has seen another car and another helpless woman with a man who has apparently stopped to help her. (This was a Bryan "plant," of course.) In Situation Two the passing motorist has seen no such earlier example of helping behavior; for him it is a fresh dilemma. Significantly more motorists who had seen someone else helping earlier stopped to help the woman.[5]

Later we shall explore other studies by Rosenhan and psychologist Silvan Tomkins in this vein—studies of the motivations of abolitionists before the Civil War and of civil rights workers in our own time. But with no more than this brief first glimpse at "goodness" studies, we can begin to assay the motivation and effect of men like John Woolman upon black and white advancement.

There is evidence, first, that both in childhood and in adult life Woolman had very strong models for altruism in his own deeply religious father and grandfather. It was his father, in fact, who upon his deathbed urged Woolman to publish his first great anti-slavery essay, which Woolman had feared was too bold for the time and had left unpublished for seven years. Furthermore, he had in the earlier evangelist John Fox and in the figure of Jesus strong spiritual models. But beyond the psychological development of John Woolman was his impact on others, and here again we see the modeling process at work. Like those motorists who stopped to help when they saw someone else helping, those whom Woolman reached in person in his time, or later through his writings and the writings of others about him, became strengthened in their own desire to end slavery and to promote black advancement.

As he was shaped by earlier models, so did Woolman shape those around him and those who came after him, as he himself was a powerful behavioral model—a continuity of leadership that has probably had more to do with the movement toward health out of the black and white sickness than anything else one might think of.

Wertheimer, Festinger, Benezet, and Dissonance Theory

Along with the study of morality under the impetus of the "Third Force" view, the study of rationality has burgeoned under pressures from an older "Third Force" known as Gestalt psychology.

Not too long after the Freudian and Pavlovian early impacts, a German scholar named Max Wertheimer became disturbed by the simplistic directions of the formal psychology of his day. The Viennese physician with his strange dream theory and the laboring physiologist with his salivating dog were hardly considered psychologists as yet, and a rather brittle view known as structuralism was dominant in many universities. Its approach was essentially to swarm over man, classifying his mind, senses, and feelings into smaller and smaller parts. It seemed to Wertheimer that much of importance was being left out as the structuralists and others tried to stuff the ballooning wonder of human existence into a small hard box of science. Over the years he was joined by a number of other scholarly revolutionaries—Wolfgang Kohler, Kurt Koffka, and, for a time, Kurt Lewin—and the Gestaltists evolved from a band of upsetters of various theoretical applecarts to become ultimately a powerful force in the shaping of current social and cognitive psychologies.[6]

The Gestaltists are generally remembered for their theories of perception, which stressed the perceiving of wholes, and posited such useful "laws" as that of closure, which states that we are physiologically impelled to fill in a broken circle or, more broadly interpreted, to round out or complete actions once begun. However, the overall Gestalt contribution was much broader. For long after structuralism passed from the scene, the Gestaltists continued to feel that Freudian, behaviorist and other contemporary theories were still leaving out much of importance about man, and their continuing criticism brought about major reforms in more dominant schools. They were particularly effective in forcing psychology to move up from the rat, sex, and simple machinery level to investigate the operation of man's most characteristic "higher-order" processes—perceiving, thinking, memory, all the mental processes that interact in man to identify, work with, solve, rearrange, organize, express, act upon, and otherwise make use of all forms of information.

Moreover, in Kurt Lewin's apostate departure from the purity of Gestalt thought into the tainted messiness of social reality, man's thinking was seen not as an insular process, but as something carried on within a vast field of forces within and about him that are continually being disturbed or aroused.[7] Lewin saw man as being motivated to bring these forces to rest within himself, to seek balance, to arrive at a state of personal equilibrium. A child is kept from reaching a toy by a screen. Tension rises as he strikes at the screen trying to reach the toy. Then he discovers that he can crawl around this barrier—and when he reaches the toy and snatches it, the tension subsides and he returns to a state of emotional balance.

Out of this stream of psychological thought have come many things, one particularly productive channel being what are generally known as the balance theories of Fritz Heider, Theodore Newcomb, Charles Osgood, and Leon Festinger.[8] Of these, Festinger's cognitive dissonance theory is the best known. The essence of the idea is appealing in its simplicity: that we humans cannot tolerate mental inconsistency, incongruity, imbalance, or dissonance. If within our minds two or more ideas are in conflict, we are driven to resolve this conflict and to re-establish cognitive consistency, congruity, balance, consonance. Moreover, this need to regain cognitive balance is a *fundamental drive that shapes our attitudes and our actions.*

The notion that ideas motivate men has long seemed obvious to philosophers and historians, but for nearly a century, during its infancy, much of modern social science has avoided this notion as being delusive and literary while it concentrated on illuminating the dark workings of such underforces as sex, life-and-death instincts, class struggle, economics, lust for territory and power. Out of such lower rumblings ideas were seen to rise like a kind of froth. While in no way discounting the working of the underforces, nor the operation of an ideational froth, the new view has been directed to the autonomous power of ideas in and of themselves. And this view and many of its implications have now been substantiated by one of the largest bodies of social psychological research to emerge within the past decade.

It is a particularly complex type of research that does not lend itself to quick summarizing. However, the essence of many experiments is to put people in various situations of mental conflict. For example, in an experiment arranged to present several possible choices that may reveal the workings of cognitive dissonance, they may be asked to carry out some task that conflicts with a cherished belief. They might then reject the task and persist in their belief. Or they might reject their belief in order to carry out the task. Or they might compromise by carrying out the task and modifying their belief slightly. Or they might modify the task to conform to the belief. The fact that these choices are indeed limited and logical eliminates considerable guesswork from the situation and can bring the analysis of conflicts of this sort within the powerful grasp of probabalistic theory.

Far from being merely the dry mentalistic play of the Ivory Tower, these theories may powerfully illuminate the past as well as the present. For example, let us look into the mind of a hypothetical colonial man who is assaulted from time to time by the verbal grapeshot of Anthony Benezet's wondrous publicity mill.

You are a slaveholding Quaker, let us say. On one hand you value having this creature to work for you, and on the other you value the Christian concept of the brotherhood of man. The two concepts are logically inconsistent; however, you are normally unaware of this inconsistency because of a number of self-protective things you tell yourself. You can tell yourself the slave is pagan, for example, and then the Christian imperative won't apply. But what if he is a churchgoer? You then tell yourself that he is really more animal than human, and thus avoid the brotherhood-of-man conflict. Or you may work overtime mentally to keep these two meaningful areas in separate compartments, as it were—you work to keep them apart. However, in a dominantly Christian democracy there will be difficulties no matter what position you take short of accepting the black as an equal. So your best strategy becomes to simply avoid anything that will remind you of this conceptual conflict.

Thus, the intuitive strategy of Benezet, Woolman, and every other advocate of black advancement, has been to persistently publicize the facts of injustice in order to force these facts past the defenses of the great majority of whites who would prefer to think of other things, and thereby so unsettle them that they might be driven to progressively resolve their conceptual conflict in the black's favor.[9]

A Glimpse Into the Dynamics of Compromise

Before we leave this look at relevant social science to return to the historical mainstream, one particularly wide-ranging aspect of dissonance theory should be noted: often, when two or more things are in conflict with one another, the dissonance is resolved by a compromise rather than by the "victory" of one force over others.

Earlier we noted a flow of events that suggested underlying social dynamics of liberative forces in conflict with repressive forces during colonial times and during the American Revolution, with compromise solutions particularly evident during the formation of our government. Concern with the workings and the meanings of this pattern recurs at every level of psychological, sociological, and historical analysis. On the cultural level, the operation of pressures toward consistency was part of the theory of Malinowski. In sociology, it is central to the theory of Talcott Parsons and others. Among historicans its analogue is the so-called consensus model of analysis.

Where one happens to enter this complex is immaterial. However, we note the fact to indicate that this glimpse into dissonance theory first lays open the body of the patient to reveal something of the incredibly complex workings of the sickness, or its possible dynamics, with which we will be increasingly concerned.

CHAPTER 6

Strange American Dreams

The early 1800s in America have not been the most popular of times for historians or their readers, and it is easy to see why. If one must go to the trouble of digging into the past, most of us prefer more dramatic times of great battles, and explorations, and more decisive events. And every so often there is something about the early 1800s that seems fuzzy and unreal, like a dream, with its enormous distortions and its slippery displacements. A time of glittering compromises, of likes, hates, hopes, and fears, at times it seems almost contemporary in a certain whispering, slithering, color-explosive, psychedelic quality.

With the end of the Revolutionary War, black hopes soared and some progress was made toward freedom, as was to happen following every American war. In the same year that the whites officially decided that the black was three-fifths of a man, 1787, the blacks also met in Philadelphia to take the vital step of organizing for group strength. They founded the Free African Society, one of the earliest group expressions of black aspiration and the precursor of every black organization existing today.[1] One of the founders, a man named Bustill, was the ancestor of Paul Robeson. Moreover, the white Uplifters were also busy. By 1793, there were antislavery societies in every state from New Hampshire to Virginia.[2]

However, as agitation for abolition of slavery and liberative impulses gained strength, counter-pressures became even stronger. King George had been replaced politically, but economically a more powerful master possessed the land. The South was ruled by King Cotton, who, for all the words of liberation, required many more slaves than ever before. The old repression versus liberation conflict radically intensified and its resolution took strange new forms—in fact, the strangest in all of American history. Nowhere was this more evident than in the church of the day, where repression was repeatedly forced into a confrontation with the liberating philosophy that was ostensibly the purpose of churchgoing.

This aspect of the years of the deepest sickness is best approached by dropping back into colonial times to exhume a fascinating bill passed by the New Jersey general assembly in 1704 that opened the way for the proselytizing of blacks.[3] The blacks then beginning to pour in from Africa in great numbers wanted to become Christian—and the impulse is certainly understandable. Torn from their own land, their own gods, and dumped from the slave ships half-alive to live in a strange land at the mercy of a strange white race, it was inevitable that they should seek to embrace the white God and his more personal and intimate human embodiment, the sweet figure of Jesus. Perhaps Jesus would protect them. Perhaps He would listen. Perhaps He would understand. Perhaps, even, He might lead them to happiness here; and when years passed and the hope grew dim, if not here, surely then in the hereafter.

The white churches were greatly agitated by this situation—partly by the plight of these poor souls, but also partly by the old American game of worldly success as measured by numbers. A slave wasn't merely a strange fellow being needing comfort. He was a potential convert from heathen hopelessness to Christianity, an accomplishment of salesmanship that could be counted to one's personal credit, a thing of definite value both here and in the hereafter. However, both desires—to save a soul and to bank him to one's own credit—ran into a problem common on the personal level to the pathological liar. His great problem is how to keep his lies consistent; sooner or later, to his great embarrassment, he will trip himself up.

The difficulty for the white churches was that, at first, in order to resolve the conflict between the need for repression and the liberation ideal, the church had based its support of slavery on the idea that the blacks were only heathen savages and beyond Christian concern. But among blacks converted to Christianity, and among their white well-wishers, there began to grow the idea that with baptism the black was made free. This problem created such dissension in some congregations—who were not about to give up their slaves for their faith—that for a time an end to black conversion seemed the only way out of the dilemma. Then in 1704 the ever-dependable New Jersey general assembly, in a masterful demonstration of the ingenuity of man, passed a bill ruling that baptism did *not* free the slave's body, only his soul. Swiftly the minions of God pounced to their duty, and black conversions surged among the Presbyterians, Lutherans, Dutch Reformed, and Quaker and Anglican congregations.[4]

One hundred years later, following the Revolutionary War, the old conflict was to surface again and take more strange forms. A surprising fact (at first glance) was that many churches at this time were integrated. For a time "it seemed that the churches of the embryonic United States would insist upon complete integration of the Negro into the religious life of the nation and would spearhead the attack against the institution of slavery."[5] Black and white often worshiped in the same building, and in numbers that testified to the success of the earlier drive for converts. But something now began to drive the blacks out of these so-called integrated churches, and it was not simple racism, as one might believe. Part of it came about because the blacks were often lost in the shuffle as American churches formed denominations separate from the mother church in Europe. But it also came in answer to the workings of more subtle human pressures, which are worth speculating about because of what began to happen nearly two hundred years later, in the late 1960s. Again, following a time of moving together, many blacks were impelled to move away from integration, and again to the relief of some whites and to the dismay of others.

For most settled and reasonably comfortable whites then, as now, it may be surmised that church was the retreat they turned to on Sunday for peace and quiet restoration rather than agitation and uplift. However sympathetic they might be to the cause of the black, their personal desire for peace and quiet and order was greater—and this is not so much deplorable as simply human. Thus, the black presence in the church, however peaceful, could be seen as a continual reminder of disturbing forces in a world that most whites devoutly wished to see more settled and orderly than it could ever possibly be. After all, they had only recently emerged from the birth agony of a new nation. Was it unreasonable to want time just to go about one's housework, one's business, one's simple duties, to live and let live?

On the other hand, this same Revolution had given the blacks good reason to aspire to a freedom they hadn't yet received, and they continued to be given reason to aspire to it by the speeches of early abolitionists and by subtle signals of sympathy from many other whites. But in the "integrated" churches they had to live among continual reminders of their low status and bondage. They stood by waiting their turn while the whites entered and stood by waiting while the whites left. The preacher generally had time for them only according to who their master was, and very little time at that. And while they were increasingly aware of white sympathy, they saw no direct benefit from this sympathy—they all stood up along the walls throughout the long service, while close physically but spiritually far away the whites sat or knelt on pillows in their comfortable devotion. Moreover, they were increasingly aware of white hatred as, under pressuring by abolitionist ministers and their sympathetic wives, the bigot's contempt swelled and cut at them with vicious looks, and words, and even blows.[6]

In answer to these situational pressures the movement toward

black and white separatism radically intensified. The black answer
was to form their own separatist churches—a move that at least
gave them the health of self-respect and the only certain institutional power base they were to have throughout the entire span of
American history into the most recent times. In 1794, Richard
Allen founded the African Methodist Episcopal Church after an
ugly incident in Philadelphia's St. George Methodist Church. The
break came in 1787 when Allen and Absolom Jones (whose names
recur in heroic contexts during this time) were told to take seats
along the wall; then later they were forced to move to the gallery;
then later still one of the church's trustees "attempted to haul
Absolom Jones to his feet during prayer." All the blacks present,
"who had recently subscribed to the refurbishment of the church,"
walked out in a body. As children, both Allen and Jones had been
pupils of the Quaker publicist and schoolmaster Anthony Benezet,
and now again the Quakers were of aid, helping them form the
Free African Society as a gathering point.[7] Jones formed the first
Negro Episcopal church in America, out of which grew the Anglican Methodist church, which Allen headed as bishop. In 1796,
James Varick led another black Methodist walkout in New York
City, and in 1805 Thomas Paul founded the first black Baptist
church in Boston.

But while the blacks busied themselves with this small-time,
self-protective separatism, the whites had much larger plans for
accomplishing the same end. Undoubtedly the strangest eruption
of the sickness ever to seize adult white males was the American
Colonization Plan, a scheme that Jefferson pondered, that became
Abraham Lincoln's favorite cure, and that was born and for a time
prospered under the aegis of some of the most respected patriots
of the day.

Over the years the noble effusions of morality and the tortuous
rationalizations have dropped away leaving only a nasty remnant
of its underlying functional thrust to survive into our time. The
plan's descendant is the radical or far-right conservative "ship 'em
back to Africa" solution of today's bull-voiced, rednecked con-
ventioneer. In 1816, however, it seemed to the Reverend Dr.
Robert Finley a most humane and lovely plan.[8] Why should the
Negro continue to suffer the indignities of slavery and remain a
displaced person in a strange white land? Why not now, before it

was too late, help him regain those verdant savannahs, those golden rivers, those mighty mountains and the manna-laden majesty of the jungle from which he had been so brutally wrested?

It was a heady concoction of many appeals. There was, for example, the uplift or parlor appeal, which Finley saw and everyone offered as its main objective in winning over black and white idealists. The nobility of this white gesture, however, masked a more powerful subterranean or basement appeal. This was the ultimate move in the logic of repression: Why not get rid of the black man entirely? Why not through this one bold stroke of social surgery dispose of all those who were no longer useful as slaves and who as free men only lowered the ethnic quality of society, spawned crime and welfare problems, or worked as agitators, like the cursed Frederick Douglass? The prospect greatly excited Southerners, who provided most of the funds for the colonization plan's operation. Beneath it all there was also the old grinding white fear of a truly massive revolt in the slave states. The seizure of nearby Santo Domingo (now Haiti) by black revolutionaries and the slaughter of all whites in 1804 greatly intensified this motivation. Thus, those who saw the black not as a passive piece of property, but as a caged human being, looked to colonization as a way to rid themselves of the danger of retaliation. And on the black side, too, there was a strong and persisting desire among a minority to take up the white's offer and go. Why stay in the cage if there was a way out? [9]

But there was also what might be called the cleanliness appeal—and our interest in the dissonance model would, of course, see this as a powerful motivation. This was the white (as well as black) desire to be clean again, to be whole, to extirpate this black-white thing that was like a cancer on the fair white body of America the Beautiful, and to be at last a country truly free. This was Jefferson's longing, and in expressing it there bubbled to the surface of his otherwise discreet *Notes on Virginia* the subterranean agonies of white America's by then 166-year-old preoccupation with the sexual aspects of the sickness.

Over the years there had gathered within the white psyche a considerable folklore of black and white sex facts. Slave traders had brought the news that blacks were the result of the mating of Africans with orangutans (there were, of course, the usual eye-witness accounts). Black men had huge penises. Black women were lascivious. Both had very loose morals, were passionate beyond belief in their love-making, and were naturally inclined to breed like flies with anything of the opposite sex that presented the opportunity. White women, on the other hand, were greatly desired by black men and in constant danger of being raped. As for white men, they were greatly desired by black women, which created the greatest social problem of the time. For this temptation of principled white males by unprincipled black females led to the breeding of hundreds of thousands of mixed-blood American Negroes. They were certainly useful as slaves, but this frenetic mating raised the horrible prospect that this degraded racial mixture might become dominant in white America. Hence, there were many (including Benjamin Franklin) who felt the slave trade should be stopped not only as a moral issue, but to keep out more sexual temptation and the inevitable corruption of race. And there came to be many who felt the solution was not only to keep out more incitement to corruption, but to export the product.[10]

"They should be colonized to such places as the circumstances of the time should render most proper," Jefferson offered in advancing the thought in 1785 that flowered into the American Colonization Society in 1817. This must be done, he first avowed, because the political incorporation of blacks into the state was probably impossible. The "deep rooted prejudices" of the whites, recollections by the blacks of "injuries they have sustained," and "new provocations" would divide the races "and produce convulsions which will probably never end but in the extermination of the one or the other race."

But the "physical" problem, Jefferson felt, was the greater—and gently at first, but then insistently and increasingly, the troubling sexual mythology worked to the surface as he wrote.

> The first difference which strikes us is that of colour. Whether the black of the negro resides in the reticular membrane between the skin and scarf skin, or in the scarf skin itself; whether it proceeds from the colour of the blood, the colour of the bile, or from that of some other secretion, the difference is fixed in nature, and is as real as if its seat and cause were better known to us. And is this difference of no importance? Is it not the foundation of a greater or less share of beauty in the two races? Are not the

fine mixtures of red and white, the expressions of every passion by greater or less suffusions of colour in the one, preferable to that eternal monotony, which reigns in the countenances, that immovable veil of black which covers all the emotions of the other race? Add to these, flowing hair, a more elegant symmetry of form, their own judgment in favour of the whites, declared by their preference of them as uniformly as is the preference of the Oran-ootan for the black women over those of his own species.

"They are more ardent after their female: but love seems with them to be more an eager desire, than a tender delicate mixture of sentiment and sensation," he muses. And again, "their love is ardent, but it kindles the senses only, not the imagination." And then he delivered himself of this careful reasoning of the problem of this sexual corruption and its tainted product, which led, of course, to the noble logic of colonization.

Will not a lover of natural history then, one who views the gradations in all the races of animals with the eye of philosophy, excuse an effort to keep those in the department of man as distinct as nature has formed them? This unfortunate difference of colour, and perhaps of faculty, is a powerful obstacle to the emancipation of these people. Many of their advocates, while they wish to vindicate the liberty of human nature, are anxious also to preserve its dignity and beauty. Some of these, embarrassed by the question "What further is to be done with them?" join themselves in opposition with those who are actuated by sordid avarice only. Among the Romans emancipation required but one effort. The slave, when made free, might mix with, without staining the blood of his master. But with us a second is necessary, unknown to history. When freed, he is to be removed beyond the reach of mixture.[11]

If one can step out of the sobering context of history to look in upon this attempt at removal "beyond the reach of mixture" as though one had just arrived from Mars, it would seem that few times in our history were more bizarre. Jefferson is known today as one of the noblest Americans, with a scientific mind remarkable for his time—and within nonblack-relevant history all this is obviously true. Yet he produces his *Notes,* and they are so weasle-minded on the subject of blacks that they are seized up and decried

as demeaning to science and to man by numerous well-equipped
and outraged critics even in his own day. Moreover, they helped
foster a gutter attack that was very damaging to him politically.
This was the bizarre charge that behind the ambivalence of his
expressions concerning blacks—behind the strange, underlying alternation of attraction and revulsion that works through his writings—lay the fact that Jefferson was actually the father of five
children by black Sally Hemmings, a favorite among his hundred
slaves. And to compound the oddity, a recent, in-depth study of
the historical evidence by W. D. Jordan indicates that however
improbable it may seem, equally good cases can be made for or
against this charge.[12]

Jefferson's involvement with the colonization scheme was followed by that of another President—in 1816 Andrew Jackson
loaned his great prestige to the founding of the Colonization Society. And he was joined by the composer of the "Star Spangled
Banner," Francis Scott Key. And the Great Compromiser, Henry
Clay.

It is possible, of course, to reconstruct a logic for all of this
within the context of the times that can make it seem normal and
inevitable, and also absolves everyone of any blame. And within
such a view these involvements and events will not loom as bizarre,
but as something "unprofessionally" pulled out of context. But this
is precisely the point we are making. Madmen and the mentally
sick are identified not by the stream of normality within which
they operate most of the time, but by a certain repetition of startling actions that are bizarre in being out of character. And the
colonization scheme, which historians have generally scooted past
on their way to the greater meaning of the abolitionists, still remains the historical episode most revealing of the mind-clouding
and emotion-warping nature of the black and white sickness.

The bizarre story of how the scheme acquired Liberia, for example, radiates many subtle matters of tensions and attitudes. The
first hauling of blacks back to Africa was in 1815 by, of all im-
probabilities, the very wealthy American *black* shipowner, land-
owner, and philanthropist Paul Cuffe, one of several remarkably
successful black men of the time.[13] Cuffe's ships unloaded at Sierra
Leone, which had been founded by British abolitionists as a haven
for freed slaves. Then, in 1826, a singular U.S. Navy vessel named

the *Alligator* put down anchor near a village along the West African coast. Its commander, Lieutenant Robert "Fighting Bob" Stockton, had brought money and goods to purchase land for the colonization plan. Early one morning, arming himself only with a pistol and taking for company a very timid white minister, "Fighting Bob" hiked twenty miles back into the jungle, walked into the council chamber of a black king with five hundred armed tribesmen, put a deed to be signed in the hand of the king, put a pistol to his head, and, upon getting what he wanted, walked out with clear title to the forty-three thousand square miles that became Liberia. (Later, "Fighting Bob," by then commodore of a larger vessel, seized California from the Mexicans. Later still, on the strength of such endearing exploits, he became a Presidential nominee of the racist Know-Nothing Party).[14]

A less flamboyant hero of the colonizationists was the plan's official historian, Dr. Archibald Alexander. As a theologian he was ranked by admirers in his time along with Jonathan Edwards in importance and in brilliance of intellect, and he was considered a remarkably sweet and lovable man personally. Yet the essential madness of the plan was seldom more clearly revealed than in the earnest words of this white saint so blind to his sickness.

His history of colonization opens honestly enough. "The best method of disposing of the free people of colour," the great cleric begins, and then plunges into an argument for colonization and against the abolitionists, which becomes increasingly tortured until finally he elevates the dispute to the realm of Higher Authority and what appears to have been an important private revelation: "Why so many of this unhappy race were ever permitted to be brought to America begins now to appear. They were sent here by a benignant Providence overruling the wicked passions of avaricious men, that they might be christianized and civilized, and might carry back to their benighted countrymen, the principles of religion, freedom, and representative government."

In other words, behind the enslavement and degradation of an entire race this man of God could only discern his Master at work arranging a free education for the black man—blind to the logic that if this were true then his God must be abysmally evil. Clothed with the authority of his personal eminence, his private God, his Presbyterianism, and the Princeton Theological Seminary, he then predicted that "the whites and blacks in this country, by no human efforts, could be amalgamated into one homogeneous mass in a thousand years." And finally, to sink these views home and squash the opposition, the good doctor hurled one last thunderbolt: "Let those, then, who oppose the scheme of African Colonization beware, lest they be found resisting what God approves." [15]

CHAPTER 7

Manifest, Latent, and Sexual Reality

Symptoms, causes, workings, and cures: The words must conjure up one figure above all others in this context, Sigmund Freud. No one else had his combination of range, ability to organize insight into a powerful theory, and gift for expressing and promoting his views. He was an uncanny scientist, artist, leader; but all of this was overshadowed by the grandeur of his courage and persistence as an explorer of the human mind.

Looking at the pictures of the pale old man with the sad eyes

and the tired mouth it is hard for those who have never been captured by Freud to understand why he means so much to those
who have. "You often estimate me too highly," he once said half-
seriously, but in words that reveal something of what it was that
seized converts. "For I am not really a man of science, not an
observer, not an experimenter, and not a thinker. I am nothing but
by temperament a *conquistador*—an adventurer, if you want to
translate that word—with the curiosity, the boldness, and the
tenacity that belong to that type of being. Such people are apt to
be treasured if they succeed, if they have really discovered something; otherwise they are thrown aside. And that is not altogether
unjust." [1]

A physician by training and economic necessity, his interest was
at first in the sickness of individual patients, and in his own emotional ills (much of the oddity he explores in his great, early
Interpretation of Dreams was his own). But the deeper he went
into the jungle of the individual mind, the more universals he encountered—the jungles were different, yes, but he kept coming
upon the same paths, the same idols, and glimpsed the same
strange beasts thrashing through the undergrowth, and heard the
same odd bird cries. It was also his contribution to show—and this
some time before Hitler made it quite evident—that this jungle
was not something removed in land space or far back in time, but
was everpresent within each of us. Freud was the first to demonstrate that it was a world all of us re-enter every night, in sleeping.
Moreover, he also showed how this underworld may shape much
of our waking thoughts and actions.

What do the cerebral explorations of a distant Viennese physician have to do with the period of the deepest sickness in the
United States? One could note that Freud, like so many social
scientists, was Jewish and knew the sickness that goes by the name
of prejudice intimately—the Nazis had to be pressured by personal
representatives of both Roosevelt and Mussolini and bribed with
thousands of dollars to allow him to escape from Austria in 1938,
and his four older sisters perished in a German incinerator. However, the matter at hand is his theory.

The early 1800s has been identified as a time of strange dreams,
and the link to Freud is more than a colorful analogy. For one of
Freud's enduring contributions was to show the linkage between

dreaming and waking sickness, and to extend this linking out from the individual into his society. "Anyone who has failed to explain the origin of dream-images can scarcely hope to understand phobias, obsessions, or delusions or to bring a therapeutic influence to bear on them," wrote the master in 1899.[2]

Two basic distinctions for Freud were between the conscious and the unconscious mind, and between the reality principle and the pleasure principle. Awake, we are mainly aware of using and being guided by our conscious mind, which operates according to the demands of reality—we work for so and so, the hours are nine to five, we go home to one wife, we vacation once a year, and so on. However, asleep is something else again. Then we return mainly to the luxuriant realm of the unconscious mind, which operates according to the pleasure principle—here we can be master, with hordes of slaves, with no work hours, with ten thousand concubines, and with an endless playtime, should we wish all this. But all is not so jolly in this netherworld. For over our past, and the past of our race and our society, through the conflict of pleasurable urges with various nonpleasurable realities, there has grown up within this netherworld a number of urges that have been denied and which now roam the jungle like hungry beasts. Sometimes they find expression in slips of the tongue, and sometimes in neurotic symptoms. The world of sleep nightly offers them their hunting ground, but even here a representative of the unpleasant old reality world is on guard, so that what emerges is that strange mishmash of sense and nonsense, of past and present, of desire in conflict with reality that we know as a dream.

In approaching the dream, Freud's first distinction was between the *manifest* and *latent* dream content, an application to the mental underworld of one of the most all-pervading concepts in modern social science—and certainly one that is crucial in gaining any understanding of the black and white sickness. Spinoza and Karl Marx had earlier concluded that much of our conscious thought is "false consciousness." Rather than the one reality that most of us feel we apprehend, there were two realities: "truth" and the distortion of social reality that has come to be known as *ideology,* or the distortions of individual reality that Freud called *rationalizations.* In sociology, for Freud's contemporary Vilfredo Pareto this distinction was between *derivation* and *residue.* More recently,

66   THE HEALING OF A NATION

sociologist Robert Merton, borrowing Freud's excellent terms, has elaborated a theory of *manifest* and *latent functions* in society.[3]

In essence, it is the difference between what we generally think of as the surface appearance of something and its underlying meaning. On the individual level, for example, it has become a psychiatric commonplace that behind the manifest oversolicitousness of a mother or a business rival can lie the latent meaning of more hatred than love. Or on the racial level, one may discern that while the manifest function of the American colonization scheme was to give blacks a change to prosper in their own new nation, the scheme's latent function is to get rid of them. Freud, then, saw the manifest content of the dream as being the strange offering, story, playlet, scenario, or extravaganza which we remember on awaking. Its latent content, however, was the dream's true underlying meaning, or what the playlet really said.

Freud believed that the mishmash of the manifest content—or more technically, the dream distortion—results from the following sequence. Everyone has unacceptable urges that are seeking expression, but before these urges can be allowed on stage in dreams they must be disguised by what he called the *dreamwork,* which makes use of four disguising or distorting devices:

1. Condensation, whereby many meanings are compressed into a single expression.

2. Displacement, whereby intense feelings about something of importance are assigned to some trivial dream element, or a feeling's opposite is used, *e.g.,* love substituted for hate.

3. Plastic representation, whereby thoughts that are normally expressed in words are translated into symbols and direct action equivalents.

4. Secondary elaboration, whereby all the odd bits and scraps of dream distortion are given some pleasing, reasonable overall shape or story line.

We have likened the colonization scheme to a strange dream; can something like the Freudian dreamwork be discerned operating within it? One could find condensation in a large complex of motives that time shrinks to the single expression: "ship 'em back to Africa." And the emphasis placed on the goodness aspects—of idealistic service to the Negroes, of how happy they would be in Africa, etc.—represents something remarkably like displacement, masking the underlying white fear and loathing. As for plastic representation, it would seem that no clearer symbol of the desire to be rid of the blacks could possibly exist than the very large and solid prospect of ships loaded with them under full sail away from America toward the new African dumping ground. And secondary elaboration can be seen at work again and again in the troubled rationalizations of Thomas Jefferson, Dr. Archibald Alexander, and hordes of other white apologists of the day.

Such hypocrisy, unfortunately, is not all long ago and far away. Colonization seems to have been merely a particularly obvious, much-inflamed symptom of the sickness. It was like a great purple boil that burst with the Civil War, compared to the more sophisticated infection that now lies within our blood. And one of the aims of relating Freud to it is to suggest the workings of a waking dreamwork that we still use to distort social reality and deceive ourselves. And the hope is to suggest an aspect of the cure, for Freud moved on to make the insights from his study of dreams the basis for his therapy, psychoanalysis, a major part of which consists of probing beneath the manifest content of dreams or disturbing symptoms to find the latent meanings and underlying causes.

This skeptical, debunking way of viewing human behavior and social processes as operating on two levels of meaning is also, we have noted, a characterizing attitude of sociology.[4] The view was also notably active by the late 1960s among young blacks and whites, who tended to discount everything Whitey or their elders said as so much manifest "bull" covering reprehensible latent intentions.

However hard it may be for some to accept, this attitude of young blacks and whites seems to be not a signal for the end of the world but evidence of the urge of the social body toward health. For the aim of all Freudian-based therapies is the patient's progressive discovery of the truth about himself, and the shedding of the distortions he has used to deceive himself and others. The catharsis is never pretty. Indeed, beneath the hair, the foul words and the bad manners may lie the strongest drive in many a generation to end the kind of hypocrisy colonization represented, and indeed to end the sickness itself.

Yet the fact also remains that in shattering idols one can destroy the temple. Moreover, debunking is only the beginning of wisdom.

And neither a sociology nor the young interested in social change can escape the great therapeutic imperative that Freud's successor Erik Erikson demonstrates in his studies of Luther and Gandhi: the need for a sensitivity to ethics.[5]

Freud, Erikson, and Black and White Sexuality

While the manifest versus latent view of realities may provide a good X-ray for examining the "bones" of the black and white disease, Freud's most famous contribution to psychology, his sexual theory, can be even more useful. However, its contribution to date has been a mixed blessing, for, as in other contexts, its application to the black and white sickness has probably obscured as much as it has revealed.

The problem is that it has been abused by psychoanalysts with little knowledge of blackness or society and by writers and literary men with no formal knowledge of psychology. In fact, one strategy in writing about any phase of the black-white story seems to be that when one feels the need to become profound and seek the causal level one tosses in something about sex, and if it can be cloaked with Freud so much the better. For example, some fairly gross examples of sexual "psychologizing" mar otherwise brilliant writings of James Baldwin and Eldridge Cleaver.[6] But it also seeps in and out of white historians and sociologists who have read the "readable" Freudians but who have not been forced through the "unreadable" contributions of more pertinent modern researchers and theorists. We shall attempt here to isolate what about sex seems to be relevant to the black and white sickness from what is not.

The mistake most generally made is to seek in sex a cause, when in fact it surfaces mainly as a symptom of more complex disturbances usually having their "cause" elsewhere. These symptoms are perhaps best described, historically, by W. D. Jordan in *White Over Black,* and currently in *Black Rage,* by two black psychiatrists, William Grier and Price Cobbs, or in Franz Fanon's *Wretched of the Earth.* We have already very briefly sketched the historical picture; to this the agonized confessions of patient to doctor in modern times adds dismal details: Black women complaining of weak husbands; black sons (all too often homosexual) complaining of weak, absent, or remote fathers; black men complaining of dominating wives who try to run everything; some black women disturbed by their lack of resistance when confronted by the sexual demands of white males; some black men disturbed by the intensity of their desire for the dangerous white woman; but also, despite all the legends of the black as a lusty beast, many complaints of no good sex life at all; and also despite the legend, many reports of black male impotency and female frigidity.[7]

Aside from the general relevance of personal therapy to this aspect of the disease—and much psychotherapy is still rooted in Freudian theory, though vastly different in method—the Freudian relevances center pretty much on what happens at two points in a lifetime: the ages one to five, and the brief time span covered by Erikson's extension of Freudian theory to adolescence and to the potentially crippling impact of our society on the young black man and the young black woman.

Freud's theory of psychosexual development was such a tremendous historical advance it seems a shame to give it only a few words. However, it is generally well known and the bare outline can be quickly stated. There is a developmental sequence of oral, anal, phallic, latent, and genital stages. Our sexual pleasure is first centered in our mothers, as we feed at their breasts; this is the oral stage, roughly extending over our first year of life. Pleasure then centers around the process of elimination, at the time of toilet training, the anal stage, roughly the second year. Then pleasure moves to the genitals, at the time of playing with oneself, the phallic stage, roughly age three to five. Then sex goes underground, during the time of latency, until age ten or so. And then, with puberty, the sexually powerful experience of the early years is reactivated, and we enter the difficult genital stage, during which we must achieve maturity of sexual expression, as well as a great deal more.

Two Freudian concepts that bring the fundamental dynamics into this picture are *fixation* and *regression*. If at any point along this line of development we encounter either overly pleasurable or overly painful experiences, something within us becomes fixated at that point. Physically we continue to grow, and to outward appearances nothing may be wrong. But it is as though we were attached by a strong rubber band to that point of fixation. Persistently, inescapably pulling upon us, this great band shapes our personality into an overtalkative orality, or a stingy anality, or a narcissistic phallicism. And then in times of great stress and anxiety we tend to regress inwardly to the early stages of these fixations, and our behavior becomes markedly, even insanely, childish in oral, anal, or phallic ways.[8]

Erik Erikson, in his *psychosocial* branching out from the original Freudian psychosexual root, extended Freud's five stages to eight, spanning *all* of life, rather than only the opening years. The first time of great relevance to the black and white sickness is the phallic stage, in Erikson's plan the third stage of life, during which the growing child faces a "nuclear conflict" of initiative versus guilt. That is, he is presented at this point with a crucial choice about the direction of his life that will determine whether he gains a sense of personal value and power mainly through a successful identification with the parent of the same sex or becomes the victim of a persisting guilt that grips him because of an unresolved hatred of this same-sex parent and the desire to possess the opposite-sex parent.

This is the involved time of the Freudian Oedipus Complex, which in Erikson's hands is given a broader significance. "Infantile sexuality and incest taboo, castration complex, and superego all unite here to bring about that specifically human crisis during which the child must turn from an exclusive, pregenital attachment to his parents to the slow process of becoming a parent, a carrier of tradition. Here the most fateful split and transformation in the emotional powerhouse occurs, a split between potential human glory and potential total destruction. For here the child becomes forever divided in himself. The instinct fragments which before had enhanced the growth of his infantile body and mind now become divided into an infantile set which perpetuates the exuberance of growth potentials, and a parental set which supports and increases self-observation, self-guidance, and self-punishment." [9]

Here, then, according to the Freudians, is the first time when the home situation is most crucial. At this point a great deal is dependent on the presence or absence of a father in the home. Or the presence of a mother counterbalanced by a father. Or whether a mother is having to go it alone. Or the presence of a lonely parent seeking too much love in a child. Or the presence of parents who are troubled by having no money and no hope.

An awareness of the black social situation in America makes it readily evident that something is wrong with the common white belief that what happens to us is exclusively individualized, and that all our ills derive from bad genes or peculiar parents. For it is apparent that the *social* problems of job and status intrude all through the psychosexual development picture in black as well as white America. Crucial absences and presences of many sorts that are directly related to psychosexual growth are tied to such every-day black facts of life as jobs for the black woman, but none for the black man. Or no jobs that offer a scrap of dignity—let alone enough money to support a family—for either.[10]

The next crucial time is the genital stage. For Erikson this is stage five, the years of adolescence, when the nuclear conflict is between choices that lead to gaining one's own clear-cut identity versus the pull toward role confusion. This is the time of the advent of puberty, the beginning of youth, a time of moving into genital maturity, when one is concerned with the problems of being a member of the right clique, of falling in love, of doubts about one's own sexual identity, of concerns about career, class, and status identity possibilities. At each point, again, the situation of being black in America intrudes upon the matter of choices, the truly crucial nature of which Erikson underlines by emphasizing that they proceed "by critical steps—'critical' being a characteristic of turning points, of moments of decision between progress and regression, integration and retardation." [11]

Here is a time for the black boy or girl to gain confidence in sex along with social mastery—to find that sexual, personal, social, and occupational wholeness known as identity—or to find the comfort of the outcast in promiscuity, self-punishment for defeat in impotency or frigidity, or now at last to resolve the Oedipal conflict in homosexuality.

In a later chapter we will take another look at Erikson's concept of *identity,* for him a major theme and contribution. For now we will close this chapter with a passage from Erikson's *Childhood and Society* that very briefly brings together an astonishing amount of Freudian psychosexual and Eriksonian psychosocial thought in relation to the black identity problem.

> Consider, for example, the chances for a continuity of identity in the American Negro child. I know a colored boy who, like our boys, listens every night to Red Rider. Then he sits up in bed, imagining that he is Red Rider. But the moment comes when he

sees himself galloping after some masked offenders and suddenly notices that in his fancy Red Rider is a colored man. He
stops his fantasy. While a small child, this boy was extremely
expressive, both in his pleasures and in his sorrows. Today he is
calm and always smiles; his language is soft and blurred; nobody
can hurry him or worry him—or please him. White people like
him.

Negro babies often receive sensual satisfactions which provide
them with enough oral and sensory surplus for a lifetime, as
clearly betrayed in the way they move, laugh, talk, sing. Their
forced symbiosis with the feudal South capitalized on this oral-
sensory treasure and helped to build a slave's identity: mild,
submissive, dependent, somewhat querulous, but always ready to
serve, with occasional empathy and childlike wisdom. But underneath a dangerous split occurred. The Negro's unavoidable identification with the dominant race, and the need of the master
race to protect its own identity against the very sensual and
oral temptations emanating from the race held to be inferior
(whence came their mammies), established in both groups an association: light—clean—clever—white, and dark—dirty—dumb—
nigger. The result, especially in those Negroes who left the poor
haven of their Southern homes, was often a violently sudden and
cruel cleanliness training, as attested to in the autobiographies of
Negro writers. It is as if by cleansing, a whiter identity could be
achieved. The attending disillusionment transmits itself to the
phallic-locomotor stage, when restrictions as to what shade of
girl one may dream of interfere with the free transfer of the
original narcissistic sensuality to the genital sphere. Three identities are formed: (1) mammy's oral-sensual honey-child—tender,
expressive, rhythmical; (2) the evil identity of the dirty, anal-
sadistic, phallic-rapist nigger; and (3) the clean, anal-compulsive
restrained, friendly, but always sad white man's Negro.[12]

CHAPTER 8

Red, White, and Black

Despite both black and white agitation against the colonization plan, between 1815 and the Civil War twelve thousand blacks shipped out from America to Liberia, their new promised land.[1] Many pressures influenced the decisions of those who left and of the majority who stayed.

Some of the reluctance of those who didn't want to go could be attributed to inertia and some to fear of the unknown and distrust of the whites. But also many blacks felt that in some way that might perhaps defy rational explanation, but was spiritually right, some part of this land they had worked and lived and died upon for so long was surely rightfully theirs. Significantly (and counter to pressures in our time), a movement began among the blacks of that time to discourage the practice of being called Africans.[2] The term was increasingly popular among whites, and the blacks sensed in this practice no honor but rather a potentially dangerous functionalism at work. Calling the Negro "African" seemed to suggest that the Negro was a subgrade savage who, if he were no longer useful as a slave, should be shipped back to the savage source-land.

Yet there still remained the siren song, the appeal of gaining some bit of personal dignity and that *sine qua non,* the respect of one's peers, in their own new country in Africa. Free Negroes had thought they would gain dignity and respect with their freedom, but they found themselves rapidly losing ground. The Continental Congress had formally ended the importing of slaves in 1775. Vermont first ended slavery in 1777, and gradually all the Northern states followed suit.[3] But the ending of slave importing was only temporary, and as more and more blacks gained freedom they found themselves with less and less power to vote, to hold a job, to buy a house, to speak out publicly.

There were sheltering social islands in New England where a particularly strong and bright black might prosper and advance himself. (The success of Massachusett's wealthy Paul Cuffe was a prime example.) But to the enlightened black of the early 1800s —and to his appalled white counterpart within the ranks of the "enemy"—America increasingly presented a nightmare vision. Throughout the vast land mass, but primarily throughout the South, there spread a horde of whites who seized, laid waste to, exploited, and engulfed everything in their path. To the whites it was just Christian homesteading and free enterprise and Manifest Destiny. But to America's colored men—the Indian and the Negro —it was Manifest Disaster. Everywhere the whites moved upon the Indian, seeding little misleading words, and the little white churches then sprang up as if from mushroom spores, and then after the words and the churches there came the horde, like giant white locusts whose jaws worked incessantly to devour anything that might be of any other color in their path.

The white treatment of Indians is particularly important in this reading of the casebook for what it reveals of something about the black and white sickness that is often overlooked, and dangerously so: its generality. That is, both blacks and whites tend to see their disease as peculiar to the two races, and this insular view leads to dangerous distortions. Both are then strongly tempted to see the whole problem as a function of genes. The white suspects (though most wouldn't admit it) that the whole mess is the result of the tainted and subgrade black gene, and the black suspects (and is increasingly vocal about it) that the problem is the innate evilness of the white gene. Such views lead logically to extermination, sterilization, or radical social removal as the only sure cure. The white treatment of the Indians, however, is an important corrective in what it reveals of a sad historical generality. It suggests that, transcending questions of race or genetics, practically any group that becomes *too* successful in its conquests becomes self-worshiping, and its arrogance and its subjugation and exploitation of others sets in motion the old dynamics that underlie the growth of the black and white sickness in our land.

Viewed in such terms, the corporate white depravity of the early 1800s is almost unimaginable. Not content with holding over three million blacks captive in a system of slavery that was designed to chew or suck from them everything of value and leave only the cleaned and hollow bones for burial,[4] the Southern whites now tried to finish off the American Indians. To the white today Andrew Jackson is a great hero. After all, wasn't he the old battler for the common man and, along with Jefferson, the spiritual founder of the Democratic party? Didn't "Old Hickory," above all others of his time, embody the idea of a democracy truly by, for and of the people? Yes, but then one must ask *whose* people? With the support of Jackson, who broke the "sacred" treaties and even defied the U.S. Supreme Court on their behalf, from 1836 to 1838 the Southern whites drove the Indians from their tribal lands in the Carolinas, Georgia, Alabama, Tennessee, and Mississippi into the dumping ground of Indian Territory.[5]

But, of course, these were savages—or so the white apologists insisted. In actuality they were the Cherokees, Choctaws, Chickasaws, Creeks, and Seminoles, who were called the Civilized Tribes for one very good reason—by any reasonable anthropological standard most of them were considerably more civilized than the

Southern whites of their day. Within six years after the Cherokee Removal, for example, a Princeton graduate, the Cherokee William P. Ross, was publishing one of the more remarkable newspapers of the time, the *Cherokee Advocate,* in Indian Territory. Published in English and in Cherokee—the only written language in human history to be developed by a single man, the great Sequoyah, and in less than one short decade—the *Advocate* included reviews of operas by correspondents in Paris, as well as the civilized local doings in the new Cherokee capitol of Tahlequah. The Cherokees also had higher education for women in advance of most whites, and certain political and legal refinements we have just barely reached—the eighteen-year-old vote, for example, and a system of justice that in its speed, humanity, rationality, and wit often made much of ours look like something out of the Middle Ages.[6] And in 1836, seven thousand Federal troops herded this advanced and peaceful people into concentration camps and then drove them through the winter across the entire length of the South, out of North Carolina and Tennessee into what is now Oklahoma. Of fourteen thousand men, women, and children who began the journey, only ten thousand reached Indian Territory, four thousand having perished along the way. But at the hub of our leadership, in the house of the Great White Father, another kind of civilization produced a characteristic assessment. "The measures . . . have had the happiest effect. The Cherokees have emigrated without any apparent reluctance," President Martin Van Buran reported to Congress at a time when a hundred Cherokees were perishing daily.[7]

If this remarkably successful, even overcivilized man with a somewhat different skin color was systematically robbed of his land, shoved about, and denied justice by a government completely subservient to the white majority, what hope could there be for the all-black person in America? So might a knowledgeable black have wondered then, debating whether to emigrate to Africa.

Few blacks, however, were given the chance to be so knowledgeable or to choose anything but life within Southern slavery's vast compound, where they were kept, and used, and exchanged, and bred—and also branded, and occasionally gutted and emasculated—like cattle. It is still hard for most whites, and even for blacks, to believe all the horror really happened and was not

merely an exaggeration for the purposes of propaganda or colorful "story telling." This reluctance is not a matter of mere accident
or happenstance; for nearly a century the legend of banjo-playing
bliss on a plantation paradise was blown up by the work of a
succession of noted white conservative historians and spread
through textbooks to blind the nation. A pretention of scientific
method was finally punctured in 1944 by historian Richard Hof-
stader, who showed how these historians had built their case upon
limited and faulty data samplings.[8] Since then increasingly more
"abolitionist exaggerations" have been shown to be quite factual.
But old movies and old books continue to extend the lovely spell
of plantation bliss, and the impression persists that Southern
slavery really couldn't have been as bad as its new critics contend.
More than 120 years ago, however, in 1845, there appeared a
document which, along with the massive evidence of the day,
should have settled the matter. It was one of the most remarkable
books ever written: the *Narrative of the Life of Frederick Douglass.*[9]

A slave in Maryland until he was twenty, when he escaped
North, this amazing human being had worked mainly as a laborer
in the fields and in shipyards, with only one brief (but crucial) time
of access to the culture of the so-called house nigger. With only
part of an alphabet to build on, he taught himself to read and
educated himself under the worst of circumstances; yet, on gaining
his freedom, Douglass wrote with a power to match that of the
greatest writers of his day about slavery from the compelling viewpoint of one who had both seen and experienced this human
devastation at its height.

There is in sociology and anthropology an important research
technique known as the participant-observer approach.[10] The
social scientist lives among his subjects experiencing life as one of
them, subjectively, while recording his observations with the objectivity of an observer from another culture. If a man can be said
to have informally made use of a research technique 150 years in
advance of its formalization, then, along with his other distinctions
—and along with Woolman—Douglass deserves credit as an early
American social scientist. Certainly no one since his time has
written more forcefully of how the slavery machine was designed
to produce disease wholesale.

The Slave as Participant-Observer

Early in the *Narrative,* Douglass notes the tactic of the separation of mother and child and surmises its purposes. "My mother and I were separated when I was but an infant—before I knew her as my mother. . . . Frequently, before the child has reached its twelfth month, its mother is taken from it, and hired out on some farm a considerable distance off. . . . For what this separation is done, I do not know, unless it be to hinder the development of the child's affection toward its mother, and to blunt and destroy the natural affection of the mother for the child." [11]

This destruction of normal human ties and emotions Douglass then records through practically every phase of the slave's life, until it becomes apparent that what is generally at work is a systematic brutalizing.

> There were no beds given the slaves, unless one coarse blanket be considered such, and none but the men and women had these . . . old and young, male and female, married and single, drop down side by side, on one common bed,—the cold, damp floor,—each covering himself or herself with their miserable blankets. . . . Our food was coarse corn meal boiled. This was called mush. It was put into a large wooden tray or trough, and set down upon the ground. The children were then called, like so many pigs, and like so many pigs they would come and devour the mush; some with oyster-shells, others with pieces of shingle, some with naked hands, and none with spoons. . . . We were all ranked together at the valuation. Men and women, old and young, married and single, were ranked with horses, sheep, and swine. There were horses and men, cattle and women, pigs and children, all holding the same rank in the scale of being, and were all subjected to the same narrow examination. . . . The holidays are part and parcel of the gross fraud, wrong, and inhumanity of slavery. . . . Their object seems to be, to disgust their slaves with freedom, by plunging them into the lowest depths of dissipation. . . . One plan is, to make bets on their slaves, as to who can drink the most whisky without getting drunk. . . . When the holidays ended, we staggered up from the filth of our wallowing, took a long breath, and marched to the field,—feeling, upon the whole, rather glad to go, from what our master had deceived us into a belief was freedom, back to the arms of slavery.[12]

The ultimate brutalizing of both black and white, however, repeatedly occurred with whippings and killings so vile it is necessary in this age of such entertainments to remind ourselves these
were not stage or television events, but actual happenings to actual
beings, beneath this same sky, and on this same American ground.

> I have often been awakened at the dawn of day by the most
> heart-rending shrieks of an own aunt of mine, whom he used to
> tie up to a joist, and whip upon her naked back till she was
> literally covered with blood. No words, no tears, no prayers,
> from his gory victim, seemed to move his iron heart from its
> bloody purpose. The louder she screamed, the harder he whipped;
> and where the blood ran fastest, there he whipped longest. . . .
> Mr. Thomas Lanman, of St. Michael's, killed two slaves, one of
> whom he killed with a hatchet, by knocking his brains out. He
> used to boast of the commission of the awful and bloody deed.
> . . . The wife of Mr. Giles Hicks, living but a short distance from
> where I used to live, murdered my wife's cousin, a young girl
> between fifteen and sixteen years of age, mangling her person
> in the most horrible manner, breaking her nose and breastbone
> with a stick. . . . It did produce sensation, but not enough to
> bring the murderess to punishment. . . . We seldom meet one
> destitute of every element of character commanding respect. My
> master was one of this rare sort. . . . Prior to his conversion, he
> relied upon his own depravity to shield and sustain him in his
> savage barbarity; but after his conversion, he found religious
> sanction and support for his slaveholding cruelty. . . . I have
> seen him tie up a lame young woman, and whip her with a
> heavy cowskin upon her naked shoulders, causing the warm red
> blood to drip; and, in justification of the bloody deed, he would
> quote this passage of Scripture—"He that knoweth his master's
> will, and doeth it not, shall be beaten with many stripes." [13]

Of the human capacities brutalized by the system none was
more readily and consistently degraded than sex—and again it is
a measure of the humanity of Douglass to note his perception of
the pathos of white as well as black degradation.

> Mr. Covey was a poor man; he was just commencing in life;
> he was only able to buy one slave; and, shocking as is the fact,
> he bought her, as he said, for a breeder. . . . After buying her,
> he hired a married man of Mr. Samuel Harrison, to live with
> him one year; and him he used to fasten up with her every night!

The result was, that, at the end of the year, the miserable woman
gave birth to twins. At this result Mr. Covey seemed to be highly
pleased, both with the man and the wretched woman. Such was
his joy, and that of his wife, that nothing they could do for
Caroline during her confinement was too good, or too hard, to
be done. The children were regarded as being quite an addition
to his wealth.[14]

The breeding of blacks by blacks was one thing, however, and
the breeding of blacks by whites another—a practice that magni-
fied the brutalizing of the whites in many subtle ways.

The whisper that my master was my father, may or may not be
true. . . . The slaveholder, in cases not a few, sustains to his
slaves the double relation of master and father . . . such slaves
invariably suffer greater hardships. . . . They are, in the first
place, a constant offence to their mistress. . . . The master is frequently compelled to sell this class of his slaves, out of deference
to the feelings of his white wife; and, cruel as the deed may strike
any one to be, for a man to sell his own children to human flesh-
mongers, it is often the dictate of humanity for him to do so; for,
unless he does this, he must not only whip them himself, but
must stand by and see one white son tie up his brother, of but
few shades darker complexion than himself, and ply the gory lash
to his naked back.[15]

Out of the years of freedom ahead, looking back, Frederick
Douglass had many more observations to make of the nature and
workings of slavery as a system. But perhaps nowhere else does he
compress so much of his vision of the enormity of the system—
so much of the economics and the sociology of inhumanity—as in
this short passage.

If any one thing in my experience, more than other, served to
deepen my conviction of the infernal character of slavery, and
to fill me with unutterable loathing of slaveholders, it was their
base ingratitude to my poor old grandmother. She had served
my old master faithfully from youth to old age. She had been
the source of all his wealth; she had peopled his plantation with
slaves; she had become a great grandmother in his service. She
had rocked him in infancy, attended him in childhood, served
him through life, and at his death wiped from his icy brow the
cold death-sweat, and closed his eyes forever. She was never-

theless left a slave—a slave for life—a slave in the hands of strangers; and in their hands she saw her children, her grandchildren, and her great-grandchildren, divided, like so many sheep, without being gratified with the small privilege of a single word, as to their or her own destiny. And, to cap the climax of their base ingratitude and fiendish barbarity, my grandmother, who was now very old, having outlived my old master and all his children, having seen the beginning and end of all of them, and her present owners finding she was of but little value, her frame already racked with the pains of old age, and complete helplessness fast stealing over her once active limbs, they took her to the woods, built her a little hut, put up a little mudchimney, and then made her welcome to the privilege of supporting herself there in perfect loneliness; thus virtually turning her out to die! [16]

Had it happened on another planet or in a nightmare, it seems that long ago we would have marveled at some fable of a voracious white insect that constructed a citadel for itself and its kind that was surrounded by a high and wondrous wall. And out from this citadel—so the fable would have it—this white insect moved only to seize black bugs, whom it imprisoned in pens just outside the wall, to eat at its leisure, and red bugs, whom it squashed in order to obtain their territory and extend the citadel and its mighty walls.

Unfortunately, men do not become insects only in fables, dreams, or in stories by Franz Kafka. Thus, how and why they undergo this strange metamorphosis becomes a question of considerable importance, which we shall next examine.

CHAPTER 9

Cognition, Conformity,
and Man as Insect

Inevitably, the historical picture of slavery and black exploitation, and the Trail of Tears and red genocide, must suggest a diminishing of humanity to a certain hard-shelled, unfeeling, voracious, predatory, swarming type of being we associate mainly with insects. Thus an extremely important question for modern social science is just how do responsible human beings become such insects? What goes on within our minds that allows us to shut out much of what makes us human and regress not merely to the animal level, but *below* it?

But this is only half of the question. The other half, larger and different in many ways, is not how man as an individual but how men *en masse* become insects. Frederick Douglass saw this vital difference, viewing slavery not simply as a consequence of an evil, predatory Southern overseer or of an evil, unfeeling Northern slave profiteer, but as a consequence of an evil social system working upon pliable men.

The relevant questions, then, are of man individually, and men within social systems. We shall first explore the curiosities of the individual mind uncovered by modern cognitive studies.

One sees the curious, dry, and somehow repellent word *cognition* everywhere in educational literature.[1] One reason for its use is (to be blunt about it) that it can make some awfully foggy and shallow pronouncements sound scholarly. A more important reason, however, is that when it is properly used no other one word conveys so much precise meaning about the "thinking processes." The process of thinking, viewed spontaneously, with no attempt to intellectualize, may seem to be a mysterious rolling about of numbers and pictures within the "brain soup" enclosed by the skull, followed by some sort of clicking into place of "solutions" out of this turbulence. The psychologist, however, has traditionally seen thinking as a sequence of three processes: *Perception,* with which we handle the stimuli that fall upon our eyes, ears, nose, skin, and other receptors, as well as those that work upon us from within (a stomach ache, or the "voice of conscience"); *memory,* that fascinating storehouse of our past experience to which we refer our present-time perceptions for some reading as to their meaning; and *thinking* itself, by which information from both perception and memory is manipulated to arrive at useful answers to questions in the broadest sense—or by which information is simply shifted around for our delight.

To the psychologist cognition is all of this—perception, memory, and thinking—and the word not only quickly conveys much meaning but also suggests that these are separate processes only for the convenience of science; in actual operation they are as closely interwoven as breathing and the pulsing of the blood. Historically, modern cognitive studies grew out of the insistence of the Gestaltists that mind mattered in itself, and the desire of many behaviorists to broaden their approach. The work of three decades now suggests that some of our failure to understand the workings of the black and white sickness, or its potential cures, may be attributed to the recency of our attention to the workings of this cognitive domain, wherein lie the foundations of insecthood.

Perception: McClelland and Bruner

In the late 1940s and 1950s the study of perception—which was still heavily concerned with the traditional debate between those preoccupied with what happens "out there" in the world of external stimuli and those preoccupied with what happens inside the mind—was rocked by a band of social-needs-oriented perceptual psychologists. They contended that perception was not merely a relatively passive process that fed highly active stimulus information from "out there" into an actively warping mind, but was in fact an actively warping process in itself. More pertinent to our purpose, there was an important shift in emphasis: Where previously the study of perception tended to be in general, philosophical, and physiological terms, this group of young Turks were interested in what it might reflect of individual personality differences that are often linked to *social* differences. David McClelland showed that hungry people looking at misty images tended to see food in the images, though no food was there. Jerome Bruner showed that, compared with children from wealthy homes, children from poor homes seemed to see coins as being larger. These experiments, they said, were evidence of how individual needs, or motivation, affect perception.[2]

On the basis of other experiments, members of this "New Look" group also posited the concept of *perceptual defense:* That we not only intensify what we want to see, making it larger or filling it in where it doesn't exist, but that we reject whatever we don't want to see—and this generally happens before we even become aware of it.[3] That is, we go about with a built-in perceptual defense system that automatically screens out anything we don't wish to see or hear.

The volleying and thundering of experimental psychologists over these findings still continues, but out of their disputes have emerged several useful "models" of perceptual processes. One of the best known was developed by Jerome Bruner, who has become an august and widely influential educational theorist (the "discovery" method of teaching, for example, is associated with him). Bruner saw perception as a filter which receives the tremendous barrage of stimuli falling upon us and allows only a tiny usable portion to pass through to our awareness. This filtering makes use of four processes: *grouping, access ordering,* a *gating process,* and a *match-mismatch* process.[4] An enduring question about the black and white sickness has been how a supposedly Christian and civilized people could tolerate the brutality of slavery and the continuing inequities of the black-white situation in America. Let us see how this might work in terms of Bruner's four processes.

You are, let us say, a truly fine, sensitive Southern gentleman, a lover of Beethoven as well as bourbon, and you are observing a slave auction. The slaves that appear before you bear various marks that an abolitionist would quickly perceive—the scars of beatings and brandings, teeth missing, possibly from blows, tears on the cheek of a mother about to be separated from her children, bare feet so split by frostbite that "one could lay a pencil in the cracks," as Frederick Douglass noted of his own experience as a child.

Curiously, as one by one and two by two the slaves pass before you to take their dismal place upon the block, you see none of this. The stimuli, along with millions of others, have reached your eye, but here they have been rejected from entry to awareness. How is this possible? The Bruner view suggests the screening could have operated somewhat in this way. The physical stimuli for the perception "scar" have reached your eye, and there is the following sequence. The *grouping process* waits to form these stimuli—a slash across the face of a certain size and redness—into the perception "scar," but a lightning-quick check via the *match-mismatch process* may find cause for a "stop order" on this perception. It may find that in your internal department for rules governing the perceptions of blacks in this situation, "scar" is not acceptable, or even if it is acceptable, "scar" may still be too low in priority to register—that is, stimuli that form the basis for more acceptable perceptions may crowd this particular stimulus out in the competition for acceptance by an *access ordering process.*

The actual rejection is then carried out by the *gating process,* and you do not see the scar—nor the frostbite, nor the tear, nor the quite literally billions of such messages of distress that have moved out from blacks toward unseeing whites over the years.

Memory: Bartlett, Autism, and the Historian's Bias

In the early 1930s a very entertaining British psychologist, Sir Frederic Bartlett, charmed his students with a seemingly light-weight experiment. He had a student read an Eskimo folk tale "The War of the Ghosts," to himself, and then write an account of it from memory. This account was given to a second student, who then wrote his version of the tale from memory and gave it to a third student, the third to the fourth, the fourth to the fifth, and so on.[5]

Sir Frederic varied the procedure in several ways. For example, he compared the results of a sequence of this sort, using British students, with a sequence using Hindu students to see how vastly different cultural backgrounds may affect memory. And he found that where in time the British dropped out the Eskimo mysticism and color to produce a simple, straightforward, no-nonsense "British" story, the Hindu end product blossomed exotically, with notably more "elaboration and adornment." This experiment initiated a great number of studies during the 1930s of what became known as the "autism" effect. And Sir Frederic himself— who for all his disarming wit was quite a heavyweight, as was this experiment, in the long run—eventually wrote of this work and his views on memory in what is still one of the most stimulating books that has been written on the subject.[6]

His conclusions were many, but essentially he found memory to be curiously like the Freudian dream. That is, he found that we do not merely forget things, but we also add things that were never there to begin with. We also condense and expand things, distort and reverse meanings, and, in short, much as a writer of fiction handles his material, we reconstruct our past to fit whatever our present needs may be.

An experiment by Gordon Allport and Leo Postman in the early 1940s demonstrated what appears to be this memory distortion effect in the black-white context. They would show a first subject a picture of a quarrel in a subway involving a Negro and a white man who was armed with a razor. Yet after a sequence of subjects retelling what they had seen—one to another, as in the Bartlett "Ghosts" story—the razor that was actually in the white man's hand to begin with had shifted over time and retelling into the black man's hand.[7]

This example, however, is nothing alongside one that has shaped the course of our nation, and that our children still encounter daily —that vast distortion of the white memory processes that our history books represent. Written and published history is, quite literally, the memory of a society. (Men die and the flesh-and-blood memory vanishes with them, but the books embodying their memories live on to become our culture, our heritage, our history, to emphasize the point.) As we now know all too well, until the 1960s American history was overwhelmingly a matter of reconstructing our past *without* the black, or with the black only presented in a denigrating or unfavorable light. Much of the black history this book presents, for example, is still unknown to most whites. Millions of blacks might serve and thousands die in our wars, and Frederick Douglass and W. E. B. Du Bois occasionally gained recognition over their long lives as being among the most remarkable men of their times, but until the past few years, for most Americans they simply did not exist in our social memory. It was as though they had never lived.

So here we see at work on a vast scale, affecting the destinies of black and white millions, a distortion of group memory that parallels the devious ways by which we forget or embellish things as individuals.

Thinking: Neobehaviorists, Neo-Pavlovians, and Osgood

Thinking is composed of processes that are still imperfectly understood. The Gestalt view, which centered about the concept of creative insight,[8] has something to do with the cure but little to do with the disease, so we shall pass on to a view that powerfully relates to the self-reduction of insecthood. The older, more powerful tradition was the associational, out of which emerged Pavlov and Watson and the behaviorists—and eventually the considerably more sophisticated neobehaviorists in this country and the neo-Pavlovians in Russia.[9]

The work of this group has much to say of relevance to the black and white sickness. So much, in fact, that we can only suggest one of many relevant channels here—the exploration of the mind through word association. The basic idea is an old one in psychology. You present a stimulus word like "car," "house," or "mother" and see what sort of words a person associates with these stimuli. Carl Jung first used an approach of this type to explore the mind of schizophrenics shortly before 1900.[10] Freud used a variant in his method of dream analysis. More recently the neobehaviorists and the neo-Pavlovians, by means of particularly ingenious experiments, have established many rules for what is aptly described as the "chaining effect" of this process. That is, one says or picks one word and asks for a response, and then asks for a response to the response word, and so on, and in this way one can discover that our minds are filled with thoughts that are linked together like strings of chain, or better still, like chain mail that is linked in a multitude of directions all at once.[11]

What happens when the stimulus word "Negro" is presented to a group of whites has been frequently explored. Probably the earliest experiment of this type was carried out in 1932 by Daniel Katz and K. W. Braley. One hundred Princeton University students were asked to select from a list of eighty-four adjectives those they felt might best describe typical members of various groups—in this case Americans, Chinese, English, Germans, Irish, Italians, Japanese, Jews, Turks, and Negroes.

Slowly but surely, as the results were tabulated, some familiar stereotypes fell in place. For example, Princeton students in 1933 reported that they thought of the Irish as being pugnacious, quick-tempered, and witty. Germans were scientifically minded, industrious, and stolid. And Negroes? Superstitious. Lazy. Happy-go-lucky. Ignorant. This same study was repeated again in 1950 with 333 Princeton students. It is of great interest that although all the stereotypes had noticeably weakened over the years, only the stereotypes for the Germans and Japanese had changed very much. The rest—and most notably the black stereotype—showed very little change over this eighteen-year span. (One encouraging finding, however, was that the students *were* considerably more sophisticated this second time around. Many balked at the "unreasonable task of making generalizations about people—especially those they had hardly ever met." [12])

Such clear evidence of "bad" associations to the word "Negro" among most whites (and prior to the 1970s, among most blacks) has been found by many different researchers in many different settings. Now let us advance this train of thought another step. The early Gestalt thinkers were the first to point out that all these associations don't merely float around in the mind as a sort of vast glittering mush, but that they are structured, or grouped, or organized in certain ways. They also stressed that how all this knowledge is used depends on how it is organized. Here a particularly useful discovery has been that our thoughts and their linkings tend to group themselves according to a fundamental good-bad, plus-minus, yes-no, off-on polarity. [13]

This polarity runs through much of modern psychology—Freud's pleasure-pain principle; the approach-avoidance view of Kurt Lewin; [14] even at the most basic level, the physiological, in the discovery by James Olds and others of what appear to be specific pleasure and specific pain centers in the brain itself. [15] And one might also add the highly suggestive off-on, binary-choice operation of the computer, which is now being used to simulate human thinking processes. However, the most extensive work on this polarity as it affects thinking has been done by Charles Osgood, an experimental and social psychologist whose general significance is still poorly grasped, but whose protean body of work is one of the more impressive in our time. [16] (His contribution of what is known as "mediation theory" to the Pavlov-Watson-Clark Hull developmental strain to conditioning or learning theory, for example, is the chief bridge from psychology into modern psycholinguistics. And his extension of advanced techniques for the measurement of meaning into areas that have been the province of the sociologist and the anthropologist could, were they understood and used, put a floor under large areas of concern for both fields.)

By means of extremely sophisticated statistical approaches, and an ingenious measure known as the Semantic Differential, Osgood has established a great deal about how this fundamental human tendency to sort our thoughts and impressions into basic "good-bad" evaluative polarities operates. The work itself is too elaborate to do more than identify here, but the fact of importance is this: Using the Semantic Differential (and other more ingenious offsprings) Osgood and his associates have tested great numbers of people not merely in America but throughout the world, and have established that underlying all the differences in color, languages, education, economic, and cultural development, men around the world are remarkably similar in how they organize their thoughts in terms of the emotional (and therefore the *motivating*) meanings they assign to everything they encounter.

They are also remarkably similar in that their basic organization of most of these meanings is in terms of only three dimensions within a hypothetical "affective meaning space." Basically we think in terms of *evaluative, potency,* and *activity* dimensions. That is, practically everything we must deal with in thought (and, eventually, action) is, in effect, assigned a place in the mind along a "good-bad" *evaluative* dimension. (This man, this woman, this object, this thought, is good, bad, indifferent.) To a somewhat lesser degree we assign to practically everything a rating along a *potency* dimension. (This man, this woman, this thought, is strong or weak.) And to a still lesser degree we give practically everything an *activity* rating. (This man, woman, object, is fast or slow.)

Moreover, Osgood's and many other studies have established the very powerful linkages between these good-bad, strong-weak, fast-slow mental ratings and the actions we do or do not take because of them. These findings can be reduced to any number of down-to-earth situations to illustrate the shaping of insecthood.

You are a Northern shopkeeper needing a helper, in the early 1800s, let us say. A black man applies. He says he is a freed slave. He says he needs the job badly, he has a wife and child, he will work long hours and be faithful. This may be true, you admit to yourself, but somehow . . . You tell yourself he may, after all, be a runaway, one shouldn't risk trouble, and you turn him away. But of course what also happened is that you have automatically assigned him to a fairly predictable place on the basic good-bad scale in your mind, and to it cluster all the "bad" associations linked to the concept "Negro" or "nigger." He could steal you blind, he could alienate customers; but, far more powerful than these specifics, he is everything strange and uncomfortable, he is that dark, bad id creature that emerges in your dreams, he is a bad, black Rorschach blot, the potential source of God-knows-what dire calamity; a deep, sure "instinct" tells you.

Moreover, as you look at him another crucial assignment will be made on the strong-weak scale. He is obviously weak, this penniless black man. Very weak indeed. And so you will deal with him accordingly. (And so will your descendants, until Malcolm X appears!)

Cognition and Conformity

"It was a society in the grip of an insecurity complex . . . heightened by having to defend against constant attack an institution it knew to be discredited throughout the civilized world. Its reaction was to withdraw increasingly from contact with the offending world . . . and to attempt by curtailing freedom of speech to avoid criticism." [17] Thus, the South's great historian, C. Vann Woodward, describes the net effect of this constriction of thinking, feeling, and perceiving that brought on the doom of the old South.

In the North, however, and in the South wherever freed slaves attempted to make a place for themselves, another monument to insecthood that was *not* doomed was being erected. And it has expanded into our day. "In the period before about 1810, one can just begin to detect the ontogeny of segregation," notes historian W. D. Jordan.[18] Stanley Elkins finds "our kind" of segregation essentially fixed in place by 1830.[19] It was to be shaken by the Civil War, but the foundation held. And the walls were then steadily strengthened with the separation of schools, jobs, homes, churches, bus seating, drinking fountains, rest rooms, lunch counters, swimming pools, beaches, movies, amusement parks—even hospitals, where life begins, blood banks, where it is maintained, and graveyards, where it ends.

Stone by stone, then, the foundations of the great perceptual wall that screens black from white were set in place in the early 1800s. And span by span went up the cognitive superstructure that still circumscribes white thought and memory. And step by step were laid down movements for white and black, prescribed according to insect fixities rather than the human potential. But for all the strength of these processes operating within the indi-

vidual mind, there was obviously something considerably more
powerful at work. The mind of the individual might very well
shrink, and harden, and become diseased; but how was it that men
en masse became insects and linked together in great antlike chains
to build their citadel?

Conformity: Tarde, LeBon, Smith, Durkheim, and Opinion Polling

Two French social thinkers were among the first to explore the
forces that might account for group inhumanities by making men
think, feel, and act alike. Everywhere Gabriel Tarde saw *imitation*
at work shaping man and society. So powerful was this force that
he felt man might resist it consciously only with great difficulty.
"Social man is a somnambulist," he asserted of the workings of
something to which William James, George Herbert Mead, and
Freud (in his concept of identification) also directed attention.

Another great early figure, the French sociologist Gustav Le-
Bon, discerned something slightly different at work. He called it
suggestibility. His classic study, *The Crowd*, examined its workings, as did Pavlov's rival, the Russian Bechterev, and more recently the late influential humanistic social psychologist Hadley
Cantril. Still others—the odd pairing of the "father" of capitalism Adam Smith, and the Russian revolutionary Peter Kropotkin,
for example—saw a third aspect to this "force." It seemed, in a
curious way, to serve to counter the sometimes harshly selfish or
ethnocentric group effects of the other two.[20] This was the force
of *sympathy*, to which in our time Pitrim Sorokin and Ashley
Montagu have directed attention in the face of much cynicism.

Perhaps the greatest single statement on all of this was the work
of the French sociologist Émile Durkheim, who drew many of
these strains together into a theory for which the beautifully self-
descriptive term *solidarity* was a central concept. After Karl Marx
and Max Weber, Durkheim is generally considered to be the most
influential figure in the history of sociology. He devoted much of
a very productive life to the pursuit of the meaning of solidarity.[21]

The area as a whole is probably one of the two or three most
important complexes of processes in all of social science. It is
certainly of central importance in understanding the hold of the

black and white sickness upon America. Yet it is an area of meaning that is not generally grasped very well. One barrier to understanding is that in practically all available accounts, this complex
of processes rapidly becomes confusing unless one is equipped
with a simple key to the whole picture. One of the most useful was
supplied by Gordon Allport in his great essay "The Historical
Background of Modern Social Psychology," which was written in
the 1930s and is still one of the best guides to the field as a whole.

Allport grounds his guide in Plato, who originally saw man as
mentally having three aspects: emotion—feelings, affects, the
affective component; reason—thoughts, cognitions, the *cognitive*
component; and striving—action, willing, doing, the *conative*
component. Allport then grouped the social processes with Plato's
components: suggestibility with the cognitive, sympathy with the
affective, and imitation with the conative. And then he added one
other piece of useful connective tissue.

In regard to the black and white sickness, one continually hears
of how attitudes are the problem, and how they must be changed.
This makes good sense to most of us, even though we may not
have any very precise sense of what an attitude actually is. The
beauty of Allport's presentation is that it defines an attitude by
placing it clearly at the juncture between the three-part personal
mental world and a social world in which the three "solidarity"
processes are operating. In a sense, it is merely a handy organizing
principle for what exists and happens at the meeting place between subject and object, or between what is "in us" and what is
"out there." On the inner, personal side, attitudes are formed of
(and by) the individual cognitive processes—perceiving, memory,
and thinking. And on the outer, social side, attitudes are linked
to the group world through the vast, scintillating, steel-threaded,
sometimes sinister, yet absolutely necessary web of imitation, suggestibility, and sympathy.

This, then, is the complex which opinion polls and similar measures tap. And it also gives some indication of why polls of attitudes can be good guides to social action. When carefully constructed and administered, attitude measures reach not only the
personal man but the social man, and each seemingly innocuous
question can, in fact, tap an incredible range of being. They can
tap the forces that determine elections, make or break new indus-

tries, bring us war or peace—or answer questions relevant to gaining health out of sickness, like whether whites believe blacks should have the vote, equal justice, and the rest of it; and whether blacks believe they are gaining these things, or whether it is an illusion.

Conformity: Sherif, Asch, Pettigrew

And so it has been obvious for many years that, whatever one might call them, some very powerful forces are at work that account for much of what men think and feel and do in groups. However, it was not until the 1930s that anyone succeeded in going much beyond observation and speculation to get an effective handle on these forces experimentally.

In 1936, an ingenious social psychologist, Muzafer Sherif, discovered a new way of studying what have come to be known (through a questionable deglamorizing) as *conformity* phenomena. A popular experimental procedure of those days involved putting students in a completely dark room and recording their reports of the movement of a single pinpoint of light. The light was actually stationary; but after one watched it for a while, with nothing in the blackness to serve as an anchoring reference point, it seemed to slowly drift, wiggle, or even dash off in various directions. This *autokinetic* effect was used to explore a number of intriguing but minor questions in experimental psychology.

However, Sherif, who is blessed with courage and a particularly fertile imagination in a field that is increasingly more timid and restrictive, saw the possibility for some productive crossbreeding. A key problem that had concerned Durkheim about the "solidarity processes" was how the social norms that generally govern our behavior are formed. Durkheim had felt that new norms were formed "during interactions in fluid, uncertain, or out-of-the-ordinary conditions." So instead of using the customary single subject in the dark room for the autokinetic effect, Sherif put several subjects together in the room to report the light's apparent movement. He found that where single subjects had reported a variety of speeds and directions, when they were brought together their reports converged, becoming quite similar to one another. It was apparent that he had at last succeeded in bringing into the laboratory, where it might be more carefully examined, the powerful but elusive force that binds men together.[22]

In the 1940s, Solomon Asch, a psychologist of central importance in the bridging of the old Gestalt into the new cognitive studies traditions, worked out an even better laboratory demonstration, and then carried out what is now the classic work in this area. In a group of seven students, six would be his confederates —that is, unknown to the seventh student the other six were working for the experimenter. Asch would show the students two cards, one with a single fat black line on it, the other with three fat black lines, one of which was the same length as the line on the first card. The students were then asked to identify which of the three lines on the second card was the same length as the single line.

Asch would run through the procedure a few times to accustom everyone to agreeing on the clear evidence before their eyes. Then he would have his six confederates begin to report that they saw two clearly *unequal* lines as being equal. What is happening here?, the poor naïve subject wonders. He can see the lines aren't equal, but a majority of his peers say they are. What shall he do?

A dismaying 75 percent of the subjects gave in to group pressure and reported a clear mistake rather than disagree with their fellows in even such a simple, nonthreatening situation. Moreover, the conformity effect was so pronounced that "even when the difference between the lines was seven inches, there were still some who yielded to the error of the majority." [23]

On this basis we might assume there was no hope for man, with the population explosion, for example, thrusting us toward the final quagmire of massed conformist bodies. However, the experiment had a reassuring feature, which was what Asch found out about *non*conformity. He found that if even one of the six confederates goes against the majority and reports the truth— what he actually sees—the seventh man is *strengthened in his own tendency to resist the group pressure and to make a truthful or veridical report.* Here we see from another angle an accounting for the impact of John Woolman, Anthony Benezet, some abolitionists we shall shortly meet, and, in fact, every dissenter, every man, however grounded, of some fearlessness and independence on this or any other issue. Through history, such have been the one in six among men who gave the seventh man strength to stand up for his own belief when put to the test.

The Asch work also indicates another possibly crucial social function of the dissenter. In another variant of this study he would have one confederate in a group of naïve subjects report as equal lines that were very obviously unequal in length. He then found that the "extremist dissenter produced a remarkable freeing of the subjects; their errors dropped to only 9 per cent." In other words, a single confederate maintaining flagrant error in a group of naïve subjects will encourage them all to be more independent and less conforming to one another. Here, it would seem, is an analogue to the situation of the extremist, who may be either for or against blacks. Though he is usually damned for his distortion and immoderation by the moderate, this finding would suggest the extremism of either white redneck or black militant frees the moderate to express himself more openly either way, for or against blacks, depending on person and circumstance.

A large body of work has now probed conformity, and another important type of finding is of personality differences. Here the picture is not merely of conformists and nonconformists (who may be simply conformists in reverse), but of two possible additional types: the truly independent, who neither conforms nor nonconforms by rote or bent, but acts according to his wits and the situation; and the erratic, who may seem to be independent or nonconforming, but is merely rudderless and therefore unpredictable.[24]

Another type of finding relates to the influence of social norms upon conforming and nonconforming personalities. And here some ingenious studies have punctured—and, let us hope, begun to end —persisting and very dangerous American myths. The picture is roughly this.

In the early 1950s, sociologist R. D. Minard observed something rather interesting about racial prejudice among coal miners in the Pocahontas Coal Field in West Virginia: That in this Southern mine white and black miners seemed to work amiably together when they were below the surface in the mine, but at the end of the work day, when they returned to the world above ground, they separated into the familiar pattern of segregated housing, churches, entertainment, etc. Nothing startling so far, of course—except that only a few hundred feet of earth separated two such radically different worlds. But then Minard observed that roughly 20 percent of the miners had antiblack attitudes both below and above ground, and 20 percent had *pro*-black attitudes in both places. And what of the remaining 60 percent? They *shifted* from problack to antiblack behavior depending on whether they were above or below ground.

The constancy or personal fixation of those with definitely liberal or definitely conservative racial attitudes also emerged in studies of interacial housing and the army. And more evidence of a majority capacity to make rather remarkable shifts in racial attitudes over a period of a few years emerged in opinion polls in Oklahoma, Delaware, and some border states during the early 1950s. (These findings were of relatively rapid shifts in the liberal direction, of course, where by contrast, since 1968, similar polls have reflected shifts toward conservatism.)

Findings of this type inspired one of the most gifted and dedicated researchers in the black-studies area, social psychologist Thomas Pettigrew of Harvard, to launch a very important study.[25] His purpose was to draw together some of these intriguing but sprawling findings by using rigorous measures and a very careful research design. Selecting for his testing sites the two most black-prejudiced countries in the world, South Africa and the United States, he gathered data on nearly a thousand blacks and whites in both countries. One type of questionnaire he used was designed to get at possible constancies of personality—it was composed of scales known as the F (for fascism) and E (for ethnocentrism), both of which can fairly accurately measure the degree to which one is consistently liberal or conservative in racial and other attitudes. And what he found, both in South Africa and in the Northern and Southern United States, were surprisingly constant proportions of the rightist, ultraconservative types that (ever since the famous study by Adorno and associates that gave rise to the name) have been known as "authoritarian personalities."

A second type of measure he used were the A (for anti-African) and N (for anti-Negro) scales to gauge differences in racial prejudice, and here he found what one might predict—South Africans and Southerners in the United States were markedly more prejudiced against Negroes than were Northerners in the United States.

These findings clearly indicated that prejudice could not be attributed solely to bigots, for the amount of prejudice varied greatly in the North versus the South, while the proportion of bigots remained roughly the same. The question then becomes what else might account for the marked quantitative difference in prejudice according to whether the group being tested lived above or below the Mason-Dixon line.

With a third type of measure Pettigrew identified two major influences. Using conformity measures (the conformity or C-scale in South Africa and biographical data analysis in the United States) he pinned the "shift" to the working of social norms upon conforming personalities. That is, by means of this careful and exacting research which grounded earlier speculation, he quite clearly recorded that a large part of racial prejudice depends on where we live and how we respond to social norm differences. More exactly and forcefully, he found that where in the South conformists were generally highly prejudiced against blacks, in the North conformists were lower in black prejudice. Moreover, in the South nonconformists had markedly more liberal racial views than the prevailing norms.

The implications of findings of this type are more profound than would appear on the surface. In every area of America there is entrenched a hoary folk wisdom that contends "you can't change human nature." Along with it one hears that "you can't change deep-seated customs or folkways by passing laws," or "you can't legislate mores." Tied to this is the old Social Darwinist belief that racial inequalities can only be ended by small, slow steps over a great span of time. Moreover, a "liberal" variant of this type of thinking feels the only solution to ending racial prejudice would be to psychoanalyze everybody!

What these findings suggest is that if you want to decrease racial prejudice and advance desegregation you do not wait for man's innate goodness to prevail over time.[26] Nor do you waste time trying to get everybody to spend years on the couch for private therapy. You simply go to work bringing certain time-tested group pressures to bear on the social conformist, which includes a majority of us. You promote lecture series. You set up discussion sessions. You write books. You lobby and you gather delegations to pressure school boards and legislatures. And you support and campaign for forceful leadership. And if you are in that leadership position, you see that influential and progressive mass circulation media reach us. You pass laws and issue executive orders. If necessary, you even move in troops—and it is interesting to see how quickly most of us will change. The vast shifts in attitudes and behavior that occurred in the South and in the North between the early 1950s and the mid-1960s, in response to just such pressures as these, suggests the validity of these methods. Moreover, the ease with which we slipped back or barely held the earlier gains *in lieu of such leadership pressures in the late sixties and early seventies* indicates how malleable most of us actually are.

But this leaves the question of what can be done about the cement-headed, suspicious, often foul-mouthed and passionately moralistic hard-core resistance that remains in both North and South. In all probability, relatively little can be done about such resistance. But research suggests the number of "fixed" antiblacks is much smaller than that of the "shift-prone" majority, and one generation gives way to another, so time would appear to be on the side of the black. The black-advancement drive of the fifties and early sixties also indicates that the influence of the entrenched antiblack can be more than offset by an aroused nonconformist or independent minority who, even if they are not personally committed to black advancement, are still generally committed to the black-advancing American ideals of liberty and equality.

And so, after a rather long journey into the caves and byways of the everyday mind, we have completed the cycle. We have ranged from the psychology out to the sociology of racism and back again. That is, we have seen how what can begin as a diminishing and hardening and encrusting infection in a single mind moves out to infect our society—and how the infection constricting the vitality of our society on an almost inconceivably vast scale can, in turn, move back to engulf the single mind.

CHAPTER 10

Two Ideas and Some Human Beings

The lamp flickered and he reached over to turn up the wick. He was a handsome man, his high forehead, the direct gaze of his blue eyes, and the firm line of his mouth expressing a jaunty confidence even in his weariness. He looked down again to the paper on his desk, writing.

"I have not one helper—not one from whom I can draw sympathy, or impart joy, on this topic! My nearest friends think it very silly in me to run against the world in a matter that cannot in any way do me any good. Even my own children appear careless and indifferent—if anything, rather disposed to look upon my views as chimerical and visionary. My nearest friends here are of the sort that are always crying out 'take care of yourself—don't meddle with other people's affairs—do nothing, say nothing, get along quietly—make money.' " [1]

The year was 1834. The man was James Birney, whom practically nobody knows today. He was forty-two years old, a white man of position, family and property, and a "seventh man" who had just announced that where others in his real-life experimental group consistently found black and white to be unequal, he could only see and report an equality. For this act of honesty he would be so abused in his hometown that he would have to move to the North, and even here he would be pursued by bloodthirsty mobs. For this Southern aristocrat, a former cotton planter, slaveowner, ex-member of the Alabama legislature and ex-Mayor of Huntsville, had announced that he was joining the abolitionists.

The stir in Danville, Kentucky, must have been something. One can hear the soft, warm, worried voices of good old Dan and Bob and Joe: "How could good old Jim Birney *do* such a thing?" He had gone from Danville to that citadel of citadels, the old "Harvard of the South," Princeton University; had returned in glory (having been kicked out twice for drunkenness, but still managing to graduate with honors); and had gone on to settle in Alabama Territory as one of the likeliest young lawyers about. Not only was he learned, but he had all the most admired virtues of the Southern male—he could drink with the best of them, loved gambling in all its great exotic Southern as well as imported forms, told a good story, could fight like a wildcat, and was a charmer with the ladies. It was obvious he was made to order for Southern politics. Why, he was elected to practically every good post around in Kentucky and Alabama, and he even gave up law to become a cotton planter with forty-three niggers on his place. How could good old Jim Birney *do* such a thing?

There was—as there always is—another side to the story. Birney had grown up in a household that was opposed to slavery even while making a living from it. Both his slaveowning father and his grandfather had fought and failed to keep Kentucky free territory. At Princeton he had influential teachers who were opposed to slavery. His cotton plantation was a failure in an acceptable Southern way—he simply gambled and drank too much; but his career in Southern politics was ended by the fact he couldn't stomach Andrew Jackson's treatment of the Indians. He refused to support Jackson, and this was political death in Alabama.

His personally ruinous support for their cause was noted by the Cherokees. When they made their final attempt to fight Removal they asked Birney to represent them as their lawyer. He fought for them in the courts in 1826, and when the Cherokees were then driven out by troops under Jackson's order—in defiance of the condemnation of Chief Justice John Marshall and a Supreme Court ruling in their favor—this idealistic young lawyer was so deeply embittered that some of those close to him felt his later direct action against slavery in defiance of the law and custom of his time dated from this episode. Others attributed his defiance to his conversion from a staid Episcopalianism to the radical evangelism taking hold among the Presbyterians during this time. In any case, both internal and external forces working upon Birney reached a crisis, and he suddenly gave up a lucrative law practice in Huntsville, Alabama, to become a poorly paid agent of Dr. Archibald Alexander's beloved American Colonization Society.

Birney, like the better-known William Lloyd Garrison and others who later became abolitionists, was at first a colonizationist—for a time the scheme was the only outlet for the antislavery impulse. But its hypocrisy, as well as its practical failure, soon soured Garrison, and later Birney. To the abolitionists there could be no compromise with slavery, and that flat statement contains a good deal of meaning.

We have noted that ideas in conflict act as drives (a core finding of cognitive dissonance work). We have also pointed out some symptomatic historical compromises. The puffed-up and preposterous nature of colonization and the constitutional three-fifths-of-a-man decision, for example, reveal the intensity of the ideational conflicts that both measures were attempting to resolve. They were compromises resulting from pressures resolved by a social policy that was neither all "good" nor all "bad" but a mixture of both. Now, however, it was as though the pressure for consistency became so great that large numbers of Americans were driven not to settle for the mixture any longer, but to press for the "all good" solution (mainly in the North), or to avoid the conflict by damning, ignoring, or trying to silence the agitators (the Southern strategy of that era).

To the abolitionists slavery was, first, a sin in relation to the Christian concepts of the brotherhood of man. Secondly, it was a social crime in relation to the equalitarian concepts of American democracy.[2]

These two driving tenets of the abolitionist faith were considerably sharpened by a remarkably contemporary happening in the spring of 1834. The nation was then amused and a bit aroused by a clash between the students and the faculty and board of overseers of an obscure midwestern college, Lane Seminary, near Cincinnati, Ohio. And behind what surfaced nationally lay an involvement of white students with the Underground Railroad, with setting up schools for blacks, and caring for other black needs that spread to Oberlin and Western Reserve. "Perhaps at no other time in American history have the colleges played such an important part in a program of social reform," John Hope Franklin believes.[3]

It was a curious happening that not only foreshadowed the Civil War but was also rife with parallels to the student protest movement and the Berkeley, Columbia, and Sorbonne clashes of our day. For eighteen months an extremely well-publicized debate on slavery had been going on at Lane. Its promoter was an irresponsible young agitator whom history later immortalized as the great abolitionist orator Theodore Weld. Over the eighteen months, as Southern cruelties and hypocrisies were revealed by many eyewitnesses and remedies for these social crimes were debated, something familiar and fairly predictable happened: the student body became more and more fervently antislavery, while the faculty and administration became progressively more concerned with cooling this radical and unseemly washing of dirty American linen in public. Finally, the college overseers (a body like today's trustees, but burdened with a most unfortunate name for the times) tried to suppress the debate—and practically the whole student body resigned.

From nearby Danville, Kentucky, Birney had closely followed the debate. Increasingly he came to feel that, externally, it mirrored the debate within himself that was raging between what, in terms of our own time, would be the voices of the 1960s crying "Freedom *now!*" and those cautioning "be practical, go slow, don't rock the boat." He finally went to the embattled school, and after talking to Weld for two days he returned to Kentucky to renounce the colonization scheme, to declare for abolitionism, and to make the gesture for which he became famous in his time.

On the morning of June 2, 1834, he called his wife, his five sons, two neighbor boys, and the six household slaves he then possessed into the living room of their home. The boys ranged in age from seventeen-year-old James and fifteen-year-old William, both in college, to two-year-old George. (The presence of his sons was especially important to Birney. Very close to his own father, with a strong sense of family, and fearing that his sons would absorb from their surroundings what he felt to be the incredible amorality of his time, he had edged northward out of Alabama into Kentucky mainly to seek a more liberal atmosphere for his children to grow in.)

The little group stood before him, waiting, no doubt somewhat baffled but curious. In one of countless affirmations of the two basic abolitionist tenets, he told them that slavery was "inconsistent with the Great Truth that all men are created equal" as well as "the great rule of benevolence delivered to us by the Savior Himself that in all things whatsoever ye would that men should do unto ye, do ye even so to them." [4] Then he read the names of his slaves, and they realized he was freeing them. Many years later, his wife dead, himself aging and badly in need of funds for the care and schooling of his youngest children, he again released more slaves, worth $12,000 (he had only recently inherited them at the death of his father).

Though these actions were obviously heartfelt, they were also done with a sure feeling for Anthony Benezet's great weapon, publicity. In dramatizing these acts Birney was not only providing a model of enlightenment for other whites to follow, he was also providing invaluable fodder for the abolitionist publicity mill. There is an unfortunate obtuseness among us about activities of this sort. We want to believe in the individualistic myth that from time to time, motivated solely by their innate goodness, men rise up spontaneously *en masse* to do good for their fellow man. This hasn't happened yet, nor is it likely to happen short of the millennium; beneath the surface of every noble movement you will invariably find the prodding leadership and the publicity machine.

Of central historic importance for black advancement was the fact that the abolitionists moved millions by assembling the most remarkable publicity mill and by mounting the most persistent propaganda campaign in our history prior to the years of World War I. They organized boycotts of slave labor products and held debates and lectures on slavery (in 1836 alone they had seventy lecturers in the field). They worked up hundreds of petitions, printed hundreds of thousands of antislavery tracts, and wrote, financed, or encouraged the writing of hundreds of forceful books like Douglass' *Narrative* and Harriet Beecher Stowe's *Uncle Tom's Cabin,* which sold three hundred thousand copies during its first year of publication alone. They not only enlisted the support but at various times had in their arsenal the powerful pens and sentiments of John Greenleaf Whittier, Henry David Thoreau, Ralph Waldo Emerson, Walt Whitman, and James Russell Lowell. They planted abolitionist propaganda in textbooks and in popular works, they pressured legislatures, they organized underground railways, and throughout the country—North, East, and West—they planted antislavery societies and antislavery newspapers.[5] James Birney headed one of these papers, Frederick Douglass another, and a host of other abolitionists, both black and white, had still others, the most famous editorial gun emplacement being that of William Lloyd Garrison and the *Liberator*.

"I will be as harsh as truth, and as uncompromising as justice. On this subject, I do not wish to think, to speak, or write, with moderation. . . . I am in earnest . . . I will not equivocate . . . I will not excuse . . . I will not retreat a single inch . . . AND I WILL BE HEARD." [6] So proclaimed the single most powerful voice in print, that of Garrison, in the first issue of the *Liberator* in 1831. Shortly this voice was to be accused (wrongly) of sparking Nat Turner's bloody rebellion, and the messianic violence of Garrison's pronouncements became the focal point for an expanding group of activists that, over the years, has given us our stereotyped view of the abolitionists as a self-righteous, self-justifying group of militants who advocated the use of any means whatsoever to end slavery. This was the extremist position that led to the strange mixture of insanity, cagey incompetence and heroic grandeur that was John Brown and to the bloodletting at Harpers Ferry, which had much to do with scaring the South and poking the North into war.[7]

Beneath the stereotyped view of the abolitionists as wild-eyed advocates of violence, however, lay a far more complex and instructive historical reality. Far from being devils blind to ethics, they were by and large an extremely moral minority radically divided among themselves over how to force morality upon an immoral white majority. The chief practical issue on which they differed was whether slavery could be ended by political action *within* the rules of the established system or whether the men and the system must be radically changed by some other means. Though initially good friends, both Birney and Douglass eventually parted with Garrison on this issue.

Not at all unlike some voices of the 1960s and 1970s, Garrison damned the U.S. Government and the Constitution and felt that any involvement whatsoever in the tainted political process was a despicable sellout to the slaveholders. Birney felt this was a very foolish position to take, and after two years of study and internal debate, Douglass came to the same conclusion. "The first duty of every American citizen," Douglass said under rather heroic circumstances, was "to use his political as well as his moral power" for slavery's overthrow.[8]

In 1840 the abolitionists split into factions, one headed by Garrison and the other by Birney. The Garrisonians maintained that one should not give an inch on principle, but should damn slavery unrelentingly and look for a massive moral conversion among whites to liberate the blacks. The Birney faction felt that word pressure simply wasn't enough, and that one must become involved in the political process, however tainted, and seek to shape it to one's own ends. To that end Birney became the presidential candidate of the new antislavery Liberty party in 1840 and in 1844. This first puny attempt to inject the ending of slavery into national politics became a stream that led to the founding of the Republican party of Abraham Lincoln and to the first vast bloody explosion of a great nation seeking relief from its central hypocrisy. And because he aligned himself with the political abolitionists in 1851, Douglass was savagely and persistently vilified by Garrison and by both black and white Garrisonians, who accused him of hanky-panky with a white female editorial assistant when loftier means of attack failed.

Underlying this byplay, however, a more powerful and perplexing issue slowly gathered intensity: whether in the end one must go beyond either "moral suasion" or political action and resort to violence to produce the needed change, a debate that is, of course, again very much evident in our time. Over history the myth-making process has made of Garrison a rabid apostle of violence. It might then seem logical that the milder Birney, who advocated change within the system, was against violence. The fact is that for most of his life, Garrison was an apostle of *non*violence, and so, for a long stretch, were both Douglass and Birney. But the dismal dialectic of human events, rather than that of pretty logic or impressive debate, eventually forced them to modify this view.[9]

Out of the rising aspirations and frustrations of the black community of that time arose more and more voices advocating direct and unequivocal violence to achieve the justice that the abolitionists only seemed to be talking about, while getting nowhere. Among the whites were those, too, who hungered for decisive action rather than more debate. Despairing of moral suasion or political action alone, the black Douglass again startled and alienated both black and white friends by advocating violence as a last resort. "I should welcome the intelligence . . . that the slaves had risen in the South, and . . . were engaged in spreading death and destruction," he said as early as 1849.[10] And then, in 1859, John Brown's bloody intervention at Harpers Ferry in a sense closed the debate for an age. The blow itself—a wild attack and seizure of a sleepy Southern town by a mixed white and black guerrilla band—so captured the headlines and men's imaginations that little room was left for quieter thoughts or lesser actions. And the subsequent hanging of Brown widened, hardened, and polarized Northern and Southern sentiment on the slavery issue, readying both sides for the ultimate violence of the Civil War.

The progression leading to this climax seems fairly clear on the intellectual level, as shown by the speeches, writings, and actions of the abolitionists. There was a huge discrepancy between the avowed American and Christian ideals of equality and brotherhood, on the one hand, and pre-Civil War realities on the other.

By every possible means the abolitionists forced this discrepancy upon the national attention with the aim of creating large-scale cognitive dissonance, which would then generate an increasingly intense desire to resolve this dissonance. And the main alternatives for this resolution were either to ignore and suppress the agitators or to make the black's situation more consonant with the American and Christian ideals.

But where, then, does violence fit into this picture? It is evident that it had its use in drawing attention to the underlying issue—to the discrepancy between avowed ideals and the reality. The violence of slavery, the whippings and killings, were, in newspaper terms, good copy; they were obviously powerful attention-gainers, as were the mob actions against the abolitionists. But this only scratches the surface, for violence is notably no cool intellectual proposition that can be kept within the chaste boundaries of cognitive theory. It is too heated, driving, explosive; and the fact serves to remind us there is far more to man than cognition—and there is also far more to man than man alone. We shall leave the historical main stream to pursue social science and the violence question in the next chapter.

Though James Birney did not live to see the Civil War (he died in 1851), few men of his time understood so well the conceptual base and the inevitable thrust to the underlying logic of events that led to it. Taking issue with the notion "that a favored few are born, ready booted and spurred, to leap into the saddle with which the backs of the many are furnished by nature," Birney felt "that the conclusion of the whole matter is, that, as a people, we are trying an experiment as unphilosophical in theory as it has been, and ever will be, found impossible in practice: to make a harmonious whole out of parts that are, in principle and essence, discordant."

So wrote this decent white American when he accepted the nomination of the new Liberty party in 1840. "It is vain to think of a sincere union between the North and the South, if the first remains true to her republican principles and habits, and the latter persists in her slaveholding despotism. . . . One or the other must, in the end, gain the entire ascendancy." [11]

CHAPTER **11**

Social Action—Violent and Nonviolent

"Some men resonated to abolitionism because slavery violated their Christian faith, or because of a general sympathy for the underdog. Others resonated to the idea of abolition because of a belief in the perfectibility of man. Still others were attracted because of a belief in the democratic assertion of the equal rights of all men, or a belief in individualism. Some were originally attracted because their own salvation required that they save others. There were those who were attracted because they hated oppression and oppressors and some because they could not tolerate humiliation, even vicariously. The plight of the slave induced resonance for these and many other reasons." [1]

Why and *how* we are motivated to act on the behalf of others remain two of the most pressing questions with which history confronts psychology. As psychologist Silvan Tomkins suggests in the paragraph above, from his remarkable study "The Psychology of Commitment," the motivations are diverse. And it would appear that in applying his clinician's sensitivity to history he has suggested many "whys,"—violation of Christian faith, sympathy for the underdog, etc. But for the persistent psychologist this level of interpretation is merely a statement of surfaces, and a much deeper probe is called for.

Earlier we indicated that studies of the modeling process seemed to hold answers to the *why* and *how* questions. We shall now take a look at an unusual linking of modeling studies in the laboratory with past and present history. Then once this base is established we will examine the workings of altruism in action—or Tomkins's view of the psychology of commitment and of producing social change. And along the way we will also see how violence enters the picture.

Tomkins happened on history quite by accident—and the fact is worth recording as a commentary on how little use is actually made by psychologists and sociologists of this vast resource. For anyone concerned about the future of social science, as well as the future of the society it ostensibly serves, this is no small matter. Within psychology both Freud and Jung made great initial use of history, and within sociology it was the laboratory for Karl Marx, Vilfredo Pareto, and Max Weber. But only Erik Erikson, Robert Lifton, a handful of other Freudians, and a lone experimentalist, David McClelland, have kept to the task in modern times in psychology. And in sociology Talcott Parsons looms today as a rather lonely figure trying to mine the past. It is true that history has, in a sense, gone underground in being to some extent involved in the data-gathering for most large studies, but few pay much attention to this "background stuff." By and large both disciplines have left history to the greater humanism of anthropology—and are diminished for it.

Tomkins became involved with the abolitionists early in the

1960s, when the activist historian and playwright Martin Duberman (*In White America*) asked him to recommend a psychologist to write a paper for a book that Duberman was compiling. "I asked him for a sample of the historical material and became so fascinated with it I offered to do it myself," Tomkins recalls. He then spent six months doing the necessary historical research, and the result was a most unusual probe into the childhood and youth of the four best-known white abolitionists: Garrison, Birney, Theodore Weld, and Wendell Phillips.

Tomkins found numerous thought-provoking similarities among the four men. Many seemed to cluster around the concept of modeling—that is, the influence of parents (or other strong figures) on the shaping of a child's character and aspirations through the child's identification with, or imitation of, the parent. For example, Tomkins found that "all four were deeply Christian. Three of the four had conversion experiences. For Garrison, Phillips, and Weld, their Christianity required that they save others if they would save themselves. Each of the three had been impressed by strong, pious Christian mothers that to be good meant to do good. The fourth, Birney, had been left motherless at the age of three, and his strongest relationship was with his father who believed not only in Christian good works, but, more specifically, had along with his father fought to make Kentucky a free state; though they lost this fight they continued to be active against slavery. In all four families, moral and Christian zeal for the salvation of their children (and other sinners) was combined with great affection for their children. The parents provided the appropriate models for future reformers. The children were taught how to combine concern and contempt for the sinner with love for those sinners who would reform."

Another similarity Tomkins found was that the parents of all four men had shown a pervasive concern with public service. "Garrison's mother, who was the sole provider, nursed the sick. Birney's father was politically active in favor of emancipation. Phillips's father was mayor of Boston. Weld's father was a minister. All were concerned with service to others and provided a model which predisposed their sons to resonate to any movement based on public service."

Further evidence of another important aspect of modeling at

work in these men's youth was that "all were exposed to, influenced by, and modeled themselves after, the great orators of their day." But with this consideration something beyond modeling enters the picture: "All four as young men were fluent and articulate and gave evidence of being able to hold audiences by their speaking powers. The combination of great energy, extroversion, and the power to influence others by oratorical ability predisposed them to resonate to a movement which required those who could influence others in just such ways."

Tomkins also found evidence of other qualities at variance with our picture of the "model" schoolboy—and with the standard American stereotype of the "do-gooder" as a person who is in some way weak or unstable. The first-rate person, according to this view, does good for himself; the second-rate does good for others. And Tomkins found that Garrison, Phillips, Weld, and Birney were all "physically active and extroverted as children. They had abundant energy which they translated into vigorous play and into fighting with their peers. This, too, contributed to their resonance to a movement which called for direct action and face to face confrontation before large groups."

Lastly, to emphasize a quality essential to altruism in action, Tomkins found that "all of them were physically courageous. They had all experienced and mastered the art of fighting with their peers, so that they had a zest for combat rather than a dread of it. No one who too much feared physical combat could afford to resonate to the defense of those held in bondage by the ever-present threat of force. The overly timid cannot entertain a rescue phantasy."

Activist Motivations: Rosenhan, Keniston, and Feuer

It is evident that Tomkins has come up with an instructive profile of what seems to underlie goodness in action in terms of early childhood influences and certain physical capacities. And to most people this would be quite enough (if indeed, not too much) information. But not to the ever-persisting psychologist. After all, despite some gains in insight this remains a general profile. And it is also something back there in history. Ideally, this generalized picture of goodness should be substantiated, made more specific, and given more present-day relevance. Almost by accident a study of present-day civil rights workers being carried on in 1963 and 1964 by a friend of Tomkins, David Rosenhan, added a second phase to this line of inquiry.[2]

Independently of Tomkins's study, Rosenhan and several associates interviewed nearly ninety civil rights workers and sympathizers about their involvement with freedom rides and other activities of this sort, which seemed to peak in the South during the spring and summer of 1961. They gathered voluminous factual information about the activists' involvement in the rides and marches. They dug into their personal histories in almost interminable detail. They found out why the activists thought they— and why they thought others—were motivated to become involved. And when it was all over, Rosenhan and his co-workers found practically no support for the now-irrelevent originating idea for the study. Their dismay can be imagined—many of the interviews had lasted as long as twelve hours! But, as frequently happens in research, they were saved by an old friend: the serendipitous, or unexpected discovery.

After letting their data lie fallow for a bit, they found that on re-examining it with fresh eyes a curious thing became apparent. The interviews revealed that instead of one large homogeneous group of persons actively committed to civil rights, there were two clearly different groups. One was composed of those who had been involved in only one or two freedom rides, who were later identified as the Partially Committed. The other had been active for at least a year, and usually longer, and had worked mainly in the South on such projects as voter registration or setting up schools for needy blacks in addition to the freedom rides; they were later identified as the Fully Committed.

After the data was sorted into these two groups according to length of commitment, two very meaningful profiles emerged. The Fully Committed person, for example, seemed to have had a positive, warm, and mutually respecting relationship with his or her parents. There were disagreements, but underlying it all there appeared to be considerable fondness between parent and child. By contrast, the Partially Committed expressed negative or ambivalent feelings toward their parents. Many, in fact, felt that the dominant parent had been hostile to them during their formative years, or else they had felt great hostility toward the parent.

Both groups were markedly concerned with moral issues, but again a radical difference emerged in parental relations. The Partially Committed fairly consistently reported a kind of moral confrontation with their parents that the interviewers labeled the "crisis of hypocrisy." Again and again they expressed the feeling that their parents said one thing and did another—in other words, that they did not practice what they preached.

In contrast, the Fully Committed exhibited some of the characteristics we have already noted in Tomkins's historical analysis. They reported having parents who were themselves fully committed to some altruistic cause during the child's own formative years. "My father carried me on his shoulders during the Sacco-Vanzetti parades," one reported. Another described how his father fought on the side of the Loyalists in the Spanish Civil War, and another of how his mother had felt close to Jesus and was warmed by his teachings. "She devoted her entire life to Christian education."

One finds these two types emerging in other in-depth studies of youthful commitment to a cause. Psychologist Kenneth Keniston, for example, often finds the close parent-child, "chip off the old block" relation in his unusually perceptive and expressive studies of young protesters and revolutionaries.[3] Yet sociologist Lewis Feuer expresses the conviction that a major drive underlying student protest throughout the world today is the pathological Freudian Oedipal desire of the son to kill the father.[4] On the surface it would seem that these two experts directly contradict one another. However, Rosenhan's Fully and Partially Committed findings indicate that there is probably no contradiction after all. Keniston and Feuer are talking about two different kinds of motivations—in a sense, the "healthy" motivation of men like Birney and Douglass as opposed to the "unhealthy" motivation of the John Browns and terrorists generally—and, in fact, both types do appear in the surveys of both men.

It is a finding that can be useful, both to the old trying to understand the young—the beleaguered college administrator, for example—and to the young trying to understand themselves and those who wish to lead them. Keniston stresses the need for society to recognize, listen to, and profit from, the voices of alienation if it is to survive. Survival is also Feuer's concern, and his view of violence is worth pondering. It is Feuer's observation that worldwide, and throughout history, with a dismaying regularity, student protest movements begin with idealism and idealistically motivated leadership. But then the "high-minded" motivations and leadership are shoved aside by the rise of pathological motivations and pathologically motivated leadership, and the violence of this type of leadership then provokes a self-defeating repressive backlash.

The progression from the idealism of Martin Luther King to the pathology of the urban black riots of 1968, and from student idealism to the Weatherman bombings of 1970, supports Feuer's view, as does the "establishment's" response of hardened attitudes and increased repression. However, there is more to this. For in extending his study of abolitionist childhoods into their adult involvement in social action, Tomkins found that all too often we are ready to settle for one cycle of a process that actually spirals, ever-changing, over history.

Tomkins and Altruism in Action

Beyond questions of childhood predispositions, Tomkins was concerned with how the adult who is so predisposed becomes a reformer, and how those he is to reform become activated. This is no small purpose. "It is our thesis," wrote Tomkins, "that the same psychological dynamic underlies the commitment of the individual and the group. More particularly, we will argue that violence and suffering are critical in a democratic society, in heightening antipathy for violations of democratic values and in heightening sympathy for the victims of such violations. A radical magnification of negative feeling toward the oppressors and of positive feeling toward the oppressed is the major dynamic which powers the commitment first of the individual reformer and then of increasing numbers who are influenced by him."

In building this thought-provoking case Tomkins makes use of a few concepts, based on clinical and other observations, that are essential to its understanding. One concept is the idea that the intensity of our feelings toward anything of importance to us builds through an alternation of positive and negative feelings. These alternations are grouped in triads of experience that cumulate over time to gather a forceful density, which then controls our thoughts, feelings, and actions toward whatever the matter is. A fear can become deep-seated, for example, through triads of this type. Some situation gives rise to the negative impact of a small fear. This is followed by the positive lift of some form of relief or rescue. But then fresh circumstances raise the same fear, and the fact that the old fear is back again suggests to us that relief was only illusory, temporary, undependable. And so out of this opening of our world to uncertainty, and through a cumulation of the negative-positive-negative triads of this type, the fear gathers in intensity.

Such sequences can also cumulate in positive directions. Tomkins sees this as the basic mechanism for producing commitment to a cause, and in the lives of the abolitionists he discerns an alternation of positive and negative events that seem to form the following sequence:

1. The individual resonates to the general idea of the salvation of others. For all four abolitionists this potential is laid down in childhood and extends into adult life as a general disposition toward doing good for others.

2. Some risk is taken in an early venture on the behalf of others. Though his knees are shaking with stage fright, for example, Garrison begins to lecture against slavery in Boston. The greenhorn Weld stages the eighteen-month-long Lane Seminary slavery debates. Or, as we have seen, Birney declares for abolitionism.

3. Suffering results from this risk-taking. As a result of his lectures Garrison is thrown in jail for seven weeks. Weld is severely reprimanded by the Lane Overseers and later attacked by angry mobs. Birney is ostracized by his friends and has to leave town.

4. This suffering is followed by an increased resonating to the cause, and an increasing identification with the oppressed and an increasing hostility toward the oppressor. "Blessed are they who die in the harness," proclaims Weld. "*I* will be harsh as truth, and as uncompromising as justice," proclaims Garrison. And all join in the increasingly fierce condemnation of the slaveholder.

5. There may now be a period of grave doubts; however, it is followed by recommitment and an increased willingness to take risks and suffer. Of the ending of slavery Birney despairs that "any exertion that I can make by writing or by showing it to be wrong is unnecessary and futile." Yet all four show this increasing willingness to take risks and suffer for the cause.

6. Increased risk-taking leads to still more suffering. A price is put upon their heads in the South, frequently their lives are threatened, and all four are beset by angry mobs.

7. The cause-committed person now accepts the suffering, intensely identifies with the oppressed, and his hatred of their oppressors becomes passionate. "I will not hold my peace on the subject of African oppression," cries Garrison. "If need be, who would not die a martyr to such a cause?"

And so a reformer is created. But a reformer is only meaningful in relation to those he reforms, so Tomkins next directed his attention to the question of how the reformer influences others and ultimately shapes the direction of his society. In the last chapter we noted what is probably involved on the subtle, more long-term, change-oriented *cognitive* level. But emotional drives are more obvious, powerful, and more immediately available. Moreover, beyond man the individual lies man the social animal. These are the sides to man which Tomkins next explored, and he found that the same "dynamics of violence and suffering" which deepened the commitment of the four abolitionists also seemed to gain the commitment of others to their cause.

The sequence is initiated by the violence inflicted upon the abolitionists, and their consequent suffering, which enlists the sympathy or outrage of others. The killing of abolitionist Elijah Lovejoy and mob action against Garrison so outraged the patrician Wendell Phillips that he gave up dabbling in many causes to concentrate wholeheartedly on abolitionism. Salmon P. Chase, a crucial problack Cabinet member during Lincoln's administration, became an abolitionist after witnessing the destruction of Birney's press and the threatening of his life by a mob in Cincinnati. There are many other such instances of violence-conversions, and, as Tomkins points out, "it was not only Garrison, Phillips, Weld, and

Birney who evoked violence, sympathy, and indignation. There were hundreds of agents who were stoned, tarred and feathered, whipped, beaten up, and in some cases killed."

Does this mean, then, that if powerful emotional drives are to adhere to the cause of social change there must be the inflicting and/or the suffering of maximum brutality with bloodshed? Tomkins makes a crucial qualification in noting that by violence he means *anything* done to another "with intent to hurt; it may be an aggressive threat or physical violence, or a verbal insult." And to suffering he gives a similar range from minimal to maximal effects by seeing it as being by no means confined to physical suffering, but including feelings of "humiliation, helpless rage, terror, or distress." This matter of degree of stress—neither too little nor too much—is a point which cannot be overstressed, and to which we will return.

"It is our argument that in a democratic society the impact of such violence and suffering on the observer is to arouse equally intense affect and to arouse vicarious distress, shame, fear, or sympathy for the victim and anger and contempt for the aggressor. Because of this identification with the victim his ideas will tend to become more influential than before such an attack," Tomkins notes in drawing his analysis together. Why this identification with the victim? "First, the tendency to identify with any human being is quite general. Second, in a democratic society there is a taboo on inflicting hurt on anyone since it denies his equal right to life, liberty, and the pursuit of happiness."

And so the process of widening identifications moves outward, enlisting fellow sufferers and adherents to the cause. The oppressors' inhumanity to the oppressed instigates the reformer's action, which activates small groups pro and con on the issue, which may then grow until ultimately, throughout the entire society, there are enough who care passionately one way or the other to actually force appreciable movement in the face of the inertia prevailing on most issues.

"Because of heightened identification with the victim, polarization between aggressor and victim increases; this magnifies the conflict and draws into the struggle, on both sides, thousands who would otherwise not have become involved. One half of the battle for radical social change is to increase the density of affect and ideation about the change. To look steadily at a social condition that violates the shared basic values of a society produces suffering for the society as a whole just as does the condition itself for a segment of the society."

Contrary to the extreme passions of the liberators and the repressors, "the Northern American citizen of the mid-nineteenth century was essentially ambivalent about slavery. He neither could approve it nor steadily disapprove it. He would have preferred to forget it." But the constant, committed abolitionists persisted in "forcing confrontation and thereby radically increased the density of affect and ideation about the issue." They would not permit the rest of the society "to look away from the ugly violation of the democratic ethos," and thus they forced goodness upon the multitude.

Historical Violence and Its Transcending

And so, bit by bit, the nature of the activist and of social action becomes somewhat clearer. In the last chapter we saw how the exposure of factual injustice apparently enlists the intellect. And now we have seen how emotion is enlisted through a widening of identification with the oppressed, and by a widespread vicarious sharing of the suffering inflicted by the oppressor upon the oppressed.

Throughout this pattern the thread of violence interweaves, depending upon circumstance and point of view, like a reptile among the vines, or like a flaming sword. Customarily, the oppression of the oppressor is seen as the starting point: The oppressor violates the rights of the oppressed by limiting his growth and restricting his freedom. And then at some point, reacting to this oppression, the oppressed violates the tranquility of the oppressor by disrupting the prevailing thoughts and systems.

We see the activist, then, violate the sacred but repressive norms, customs, beliefs, myths, and prevailing hierarchies of his time. He suffers psychological, social, and sometimes physical abuse, which may then encourage him to a greater disruption of the status quo, which can lead to greater efforts of repression, through all of which tensions build and the potential for violence escalates. We see the well-known abolitionists begin nonviolently, and by relatively peaceful means successfully force the slavery issue upon the national awareness. But when the strength of the system—of the resistance entrenched at every level of social and individual being—seems to be too great for milder methods, another mood and another set of activists takes over, and under the John Browns of the time a few incidents of small-scale violence seem to create the potential for the large-scale, blood-spilling violence of the Civil War.

The final violation comes with the firing on Fort Sumter. Before the attack, Tomkins notes, it was widely said that the North couldn't possibly enter a war with the South. But the "attack produced an immediate identification with the nation which had suffered such violence." Gradually more and more Northerners came to experience "the suffering of violence, at first vicariously and then more directly, until the firing on Fort Sumter suddenly galvanized all to respond in kind." Moreover, it is evident that the trial of John Brown and its attendant massive publicity interacted with private needs to create a martyr with whom legions in the North identified, and the state-sanctioned violence of his hanging then increased the suffering, and this in turn increased the polarization into hostile camps.

However much we may wish to avoid facing it, the historical record clearly shows that violence—and a considerable dose of it —was necessary to promote the social change required for black advancement through the ending of slavery. But does this mean that violence is *always* necessary? Again the record is clear, but this time not the record of much history and a little bit of social science, but of the reverse. A tiny bit of hopeful history (the lives of Woolman, Gandhi, and Martin Luther King, for example) and a large helping of a relatively new social science suggest hopeful alternatives.

For example, one might ask how was it that Woolman actually succeeded in moving people in his time nonviolently? For he was so mild a figure that his success can only be attributed to some nonviolent approach. It is worth knowing, then, that cognitive dissonance and other theories relating to attitudinal change indicate there are optimal levels of conflict or dissonance for motivating people in a desired direction. There can be too little conflict or dissonance, but also there can be too much. Within this optimal range—and depending on circumstances, there may be many, many variables—a surprisingly slight degree of dissonance or conflict may motivate change in the desired direction. *But if the conflict or dissonance is too great, the target individual or group has the options of either withdrawing from the problem or taking action to suppress or do away with those calling attention to it.*[5]

It is also worth noting the possible relevance of B. F. Skinner's work with operant conditioning, whereby pigeons are taught to play Ping-Pong, chickens and cats to play the piano, the mentally retarded to read, and the insane to feed and care for themselves, on the principle that large-scale behavioral changes can be brought about through a lengthy sequence of rewarding very small steps in the desired direction.[6] This would suggest, then, that a series of relatively small dissonance-producing situations can produce a large-scale change of attitudes and behavior, and that intelligent planning—rather than the traditional floundering, hit or miss, with which history is filled—could radically shorten the invested time.

Actually both of these methods have been extensively field-tested with many millions of people (but, characteristically, relatively few social scientists are aware of the fact because it has never appeared in the formal research literature). The underlying principles in both instances were appreciated and used by the master strategist of nonviolence, Mahatma Gandhi, in his successful strategy to win independence for India.[7] Moreover, the perceptive reader of Erikson's *Gandhi's Truth* will have noted Gandhian overtones in Tomkins's analysis of how the violence inflicted upon the abolitionists enlisted widespread emotion to the cause of social change. And the abolitionists' exposure of factual injustice, and, by implication, the cognitive mechanisms we have outlined, are also aspects of Gandhi's Satyagraha, or the social therapy of Truth-Force, to which Erikson so brilliantly relates Freud's insight method of individual therapy.

From sources such as these the answer appears to be: No, blood-spilling violence is *not* always necessary. It appears that it has been used throughout history not only because the economic and social subconditions for nonviolence were not right, but because the techniques for successful alternatives to violence were unknown or poorly understood by both leaders and followers. And the closing of our last escape route by the atomic bomb is at last quickening interest in exploring this alternative.[8]

So far this reading of the casebook has been mainly from the viewpoint of psychology. But no single field can describe, let alone attempt to prescribe for, the black and white sickness. From here on we shall expand the view somewhat into sociology and other fields in the chapters on relevant social science that alternate with sketches of the history.

CHAPTER **12**

*Abraham Lincoln
and Frederick Douglass*

The guns roared on Sumter. The Blue and Gray armies formed
and marched and the awesome roll of battles began: Bull Run,
Fort Henry, Fort Donelson, Shiloh. On August 14, 1862, President Lincoln called the first official group of Negroes to the White
House for a little talk.

The black community waited for news of what took place with
a mixture of feelings. When, after the fall of Sumter, the new
President called for seventy-five thousand volunteers for the Union

Army, blacks rushed forward throughout the North. But as had happened eighty years before at the start of the War of Independence, everywhere they were refused. Then they witnessed this baffling and distressing sequence. Thousands of slaves were freed by three Union generals only to be, in effect, re-enslaved when the new President countermanded the orders. "Most beautiful, missis; onspeakable," one Sea Island black said when asked how it had felt to be free for even so short a time.[1] Now five handpicked blacks, who supposedly represented four million black Americans, were to receive President Lincoln's deepest, personal thoughts on their behalf.

As was the official way with whites speaking to blacks, Lincoln offered a monologue that quickly made the following points. He had been given $600,000 by Congress to colonize blacks. He had long felt it to be to the advantage of both races for blacks to settle elsewhere—the fact that white men were now cutting one another's throats because of the colored man made it doubly urgent. His personal preference was a site in Central America, where they would be able to support themselves by digging coal in the mines. Now he hoped they would go about finding some black families to help begin the exodus—and the interview was over.[2]

"Can anything be more puerile, absurd, illogical, impertinent, and untimely!" roared Garrison in the *Liberator*.[3]

Frederick Douglass was even more deeply moved. Editor of his own *Douglass' Monthly,* and particularly infuriated by Lincoln's suggestion that the blacks were the cause of the war, he felt that "a horse thief pleading the existence of the horse as the apology for his theft, or a highwayman contending that the money in the traveler's pocket is the sole first cause of his robbery are about as much entitled to respect as is the President's reasoning at this point." He attacked Lincoln's language as "coarse-threaded." As for Lincoln's reported graciousness to the five black visitors, it only reminded Douglass of the "politeness which a man might try to bow out of his house some troublesome creditor or the witness of some old guilt." [4]

Douglass had considerable cause for dissapointment. Following the great success of the *Narrative* of his life, he had had to flee to England to avoid being captured in the North under the Fugitive Slave Law and shipped back to his legal master in the South. He had become a highly popular lecturer abroad, and not only on black slavery in America. His vision had broadened—and in a way that prefigured the exceptionally meaningful experience of blacks as diverse as W. E. B. Du Bois, Paul Robeson, Malcolm X, and Martin Luther King. This journeying beyond the physical and mental boundaries of America, rare for a black both in his time and, until very recently, in our own, profoundly affected Douglass, and in England, Scotland, and Ireland the plight of the poor workers greatly intensified his feeling for the human condition. "I am not only an American slave, but a man, and as such, am bound to use my powers for the welfare of the whole human brotherhood. . . . I believe that the sooner the wrongs of the whole human family are made known, the sooner these wrongs will be reached," he wrote back to his readership in Garrison's *Liberator*.[5]

He returned to the States, his freedom was purchased for $750, and he founded his own newspaper, the *North Star*. (This move was opposed by Garrison and Wendell Phillips, who, among other motives, didn't want to see their best black speaker go into business for himself. Douglass, however, felt the paper was personally and racially essential as "powerful evidence that the Negro was too much of a man to be held a chattel." [6]). He had known John Brown and had tried to persuade him *not* to attack Harper's Ferry. Then he fled again, this time to Canada to avoid standing trial, and returned once more, to found *Douglass' Monthly*. By now he was known not only as the most eloquent speaker of his time, black or white, but—among those able to overlook his color —as one of the nation's most powerful minds.

But, however exceptional Douglass was personally, he had come to represent more than a single man. To many throughout the civilized world he was his race and embodied all the meanings of slavery in relation to its past and all the hope in relation to its future. Soon this assumption of a larger identity would be even more deeply true of Lincoln, but his hour had not yet arrived. He was still Lincoln the relatively unknown, while over twenty years Douglass had become the chief living proof of the black's right to equality. ("There is no sadder commentary upon American slavery than the life of Frederick Douglass. He put it under his feet and stood erect in the majesty of his intellect; but how many intellects as brilliant and as powerful as his it stamped upon and crushed no mortal can tell," a newspaper in Rochester commented toward the end of Douglass' life.[7]) From this position, then, Douglass had heralded the election of Abraham Lincoln as the beginning of the end for slavery, and when Sumter was fired on and Lincoln called for volunteers he had thrown himself with demonic energy into publicizing the blacks' readiness to serve the Union Army. And now this man he so greatly hungered to believe in had not only rejected an offer that might give blacks dignity, even if they must die for it, but he was offering the stale old racism of colonization— a scheme most thoughtful men, black or white, had rejected as unfeasible and hypocritical twenty years earlier.

It was, on the surface of it, a crushing blow. But Douglass was too wily, too knowledgeable, to accept the stale offering. He knew the times and thought he knew the man somewhat. After one horrified blast he returned to his basic strategy of again and again pointing out the high road and expressing faith that Lincoln would take it. There was reason for doubt about the new President, but Douglass had an intimate practical knowledge of the shaping power of high expectation. (It was called "moral suasion" in those days, and Douglass, Garrison, and Birney were leading advocates of its use among the abolitionists.) And shortly his faith (or his strategy, whichever one chooses) was to pay off.

The puzzle of Lincoln is difficult to penetrate if one knows no more about him than Douglass did then—or than Lincoln may have known about himself at the time; or if one is determined, from today's perspective, to portray him as either a saint or a racist, which is the new pastime.[8] However, if one simply examines what is known about him, as a man of exceptional strengths and some large weaknesses, nearly everything falls in place. Before he became President he had been deeply concerned by the slave's plight. He had known free blacks with some intimacy during his years as a notably kind, humane, small-town lawyer who had many poor blacks for clients. He also happened to have a very deep and enduring belief in the Declaration of Independence. He had long been fired with an awareness that slavery was inconsistent with the Declaration's ideals and was the nation's central moral and political problem, and, being at times extremely ambitious, he had decided to make this the issue on which he would rise in public life. Then suddenly he was President and the full weight of the nation descended upon him—or, to return to our overriding metaphor, suddenly he was an old, comfortable, storytelling country doctor with a satchel of doubtful pills who had been called in to quell the bubonic plague.

The pressures upon him were almost inconceivable. He had taken on the enormous job of bringing together a country a good part of which was committed to not listening to him—not only had the South stopped its ears, but his own Cabinet and Congress included both men of culture who considered him a coarse bumpkin and vulgar jokester and men of political stature who considered him a greenhorn hack from the sticks. And then when he couldn't bring the country together, he was forced to wage a war conducted by one of the strangest assortments of military incompetents in history. But grinding away beneath all of this, nudging, shaping, poking, stirring it up, and even embracing it, was the working of the old compromise process affecting the blacks.

On one hand Lincoln was being importuned, wheedled, and threatened by all those resonating to the cause of black liberation— Douglass and a host of eloquent abolitionists, powerful legislators like Charles Sumner and Thaddeus Stevens, famous men and women of letters like Emerson and Harriet Beecher Stowe, journalists like Horace Greeley, in short, practically the full weight of the notably decent, thinking Americans of the day. On the other hand he was confronted with the strategic necessity of hanging onto the border states, which could swing to the South if he advocated freeing the slaves. He was also constrained by the fact that his sure political sense told him that black freedom was a doubtful issue as far as the rank and file Americans of the day were concerned. ("The position in which I am placed brings me into some knowledge of opinion in all parts of the country," he told one visiting clergyman, "and it appears to me that great masses of this country care comparatively little about the negro." [9]) He was also encouraged to go slow by the revelation of widespread white resistance such as was manifested in the bloody riots by Irish and German laborers, who shot up New York City, with a thousand casualties, and rampaged in other places to make it plain they did not want to fight to free blacks who would then compete with them for jobs that were bare subsistence as it was.

Until the outbreak of the Civil War these pressures, liberative

versus repressive, had ground upon each other within the minds
of individual men and throughout the system as a whole. But now
much of their weight pressed down upon this one tall, wry, slightly
stooped, slightly uncertain man with the melancholy eyes and the
sardonic smile. Obviously, a smaller being would have been ground
under. Though he said some foolish things at first under this pressure, he also did some very wise things. He avoided every decision
he could, for one, buying time to get some feel for the situation
and to marshal what was best in him to meet it. He dropped his
cherished colonization notion, and with it possibly a good portion
of what remained in him of the old black and white sickness. On
the advice of a child he grew a beard to project a greater authority.
And with the issuing of the Emancipation Proclamation—a pre-
liminary version was announced just one month after the colonization "bombshell" and the final version came on January 1, 1863—
Lincoln began to fashion and consolidate his larger identity.

Part of the mystery surrounding Lincoln is his growth into a
superhuman figure conveying the stature and aura of the Patriarch
Abraham, Moses, Jesus, and even God Himself. It is interesting,
then, to note four extremely powerful forces that were at work
within the four million blacks of his time that somehow may have
been related to this giantic creation. There was, first, most blacks'
strong feeling for the Bible, for so long their chief emotional and
mythic support. There was the slavery-induced lack of known
fathers. There was drawn up within them the intensity of two centuries of yearning for freedom that, with Lincoln's Proclamation,
came pouring out like an organ blast. And there was finally, the
very great shaping power of their high expectations. And so to the
fatherless—including Douglass—he was Father Abraham. To
those yearning for freedom, he was the culmination of Genesis, the
Moses of Exodus, who would lead them to the Promised Land.
While he was still living, to many a freed, unlettered black he was,
quite simply, God Himself, no question about it. And in death he
was the Martyred Jesus, who took upon Himself the sins of the
world.

This is not to suggest that Lincoln was only a myth created by
black longing and white guilt and admiration. Far from it. Whatever his weaknesses, and they definitely included racism, he was
a very large, potentially great, man who was one of few in history

to receive the intense adoration and high expectations of four million people just freed from long bondage. And as men will do, it would seem that he grew to live up to their expectations.[10] Few expressed it better than Frederick Douglass at the unveiling of the freedmen's memorial monument to Lincoln, in Washington, D.C., on April 14, 1876.

"Truth compels me to admit, even here in the presence of the monument we have erected to his memory, Abraham Lincoln was not, in the fullest sense of the word, either our man or our model. In his interests, in his associations, in his habits of thought, and in his prejudices, he was a white man. . . . You are the children of Abraham Lincoln. We are at best only his stepchildren," he told his audience.[11] However, Douglass continued:

> We were able to take a comprehensive view of Abraham Lincoln, and to make reasonable allowance for the circumstances of his position . . . and in view of that divinity which shapes our ends, rough hew them how we will, we came to the conclusion that the hour and the man of our redemption had somehow met in the person of Abraham Lincoln. . . . He was a mystery to no man who saw him and heard him. Though high in position, the humblest could approach him and feel at home in his presence. Though deep, he was transparent; though strong, he was gentle; though decided and pronounced in his convictions, he was tolerant toward those who differed from him, and patient under reproaches. . . . His moral training was against his saying one thing when he meant another. . . .
>
> But dying as he did die, by the red hand of violence, killed, assassinated, taken off without warning, not because of personal hate—for no man who knew Abraham Lincoln could hate him—but because of his fidelity to union and liberty, he is doubly dear to us, and his memory will be precious forever.[12]

And seven years later to the month—in April 1883—Douglass evoked Lincoln once more to hurl this challenge toward us across a century:

> What Abraham Lincoln said in respect of the United States is as true of the colored people as of the relation of those States. They cannot remain half slave and half free. You must give them

all or take from them all. Until this half-and-half condition is
ended, there will be just ground of complaint. You will have an
aggrieved class, and this discussion will go on. Until the public
schools shall cease to be caste schools in every part of this country, this discussion will go on. Until the colored man's pathway
to the American ballot box, North and South, shall be as smooth
and as safe as the same is for the white citizen, this discussion
will go on. Until the colored man's right to practice at the bar
of our courts, and sit upon juries, shall be the universal law and
practice of the land, this discussion will go on. Until the courts
of the country shall grant the colored man a fair trial and a just
verdict, this discussion will go on. Until color shall cease to be a
bar to equal participation in offices and honors of the country,
this discussion will go on. Until the trades-unions and the work-
shops of the country shall cease to proscribe the colored man
and prevent his children from learning useful trades, this discussion will go on. Until the American people shall make character
and not color, the criterion of respectability, the discussion will
go on.[13]

CHAPTER 13

Marx, Conflict Models, and the Anti-American Creed

Douglass was the first black critic of great stature to challenge white America, saying, in effect, "Where, for us, is this liberty you speak of? Where is the equality? Prove to us this system is not based on lies." And Lincoln was the first white President forced to attempt a serious answer. By 1970, many felt the country faced the same question, with little changed. They looked for a new Civil War to resolve it, this time between black and white, or between young and old. And their conviction of the rottenness of the system was, for many, the fiery core of their being.

By one of those historical happenings that are more than coincidence, many of the disillusioned of today draw their fire from a famous contemporary of Lincoln and Douglass, the mighty Karl Marx. His contribution has been widely distorted, but in one way this is a tribute to his phenomenal breadth as a social-scientific pioneer. For no one else in all of this venturing, including Freud, had a greater effect both on history and on those who followed him in the social sciences. Weber and Durkheim, who laid the foundations of modern sociology, and Pareto, who greatly figured in sociology, economics, and political science, all found themselves intellectually out of the scholar's conversation with Marx, accepting a little, rejecting more, but mainly arguing to differentiate themselves and their ideas from this often overwhelming father figure.

Before pursuing the relevance of Marx to the black and white sickness, however, it might be worthwhile to take a brief look at Marx the man. A comparison with his contemporaries Lincoln and Douglass suggests itself, and it is startling to discover how much they had in common. They were alike, for example, in being exceptionally eloquent men. Marx is the greater orchestrator, at his best his logic, wit, and words volleying like a Bach concerto. But underlying the elaboration all three were poets in action, with much the same very rare, blunt, no-nonsense feel for putting reality into words.

They also shared something too little remarked of men of strength: a deep love of women and children. Lincoln's love for his own and for children everywhere is well known. Douglass became a great champion and fighter for women's rights. And the revolutionary Marx—who, many assume, must have snarled his way through London like a hairy Scrooge—in actuality was the favorite person of the children of his neighborhood, a very loving father and a great storyteller; and to many, the love story of Jenny and Karl Marx is one of the saddest and most beautiful of all time.[1]

They were also alike in being shaped by years of incredible struggle—Douglass and Lincoln struggling in their youth to emerge from the deep pit of ignorance, poverty, and slavery; Marx in his maturity struggling year after year to gain a few potatoes here, a few shillings there, to keep himself and his family and his angry outpouring of manuscript alive. They were also alike in being men of great intellect and wit, and in their very active contempt for stupidity (this was Marx's most alienating stock-in-trade, but it was also strong in Lincoln, though softened by other qualities and masked by the necessities of politics).[2] However, most important of all was the fact that all three were appalled by the condition of man on earth, and were driven to sacrifice themselves to try to improve our lot. They were humanitarians of a grandeur that shames our age.

Karl Marx's great contribution was the most forceful statement ever made of the liberating notion that men need not be saddled with history, but can change it. This was Freud's message for the modern individual—that he could, through psychoanalysis, be changed. But Marx was saying something much larger. "The philosophers hitherto have only interpreted the world in various ways: the thing is, however, to change it."[3] In the 1840s, the young Marx was beginning to say not merely that men, individually, might improve themselves but that men collectively could change their whole social system for the better.

A staggering thought indeed. Since his time it has shaken and shaped our world. But the question must intrude: Was this really news? Undoubtedly among the reasons that Marx has failed to excite many Americans is that the idea of men making their own history is so integral to the American ethos that we find it hard to appreciate its historical novelty. Moreover, the political scientist and the historian know that our own revolution, when collectively we radically changed our social system for the better, made the point well before Marx was born, and in action rather than words.[4] And many of the rest of us take our own revolution so much for granted that it is hard to appreciate what a phenomenal social advancement it was for mankind.

What Marx contributed was the most forceful and comprehensive *articulation* of revolution in history. He tried to elevate the means whereby men might better themselves and their society into a science, with both theoretical underpinnings and a plan for action. He also tried, in the wake of the breakdown of the old religion, to advance a new secular evangelism and a new vision of utopia. His dream was of something that might be reasonably nearer to heaven on earth than anything man has yet known;

something more certain of accomplishment than the earlier visions of Vico and Saint-Simon of the scientifically perfected society; something that would be brought on by more carefully considered techniques than the relatively hit-or-miss extemporizing of the social reformers of his day.

Central to both his social science and his dream of the New Jerusalem was Marx's vision of the workings of the dialectical process. This is one of the most meaningful concepts man has chanced upon in his search to understand what is happening to us as, caught up in a whirl of change, we shoot through space and time on this round projectile of earth. Yet it has generally been buried within a wordy cloud of philosophy, avoided as the tainted and exclusive property of communism, or lost through over-simplification.[5]

For Aristotle dialectic lay within the heart of formal discourse or debate—a give-and-take sequence of thesis, antithesis, and the ongoing combination of the two, synthesis. It appears in contexts as diverse as Hindu, Buddhist, and early Christian and medieval European theology. For the master synthesizer, Hegel, it was the key to history, the core dynamic of the onrush of man and society through space and time. Marx then "stood Hegel on his head," finding the dialectic at work not through some grand disembodied Hegelian Idea, but in *praxis,* in the very down-to-earth struggle of man to scratch out an existence on this earth, to gain some mastery of himself and his surroundings with some work to do, to create for himself a language and bit by bit his entire social world.

In his youth Marx stated his vision of the workings of dialectical processes in terms of a brilliant philosophy, sociology, and psychology. It was an interaction of subject and object; a progression of the internal contents of man externalized into the institutions of society, to be internalized in man again through child training.[6] But to this looser vision of dialectical process Marx added the familiar concept of class struggle and introduced a new compulsiveness and rigidity. The dialectic became the action of the sacred proletariat in conflict with the depraved bourgeoisie, with a classless society looming as the synthetic end product following the triumph of the proletariat. It made of history and society a beautifully logical mechanism—and for this reason it has traditionally appealed to many who seek the comfort of seemingly absolute knowledge in a world of dismaying uncertainties. But while it seemed to account for the dynamics of social change in many instances, it just didn't fit the facts in others.

The Marxist dynamic can be made relevant by dropping the notion of an inflexibly sacred proletariat (which has shown a minimal interest in revolution wherever it has gained itself labor unions, regular paychecks, and homes in the suburbs), and by thinking in terms of denied undercastes and classes in conflict with denying overcastes and classes, of have-nots versus haves, of the excluded versus the power-possessors, of the liberators versus the repressors.[7] But beyond somewhat more useful particulars of this sort, the idea of dialectical processes only seems to add a confusion that delights scholars, and does little to aid practical understanding.

It all seems to become workable again—and more meaningful in this context, we would contend—if one drops back into the psychology which briefly interested the young Marx. On this level, another ancient Greek view seems more fitting than the thesis-antithesis progression, a sequence of *unity* (moné), followed by a *going out of oneself* (próhodos), followed by a *return into oneself* (epistrophé).[8] In psychology this has been expressed by such popular concepts as "interaction" or "transaction," and we have seen it at work in Bartlett's "War of Ghosts" experiment, where the story undergoes significant changes as it is passed from person to person over time. It emerges in an intimate and fascinating form in Skinner's operant conditioning, where in learning new techniques the organism creates for itself a new social world through interaction with a responsive environment. It also appears in cybernetics, in the concept of change based on *feedback,* and in the system-analytical psychological theorizing which makes use of the feedback idea—perhaps best captured by George Miller's TOTE (Test-Operate-Test-Exit) concept which he developed as a radical improvement over the relatively static S-R unit, or the stimulus-response idea.[9] Most recently, in this context, we have seen it working outward from psychology into sociology through Tomkins's stages of interaction between reformer, resistors, and the reformed, where each stage, interacting sequentially, works a change upon the other.

It is an exciting view of man's being and is exceptionally meaningful in the context of the black and white sickness because it asserts that man is not only *being* but *becoming*—that whatever exists today is not sacred and inflexible beyond redemption, but will and can be changed. For this reason the dialectical idea has been appropriated by most ideologies that appeal to the oppressed or to those eager for a better tomorrow, while it has been feared or deprecated by those who, understandably, are so settled or well off today that they have little reason to hunger for tomorrow.

Marx and the Anti-American Creed

With only the preceding knowledge about Marx (which is all that many care to retain) it would be hard to see why Marx and the Marxians are viewed as such a dangerous foreign contagion by most Americans. The reasons for American fears, of course, were (and are) that Marx advocated hastening the predicted death of capitalism and colonialism by revolt; he advocated abolishing private property; he advocated eliminating all classes above the proletariat; he advocated establishing new governments that would be dictatorships in the name of this proletariat—that is, governments run by a self-appointed elite until such time as the mass of men had learned, through a prolonged and often painful social conditioning, to be dependably "good" (the optimistic Marx hoped for a natural unfolding of man's innate goodness after the revolution, but implicitly both his revolution and governing its result called for painful constraints, as the Soviet experience demonstrates). If necessary, Marx also advocated violence to accomplish his ultimately humanitarian ends, and his successors have all proceeded pretty much according to this plan.[10]

It is surely evident that however appropriate such an approach might be elsewhere on this earth, it was hardly calculated to appeal to many Americans—not to the capitalism-based, propertied, middle and upper classes that valued the right to elect their own representative government; nor to a lower class that, however pinched it might be, still generally aspired to or already enjoyed some tantalizing small degree of capital, property, and social participation. Nor was it designed to win over in droves a people who saw themselves as having had the *original* revolution through which it had created an ingenious, self-advancing, self-correcting, self-healing social system that could, through peaceful means, over time, remedy all social evil and accomplish the same humanitarian ends that Marx envisaged.

The first great test of whether this American dream was, in fact, true came with the Civil War. While the war demonstrated that the new system could indeed improve itself and could endure, it also demonstrated that, at least in this instance, following the breakdown of all the ingenious self-correcting mechanisms, the solution had to be found in temporary tyranny, *outside* the new system's rules. Eventually there was nothing to do but split apart and fall back on the age-old procedure of violence, where adversaries club one another until they grow tired, or die, or a victor emerges. Moreover, while the war ended slavery, it obviously did not end our very deeply entrenched racism—and it sometimes seems that we will never learn that world communism has long seen this failure as the key to our overthrow. Marx himself both admired and deprecated the American system, and, true to his factual-embedded rather than his speculative side, generally avoided trying to predict our course. If one wholeheartedly embraces the doctrine that has grown out of his works, however, one is forced to view whatever success our system has shown as being only temporary, an illusion that class struggle and the "death instinct" of capitalism will bring to its inevitable end.

World communists, then, have seized on every possible scrap of our bumbling or our villainy to support this vision of our downfall, and, worldwide, to build the case against us; and year in, year out, in the grandeur of our almost inconceivable arrogance and ignorance, we have consistently offered them at least one monumentally useful piece of damning evidence. At the heart of America the communist sees the fatal flaw of a capitalism based on the degrading, dehumanizing, and alienating exploitation of man by man. And over much of our history the white treatment of the black in America has supported their case with very little distortion.[11]

"The discovery of gold and silver in America, the extirpation, enslavement and entombment in mines of the aboriginal population, the beginning of the conquest and looting of the East Indies,

the turning of Africa into a warren for the commercial hunting of
black-skins, signalized the rosy dawn of capitalist production,"
Marx wrote with characteristic verve toward the end of *Capital*.[12]

Only economists and Marxist scholars are equipped to treasure
the convolutions of the Marxist economic analysis, but his linking
of black exploitation to the basic economic dynamism of the American system was the beginning of something else again. Here was
something that required no sophistication to understand; all you
needed was some reason to hate, fear, or envy America. And so
the words established a linkage that has been expanded over a
century into the vivid, rigid, simplistic view that has sustained revolutionaries from Frantz Fanon to Che Guevara—a view that
couples capitalism with colonialism and so ultimately focuses on
the most powerful capitalist nation, the United States, as the chief
support for most of the evil in today's world.[13]

However our system may have confounded the grim Marxian
prognosis to date by profiting from his (and our own) criticism
and managing somewhat to level extremes, spread the wealth, shed
our outright colonial aspirations and acquisitions, and in many
ways to modify capitalism and collectivize, as long as the great
gap has remained between promise and reality for the black in
America the Marxian critic has been able to sustain the hard-core
anti-American Creed. "See, for all their pretensions, they are the
worst of liars," he can say.

Old hands thought the Harpies of Marx were downed with the
disillusionment of the thirties and the repression of the forties and
fifties, but in the late sixties they began to rise again, and again
Marx began to seize the brightest and best as well as the worst of
our youth. And again the black man became the symbol of alienation, the legitimizing rallying point.

The reasons for the deathless appeal of Marx to the young are
a pulsating compounding of love and hate, to which large numbers
of their elders also resonate. To our hating, Marx appeals with his
expression of the theme of *alienation* or estrangement, to the gnaw-
ing sense across races, classes, and ages of being aliens in our
schools, our jobs, in our own land. Though this is a common theme
among visionaries of the dark side of industrialization from William Blake through Max Weber, in Marx it comes equipped with
an intricate rationale and the promise of a release. With his por-

trait of the insular, vulgar, grasping, all-engulfing bourgeoisie, he gives to the young hating products of white suburbia, the black ghetto, and the decolonializing nations a recognizable surrogate for the experience of both whiteness and middle-classness that they are conjointly trying to throw off. In his portrayal of the entrenched strength of capitalism he offers something salient and (deceptively) simple to account for the mountainous inertia we encounter everywhere, and an expression of the frustration of pushing against it. And in his writing of *coup d'états* and revolution he gives vent to the need for, and legitimizes, violent action, the need to blow the lid off, to punch through this compression to freedom.

But he is also speaking to love, and this is the bewildering part of it both to those involved with these feelings and those, on the outside, who must try to understand them. For he writes with real caring and passion of love, of children, family life, work, of mankind, of a feeling for the brotherhood of man, of a good laugh, of sex, of wit, of an unquenchable optimism, of competence, of craftsmanship, of the beauty of style, of good words, of the craft of self-expression, and of the zest of battling for the good cause. He caters, then, to the bewilderment of a transitional age, when men and women are confronted with inconceivably complex questions of loving versus hating, in a time of shifting norms. (Continually, in effect, we must ask ourselves, which is me, which is them, which is us, what applies this particular year and in this particular place?)

But within the bewildering appeal of this ever-shifting, loving-hating complex lie two oases apparently grounded on the rock of an enduring social reality—two pressing questions for young and old activists to which Marx and his disciples seem to speak clearly and boldly where most everyone else seems to speak in pussy-footing ambiguities.

Despairing of slower means to ideal ends, the activists and the alienated feel (and all too often see the supporting social and historical evidence) that only violence will bring these desired ends—and the Marxist speaks clearly to this issue.

But to move with certainty toward any ends one must have some firm notion of social dynamics—not of how things seem to be put together but of what really happens beneath surfaces. And here again the Marxist seems to speak clearly where others are

prolix and unsure. Activists and the alienated tell themselves they
have seen enough of the dismal, drab results of governance by
committee, consensus, and compromise. And the Marxist asserts
the thrilling primacy of conflict.

Violence in the Social Context

"Force is the midwife to every old society pregnant with a new
one," Marx wrote with the sense for metaphor that so endears him
to those who are turned off by the earnest pedantry of most sociological writing.[14] Over the years this aphorism has been used by
many to justify violence, and certainly it seems at first glance to
support such an interpretation.

We noted earlier some psychological research evidence that
suggests that extreme violence is not needed and can, in fact, work
against the production of social change (*i.e.*, operant conditioning
work indicates that dramatic overall change can be produced by a
planned sequence of very small steps, and other studies indicate
that too much dissonance or conflict can drive away the person to
be changed, or harden resistance and repression). This pattern is
also borne out by clinical experience, where the therapist must
play a careful game, for too much pain can drive the patient out
of therapy. But these were (and are) effects produced with lone
individuals in laboratories and the clinician's office, and there is
quite literally a world of difference between this sort of effect and
what happens in a society. The operations may be qualitatively
similar, but the quantitative difference is almost incalculable. For
aside from the disparity in the degree of control one has over
what is happening in the two situations, the problem of social
inertia is not merely one of individual resistances that are multi-
plied, but of an overriding complex of inertia and resistance that
is held together by the social glue of historical experience and
conformity processes.

As the great prophet of social fixity Émile Durkheim put it,
we are enmeshed in hard social factualities "endowed with coercive
power, by virtue of which they impose themselves upon [us] independent of [our] individual will. . . . If the complacency with which
we permit ourselves to be carried along conceals the pressure

undergone, nevertheless it does not abolish it. . . . Air is no less heavy because we do not detect its weight." [15]

Is it any wonder, then, that when repression joins forces with this "normal" social inertia, and is unresponsive to gentler means, that men have historically been driven to revolution? But still the fact that historically it has often taken violence to crack the shell of extreme repression and indifference and to open societies to change is again no proof that it *must* be this way.

It might also be wise to look again at what Marx said about force as the midwife, for he was a milder and more thoughtful man than many of his successors, and generally a careful writer. And the overall context of his work suggests that among the meanings intended for this metaphor was also something of this sort: that a midwife has a specific and time-honored job, which she does with competence, respect, and understanding. That is, she does not jump upon the mother's belly, chanting vile slogans, while attempting to force the infant to issue through an ear. Nor does she arrive in the third or fourth month of pregnancy and insist on an immediate delivery.

The Nature of Social Dynamics: Conflict vs. Compromise

To this point in our examination of the casebook of the black and white sickness we have seen frequent evidence of a compromise process at work. It lies at the heart of our—and indeed all—governments. Along the black-relevant dimension it dictates Jefferson's omission of a slavery-dawning clause from the Declaration of Independence, and the Constitution's three-fifths of a voting right for each black. We have seen Lincoln at the vortex of its pressures at the start of the Civil War, and ahead lie its workings through practically every American President, acting, or not acting, in the sacred name of consensus.

But by the 1960s, a growing body of Americans were decrying compromise and consensus. Moreover, even the staid social sciences were cracking open under the pressures, and everywhere a militant body of young Turks confronted an outraged old guard. The conflict has been most intense in sociology, where the Turks clustered to the banner of C. Wright Mills and a Marxist conflict

142   THE HEALING OF A NATION

model, while the old guard closed ranks around Talcott Parsons and the sprawling fortress of a structural-functionalist equilibrium model, out of Malinowski, Marshall, Spencer, Durkheim, and Pareto. In history the civil rights drive of the fifties and the black-history eruption forced the same basic conflict to the surface. Such men as Staughton Lynd, Martin Duberman, and Howard Zinn have insisted that a conflict model of historical interpretation be emphasized, rather than the consensus model used by the bulk of historians into recent times.[16]

In psychology, the controversy has been quieter—in fact, almost devoid of bad feeling—but no less profound in its implications. For what are known (after Clark Hull) as drive-*reduction* theories have been subjected to increasing question by findings that support drive-*inducing* theories. The implications of this struggle may be indicated by noting that among those who could be classified as old guard are Sigmund Freud, Ivan Pavlov, and Kurt Lewin, as well as the cognitive dissonance theorists. Whereas the opposition includes the brilliant Canadian psychologist Donald Hebb and a number of others who, under the banners of physiology, information theory, animal psychology, and a variety of other methods and views, are re-exploring the implications of some very old ideas in psychology, such as the notion of a *curiosity* drive.[17]

Though the complexities are many books in length, the crux of the issue can be quickly stated. Is the driving force in man and in his society a need for activity (the drive-inducing, stimulus-seeking, social-conflict positions), or is it a need to resolve or come to rest after activity (the drive-reduction, cognitive dissonance, equilibrium, compromise, consensus positions)? Let us see how the history we have examined may reflect these urges.

As we follow the attempts by whites and blacks to liberate the blacks and gain equality, the pattern that excites those interested in conflict models is certainly evident. In Woolman, Benezet, Birney, Garrison, Douglass, and John Brown we see highly active, individual liberators in conflict with increasingly reactive repressors and forces of repression. And on both sides we see this struggle move out from the individuals involved to seize and polarize large segments of our society, until the entire social organism has split in two and the nation writhes in the throes of the Civil War.[18]

Here, then, is evidence to delight the model-building desire of liberals and conflict-theorists. But let us return to history again. The highly active struggle of Woolman, Benezet, and others to end slavery leads *not* to its ending (except among Quakers) but to the social compromise that was worked out during the formation of the new American government. The Declaration of Independence offers the gain of a statement of the equality of all men that commits the nation to and publicizes this equality as a goal. But the Constitution fails to lift the curse of slavery. So we have a compromise that is only partially black-advancing, but nonetheless more advancing than regressing.

Later, the drive of Garrison, Birney, Douglass, and other abolitionists to end slavery and bring equality to the black did lead to the formal ending of slavery. But the chief instrument of liberation was a war that was pursued according to a compromise of pressures involving many considerations in addition to black advancement, and that ended with a compromise that freed the black from slavery, but did little else to promote equality.

So it would seem that however we may wish to avoid the conservative settlement of compromise, it is, in the last analysis, personally, socially, and historically unavoidable. But this, again, is no stopping point. For how do we really know which is the right model? A problem here is that the social scientists are often victims of the psychology and sociology of knowledge. Those with an interest in change, the liberals, tend to stress the conflict model. And those with a vested interest in social stasis, the conservatives, tend to stress the compromise or equilibrium models. Moreover, to the normal ideological weighting in the conservative direction is added the functional conservatism of social science as a profession. Whether they are ideologically liberal or conservative, there is a tendency among social scientists to treat everything as though it were stopped in motion. They want to transfix it in order to examine it over a period of days, months, weeks, or years. But reality is not like that. It changes. As we hurtle through space and time each of us, and our societies as well, are undergoing a continuous upheaval in relationships.

But here, again, is no stopping point. For it is apparent that neither view is exclusively "right," but that both operate simultaneously; and thus today any really sophisticated model of individual and social dynamics must account for both conflict and equilibrium. Though on the surface this might seem a simple task, and though the fact is widely recognized among psychological and social theorists and many have wrestled with it, few would agree that anyone has yet tied the two together satisfactorily.

And this, again, is no stopping point. For the truly advanced theorizing in all fields moves on from this point to investigate this interaction not in a few isolated episodes of individual or social behavior, but in a chain-linking of one episode to another. In short, movement through space and time is added. And again we confront a reason for the endless fascination of cycling and dialectical movement that has, from time to time, seized the imagination of social scientist and historian alike.

CHAPTER 14

Reconstruction:
The Freedmen's Bureau

The war has naught to do with slaves, cried Congress, the President, and the Nation, and yet no sooner had the armies, East and West, penetrated Virginia and Tennessee than fugitive slaves appeared within their lines. They came at night, when the flickering campfires shone like vast unsteady stars along the black horizon: old men and thin, with gray and tufted hair; women, with frightened eyes, dragging whimpering hungry children; men and girls, stalwart and gaunt,—a horde of starving vagabonds, homeless, helpless, and pitiable, in their dark distress. . . . The

stream of fugitives swelled to a flood, and anxious army officers
kept inquiring: "What must be done with slaves, arriving almost
daily? Are we to find food and shelter for women and children?" [1]

Thus the greatest black leader after Douglass wrote of the needs
that brought on the first serious attempt by this nation to heal the
sickness. The writer was W. E. B. Du Bois. His theme was the
Freedman's Bureau, and seldom have a subject and its interpreter
been so well matched.

Today our impression of Reconstruction is of a giant mess,
which it was. But thanks mainly to Du Bois's black historical
pioneering, out of the swamp of those years the maligned Freedmen's Bureau now looms as a ruin of considerable grandeur and
meaning for our time.[2] Only three times within the 350 years of
the black and white sickness has the nation been sufficiently motivated seriously to attempt a cure—during the New Deal era under
Franklin Roosevelt, during the Great Society years of Lyndon
Johnson, and this first time so long ago in years, yet uncomfortably
close in its similarity to our more recent derelictions. Schools, jobs,
votes, money, housing, the courts, some land to call one's own—
the Bureau tackled them all, with hauntingly familiar degrees of
success and failure—that is, the successes that only a handful of
experts are aware of, and the failure that becomes the popular
identity for so much noble human effort when political fashions
and administrations change; a failure in the case of the Bureau
not so much of a flawed instrument and flawed people applying it,
as of a nation lacking the goodness, the will, the intelligence, the
leadership, and the social maturity to insist on the pursuit of
health above the pursuit of war, gold, western lands, and other
aggrandizements.

To his account of this crucial social experiment Du Bois brought
an unusual personal interest. He was America's first black social
scientist, a historian and sociologist, still relatively fresh out of
Harvard and the University of Berlin but already nationally known
in 1901, when his first article on the Bureau appeared. He was
also within a few years of wresting the black leadership mantle
from Booker T. Washington. And he was also at the early peak
of a vision that, periodically, over his ninety-five years was to
take him far beyond questions of blackness or whiteness to make

him a seer in an age, and among nations, of the deaf, dumb, and blind.

His later works were often marred by the strain of juggling too many roles, but the best of Du Bois as historian, social scientist, politician, poet, and seer melds in "The Dawn of Freedom." Historians are familiar with this essay, but dismally few other social scientists are. Moreover, not only has no one ever written a better account of the Bureau, but because of the power of Du Bois's young vision he lifts this bit of history out of history and makes of it a free-floating and persisting commentary on all of our attempts to cure the black and white sickness through social engineering to this very day. With but a change of names and dates, the account could be that of the rise and fall of the Great Society programs of the 1960s. This account is, of necessity, an editorial reduction by a good half, and the reader is urged to read the haunting original.

> The bill finally passed by the Senate in 1865 was a hasty bit of legislation, vague and uncertain in outline. A Bureau was created, "to continue during the present War of Rebellion, and for one year thereafter," to which was given "the supervision and management of all abandoned lands and the control of all subjects relating to refugees and freedmen." . . . A Commissioner, appointed by the President and Senate, was to control the Bureau, with an office force not exceeding ten clerks. The President might also appoint assistant commissioners in the seceded States, and to all these offices military officials might be detailed at regular pay. The Secretary of War could issue rations, clothing, and fuel to the destitute, and all abandoned property was placed in the hands of the Bureau for eventual lease and sale to ex-slaves in forty-acre parcels.
>
> Thus did the United States government definitely assume charge of the emancipated Negro as the ward of the nation. It was a tremendous undertaking. Here at a stroke of the pen was erected a government of millions of men, and not ordinary men either, but black men emasculated by a peculiarly complete system of slavery, centuries old; and now, suddenly, violently, they come into a new birthright, at a time of war and passion, in the midst of the stricken and embittered population of their former masters. . . .
>
> Less than a month after the weary Emancipator passed to his rest, his successor assigned Major-Gen. Oliver O. Howard to duty

as Commissioner of the new Bureau. He was a Maine man, then only thirty-five years of age. He had marched with Sherman to the sea, had fought well at Gettysburg, and but the year before had been assigned to the command of the Department of Tennessee. An honest man, with too much faith in human nature, little aptitude for business and intricate detail, he had large opportunity of becoming acquainted at first hand with much of the work before him. . . . On the 15th, [he] began examining the field of work. A curious mess he looked upon: little despotisms, communistic experiments, slavery, peonage, business speculations, organized charity, unorganized almsgiving—all reeling on under the guise of helping the freedmen, and all enshrined in the smoke and blood of war and the cursing and silence of angry men. On May 19 the new government—for a government it really was—issued its constitution; commissioners were to be appointed in each of the seceded states, who were to take charge of "all subjects relating to refugees and freedmen," and all relief and rations were to be given by their consent alone. The Bureau invited continued cooperation with benevolent societies, and declared: "I will be the object of all commissioners to introduce practicable systems of compensated labor," and to establish schools. Forthwith nine assistant commissioners were appointed. They were to hasten to their fields of work; seek gradually to close relief establishments, and make the destitute self-supporting; act as courts of law where there were no courts, or where Negroes were not recognized in them as free; establish the institution of marriage among ex-slaves, and keep records; see that freedmen were free to choose their employers, and help in making fair contracts for them. . . .

No sooner was the work thus started, and the general system and local organization in some measure begun, than two grave difficulties appeared which changed largely the theory and outcome of Bureau work. First, there were the abandoned lands of the South. It had long been the more or less definitely expressed theory of the North that all the chief problems of Emancipation might be settled by establishing the slaves on the forfeited lands of their masters—a sort of poetic justice, said some. But this poetry done into solemn prose meant either wholesale confiscation of private property in the South, or vast appropriations. Now Congress had not appropriated a cent, and no sooner did the proclamations of general amnesty appear than the eight hundred thousand acres of abandoned lands in the hands of the

Freedmen's Bureau melted quickly away. The second difficulty lay in perfecting the local organization of the Bureau throughout the wide field of work. Making a new machine and sending out officials of duly ascertained fitness for a great work of social reform is no child's task; but this task was even harder, for a new central organization had to be fitted on a heterogeneous and confused but already existing system of relief and control of ex-slaves; and the agents available for this work must be sought for in an army still busy with war operations—men in the very nature of the case ill fitted for delicate social work—or among the questionable camp followers of an invading host. Thus, after a year's work, vigorously as it was pushed, the problems looked even more difficult to grasp and solve than at the beginning. Nevertheless, three things that year's work did, well worth the doing: it relieved a vast amount of physical suffering; it transported seven thousand fugitives from congested centres back to the farm; and, best of all, it inaugurated the crusade of the New England schoolma'am.

The annals of this Ninth Crusade are yet to be written—the tale of a mission that seemed to our age far more quixotic than the quest of St. Louis seemed to his. Behind the mists of ruin and rapine waved the calico dresses of women who dared, and after the hoarse mouthings of the field guns rang the rhythm of the alphabet. Rich and poor they were, serious and curious. Bereaved now of a father, now of a brother, now of more than these, they came seeking a life work in planting New England schoolhouses among the white and black of the South. . . . They did their work well. In that first year they taught one hundred thousand souls, and more. . . .

The act of 1866 gave the Freedmen's Bureau its final form— the form by which it will be known to posterity and judged of men. It extended the existence of the Bureau to July, 1868 . . . [and it] became a full-fledged government of men. It made laws, executed them and interpreted them; it laid and collected taxes, defined and punished crime, maintained and used military force, and dictated such measures as it thought necessary and proper for the accomplishment of its varied ends. Naturally, all these powers were not exercised continuously nor to their fullest extent; and yet, as General Howard has said, "scarcely any subject that has to be legislated upon in civil society failed, at one time or another, to demand the action of this singular Bureau."

To understand and criticize intelligently so vast a work, one

must not forget for an instant the drift of things in the later sixties. Lee had surrendered, Lincoln was dead, and Johnson and
Congress were at loggerheads; the Thirteenth Amendment was
adopted, the Fourteenth pending, and the Fifteenth declared in
force in 1870. Guerilla raiding, the ever-present flickering after-
flame of war, was spending its forces against the Negroes, and
all the Southern land was awakening as from some wild dream
to poverty and social revolution. In a time of perfect calm, amid
willing neighbors and streaming wealth, the social uplifting of
four million slaves to an assured and self-sustaining place in the
body politic and economic would have been a herculean task;
but when to the inherent difficulties of so delicate and nice a
social operation were added the spite and hate of conflict, the
hell of war; when suspicion and cruelty were rife, and gaunt
Hunger wept beside Bereavement—in such a case, the work of
any instrument of social regeneration was in large part fore-
doomed to failure. The very name of the Bureau stood for a
thing in the South which for two centuries and better men had
refused even to argue—that life amid free Negroes was simply
unthinkable, the maddest of experiments. . . .

Here, then, was the field of work for the Freedmen's Bureau;
and since, with some hesitation, it was continued by the act of
1868 until 1869, let us look upon four years of its work as a
whole. There were, in 1868, nine hundred Bureau officials scat-
tered from Washington to Texas, ruling, directly and indirectly,
many millions of men. The deeds of these rulers fell mainly
under seven heads: the relief of physical suffering, the overseeing
of the beginnings of free labor, the buying and selling of land,
the establishment of schools, the paying of bounties, the administration of justice, and the financiering of all these activities.

Up to June, 1869, over half a million patients had been treated
by Bureau physicians and surgeons, and sixty hospitals and asy-
lums had been in operation. In fifty months twenty-one million
free rations were distributed at a cost of over four million dollars. Next came the difficult question of labor. First, thirty thousand black men were transported from the refuges and relief
stations back to the farms, back to the critical trial of a new way
of working. Plain instructions went out from Washington: the
laborers must be free to choose their employers, no fixed rate of
wages was prescribed, and there was to be no peonage or forced
labor. So far, so good; but where local agents differed *toto coelo*
in capacity and character, where the *personnel* was continually

changing, the outcome was necessarily varied. The largest element of success lay in the fact that the majority of the freedmen were willing, even eager, to work. So labor contracts were written—fifty thousand in a single State—laborers advised, wages guaranteed, and employers supplied. In truth, the organization became a vast labor bureau—not perfect, indeed, notably defective here and there, but on the whole successful beyond the dreams of thoughtful men. . . .

In the work of establishing the Negroes as peasant proprietors, the Bureau was from the first handicapped and at least absolutely checked. Something was done, and larger things were planned; abandoned lands were leased so long as they remained in the hands of the Bureau, and a total revenue of nearly half a million dollars derived from black tenants. Some other lands to which the nation had gained title were sold on easy terms, and public lands were opened for settlement to the very few freedmen who had tools and capital. But the vision of "forty acres and a mule" —the righteous and reasonable ambition to become a landholder, which the nation had all but categorically promised the freedmen—was destined in most cases to bitter disappointment. . . . The Commissioner of the Freedmen's Bureau had to go to South Carolina and tell the weeping freedmen, after their years of toil, that their land was not theirs, that there was a mistake—somewhere. If by 1874 the Georgia Negro alone owned three hundred and fifty thousand acres of land, it was by grace of his thrift rather than by bounty of the government.

The greatest success of the Freedmen's Bureau lay in the planting of the free school among Negroes, and the idea of free elementary education among all classes in the South. It not only called the school-mistresses through the benevolent agencies and built them school-houses, but it helped discover and support such apostles of human culture as Edmund Ware, Samuel Armstrong, and Erastus Cravath. The opposition to Negro education in the South was at first bitter, and showed itself in ashes, insult, and blood; for the South believed an educated Negro to be a dangerous Negro. And the South was not wholly wrong; for education among all kinds of men always has had, and always will have, an element of danger and revolution, of dissatisfaction and discontent. Nevertheless, men strive to know. Perhaps some inkling of this paradox, even in the unquiet days of the Bureau, helped the bayonets allay an opposition to human training which still to-day lies smouldering in the South, but not flaming. Fisk,

Atlanta, Howard, and Hampton were founded in these days, and
six million dollars were expended for educational work, seven
hundred and fifty thousand dollars of which the freedmen themselves gave of their poverty. . . .

The most perplexing and least successful part of the Bureau's
work lay in the exercise of its judicial functions. . . . Bureau
courts tended to become centres simply for punishing whites,
while the regular civil courts tended to become solely institutions
for perpetuating the slavery of blacks. Almost every law and
method ingenuity could devise was employed by the legislatures
to reduce the Negroes to serfdom—to make them the slaves of
the State, if not of individual owners; while the Bureau officials
too often were found striving to put the "bottom rail on top,"
and gave the freedmen a power and independence which they
could not yet use. It is all well enough for us of another generation to wax wise with advice to those who bore the burden
in the heat of the day. It is full easy now to see that the man
who lost home, fortune, and family at a stroke, and saw his land
ruled by "mules and niggers," was really benefited by the passing
of slavery. It is not difficult now to say to the young freedman,
cheated and cuffed about who has seen his father's head beaten
to a jelly and his own mother namelessly assaulted, that the meek
shall inherit the earth. Above all, nothing is more convenient
than to heap on the Freedmen's Bureau all the evils of that evil
day, and damn it utterly for every mistake and blunder that was
made.

All this is easy, but it is neither sensible nor just. Some one
had blundered, but that was long before Oliver Howard was
born; there was criminal aggression and heedless neglect, but
without some system of control there would have been far more
than there was. Had that control been from within, the Negro
would have been re-enslaved, to all intents and purposes. Coming as the control did from without, perfect men and methods
would have bettered all things; and even with imperfect agents
and questionable methods, the work accomplished was not unde-
serving of commendation.

Such was the dawn of Freedom; such was the work of the
Freedmen's Bureau, which, summed up in brief, may be epito-
mized thus: for some fifteen million dollars, beside the sums
spent before 1865, and the dole of benevolent societies, this
Bureau set going a system of free labor, established a beginning
of peasant proprietorship, secured the recognition of black freed-

men before courts of law, and founded the free common school in the South. On the other hand, it failed to begin the establishment of good-will between ex-masters and freedmen, to guard its work wholly from paternalistic methods which discouraged self-reliance, and to carry out to any considerable extent its implied promises to furnish the freedmen with land. Its successes were the result of hard work, supplemented by the aid of philanthropists and the eager striving of black men. Its failures were the result of bad local agents, the inherent difficulties of the work, and national neglect. . . .

Had political exigencies been less pressing, the opposition to government guardianship of Negroes less bitter, and the attachment to the slave system less strong, the social seer can well imagine a far better policy—a permanent Freedmen's Bureau, with a national system of Negro schools; a carefully supervised employment and labor office; a system of impartial protection before the regular courts; and such institutions for social betterment as savings-banks, land and building associations, and social settlements. All this vast expenditure of money and brains might have formed a great school of prospective citizenship, and solved in a way we have not yet solved the most perplexing and persistent of the Negro problems. . . .

The passing of a great human institution before its work is done, like the untimely passing of a single soul, but leaves a legacy of striving for other men. The legacy of the Freedmen's Bureau is the heavy heritage of this generation. Today, when new and vaster problems are destined to strain every fibre of the national mind and soul, would it not be well to count this legacy honestly and carefully? For this much all men know: despite compromise, war, and struggle, the Negro is not free. . . . And the result of all this is, and in nature must have been, lawlessness and crime. That is the large legacy of the Freedmen's Bureau, the work it did not do because it could not.[3]

CHAPTER **15**

Intervention and Frustration-Aggression Theory

Gestalt theorists were fascinated by the implications of the background in relation to foreground sights and sounds. A midget is seen as small, for example, because of the background against which he appears. He looks small in the usual surroundings, but he would look like a giant if he were photographed beside a doll house. This line of thinking was extended by the great social psychologist Kurt Lewin into social research, and the point he repeatedly made has been repeatedly ignored: One can completely miss the real truth about something by becoming immersed in what most immediately interests one—the foreground—because it is the *background* that gives it meaning.

Thus, the Freedmen's Bureau only becomes fully meaningful in terms of a background that widens out through history to take in our time, and we will briefly examine this aspect of its meaning in a later chapter. But it also takes on meaning from something very large that was moving within the background of the 1870s and that still acts upon and shapes the tensions of our time.

We have examined the import of Karl Marx's thought with its activist thrust and its assertion that man *must* intervene in history and that government is the means of intervention. Though probably not a soul involved with the Freedmen's Bureau had ever heard of Karl Marx, their move was activated by such a philosophy, gained not from books but from the pressure of social necessity. It was, in this instance, simply a logical response to the situation at hand. However, during Marx's years of relative obscurity an opposing theory was being developed by Herbert Spencer. It was far better known, far more influential, and what it fundamentally represented can help us understand not only the collapse of the Freedmen's Bureau in the 1870s, but the diminishing impact of the Great Society programs in our time.

With only three months of formal schooling—he was taught at home by his father and his uncle, but he was, throughout his life, self-educated—Herbert Spencer is quite possibly history's most interesting product of an education pinned to the interests of the exceptional pupil rather than to the requirements of the unexceptional teacher or school. Several years before Darwin he expressed the main thrust of evolutionary theory, and he made major contributions to biology and anthropology as well as sociology. Yet much as Marx was later cast into the outer darkness for being a communist, so has Spencer been relegated to the dust bin for his contribution to Social Darwinism, which we will examine in a later chapter. Both men, however, were more the victims than the promoters of social movements, and much of modern sociology grew out of the dialogue of their successors with them (*e.g.,* Durkheim, Pareto, and Weber).

Earlier we noted that Marx propounded a theory of a tension-seeking conflict model of social processes, and that counterposed to Marx's hell-raising views are those of a more settling and comfortable sort—of social and personal systems that operate according to pressures to compromise, reach a consensus, reduce tensions and dissonance, and return to a "normal" state of balance, consonance, or social equilibrium. We also noted that liberals and leftists tend to identify with the conflict model while conservatives veer toward consensus models.

To Spencer, society was a vast living organism of interlinking, mutually dependent parts that, "living by and for one another, form an aggregate constituted on the same general principle as is an individual organism. The analogy of a society to an organism becomes still clearer on learning that every organism of appreciable size is a society, and on further learning that in both, the lives of the units continue for some time if the life of the aggregate is suddenly arrested." [1]

An important implication of Spencer's theory was its equilibrium tendency: "It inevitably happens that in the body politic, as in the living body, there arises a regulating system and within itself this differentiates as the sets of organs evolve." [2] Or as Vilfredo Pareto, who was indebted to Spencer and was also an engineer by profession, more specifically noted, "Accidental movements arising in a society are neutralized by the counteracting movements they provoke; and ultimately, as a rule, they die away, and society reverts to its previous state. A society where this occurs can therefore be considered as being in a state of equilibrium." [3]

It is useful to counterpose this view with the Marxist tradition for two reasons. As the study of the psychology and sociology of knowledge makes quite plain,[4] they can be seen as the basic statements of a polarity that repeatedly surfaces in modern times according to differences of personality and social condition. For example, within the context of this book liberals concerned with black advancement will orient to the "Marxist" strain, while conservatives who do not want the disruption of social change and who do not believe we should tamper with the social organism— and certainly that we should do nothing so ungodly as to launch *governmental* intervention—will orient to the "Spencerian" strain. However—and this is the more important aspect of the matter— they can also be seen as indicating two basic aspects of social reality that exist independently of personal ideology, and any comprehensive theory of social reality must account for both strains.

THE "SPENCERIAN" STRAIN		THE "MARXIST" STRAIN
Evolutionary change	versus	Revolutionary change
Society is a ponderous organism	versus	Society is a fragile fabrication by man
The necessity to establish and preserve norms, structures, and regulatory mechanisms	versus	The necessity to shatter or expand norms and structures
The importance of perfecting and rationalizing the existing system	versus	The importance of creativity and charisma
Social stability	versus	Social change
Consonance	versus	Dissonance
Social catabolism	versus	Social Anabolism

Or in the powerfully suggestive but easily misread and misused overview of Freud: [5]

Thanatos	versus	Eros

This "background" suggests that those who wish to launch healing interventions such as the Freedmen's Bureau and its latter-day Great Society progeny should be aware of both forces. It is likely that governmental intervention will always be viewed with suspicion by many; they will oppose its use, and once it is in motion will seek to undermine it. And this background further suggests that they do it not because they are in any way evil (a conclusion that some find it easy to jump to), but simply because it seems to them to be a tainted, man-made violation to the sacred social organism.

Frustration and Aggression

There was at work in both the background and the foreground of the Reconstruction era a particular interaction of forces that social science has been very concerned with. Sigmund Freud noted that when an individual was frustrated in reaching a desired goal his energies were then channeled through *displacement* into other outlets—among them hostility and aggression. Later, Kurt Lewin advanced a view of barriers that provoke tension in an organism, which motivate the organism to seek ways to reduce the tension.

Lewin's theory was explored in a series of experiments by some of his students—Bluma Zeigarnik, Maria Ovsiankina, and Tamara Dembo—and theirs was probably the earliest and most remarkable work dealing with frustration phenomena. By means of experiments in which the subjects were interrupted and redirected to other tasks, and in which children were denied toys they greatly desired, the researchers learned an astounding amount about the effects of frustration in a wide variety of contexts.[6] However, we will concentrate here on the much better-known work of John Dollard, Neal Miller, Robert Sears, and other psychologists who in the late 1930s developed a specific theory of how frustration relates to aggression.[7]

They applied their own great ingenuity and background in modern learning theory to Freud's observations (Lewin was then just a mystifying, relatively recent arrival to America), and carried out experiments to substantiate their views. First, they hypothesized that aggression *is* (not *may be*) the result of frustrating or interfering with some goal-directed activity (which was a more precise way of stating "wish" or "desire"). Second, they stated that the amount of this aggression depends on three things—the strength of the desire being frustrated; the strength of whatever is doing the frustrating; and the number of times the desire is frustrated.

These tenets have since been substantiated by many studies, but undoubtedly the most dramatic was that carried out in 1940 by Carl Hovland and Robert Sears, in which they probed the relation of economic conditions to lynching in the South.[8] Hovland and Sears, seeking to relate theory to real life (and vice versa), wondered if there might be a productive cross-disciplinary tie between economics, sociology, and psychology. It seemed logical, for example, to assume that bad economic conditions would frustrate numerous desires of people living in economically depressed areas, since they would not have as much money to buy the things they had come to take for granted in more prosperous times—cars, refrigerators, steaks, and the like. Moreover, they would be aware that people in more prosperous areas were still able to have all these desired goods. Also, they would probably feel that the economic pinch threatened not only their present status but their future security. If all this were true, Hovland and Sears reasoned, then frustration would increase as economic conditions worsened

—and so would evidence of aggression. Likewise, as economic conditions improved, there might be a drop in aggression.

The American South as a whole seemed an ideal test area. It was notably dependent on cotton, so it seemed logical that the annual per-acre value of cotton would serve as a good index of the Southern economic well-being. The cotton market was also subject to great fluctuations, so this index ought to provide a rather clear picture of risings and fallings over a number of years. Finally, the violence that whites directed against blacks was a well-known fact of Southern life. The number of lynchings could be plotted on a graph, and the resulting curve could be related to the cotton-price curve for the same years.

Hovland and Sears computed the trend lines for both cotton prices and lynchings over the forty-eight years from 1882 to 1930, and when they examined all the breaks or departures from the trend lines very carefully—that is, sudden risings or fallings in either cotton prices or lynchings—a clear relationship could be discerned. Whenever there was a sudden drop in the cotton market that produced severe and unanticipated losses for many southerners, there was usually a sharp rise in the number of lynchings.

Repeated studies since then have generally borne out this finding, and it is an important one. The cumulation of a great number of studies of all types proving this type of theory has given social scientists a very valuable social tool. They are on firm ground when they point to the connection between abnormally frustrating social conditions and the prevalence of crime, violence, and the more subtle hostilities that exist at all levels of society. By such persistent demonstrations of the way things are actually linked together, men slowly become convinced that this is, in fact, the shape of reality, and not merely one man's opinion versus another's.

Not only does this work help explain the relation of social and economic depression to the brutality of Southern whites during and after Reconstruction, but it also gave social scientific support to the conviction of many that improving the Southern economy would be the first step in healing the South of its sickness.

Moreover, it helps explain the raging of the sickness in the cities of the North and among blacks everywhere. Again, frustration leads to aggression. Coop blacks up in crowded ghettos and then over television pipe in the visions of everything they are denied, and you will have a monumental frustration, with constantly mounting pressure for a monumental aggression. And not the least of the frustration for those both in the ghetto and in the larger society who are concerned about this is knowing what could and should be done about the situation, and seeing so little motion.

CHAPTER **16**

Backlash and the
Failure of Leadership

The cloaked riders of the White Camellia and the Ku Klux Klan, and the burnings, maimings, and lynchings remain to symbolize the fierce resistance to Reconstruction and the brutality and depravity of the South following the Civil War. But behind this lurid eruption lay a society of white men and white women who were convulsed by the deepest fear known to man. They feared the ending of their lives, both individually and socially.

On the more apparent level, powered by at least a hundred

years of guilt (and no doubt also based on their conscious estimate
of what *they* might have done under the same circumstances with
the roles reversed), they feared that these black hordes, now free
after such a long suppression, would fall slavering upon them and
kill the men and rape the women. But more hidden and intense
was the basic human fear of loss of support. The infant knows no
sharper terror than loss of his footing or loss of the security of his
mother's arms.[1] Grown up, we are still like infants, dependent
upon our sure footing on a vast social flooring and our secure
place within the warm arms of caste and economics. Suddenly for
the South both floor and arms were gone. As C. Vann Woodward
has noted, "the temporary anarchy that followed the collapse of
the old discipline produced a state of mind bordering on hysteria
among Southern white people." [2]

Even before the war ended, Southern leaders, foreseeing defeat,
met to plan an aftermath that would keep the black suppressed
and the white supremacist society intact. With the end of the war
they went swiftly to work, and with great initial success—the range
of ingenious methods Southerners have employed to keep blacks
from the polls date from these days. Besides the well-known
Knights of the Camellia and the Ku Klux Klan, a number of other
terrorist groups were formed. One such group, the Rifle Clubs of
South Carolina, has modern overtones. Others who called themselves "Regulators, Jayhawkers, and the Black Horse Cavalry
were committing the 'most fiendish and diabolical outrages on the
freedmen' with the sympathy not only of the populace but of the
unreconstructed governments." [3]

Such gory evidence of the Southern whites' incapacity to reconstruct themselves, and the complicity of Andrew Johnson, stirred
the North to support Thaddeus Stevens, Charles Sumner, and the
so-called Radical Republicans in their seizure of congressional control of the government and the imposition of military rule upon the
South. And as the Klan persisted, their atrocities and other nause-
ous evidence of a Southern determination to re-enslave the blacks
fueled popular support in the North for the congressional passage
of an amazing series of progressive measures. During Reconstruction days, the Radicals were able to build a seemingly impregnable
legal bastion against denial of black rights. The sequence began
with the wartime passage of the thirteenth amendment to the Con-

stitution in 1865, which formally abolished slavery and guaranteed equal protection of the laws. The Civil Rights Act of 1866 further spelled out legal protection. The fourteenth and fifteenth amendments did more of the same—and added federal protection for the black voter. And the Radicals also re-enacted the Civil Rights Act to further protect the black voter, and passed another bill to effect the rights supposedly guaranteed by the fourteenth amendment.

Finally, to crown this achievement, they passed the Civil Rights Act of 1875, which provided that "all persons within the jurisdiction of the United States shall be entitled to the full and equal enjoyment of the accommodations, advantages, facilities, and privileges of inns, public conveyances on land or water, theatres, and other places of public amusement, subject only to the conditions and limitations established by law and applicate alike to citizens of every race and color, regardless of any previous condition of servitude." [4]

It was seemingly a beautiful, noble, and permanent accomplishment, to the everlasting credit of the nation. Yet after the blacks' 250-year agony, after the suffering of the abolitionists, after the death of 622,000 men in the Civil War, after the assassination of Lincoln, and after the vast effort of the Freedmen's Bureau and the driving years of Stevens and Sumner in Congress, *within two short years the formal dismantling of these Acts and all this effort had begun, and within twenty-five years their destruction was completed.*

How this destruction came about is a crucial piece of social wisdom, for of all the dismal periods of our history this is the one we can least afford to repeat in any aspect. The Reconstruction era forces of destruction were of three types: Southern, Northern, and a failure of leadership that embraced both regions.

We have already noted how, out of the postwar chaos, Southerners were motivated to restore order by the strongest of drives, for personal and social survival. To most of them nothing was more urgent or sacred than ending the social shambles of Reconstruction and restoring the golden age of the plantation, when—if one could just overlook the admittedly bad master-slave aspects— rich and poor alike were players in a courtly and truly magnificent social drama. However, it wasn't merely the vision of a golden past that drew them. Many were also repelled by the particular kind of future that Northern industrialism seemed bent on forcing upon them, along with the hateful black equality. The driving Northern passion for money and power, to the detriment of the virtues of taking one's time and enjoying life, seemed to the easy-going Southerner a very questionable social direction.

But also while Stevens and Sumner moved in majesty along the high road, perceptive Southerners saw something else moving along the low road. They saw a Republican party that had discerned in the black man a great chance to consolidate Republican party control of the country. They saw chapters of the Union League pop up all over the South, which then faithfully delivered the Southern black vote to the Republican party until Redemption—the Southern term for the Compromise of 1877. They saw the military control of the region as an airtight means of maintaining Republican party hegemony. And behind the party interests they saw Northern business interests increasingly nakedly at work. The Reconstruction years were a time for incredible economic creativity and expansion in America. The lovely, reasonably strong, and rather dull economy we enjoy today derives from the base laid down by the ugly but vital and exciting economic drive of those days, which encouraged the inventions, developed the industries, created the financial structures, and established the markets and marketing techniques.[5] Northern businessmen, then, saw in the South an enticing source of cheap labor and a great new market for exploitation. So from business flowed the funds for campaigns, and from the politicians flowed the measures to extend Northern industrial power throughout the South, and, in reaction (and divine justice?), from the white Southerner there flowed a resentment at being exploited very like that which the black had felt under the Southerner's domination.

Enraged by Republican perfidy, and driven by the need to reassert their independence and suppress the black, the Southerners poured much of their fury and their aspirations into building the Democratic party in the South. They succeeded so well that the antinigger, anti-Yankee core to the Southern Democratic party still persists today, after a hundred years. And with this weapon, they shattered Northern control in 1877, and then shut the door on the black for seventy years.

While the Southerners were busy building this antiblack political missile and stoking it with hate, in the North another kind of labor was underway. Where once the cause of black advancement had been hard as a cannonball, now it was more like a balloon swelling up with hot air, until, gossamer light, a tempting target, it floated out of sight over America. As the nation's attention turned from the Civil War to postwar economic and territorial expansion, the black issue became progressively less salient, and uncertainty grew as to what policy should be pursued. Was it really sensible, or right, to go on trying to force the South to comply with the national and Christian ideals of liberty and equality? Or should one have faith in the innate goodness of men and let Southern blacks and whites work it out among themselves over a period of time? Feelings toward the latter option were greatly intensified by the rise and spread of Social Darwinism, with its implications that, like animals, man was arranged in a hierarchy of lesser and more advanced races; that social change, like evolutionary biological change, must come slowly, over eons; and that one should not tamper with the social organism but leave it to develop according to its "natural" laws.

Against such trends as these, blacks like Douglass and white sympathizers fought heroically. There is a widespread impression that in addition to not having a program of rehabilitation to offer, the white abolitionists abandoned the blacks following the Civil War. But this is a gross distortion of history. In fact, the abolitionists were active in shaping the laws, the education, and the other forms of social engineering, and they and their descendants persisted in pushing for black advancement well into the twentieth century.[6]

"Beware of the siren cry of 'conciliation' when it means humoring the old dragon spirit of slavery," Garrison warned in 1874.[7] "To trust a Southern promise would be fair evidence of insanity," Wendell Phillips said of assurances that it would be safe to end federal troop protection of Southern blacks in 1877.[8] Garrison died in 1879, Phillips in 1884, but a handful of followers carried on the fight and founded the NAACP, in 1910. It was an uphill battle against nearly hopeless odds, however, and of the forces ranked against them the most overwhelming was the retrograde and inertial leadership in all areas of national life.

Through the condensation process that seems to work in history as it does in dreams, this colossal failure of national leadership has come to be symbolized by the Compromise (or sellout) of 1877. Because it is difficult to explain its complexity in few words, what really happened is seldom clear; and, because of the greater failure it has come to symbolize, its significance is not always evident. In 1876 the Democratic candidate for the Presidency, Tilden, received more popular votes than the Republican Hayes. However, in three "unredeemed" Southern states and in Oregon there were two sets of electoral returns. Since the results were so ambiguous, both sides claimed victory. But while the Democrats had the edge in popular strength, the Republicans had the greater entrenched political power. The ostensibly objective Electoral College deliberated for a time and then gave the election to Hayes. Immediately the Democrats screamed fraud, and when this seemed to make little impression they quite seriously threatened to seize the government, which forced the Republicans to create an "impartial" fifteen-man Electoral Commission to puzzle over the matter at further length. But as this new group puzzled it became evident that Republican ingenuity had triumphed again. True, there were roughly equal numbers of Democrats and Republicans on the Commission, seven each; but seven plus *eight* equals fifteen, and the Republicans seemed to have the extra man.

And so nearly a hundred years before a similar action reportedly involving Senator Strom Thurmond and Republican presidential candidate Richard Nixon on the matter of Southern appointees to the Supreme Court, in 1877 the Southern Democrats moved in to bargain. They wouldn't protest the inevitable Commission decision favoring Hayes, they said, if Hayes in turn would promise to pull the federal troops out of the South. He promised, and gained the Presidency, and so began what is undoubtedly the saddest—and still one of the least understood—episodes in the entire history of the black and white sickness in America.[9]

While it is true that leaders are nowhere near as independent as the ancient Great Man mystique holds, it is also evident that the leader is by no means simply the servant of forces beyond his control. If leaders were elected and supported only to give voice to the pressures of their time, the human race would long ago have perished in its ignorance. Rather, another function of leadership is to make choices within an often wide range of alternatives, and

then to explain and promote the hard choice that is socially necessary but that may be unpopular or hard to understand.[10] Within
such a perspective, the action of Hayes and the leadership involved
in the Compromise of 1877 must not be seen as socially inevitable,
and thus excusable; there were, however hard, other choices that
could have been made, and thus their action was reprehensible.
The Hayes Compromise, and the mighty failure in leadership that
extended throughout our society which it has come to symbolize,
lost for seventy years our one chance, however slim it might have
been, to end the black and white sickness.

This leadership failure was first most evident in the Republican
party. The party's alignment with the Civil War victory and the
end of slavery, with Abraham Lincoln, Thaddeus Stevens, and
Charles Summer, had given it a moral leadership stance that for a
time kept at bay the political and business concerns to which the
jaundiced Southern eye was so sensitive. But with the passing of
time and of Stevens and Sumner, the leadership fell to men with no
past experience with or commitment to the black cause. Increasingly their waving of the bloody shirt was an empty oratorical
gesture. By 1877, the transition from a moral to an expedient
leadership—or from idealism to pragmatism, if you will—was well
underway, and the party of Lincoln was ready to trade the black's
(and perhaps the nation's) long-term fate in return for short-term
political and economic gains.[11]

A second major failure of leadership was in the nation's press.
Before the Civil War hundreds of editors had played perhaps the
key role in exhorting, cajoling, poking, and prodding a reluctant
populace and a reluctant political leadership to face up to the
social necessity of ending slavery. This injection of a higher, freer
social intelligence ranged from the mass impact of Horace Greeley
of the *New York Herald Tribune* to the partisan impact of the
avowedly abolitionist press. For a time following the war and
during Reconstruction many editors kept the pressure up. But then
a softening and a weaseling on the issue began to take over the
editorial pages of a number of journals, many of which had originally been founded by abolitionists, notably *Harper's Weekly,* the
Independent, and the extremely influential *Nation,* of which Garrison's son, Wendell Phillips Garrison, was assistant editor from
1865 to 1881, and editor from 1881 to 1906. All three were at

first hard-driving Reconstructionists, but from 1873 through 1877 a rather abrupt change of attitude took place.

"The difficulties of the social problem in Southern society must mainly be disposed of by Southern society itself, and not by any outside power coming from Washington," the *Independent* ventured in 1874. "[It] is not wise to expect the national power to do by force of arms what can be done only by moral processes and by time," *Harper's Weekly* opined in 1875. "As a 'ward of the nation' he [the black] can no longer be singled out for especial guardianship," the *Nation* concluded of the federal troop withdrawals in 1877.[12]

Why did this change take place? Undoubtedly economic depressions in 1873 and 1893 were powerful forces—as the frustration-aggression research described in the previous chapter would suggest. However, cognitive dissonance mechanisms and other psychological theory suggest a pattern of this sort also at work. There were numerous dissonance-producing factors: the highly publicized corruption of Reconstruction governments; the general appearance of a mess to be avoided; the fear of, desire to avoid, and guilt concerning, an apparent large-scale social failure after such high hopes. And also people were simply becoming bored with the same old issue—a particularly powerful motivation in an industry and among a people attuned to the seeking of novelty.[13] Then along came Social Darwinism to provide an excuse for resolving the dissonance by abandoning the black to "natural" social law. Whatever the forces at work, however, they do not excuse men of intelligence from using it. The fact of a failure of leadership remains. And as the newsman and his editor are traditionally among the best-informed of Americans, this failure seems particularly deplorable, as do efforts in our time to sap the courage, deflect the gaze, and curb the tongue of this crucial source of social criticism.

A third leadership failure was in the South. When Federal troops were withdrawn under the Compromise arrangement, the old aristocracy of Southern leadership in all sincerity promised that the rights of the black would be protected. But with the passing of this leadership, demagogues catering to redneck lusts, like Vardaman and Tillman, took over, and with them came a rapid rise in lynchings and the imposition of Jim Crow laws everywhere.

The fourth leadership failure was among the blacks. Well into the beginning of the end Frederick Douglass pressed relentlessly for black advancement, but in 1895 he died and Booker T. Washington rose to replace Douglass' intransigence with a policy of accommodation. And while it is true that beneath this outward show Washington did keep more going for the black than he is generally credited with, the effect of his speeches and his policies was to bless and sanctify the failure of white leadership, while discouraging the rise of the hell-raising kind of black leadership which the times increasingly required.

The fifth leadership failure was that of the makers, interpreters, and enforcers of the law. Here—and again with overtones for our times, but of a favorable comparison—the central symbolic failure was in the Supreme Court. The undermining of the grand black-advancing constitutional amendments began in 1875 with the refusal by the Supreme Court to uphold the Fifteenth Amendment's supposed protection for black voting rights (*United States* v *Reese,* and *United States* v. *Cruikshank*). And in 1896 the Supreme Court completed the devastation with a repressive and regressive masterstroke, the famous decision upholding "separate but equal" facilities in *Plessy* v. *Fergusson* that sanctioned school segregation and fixed upon the nation a straitjacket and a set of blinders we are still trying to cast off.

In retrospect, however, all these failures of leadership seem secondary to the greatest failure of all, which was in the Presidency. For however one may try to excuse American Presidents by pointing to the political facts of life and the complex of concerns they must resolve, this hard, uncomfortable fact remains. This was the fundamental issue for a nation ostensibly based on the ideals of Christianity and democracy, yet no President from the time of Grant until the time of Franklin Roosevelt felt called upon to do more than make a few token gestures toward black advancement. Whatever noble words they might from time to time offer, all faithfully followed the precedent of the policy of federal neglect successfully established by Hayes and his immediate successors. And even Franklin Roosevelt's personal concern is a matter of debate. It was not until the emergence of Harry Truman, John Kennedy, and Lyndon Johnson that a President was sufficiently moved to brave white disapproval and advocate black advancement on a partisan basis.

It would be hard to overstate the social devastation that followed this combined failure of American leadership. From this time the final separation of black and white was imposed by fiat, look, and terror, if need be, practically everywhere—specifically, by law or custom, in train, streetcar, steamboat, theaters, boardinghouses, toilets, water fountains, waiting rooms, ticket windows, factory entrances, pay windows, exits, doorways, stairways, trade unions, hospitals, penal institutions, chain gangs, homes for the aged, the indigent, the orphaned, and on up to housing areas and entire towns. ("In 1914 there were six such towns in Texas, five in Oklahoma, and two in Alabama." [14])

"The extremes to which caste penalties and separation were carried in parts of the South could hardly find a counterpart short of the latitudes of India and South Africa," C. Vann Woodward noted in *The Strange Career of Jim Crow,* which lured the reluctant back to gaze into and ponder the implications of this historical abyss. "In 1909 Mobile passed a curfew law applying exclusively to Negroes and requiring them to be off the streets by 10 p.m. The Oklahoma legislature in 1915 authorized its Corporation Commission to require telephone companies 'to maintain separate booths for white and colored patrons.' North Carolina and Florida required that textbooks used by the public-school children of one race be kept separate from those used by the other, and the Florida law specified separation even while the books were in storage." [15]

A crucial point that Woodward made, and that others have since amplified, is that this devastation did not come immediately. For a time following the abandonment of the issue to the "natural" goodness of the individual and to the supposedly benign "natural" workings of society and the marketplace, the health of the nation did seem to be improving, racism seemed to be waning, and blacks and whites here and there appeared to have reached the doorstep of the millennium.

In 1878, Thomas Wentworth Higginson, commander of a black regiment in the Civil War, again visited the South, this time to view the results of the Hayes federal troop withdrawal with "the eyes of a tolerably suspicious abolitionist." Everywhere he found evidence of black prosperity and advancement that (although the President had only been in office a year) he attributed to the Hayes policy. Moreover, Southern white promises of protection of voting rights and political advancement were seemingly being kept. Most of the black veterans from his old regiment, said Higginson, "agreed that wherever the Democratic party itself began to divide on internal or local questions, each wing was ready to conciliate and consequently defend the colored vote, for its own interest, just as Northern politicians conciliate the Irish vote, even while they denounce it." [16]

In 1879, Sir George Campbell, a member of the British Parliament, after traveling throughout the South remarked that "the humblest black rides with the proudest white on terms of perfect equality, and without the smallest symptom of malice or dislike on either side. I was, I confess, surprised to see how completely this is the case; even an English Radical is a little taken aback at first." A Negro newsman, T. McCants Stewart, returning in 1885 to his native South Carolina after an absence of ten years in Boston, was amazed at the acceptance he found everywhere. "I think the whites of the South are really less afraid to have contact with colored people than the whites of the North," he said in commenting on how easily whites entered into conversation with him for no other purpose than to pass the time of day. Even as late as 1897, a Charleston editor wrote of a proposed Jim Crow law for trains that it would be "a needless affront to our respectable and well-behaved colored people." [17]

Thus, everywhere intelligent and well-meaning men—and those who were simply tired of it all—worked hard to see the millennium (and wanting to see it, they *did,* despite all evidence to the contrary). But behind this hopeful façade the whirlwind that no one wanted to see was not only gathering strength but was *already* hard at work. "It would certainly be preposterous to leave the impression that any evidence I have submitted indicates a golden age of race relations in the period between Redemption and complete segregation," C. Vann Woodward concluded in *Jim Crow.* "On the contrary, the evidence of race conflict and violence, brutality, and exploitation in this very period is overwhelming. It was, after all, in the eighties and early nineties that lynching attained the most staggering proportions ever reached in the history of that crime. Moreover, the fanatical advocates of racism, whose doctrines of total segregation, disfranchisement, and ostracism eventually triumphed over all opposition and became universal practice in the

South, were already at work and already beginning to establish dominance over some phases of Southern life. Before their triumph was complete, however, there transpired a period of history whose significance has been neglected." [18]

It was a bewildering interlude of liberation and repression, of good and bad, of pro and con. And to understand what was at work would seem of considerable importance to us now, in a new age of ambivalence on the black issue. One sees, then, a people and a region torn between repression and liberation, disturbed but still fluid, still able to swing either way. On one hand is their impulse toward health—that composite of a gentle urge and some fierce old internal voices of morality and good sense urging them toward individual and social growth. But ranked against this impulse are all the old lusts, the fears, the immaturities. What is to decide this struggle? For it must be decided, and soon now, for pressing upon them are all the old processes demanding consistency and fixities of perception, thinking, memory, roles, norms, caste. And it is at this crucial point, it would seem, that the failure of Presidential, party, press, racial, regional, congressional and judicial leadership was devastating. For wherever the people looked they found confusion, evasion, or very poor counsel. And so the old associations of good with white and bad with black proved overwhelming in the end, and cognitive dissonance was resolved with a great rolling backward toward repression. Yet, as Woodward so hauntingly suggested, it might have been different.

"The era of stiff conformity and fanatical rigidity that was to come had not yet closed in and shut off all contact between the races, driven the Negroes from all public forums, silenced all white dissenters, put a stop to all rational discussion and exchange of views, and precluded all variety and experiment in types of interracial association. There were still real choices to be made, and alternatives to the course eventually pursued with such single-minded equanimity and unquestioning conformity were still available." [19]

CHAPTER 17

Social Darwinism
and the Jensen Affair

"Mr. Herbert Spencer is already a power in the world. . . . Mr. Spencer represents the scientific spirit of the age. . . . Mr. Spencer has already established principles which, however compelled for a time to compromise with prejudice and vested interests, will become the recognized basis of an improved society." [1]

So trumpeted the *Atlantic Monthly* in the 1860s. The subject of its enthusiasm was, as we have seen, indeed amazing. Herbert Spencer was a successful designer of railway lines and bridges who

"remained till forty an uneducated man" and who reportedly had
never read a book all the way through.[2] Yet, with the exception of
Charles Darwin, this British engineer was probably the most
powerful intellectual influence in the world from roughly 1870 to
1890. It is for this reason that Spencer, more than any other one
man, was the key figure in relation to the black and white sickness
in America at that time, for the great influence of this kind and
decent man, himself no racist, unwittingly helped cut away the
little bit of social ground the black man had gained during the
early, favorable years of Reconstruction.

On the other hand, Spencer, more than anyone else, is responsible for the development of American social science as a healing
intervention—not because of what he believed, but because of the
driving intellectual fury of the reaction to his beliefs and their
social effect. Thus, to bring out the social scientific concepts relevant to that age—and even more greatly to our own—it is necessary to take a look at more of their history.

The sciences of man were relatively new, amorphous, weak, and
speculative when Spencer appeared. A synthesis of what seemed to
be known was needed, and this he provided. With a clarity of expression that was rare for the time and that drugged his readers
with a mighty vision of the realm of human knowledge, his works
won disciples by carload lots and gave the new sciences of man
their first forceful statements in the wake of the general Darwinian
excitement. The books emerged as though on an assembly line—
a philosophy (*First Principles*), two volumes on biology, three on
psychology, three on sociology, and one on ethics. Their impact on
all the social sciences of that time was enormous, and Spencer,
along with Auguste Comte, was a principal founder of sociology.
Thus, when he visited the United States in 1882, many younger
men who were to make their mark on psychology, like William
James, and on sociology, like Charles Cooley, no doubt glowed
with some feeling of an old debt. Though by the time of his visit
they were disillusioned by him, more than any other one man
Spencer had fired them and opened the future to them when they
were very young.[3]

But their mixed pleasure was nothing compared to the uncommon acclaim given Spencer's theories by the American business
community and their conservative academic supporters. Industrial-

ists like John D. Rockefeller and James J. Hill were then beginning to cite Darwin's "survival of the fittest" theories as the natural justification for their ruthless drive to crush competition, expand their industrial empires, and accumulate great personal wealth. Indeed, much of the business community, the government, and the country as a whole was caught up in a "survival of the fittest" mood; it seemed tailor-made for a nation that worshiped the Anglo-Saxon and felt it had a special destiny because it was so blessed as to be under relatively pure WASP leadership. But again it was the old American story of a blessing for one group that was a curse for another. For aside from its grim implications for the blacks, this buoyant and seemingly harmless reveling in racism and expansionism went along with new attempts to slaughter the remaining American Indians and led to the American seizure of Cuba and the "colored" Philippines.[4]

Spencer, then, was the right man for the times. It was as though the God who looked after white America was, in Spencer, responding to an order for a custom design. Here was no wordy Doktor with a German accent, nor an alien Frenchman, but a safe man of practical affairs from the source-land for the Anglo-Saxon, a comfortably *British* engineer, a designer of bridges, who (next to Darwin) was by all accounts the greatest living intellectual—and he was saying exactly what the right people in America wanted to hear. And so began a devastating interaction between a sage and those who became known as Social Darwinists, on the one hand, and many of the practical and powerful leaders of the times, on the other. Like schoolboys entranced with a new game, the great industrialists—Hill, Rockefeller, Chauncey Depew, and Andrew Carnegie—vied with one another in becoming amateur social scientists. Of the "law" of competition, for example, steel magnate Carnegie, who considered himself to be Spencer's closest American friend, wrote in the *North American Review* that while it "may sometimes be hard for the individual, it is best for the race, because it insures the survival of the fittest in every department." [5]

But stranger still was that social scientists like Spencer talked like industrialists, many of them with a racist thrust. Another acceptable Englishman whose views helped strengthen Social Darwinism was Sir Francis Galton, Darwin's almost superhumanly brilliant cousin. Galton, who ranks with Freud, James, and Wilhelm

Wundt as a founder of psychology, was the father of psychometrics and all mental testing. He was also the first and most persuasive advocate of a view that psychologist Arthur Jensen revived in 1969—that intelligence is not only overwhelmingly determined by genetics, but also by race, with the Negro belonging to an obviously inferior order. Galton's disciple, Karl Pearson, a psychologist of central importance in intelligence testing and the perfection of statistics (for example, all the ingenious ramifications of the concept of *correlation*) also made a contribution to the racist aspect of Social Darwinism, as did William McDougall, an early-day giant in the field of social psychology. G. Stanley Hall, who founded the American Psychological Association, introduced Sigmund Freud to America, and did important early work in the study of childhood and adolescence, was for a time of this alignment, and so was Edward L. Thorndike, founder of educational psychology in America, propounder of the famous "Law of Effect," and a pioneer figure in American learning theory. While most of these men avoided the social undesirability of the flat statement that the black man was inferior, it was the logical implication of what they were saying, and many laymen got the signal.[6]

With one major exception, Social Darwinism found no comparable support among American sociologists. By the nature of their discipline most sociologists were attuned more to the external than to the internal forces that shape man and were more aware of the valid import of Darwinism—that is, of the vast impact of environment in turning out one kind of man rather than another. Moreover, sociology has traditionally been more liberal than psychology. But while the psychologists only contributed passive racist views that were very much incidental to their larger purposes, one sociologist made of Social Darwinism a holy war and had a direct and impelling impact on the attitudes of his time. This was caustic, brilliant William Graham Sumner, one of the most popular professors in the history of Yale University.

"Poverty belongs to the struggle for existence," Sumner proclaimed. Reformers were "puny meddlers" and "social quacks"; the "greatest folly" of man was the attempt to "plan a new social world." [7] In *Folkways* he laid the intellectual groundwork for a familiar and still well-entrenched folk wisdom with his dictum that "legislation cannot make mores." [8] And the hero of his numerous essays, oddly enough, was the same figure Richard Nixon was to evoke in the Presidential campaign of 1968: The Forgotten Man, the decent white middle-class citizen who went quietly about his business while overburdened with taxes.[9]

The destruction wreaked by the "doctrine" of Social Darwinism was the product of a simple but extremely powerful social mechanism. The doctrine seems first to have worked upon a complex of white beliefs and attitudes toward blacks, producing a radical change in these attitudes, which in turn influenced white *behavior* toward blacks. Particularly notable was the way by which Social Darwinism created the intellectual climate wherein the "higher-minded" segments of society, the so-called leaders, acted to bless the racist urges of the "lower-minded" followers. No single authority went around proclaiming a formal list of the principles that comprised this doctrine, of course, but underlying the statements of authorities who loosely tended to talk and think alike several fairly hard tenets can be identified—and their persistence is frightening.[10]

A first principle was that just as Darwin's theory of evolution revealed a developmental hierarchy of organisms in the animal kingdom, so was there a hierarchy of races among humans. The white race was, of course, the most advanced, the natural leader. Consequently, one could not expect much from the blacks or any of the other lesser, follower races.

Second, the record of the rocks showed that evolutionary change could take place only very slowly, over eons of time. Consequently, it was again foolish to hope for much from the black within the foreseeable future. One could do nothing but wait patiently for the helpful eons to transform him into something more acceptable.

Third, intelligence was an innate thing, fixed at birth; some men were born exceptionally smart and gifted, many were born stupid. Thus since little could be done about intelligence after birth, it was best that the generally inferior black give up the frustrating delusion of rapid self-improvement.

Fourth, the ideas of natural selection and the survival of the fittest were actually sacred laws vital to the preservation and advancement of society. If the black should be ground under or lose out in the process, it was certainly pitiable, but an inexorable natural law decreed that inferior specimens and species must perish.

Fifth—and central to everything else—society itself was a sacred organism that must not be tampered with by men. Men did so at their peril, for inevitably the great organism would reject all artifice, and it must be left to work itself out according to the evolutionary process. (The Freedmen's Bureau or Head Start or social welfare in any form would be seen as tampering.) And the implication of this view for social science was that its purpose was to understand, *but not to act on that understanding.*

Sixth—and this was supposedly Social Darwinism's saving grace —things in general would progressively get better and better. As the glory that was man had evolved from the lowly amoeba, so would the social organism become ever more delightful and bountiful. We all basked within the protection of a giant natural, social problem-solver. Things might not be going well for the blacks now, but if you didn't tamper with anything and just went on about your own business, it would all work out for the best somehow, sometime.

This, then, was the dubious fruit of the first major formalizing of social science in America. It is a point worth remembering. The curing of our social ills will probably bring on a day when the social scientist, like today's doctor, will be tempted to think of himself as God, and it will be well to remember that this science had, and still has, feet of clay.

As for Social Darwinism's historical relevance to the sorry drama that entrenched Jim Crow in the South and segregation in the North, underlying political and economic forces were undoubtedly of greater initiating or impelling importance, but it would appear that nothing else was so effective as a means of justifying the regressive attitudes and actions of both good and bad men. Everywhere one looks in the journals that reflected the changing position on the black issue, one encounters the soft purring voice of Social Darwinism. And stepping back, one can see the cycle of sanctification for social disaster. From the prestigious mouths of scholars and moguls the doctrine issues, to worm its way out through the press to lull the people, to soften the minds of Presidents, party politicians, and Supreme Court justices, to strengthen the racist resolve of Southern leadership, and to sap the hopes of the black leadership.

Besides all its other implications, this episode should serve as a warning of the very great danger of social science misused. More-over, notwithstanding the many scholars who treat Social Darwin-ism as part of the dead past, the extent to which the attitudes it promulgated are still alive and virulent, sapping initiative and strengthening resistance to change in our land, cannot be over-emphasized. They are expressed overtly by some, unconsciously by many more, and are definitely not confined to the Southern taxi driver, the Northern coupon-clipper, or the new Babbitts, as some might wish to believe. These attitudes still exist to an alarming degree among some who call themselves social scientists, and among many who supposedly orient to social science, particularly in education.

In 1968, it would have been possible for anyone not intimately acquainted with the facts to question this statement. However, in 1969 there occurred a particularly dramatic eruption of the old sickness that left little room for doubt.

The Jensen Affair

One of the highlights of the winter of 1969 for social scientists was the publication of an article by the psychologist Arthur Jensen in the prestigious *Harvard Educational Review* entitled "How Much Can We Boost IQ and Scholastic Achievement?" Its rapid injection into the social body and the resulting convulsions made it one of the most famous professional papers of our time.[11]

Within the Nixon administration there were those who pounced upon its revelations as something quite new. However, every dec-ade since the supposed death of Social Darwinism there has emerged, mainly out of the statistical and mental testing tradition established by Francis Galton, a fresh spokesman to assert that, genetically, blacks are intellectually inferior to whites. Most re-cently, during the 1940s, the 1950s and early 1960s the spokesman had been Professor Henry Garrett, who was, as Thomas Pettigrew noted, "publicly joined by two other psychologists out of the roughly twenty-two thousand who belong to the American Psy-chological Association." [12] But now Galton's old points were being revived by a psychologist so widely respected as to be elected vice president of the American Educational Research Association for 1968 through 1970. *Time, Newsweek, U.S. News and World Report,* the *New York Times,* and a dozen syndicated columnists quickly spread the news throughout the nation.

The first professional reaction to the Jensen article was relatively mild, for only slowly did it dawn on both Jensen and his critics—isolated as they were in academia—that they had a serious fire on their hands. The spring issue of the *Harvard Educational Review* carried follow-up articles in which a number of contributors discreetly parted company with Jensen on some of his main points, while heartily agreeing with most of his minor points.[13] In general, the effect was that of a comfortable group of scholars gathered about a fireplace, alternately warming their hands and their backsides, while jovially sorting through the matter. And there, in the best of all possible worlds, the discussion would have remained.

But by the time this follow-up issue appeared (after the usual production lag) both Jensen and his critics found that their little blaze had suddenly spread and was threatening the house. For the Jensen paper had been taken up by lawyers to fight desegregation in court cases in the South. Legislators seeking excuses for cutting the appropriations for compensatory education were citing it and calling upon Jensen to testify. Copies were being circulated within the Nixon administration, it was reportedly discussed at a Cabinet meeting, and the word was passed around that Jensen had at last pinned down the whole sorry mess.

Now thoroughly aroused, many psychologists, sociologists, anthropologists, and educators flew to the attack. The main problem was the widespread publicity being given to Jensen's views in radically oversimplified and distorted accounts. To counter this, the social scientists began to besiege the popular organs and journalists with corrective information, only to discover one of the true minor horrors of our time—that to all but a handful of people in America what they had to say was just so much jargon. Oversimplifications of Jensen's views were quickly absorbed and easy to understand (after all, the gist of it had been around since Thomas Jefferson's time), but the rebuttal tended to be labored, cumbersome, and beyond the time and capacity of even the best of journalists to comprehend, and thus very little of it ever appeared in the mass media. The combined agony of the opposition was mainly poured into two issues of professional journals of extremely limited circulation, the summer 1969 *Harvard Educational Review* and the autumn 1969 *Journal of Social Issues,* with some spillover into the generally excellent *Psychology Today.* Meanwhile, Jensen, rather than simply washing his hands of the whole miserable affair and refusing to talk to anyone who looked like a reporter, granted more interviews, gave speeches, and endlessly belabored and defended his case, much of which by now wasn't what he said originally.

The episode is worth recounting and examining because of its transhistorical as well as its contemporary meaning, for it dramatically highlights additional disturbing similarities between the post-Reconstruction era and our own time. Again, quite frighteningly, we see a confusion of counsel, an ambiguity of feeling and action, and, in general, many of the signs of a social climate that has been ripe for something out of social science to *justify* abandoning the black. We see a social scientist—who is much like Spencer in clearly not being a racist personally, who is by all accounts a decent person with nothing but the best of intentions toward his fellow man—produce an excellent, long paper, devoted to many other matters, which strays into the vortex of racism. And we see this man seized up and lionized by the press and the politicians, and his suspect wisdom being used in the courts and in the counsels of the Presidency. And it is 1969, almost exactly a hundred years after the eugenicist doctrine helped bring on the debacle of Jim Crow and the great seventy-year freeze following Reconstruction. One is haunted by a sense of *déjà vu;* it is as though no time at all has passed. But while there is a great qualitative similarity in the eras, quantitatively there is a vast difference. Where then this sort of thinking once dominated social science and the thoughts of leadership, it is now a very small minority position.

Let us quickly recount Jensen's main points, and then examine their pros and cons. He contends, first that compensatory education has failed in America, and conjectures that perhaps the explanation can be found in the fifteen point gap between the IQ of blacks as a group and whites as a group, which all IQ measures generally record. For years the environmentalists have claimed that this gap is caused by the social deprivation of the black, and that environment is generally far more important in determining intelligence than heredity. However, Jensen's thorough examina-

tion of hundreds of psychometric studies has convinced him that
the psychological and sociological reasons given by the environmentalists are questionable, and that the primary cause is biological—there very well may be a basic genetic racial difference affecting intelligence. He finds in his own experimental studies that
intelligence reduces to two types: Level I—simple, associative
intelligence; and a more complex Level II—abstracting intelligence.
He also finds in his studies that while black and white children do
equally well in Level I testing, whites do considerably better with
tests of Level II. He then recommends that different schooling be
instituted—and though he stipulates that this be done on an individual basis, setting race aside, the only logical implication is
that in practice blacks face a new kind of segregation, being given
Level I training while whites are given Level II.

Now let us take a closer look at the matter, first from the favorable side. The Jensen paper was surprisingly good, being much
better written and better organized than most papers by educational
researchers—in fact, from the standpoint of academic showman-
ship, it was one of the best to appear in some time. Moreover, it
was written *not* as a statement of fact (Jensen makes this point
repeatedly), but to present a forceful case for investigating an area
of great fuzziness and general mystery. What the furor is about is
not so much what Jensen actually said, but the conclusions that
have been logically drawn from his paper by those (like the press,
and like myself, in summarizing it) who must boil it down to its
essential meanings.

It also contains an excellent attack on educational and social
systems that require all of us to look, think, and be alike, and an
eloquent appeal for pluralism and respect for cultural and individual diversity in our society. His contention that heredity tends to be
unfairly and unscientifically downgraded as a factor in social research in America is also generally true.

Having said all this, however, we must return to the perspective
of American history and the trouble of our times, which forces us
to see this episode in a very bitter light. Here are only a fraction
of innumerable points of disagreement raised by his peers and
critics.

He opens his paper with a forceful and very damaging contention that compensatory education programs such as Head Start

have everywhere failed. But then far within the paper, on page 98, he introduces evidence that it hasn't—specifically he reports on successful small-scale compensatory education programs, but even here he leaves out the most favorable results of the programs he mentions. Moreover, his critics have presented considerable additional evidence to indicate that where the right program is pursued over a sufficient length of time compensatory education does work.

One consistently forceful set of points his critics make is that Jensen centers his case almost entirely on statistical studies either not of blacks at all or of black-white comparisons within the basic American context, in which it is impossible to exclude social-deprivation factors. They note that his case rests in biology—and that he is *not* a biologist, nor has he received much support from this quarter. They note also that contrary to his contention that black genes may be deficient in Level II capacities, one of the highest IQs ever recorded among children was of a black girl with no trace whatsoever of white blood.

But it is what he leaves out that has most consistently infuriated his critics, for in a few lines he discounts seventy years of work by the descendants of William James, Franz Boas and Lester Ward to gain social-psychological evidence to account for the black-white general performance gap. In a later chapter we will take a brief look at the Rosenthal study of expectation; Jensen's use of this study is characteristic. Out of a vast number of persuasive studies of social-psychological phenomena bearing on intelligence, he picked only this one to use as a straw man. And on the basis of methodological flaws in this particular study, which are possibly quite serious but not at all uncommon to pioneering or early work, he rules out *expectancy* as an effect—even though, as we will later demonstrate, it has been observed at work in a wide range of contexts by noted social scientists for seventy years and has been explored experimentally by the Lewin group since the 1920s. This entire book, in fact, can be seen as a compilation of much of what Jensen leaves out in the way of the relevant history, psychology, and sociology that bears on the gap between black and white in practically all areas, including measured intelligence. From the insights of John Woolman through the experiments of Kurt Lewin, the vast gathering of ancient and modern social psychology has been almost completely ignored by Jensen.

But let us end with a few points made by a man who was formerly one of Jensen's closest associates, the noted social psychologist Martin Deutsch, president in 1969 of that refuge for the disciples of Kurt Lewin, the Society for the Psychological Study of Social Issues.

In his SPSSI presidential address in 1969 Deutsch noted—and more in sorrow than in anger—that Jensen's paper had had a "destructive" impact, that his conclusions were "unwarranted by the existing data," that the paper as a whole displayed a "consistent bias toward a racist hypothesis" [14] and that it "completely lacks a sophisticated understanding of the magnificent complexity of environment-organism interaction." The SPSSI membership had been so disturbed by this and other aspects of the affair that it had issued a comprehensive statement, from which Deutsch quoted: "When research has bearing on social issues and social policy, the scientist must examine the competing explanations for his findings and must exercise the greatest care in his interpretation. Only in this way can he minimize the possibility that others will overgeneralize or misunderstand the social implications of his work." [15]

One aspect of Jensen's report was particularly damning, in Deutsch's view, and he twice quoted the noted geneticist Dobzhansky to underline his feelings. "The opinions uttered by scientists are, however, prone to be utilized by politicians and propagandists for purposes of their own. Is a scientist accountable for misuses of his discoveries and utterances? He ought to be articulate enough at least to disown such misuses." [16]

As for Jensen's deriding of compensatory education, Deutsch felt that with "the paucity of funds available for so-called compensatory education, we have never really had a national compensatory effort. We simply must face the grim truth that while we have had social destruction and urban decay, our overall thrust as an organized society has placed our major resources in the arena of war." [17]

He also found that in discounting all efforts to raise intelligence, Jensen had committed the unforgivable professional sin of reporting the failures *but not the successes within the same program* carried out by Deutsch himself. Nor had Jensen had a word to say about the dramatic work in Israel kibbutzim with Oriental Jewish children, where IQ gains of from 85 to 115 were produced. Nor had he seen fit to consider the significance of the famous study by Otto Klineberg in 1935 showing the rise in measured IQ that took place among Southern Negroes who moved to the North.

Clearly recognizing the historical source of Jensen's position, Deutsch noted that the paper represented "a restatement of the old Galtonian eugenic point of view, which essentially hypothesizes high positive correlations among social class, intelligence, and neural factors. The social implications of this are enormous, obvious, and totally antidemocratic, and would tend to create a permanent caste society in which those of lower caste (mostly black) would be forever doomed by their hypothesized neural structures to remain in an inferior position, with all that it implies for future occupational attainment and the antecedent educational opportunities.[18]

"Unfortunately, Jensen's article," Deutsch observed of its social impact, "through its use by attorneys in some desegregation cases and by legislators with respect to appropriations bills (aside from its overinterpretation in public media), has had a negative effect on social progress: less money for education cannot lead to better education; casting aside court desegregation decisions cannot lead to greater social equality.[19]

"It would be in the social and scientific interest if Arthur Jensen would summon the social courage necessary to repudiate the positions which have been taken in his name," Deutsch concluded. And he called upon his old colleague to "re-examine his thinking, re-evaluate his sources of information, reassess his argument, and retract his genetic conclusions in the light of data about and understanding of environmental factors with which he was apparently not familiar at the time he wrote the article. In times of serious social crisis, when the barriers to social change are so enormous and when young people are venting such frustration, a senior social scientist's manifestation of the courage to reformulate a well-publicized opinion would be a positive example of the conquering of discomfort by the inner conviction of the necessity for scientific objectivity."[20]

CHAPTER 18

Black Aspiration and Leadership

The aspiration of a people is expressed in many ways, but most strikingly and memorably in its leadership. And while the white leadership of the late 1800s was inexorably moving to abandon the black—and sensitive black leaders were readying themselves to accommodate this desire—within the black community another kind of leadership was beginning to find itself. This was the counterleadership of a new kind of revolt that has grown over the years to flower in our time—a revolt that consists, at the core, of finding, first, a new way for blacks to see themselves as a group; second, a new way to see themselves individually as part of this group, but also as unique entities, beyond all matters of race; and third, a new way to see and feel about the whites who surround and outnumber them.

Frederick Douglass had begun to articulate the complexities of this vision, but the significance of what he was saying had been missed, being generally put down as only the rhetoric of a famous orator. Now, in the late 1800s, the very young W. E. B. Du Bois began to seek ways to understand and, with this understanding, launch a new kind of revolution in black-white relationships.

The problem he faced was incredibly difficult. Merely to achieve the first goal—understanding—required all his skills as a poet, historian, and fledgling social scientist. In retrospect the problem he wanted to solve can be seen as having many intricately interrelated aspects. It was important, first, to set aside in mind the social exceptions in order to get at a crucial general rule of black-white relationships, the exceptions being the handful of blacks and whites who had come to know and value one another by the late 1800s —whites with a good opinion of blacks, and blacks who were successful in white society. Among the rest—the majority of blacks and whites—there were persistent symptoms of the sickness, which Social Darwinism had radically increased in virulence. The blacks (in relation to what whites aspired to and expected of themselves) generally had low opinions of themselves, low aspirations and low self-expectancies. For a black to aspire to college, as Du Bois did, was seen by most other blacks as something akin to wanting to fly to the moon. Moreover, there was not a single area or aspect of national life, no matter how low in status, in which most blacks believed themselves capable of competing successfully with whites.

Added to this low self-expectancy was the very low opinion of blacks held by the powerful white majority, which continually acted like the heaviest of lids on a pot that only occasionally came to a feeble boil. This low white expectancy encouraged lower black performance, which in turn confirmed the low expectancies of both races, which in turn continually depressed black aspirations.

It was a vicious cycle of the worst sort that must somehow be broken; even in the face of massive white opposition black aspirations must somehow be raised. But this not only raised the difficult question of how to do it but of what the black was to aspire to. What *should* he expect of himself? Thus, Du Bois was also forced to confront anew the questions of identity that have baffled the black ever since he was torn away from his old identities in Africa and cast upon the American shore relatively naked and unprotected in this fundamental aspect of human psychology. And this dilemma was further complicated by the fact that blacks not only had to discover useful identities but, following the Civil War and the impetus of Reconstruction, they were also plagued by the question of rightful identities.

For a long time most of them had been preoccupied with the problem of taking on whatever identity was most useful in terms of surviving in relation to the white—the shambling gaiety of Sambo that was acceptable to the slavemaster, for example. But with their emancipation, freedom had imposed upon them the need to consider what they should aspire to. Being classified as men rather than as animals had opened the door to an enticing but bewildering new range of human identities.

The search for answers to such questions began to lead the young Du Bois in the three directions that were alternately to lure him and to tear at him for the rest of his life. Du Bois the fledgling historian was impelled to explore the past of his people in America and in Africa for models of heroic individual achievement—and for the group dynamics that seemed to underlie successful black leadership. Du Bois the fledgling social scientist was impelled to seek ways of intervening and transforming a history that was going badly for the black in America. And both concerns were to be shaped—and given their eventual point and social impact—by the third role he was eventually to assume, as himself a leader and a model for black aspiration.

The Du Bois Leadership Analysis

In studying the past of the black in America and in Africa, Du Bois discerned a particular kind of aspiration that has surfaced in many contexts. Hegel, examining all of human history up to his time, saw this aspiration as a desire for freedom that had animated man from the earliest time. More recently, within the past two decades, modern psychologists have begun to approach it within the context of the Third Force "school" and the concept of *self-actualizing*. These sources suggest that this aspiration can be seen as the core of an urge to health that shapes both man's society and his history. Du Bois found it working within the black in America in three ways, each of which found black leaders to give these liberative eruptions their driving edge.

> Now in the past the American Negro has had instructive experience in the choosing of group leaders, founding thus a peculiar dynasty which in the light of present conditions is worthwhile studying. When sticks and stones and beasts form the sole environment of a people, their attitude is largely one of determined opposition to and conquest of natural forces. But when to earth and brute is added an environment of men and ideas, then the attitude of the imprisoned group may take three main forms—a feeling of revolt and revenge; an attempt to adjust all thought and action to the will of the greater group; or, finally, a determined effort at self-realization and self-development despite environing opinion. The influence of all of these attitudes at various times can be traced in the history of the American Negro, and in the evolution of his successive leaders.[1]

Before 1750, "while the fire of African freedom still burned in the veins of the slaves," Du Bois discerned in all leadership or attempted leadership "but the one motive of revolt and revenge—typified in the terrible Maroons, the Danish blacks, and Cato of Stono." Later, the slaves in the South, "aroused undoubtedly by vague rumors of the Haitian revolt, made three fierce attempts at insurrection—in 1800 under Gabriel in Virginia, in 1822 under Vesey in Carolina, and in 1831 again in Virginia under the terrible Nat Turner." But alongside this ferocious and vengeful drive for self-assertion there arose a milder, hopeful aspiration. "The liberalizing tendencies of the latter half of the eighteenth century brought, along with kindlier relations between black and white, thoughts of ultimate adjustment and assimilation. Such aspiration was especially voiced in the earnest songs of Phyllis, in the martyrdom of Attucks, the fighting of Salem and Poor, the intellectual accomplishments of Banneker and Derham, and the political demands of the Cuffes."[2]

We have earlier noted how, as the hope for this acceptance soured, blacks withdrew from the white churches to create two small bastions of self-assertion and group strength, the African church and the African social club. And ultimately, with the rise of black abolitionists before the Civil War and black leadership during Reconstruction, with the rise of men like "Remond, Nell, Wells-Brown, and Douglass, a new period of self-assertion and self-development dawned." [3]

Thus Du Bois found at work in history these three expressions of black aspiration—the knife-edged, violent thrust of Gabriel Prosser, Denmark Vesey, and Nat Turner; a milder drive that sought assimilation into the white society via the avenue of remarkable achievement by such black individuals as the poetess Phyllis Wheatley and the entrepreneur Paul Cuffe; and the surge of self-development and self-assertion that was to embrace blacks as a whole, represented by Frederick Douglass, John Langston, Blanche Bruce, and other black leaders of the Reconstruction era.

All three expressions, it should be noted, were not only historical events established by a living leadership, but, perpetuated by the black historian, they continued to resonate within the black subculture, existing as choices that have been more or less open to each new generation of young blacks and black leaders seeking to form their own personal and group identities. Considering these choices and the trends and personalities as the 1800s gave way to the 1900s, the young Du Bois came to a conclusion that made black history in his time.

Du Bois Versus Booker T. Washington

"Douglass, in his old age, still bravely stood for the ideals of his early manhood—ultimate assimilation *through* self-assertion, and on no other terms," Du Bois remarked of the old warrior who more than any other seemed to him worth emulating.[4] But as we have seen, in the late 1800s the urge to health in both the black and white communities was shrinking, the mood was for accepting the sickness and making the most of it, and in answer to this need the most powerful of the black leaders arose.

"Easily the most striking thing in the history of the American

Negro since 1876 is the ascendancy of Mr. Booker T. Washington," Du Bois wrote in the respectful but ultimately coldblooded piece of literary surgery that was the beginning of his own gradual assumption of black leadership and of the even more gradual decline of Washington.[5]

In 1903, Du Bois saw Washington as "certainly the most distinguished Southerner since Jefferson Davis, and the one with the largest personal following." [6] Carefully, steadily, with hardly a false move, through a combination of great shrewdness, tact and charm, Washington had gained the support of many of the influential whites of his time, and this alignment gave him the strength to override his black opposition, if he so wished, and to be almost all-powerful in the black community.

How Washington came to power, and the relevance of his emergence to the situation of the black today, can be placed in perspective by recalling how eagerly the great American industrialists and conservatives in government and academia embraced Herbert Spencer. Now here was a lesser but in some subtle ways more important partner to take into the fold. "In all things purely social we can be as separate as the five fingers, and yet one as the hand in all things essential to mutual progress," Washington proclaimed in his famous address of 1895, known as the Atlanta Compromise. "It is at the bottom of life we must begin, not at the top," he told his audience—and via the newswire—the nation, black and white. And again: "The wisest among my race understand that agitation of the questions of social equality is the extremest folly." And again: "Progress in the enjoyment of all the privileges that will come to us must be the result of severe and constant struggle rather than of artificial forcing." [7]

It was the black masterwork of compromise, a beautifully crafted response to the white need to justify the low status of a people for whom, try as they might, they simply had no use except as servants and menial laborers. It was also greatly responsive to the needs of many blacks who deeply desired—because of so much unsettlement—some settled, easy goals. And for perhaps a majority in both races it was a welcome response to a profound weariness—the whites weary of the "problem" and the blacks weary of aspiring. Moreover, here at last was the ultimate, the perfect, the unimpeachable confirmation of everything the Social Darwinists were preaching: The blacks' great leader had said, in effect, Yes, you are right; all we can do is quietly, gratefully, over the eons, crawl up from the slime to your level.

The apparent relief of so many tensions was so great that when Washington ended his Atlanta address Governor Bullock of Georgia literally rushed across the platform to seize his hand. President Grover Cleveland wired a special letter of congratulations. And on the strength of this and other endearments, Andrew Carnegie and other great Northern philanthropists poured millions into Tuskegee, into the support of George Washington Carver's phenomenal agricultural research at Tuskegee, and into Booker T. Washington's other ventures.

For a time Du Bois seethed in relative silence. By the turn of the century, he was not only deploring the social conspiracy against the black, both North and South, but was already aware of linkings that many white and black scholars were only beginning to discern clearly in the 1960s. And at the heart of this conspiracy he saw Booker T. Washington at work, often with the best of intentions, but functionally serving continually to bless and sanctify black degradation. Somehow the black Goliath and all that he represented must be felled. And however he might, as a black man and as a scholar, shrink from this difficult task, by stages Du Bois came to see that it was up to him to do it.

In 1903, he let fly his first pebble—the key essay in his masterpiece, *The Souls of Black Folk*. But the black Goliath was apparently untouched. Du Bois tried again in 1905, calling together a handful of black intellectuals to meet in Niagara Falls, selected for its symbolic impact—Niagara Falls had been the terminus of the old Underground Railroad. Now after forty years of freedom, these black intellectuals, the supposed pride of their race, had to meet on the Canadian side to avoid being denied a hotel, and white indifference and Washington's control of much of the black press guaranteed that the message would be lost.

Du Bois tried again, calling a meeting in 1906 at Harper's Ferry, to evoke the memory of John Brown. The group issued another proclamation, and among the goals that both whites and blacks found dangerously radical in those days were the following: "We want full manhood suffrage and we want it now. . . . We want discrimination in public accommodation to cease. . . . We claim the right of freemen to walk, talk, and be with them that wish to be with us. . . . We want the Constitution of the country enforced. . . . We want our children educated. . . . And here on the scene of John Brown's martyrdom we reconsecrate ourselves, our honor, our property to the final emancipation of the race which John Brown died to make free. . . . We are men! We will be treated as men. And we shall win." [8]

They met again in 1907 at Fanueil Hall in Boston (the old focal point of Boston abolitionism) and in 1908 at Oberlin (the old capital of Western abolitionism), and both these gatherings and Du Bois's passionate statements decrying what was being done to the black in America were either mocked as romantic, melodramatic, and ridiculous or magnificently ignored by the majority of both whites and blacks. Then in August of 1908 something happened in Springfield, Illinois, that began radically to change the nature of black aspiration and the nature of both black and white leadership. It was the result of the bloody legacy of thirty years of an indifferent white leadership, an accommodating black leadership, and nationwide inaction sanctified by Social Darwinism, and it impelled truly horrified whites—the grandson of William Lloyd Garrison and John Dewey among them—to found the NAACP. A white woman in Springfield had accused—falsely, it was proved in court—a black man of rape; what then happened is best told, soberly and factually, by the great black historian John Hope Franklin.

The town officials saw that the mob was becoming unruly and several unsuccessful efforts were made to disperse it. Finally the governor called out the militia. The mob, oblivious to the appeals of high state officials to respect the law, raided secondhand stores, secured guns, axes, and other weapons, and began to destroy Negro businesses and to drive Negroes from their homes. They set fire to a building in which a Negro owned a barber shop. The barber was lynched in the yard behind his shop, and the mob, after dragging his body through the streets, was preparing to burn it when the militia from Decatur dispersed the crowd by firing into it. On the following night an 84-year-old Negro, who had been married to a white woman for more than 30 years, was lynched within a block of the State House. Before order was restored more than 5,000 militia men were patrolling the streets.

In the final count, 2 Negroes had been lynched, 4 white men had been killed, and more than 70 persons had been injured. More than 100 arrests were made and approximately 50 indictments were returned. The alleged leaders of the mob went unpunished.

The news of the riot was almost more than Negroes could bear. It seemed to them a perverse manner in which to celebrate the one hundredth anniversary of the birth of Lincoln. Negroes were actually lynched within half a mile of the only home Lincoln ever owned and within two miles of his final resting place. Their cup was filled, and they hardly had the voice to cry out against this most recent outrage. It was a time for drastic action. Somehow, some solution must be found to the problem of color, which Du Bois had already called the greatest problem of the twentieth century.[9]

CHAPTER 19

Expectancy, Self-Actualizing, and Identity

Social science has a great deal to say about the processes underlying the historical events sketched in the last chapter—about such concepts as aspiration, expectancy, self-actualizing, and identity. It has, in fact, so much to say that we must call a familiar analogy into service to help keep it all untangled.

The birth of blacks and whites in America can be compared to the falling of seed upon the soil. This seed may fall either upon barren soil, receive little rainfall and be afflicted with extremes of heat and chill, or it may fall upon fertile soil, with a good rainfall and a favoring climate. How the two conditions correspond to the general situation of the black seed versus the white seed will, of course, be obvious; and the relation to the concepts we will develop is this: The potential drive within each seed for growth can be seen as its potential for *self-actualizing*. The watering or lack of watering of the seed, and the favorable or unfavorable climate, can be seen as the effect of high or low *aspirations* and *expectancies*. And the shapes the seed takes as it begins to grow can be seen as its succession of *identities*.

Expectancy phenomena have fascinated psychologists, sociologists and, to some degree, economists for well over seventy years, so we will examine them first. In 1898, Albert Moll, a clinician who was brave enough to ignore the raised eyebrows of his peers, experimented with hypnosis and noticed that "the prophecy causes its own fulfillment"—that is, patients with hysterical (or mind-induced) symptoms were "cured" as soon as they believed a cure was possible. As for the effects of the hypnosis, it seemed interesting to Moll that the subjects were so strongly impelled to act out the expectations of the hypnotist.[1]

In 1948 sociologist Robert Merton expanded this line of thinking into the concept of the *self-fulfilling prophecy*. Perfectly healthy banks failed, he noted, when depositors began to fear failure— and thus *expected* failure—and made a disastrous run on the funds. Merton also pointed out that the self-fulfilling prophecy operated in racial relations. In a state where whites felt that blacks had little capacity for achievement, only a fifth of the amount spent on the education of whites was spent on blacks, which seemed to lead in turn to the low black achievement originally prophesied.[2] Gunnar Myrdal also noted such processes in many areas of black life, finding that they seemed to produce a negatively cumulative effect, which he developed in his theory of the vicious circle.[3] Gordon Allport found the force working on the broadest possible scale —in world affairs: Nations that expect to go to war, he suggested, eventually do go to war, while somehow nations that expect to stay out of wars avoid them. And on a more lighthearted level, William Whyte, observing his famous street-corner gang, found that the gang's expectations of who would win and who would lose—expressed in *advance* of the evening's bowling games—actually seemed to determine the games' outcomes.[4]

In experimental psychology, phenomena of this sort were explored throughout the 1930s and 1940s by students of Kurt Lewin investigating the concept of a *level of aspiration*. However, it is only relatively recently that experiments have been conducted to relate expectancy to the situation of a disadvantaged minority. The best-known study of this type was one of the earliest, the Oak School study of teacher expectation by social psychologist Robert Rosenthal and educator Lenore Jacobsen in 1964. Soon after its publication in a very readable account—rare for experimental work—*Pygmalion in the Classroom,* it was roundly criticized by some leading educational psychologists for faulty methodology. However, it was defended by others, succeeding studies have supported its findings, and it remains one of few readable accounts of educational research.[5]

Oak School, a fictitious name for screening purposes, is in a predominantly lower-class community in the Far West. At the time of the study it had 650 students, approximately one-sixth of whom were Mexican-Americans, in six elementary grades, sorted into three ability tracks—high, average, and slow. Rosenthal and Jacobsen gave the entire student body a test they identified as the "Harvard Test of Inflected Acquisition," which was described as an accurate predicter of which children would suddenly "bloom" or show a spurt of learning within the near future.

Actually the test was a standardized, relatively nonverbal test of intelligence known in the trade as TOGA (Flanagan's Tests of General Ability). Moreover, all the talk of "bloomer-predicters" was simply to prime the teachers for the *real* test, which was of themselves and the effect of their heightened expectations. On a purely random basis, the experimenters selected 20 per cent of the class, announced that a group had been identified by the "Harvard" test, and then—a crucial move—gave each teacher a private list of the supposed potential "bloomers" in her class. The children were retested after a four-month semester, at the end of the academic year, and again after two years. The results range from curious to remarkable.

It was found, for example, that over all six grades the children on the teachers' lists (the experimental group) gained four IQ points over the control group—a comparison group of Oak School children who were not on the list but who were, according to the rationale of random selection, of equal ability. This widely reported finding is interesting, but not overly impressive. However, underlying the Oak School results was something of much greater interest that, as noted earlier, psychologist Arthur Jensen left out in his critical summary of this study. In a sense, the significance of the findings is deflated by lumping all six grades together. And when one looks at the results for the first grade alone, a singularly dramatic fact leaps out of the welter of figures and tables: The gain in IQ for the favored *first* graders was *fifteen points*.

What can fifteen IQ points mean? According to the crude scale in practical usage for many years, fifteen IQ points is the difference between a moron and an average child (that is, the difference between an IQ of 85 and 100). It is also the difference between those whom counselors later discourage and those whom they encourage to enter college (that is, the difference between an IQ of 100 and 115). It is *also, as we have seen, the overall group difference found between blacks and whites on IQ tests that Arthur Jensen would account for by genetic racial differences.*

Such a finding at the beginning of a child's educational experience can be laden with exceptional meaning. It is at this stage that vital first impressions are made—of the child upon the teacher and of teacher and the school upon the child. Most importantly, it is at this time that the child's own first groping for some sense of his own potential in this new, vast, exciting but often frightening real world beyond the cocoon of home and family begins to solidify. It is at this point that he may most actively search for some firm sense of what he himself, as well as others, may reasonably expect of him over a lifetime.

It takes no great imagination to appreciate what it can mean during this crucially formative year for a still alert and open first grader to sense himself to be *not* a moron, but average. Or not average, but *above* average. Or not a stupid black child, but a human being. Rosenthal and Jacobsen also found that the gains for the experimental group were not transitory, but held up over time. The plotted curves for retestings show that Oak School girls in the experimental group exhibited the expectancy advantage early, maintained it at a high level, and lost virtually none of it over twenty months. The boys' gains were more moderate, but even so their expectancy advantage was greater after twenty months than it had been at the first testing after four months.

What does this suggest about the black situation in America beyond what we've already attempted to express? Again, something John Woolman may have first discerned: the power of the cumulative, or "snowballing," effect of expectancy. One of the most interesting things about Gunnar Myrdal's great study is its leftovers. After page 1024 the remarkable appendices begin, wherein he attempted to bottle for posterity some social scientific distillates out of his sifting of the American dilemma, and here Myrdal discusses the "principle of cumulation." Bypassing the fairly complex economic theory involved, the essence of the notion is that like a snowball rolling downhill, once things are set in motion they can gather weight, size, and momentum. The crucial factor in the blacks' situation, Myrdal points out, is the matter of the snowball's direction: whether the cumulation is a "vicious circle" spiraling downward, or whether it is a bolstering, burgeoning, upward trend.

The Rosenthal work suggests not only the immediate power of expectancy, but also, in the light of Woolman's vision and Myrdal's more recent insight, its potentially immeasurably greater cumulative power. In the view of man and his society as *systems,* one thing triggers another, until—moving inward into the psychology and the biology of it, or outward into the sociology and economics—one comes to see a vast, shifting network of cumulatively more or less powerful, more or less tightly interlocked forces in motion. Though much remains to be learned about it, it is evident that expectancy is one of the most powerful forces working upon the black to raise his aspirations and encourage his growth —or to stunt him, blight him, warp him, press him under.

Maslow and the Self-Actualizing Revolution

When the philosophy of man changes, then everything changes, not only the philosophy of politics, of economics, of ethics and values, of interpersonal relations and of history itself, but also the philosophy of education, the theory of how to help men become what they can and deeply need to become.

We are now in the middle of such a change in the conception of man's capacities, potentialities, and goals. A new vision is emerging of the possibilities of man and of his destiny, and its implications are many.

We have, each one of us, an essential inner nature which is instinctoid, intrinsic, given, "natural," *i.e.*, with an appreciable hereditary determinant, and which tends strongly to persist.

If this essential core of the person is frustrated, denied or suppressed, sickness results, sometimes in obvious forms, sometimes in subtle and devious forms, sometimes immediately, sometimes later.[6]

As we have already noted, there is now working within and transforming psychology a group known informally as the Third Force, in the sense that Freud was the first force, Pavlov the second, and this loose grouping is the third—Carl Rogers, Rollo May, Erik Erikson, Gordon Allport, Erich Fromm, Karen Horney, Carl Jung, Gardner Murphy, Henry Murray, Kurt Goldstein, Chris Angyal, Clark Moustakas, and many others.[7]

A central question for this group, as we have indicated, is: What is man's essential nature? What is really there underneath it all, before life starts opening avenues for this potential or alternatively thrusts bad news upon us? Their explorations have generally centered about the concept of self, and out of this concern has emerged the compelling notion that we are by nature motivated to be *self-fulfilling* or *self-actualizing*.

This exploration is particularly relevant to the understanding and curing of the black-and-white sickness for several reasons. First, there runs through the work of this clinically oriented group the belief that the drive toward self-actualizing is the basic therapeutic force working within us to impel us toward health, guiding our choices of healthful personal directions and self-liberating identities.

Secondly, this drive is seen as the basis for a quiet revolution in both man and society. It can be easily blocked, repressed, denied, or ignored, but it is remarkably persistent—like a seed buried beneath a new sidewalk, it will persist until the concrete has been shattered and a tree emerges.

And finally (for now—there are many other implications), this group generally agrees that sickness results from the denial, falsification, or radical distortion of this drive to fulfill one's own potential, to realize one's own uniqueness, to *self-actualize*.

The quote opening this section is from one of the group's great-est and (among many men about whom this odd but reassuring thing may be said) most beloved members, the late Abraham Maslow. Active as a teacher, researcher and psychotherapist, Mas-low managed to bridge the gap that usually separates the clinically oriented psychologist interested in *changing* what exists and the experimental and academic psychologist interested mainly only in understanding what exists. He was also a remarkable integrator of theory during an age of men pursuing fragments. Pavlov, Freud, Marx, Gestalt theory, and existentialist philosophy all came to-gether within Maslow to be reworked into one of the most inspir-ing, useful, and comprehensive views of man available to our time.[8]

Reflecting a crucial general trend in psychology, throughout his life Maslow moved from an absorption with abnormality—he was, in fact, the co-author of one of the most successful texts on the sub-ject—to an overwhelming preoccupation with the psychology of health and normality. But Maslow was not concerned with nor-mality in the sense of the average or "normal" common man; he was concerned with a highly selective, uncommon, and even elite normality that he found expressed in a minority of people who seemed to him to represent self-actualizing at its peak. That is, he found among us, in all races and in all walks of life, a particular kind of human being who seemed to have attained the health that both white and black seek in America.[9]

He came upon these self-actualizers in a way that, in itself, is a short parable on the times. Maslow first gained recognition as a researcher in sex life, although few know this today. While Kinsey was gaining fame for his vast packrat collecting of statistics on activities in bedrooms and public toilets—for all its usefulness, essentially a workaday reduction of sex to joyless numbers and a bizarre repertoire—Maslow was exploring more challenging terri-tory. He felt that the Freudian view of sex as a key to creativity and personal fulfillment should be thoroughly investigated, and was particularly intrigued by the potential meaning of what he called *peak* experiences. Through the reports of artists, drug ad-dicts, religious mystics, and the everyday person with a good sex life there ran a commonality of expression: for each of them crea-tivity, the drug experience, mystic ecstasy, or sexual orgasm seemed to offer a centrally meaningful experience of self-expansion, self-transcendance, and ultimately self-integration.

This was fascinating, but over a period of time, as he pursued this line of inquiry with more and more people, the interviews began to change his views about many things—and ultimately this strange journey reshaped his life. It led him away from the questions that customarily absorb the clinician to a set of questions science had relegated to poets and philosophers. It led him out of an all-absorbing concern with the pathology of the sexually disturbed, warped, or unfulfilled, the creatively bottled-up or constricted, the addict able to get his "high" only from self-destructive drugs or alcohol, to some remarkable people whom the clinician seldom saw mainly because they didn't need him.

These people usually had little to report about sex because they frankly and matter-of-factly enjoyed it but weren't particularly interested in advertising the fact. They were without exception extremely creative, but although some were famous creative people in the usual sense, many were not. Whatever their position or occupation, they seemed to be characterized by an unusual freedom, spontaneity, and independence of thought and movement. Although they were quite mature in terms of responsibility and concern for others, they tended to be playful and had managed to retain a childlike sense of wonder and openness. Their sense of humor also had a different quality; where most humor tends to be frenetic and is based in hostility, theirs was quieter, philosophic, dependent for effect on the surprise of offbeat insights. They also reported a high ratio of peak experiences without the use of drugs or alcohol, and they expressed this experience in terms of being filled with a sense of the joy and wonder of life, of being at one with the universe— an "oceanic" feeling, in Freud's apt term.

Going more deeply into the matter, Maslow found that these people who fascinated him so much seemed to be leading unusually rich and satisfying lives along many dimensions. Moreover, they seemed to exist among all ages, classes, and within occupations of both high and low prestige.

Most notable in the black and white context were these four qualities in Maslow's self-actualizers: They had a superior perception of reality (they were not blinded by perceptual defense or the other distorting mechanisms examined in an earlier chapter); they were more tolerant of themselves and of others; they had a more democratic (as opposed to authoritarian) character structure; and they notably identified with the human species as a whole, rather than limiting themselves to certain in-groups and excluding out-groups (they were *species,* rather than *pseudospecies,* oriented, in Erik Erikson's terms).

Maslow estimated that only 1 per cent of our population may be considered full-fledged self-actualizers. And in a screening of three thousand college students he found "only one immediately usable subject and a dozen or so possible future subjects." [10] The prospect, however, is far more promising than these findings suggest. For within all of us, Maslow sees a striving toward self-actualizing at work. The profound implications of this view become evident when self-actualizing is seen in relation to the motivational matrix out of which it rises. That is, Maslow views self-actualizing as rising out of a magnificent personal, social, and historical struggle that involves two levels of human motivation, both having implications for the persistence of the black and white sickness, and for therapy to end it.

Drawing together the ponderings and research of men in all branches of social science and in physiology, Maslow sees us as being motivated by both lower-order *deficiency* and higher-order *being* needs. Another highly suggestive way he has expressed this is as the difference between *defense* and *growth* needs. [11]

On one hand we are motivated by such primary, egocentric needs as those of food, sex, selfish love, safety (from our fellows or the elements), belongingness (to some group, to some other persons), stimulation (we have basic needs for information, for novelty), and by needs for something to work with, to manipulate, and needs for status and personal power. These kinds of needs are fundamental—they must be met for our basic health. And they are elementary—they emerge earliest in the development of human beings, in childhood, and they remain highest in the priorities of most adults. They are also predominantly the needs that were studied by the early Freudians and behaviorists, those of the id and the autonomic nervous system. They are also the "fixed" needs in the two-level view of motivation used by the young Karl Marx, by Émile Durkheim, and by other sociologists in the construction of social theories.

But once these lower-order defense or deficiency needs have been satisfied, another kind of more gentle, less urgent but quite persistent needs begins to act upon us, to guide our thoughts and shape our actions. These are the *being* or *growth* needs—for expressing an unselfish or unneeding love, for growth itself and a fuller realization of one's skills, talents, and other potentials, for the discovery of suitable goals and a worthwhile task or mission in life. These are the needs of which the self-actualizing drive is composed, and though they may be denied and blocked during one's personal and social history, they persist in seeking liberation, freedom, self-fulfillment.

The implications of this motivational structure for the ending of the black and white sickness are endlessly suggestive. On the one hand, those dominantly motivated by self-protective defense needs tend to horde for themselves, to fear differences, to be ethnocentric as well as egocentric and to exclude and denigrate the outsider, to be prejudiced; in short, among *both* races, they are motivated to perpetuate the sickness. On the other hand, those dominantly motivated by self-enlarging and self-transcendant growth tend to share, to welcome differences, to value human brotherhood transcending the usual barriers, to be relatively unprejudiced.

Coupled with other research (the Minard and Pettigrew studies discussed in Chapter 9, for example), Maslow's theory suggests that some of us are more or less held to the defense-needs level and fixed in a tendency toward bigotry, while others tend to operate mainly according to the more sublime dictates of growth needs. But for most of us life is a mixture of both levels. We worry about ourselves, our immediate needs, our own position—as we must for survival—and within this perspective we are perfectly willing to let our neighbor (and our own higher self) perish if this will just happen out of sight, without involving us even vicariously. But we are also driven by the being and growth needs—by all the worrisome ideals that tie us to our neighbor and to the best in ourselves, and that now and then force us to open our eyes and our hearts to these disturbing but uplifting sights and voices.

One extremely thought-provoking variable that seems to tip the scale one way or another is the matter of security—the confidence and security that comes from love and a stable home when one is a child, and from having a decent job, a sure source of income, and the respect of one's neighbors when one is an adult. Such personal securities act to satisfy our defense needs and leave us open to the influence of growth needs. And this in turn suggests the importance of a larger sense of security within which the person exists as an island or an oasis—the sense of security that comes from living within a social system equipped to satisfy both the needs of defense and the needs of growth.

Erikson and the Search for a Wider Identity

We have briefly glimpsed, in self-actualizing, something of the nature of the human seed, and we have examined, in expectancy, how it may be watered and cultivated. Now we will consider the question of the forms the seed may take as it grows.

Identity is Erik Erikson's great theme. Growing out of the Freudian sexual exploration, the concept was widened by Erikson to become the centering device for his approach to much of life. It is also the basis for a diagnosis of the causes and a prescription for a cure of the black and white sickness. In this context, identity can probably be most easily approached by first looking at how Erikson applied it to the situation of individual blacks and whites and then looking at how he extended it to the larger problem of significant *group* identities, which concerned the young Du Bois and has from time to time absorbed all great leaders, black or white.

Let us first firmly ground a concept that has generally received a very loose, and even slippery, usage. For Erikson *identity* is similar to William James's concept of *character,* a recognizable wholeness of person, both mental and moral. It relates to the concepts of *role* and *self,* being both a composite and the meeting place of the *personal* self and the *social* role. "We may speak, then, of a *complementarity* of an *inner synthesis* in the individual and of *role integration* in his group." [12]

This passage, stressing a gathering together of meanings, suggests that a personal and social rounding and completion is the goal of each of us as we seek a firm identity. However, it also evokes its obverse—that is, the *in*completion that we must all suffer for much of our lives, for it is in the nature of things that we spend more time moving *toward* goals than in achieving them. As we move through time, then, generally in a state of seeking and incompletion, we are pushed by growth to confront the choice points that correspond to Erikson's eight stages of man. And at each of these points—infancy, early childhood, adolescence, young adulthood, etc.—we must resolve the crucial questions that govern the building and the liberating of our personal identities.

In addition to the identity problems common to all of us, blacks must contend with special problems of personal and social disjointedness—the horrendous identity complications of the black-white relationship. It is as though all of us, like jugglers in training, must learn to keep eight balls in the air at once, while the black must also balance a plate on a stick on his head and another on one foot. One basic problem, for example, is that whites, in a social world where they are dominant, have a wide range of heroic, respectable, and otherwise useful models or identity choices, but until very recently blacks have been offered only the suspect identity choices that whites found useful in maintaining black suppression (such as the "Sambo" identity that Stanley Elkins found American slavery dictated, or the accommodating "Uncle Tom" identity of our time). But if he rejects these offerings, the black has the problem of developing useful alternatives out of *his* world. The development of black identities, Erikson notes, "is one aspect of the struggle for ethnic survival: One person's or group's identity may be relative to another's; and identity awareness may have to do with matters of an *inner emancipation* from a more dominant identity." [13]

Erikson notes that the longtime dominance of the white majority has left personal and social disaster in its wake for blacks seeking identities in their own world, for until very recently two of the most prevalent forms available to the black were the "surrendered" and the "negative" identity. The first is that *absence* of identity that Du Bois, Ralph Ellison, and James Baldwin have characterized so passionately as the black sense of being inaudible, invisible, nameless, and faceless. Erikson prefers to use C. Vann Woodward's term "surrendered identity" because the term "does not assume total absence, as many contemporary writings do—something to be searched for and found, to be granted or given, to be created or fabricated—but something to be liberated." [14]

The negative identity for the black raises a more complex problem because it involves a particularly intimate and meaningful interaction with the white. Within each of us, Erikson says, there are at work negative as well as positive identities. Along with the sense of a positive identity that expresses what we wish to be and guides our preferred actions, there exists a negative identity composed of all we wish to avoid being and doing—all the quirks, traits, gestures, qualities we have come to be repulsed by, a quivering composite of childhood "don'ts" and social evils. And now the plot thickens: "The individual belonging to an oppressed and exploited minority, which is aware of the dominant cultural ideals but prevented from emulating them, is apt to fuse the negative images held up to him by the dominant majority with the negative identity cultivated in his own group." [15]

This fusion of the black negative identities with the negative identities of the white *over*-culture has three disturbing consequences, according to Erikson. It produces and reinforces feelings of inferiority; it generates a particularly virulent and destructive hatred of oneself; it can also, like a superhumanly endowed evil genie, cause an outburst of "totalism"—that is, a total rejection of all positive identity elements and a wholehearted embracing of the negative identity. This happens with infants at certain stages, with adolescents during periods of extreme rebellion, and even with nations, as in the case of Nazi Germany. And it has happened repeatedly among blacks, ranging from Nat Turner to the totalism of a Malcolm X during both the violence of his criminal years and his years as the prophet of antiwhiteness.

Most disturbing of all, however, is the "unpleasant fact that our God-given identities often live off the degradation of others." At the heart of the black and white sickness Erikson finds a peculiarly perverse and degrading feeding upon one another: "The oppressor has a vested interest in the negative identity of the oppressed because that negative identity is a projection of his own unconscious negative identity—a projection which, up to a point, makes him feel superior but also, in a brittle way, whole." In other words, he confirms what some historians have suspected: that one of the functions of the black historically was to serve as the involved symbolic means by which the white might rid himself of guilt, a sense of sin, and everything else from the dark underside that troubled him; his repressing, whipping, or killing the black serving to keep down something he feared within himself.

Doting on such discoveries within the hades of our psyche, the psychological and literary sensationalists of our day will, with a great drum roll, point into the pit and say that this is the end. But, characteristically, Erikson rolls majestically out of the pit to spread before us the therapeutic vistas of self and social fulfillment by finding the release from racism in the worldwide search for wider identities.

> In many parts of the world the struggle now is for anticipatory and *more inclusive identities*. . . . Revolutionary doctrines promise the new identity of peasant-and-worker to the youth of countries which must overcome their tribal, feudal, or colonial past . . . world space is extended to include outer space as the proper "environment" for a universal technological identity.
>
> At this point, we are beyond the question (and Gandhi did much to teach this at least to the British) of how a remorseful or scared colonialist may dispense corrective welfare in order to appease the need for a wider identity. The problem is rather how he includes himself in the wider pattern, for a more inclusive identity is a development by which two groups who previously had come to depend on each other's negative identities (by living in a traditional situation of mutual enmity or in a symbiotic accommodation to one-sided exploitation) join their identities in such a way that new potentials are activated in both.

According to Erikson, however, this goal is not reached by an unrealistic giving up of smaller identities and loyalties in order solely to merge into an evanescent, mystic union with all humanity. Human relations are made up of specifics—"man meets man always in categories"—and categories of age, sex, occupation, class, and race must remain significant. The strategy is not to give up black power for integration, or integration for black power but, paradoxically, to live in both worlds, to reconcile the two and be expert in both life styles.

For the black, Erikson sees the way to health in casting off the negative identities of "invisibility" and the violence of totalism, and moving out of the identity confusion prevalent during a time of rapid social advancement (in contrast to the snail's pace of the past). In place of the old identities, Erikson sees wider alternatives opening to the black which he will construct for himself out of the following identity elements.

The first, most inclusive, and absorbing of identities—to which both Kurt Lewin and Booker T. Washington directed major portions of their interest—is that of *technical skill*. "This is, no doubt, what Lenin meant when he advocated that first of all the *mushik* be put on a tractor. True, he meant it as a preparation for the identity of a class-conscious proletarian. But it has come to mean more today, namely, the participation in an area of activity and experience which (for better or for worse . . .) verifies modern man as a worker and planner."

The African identity is a second, and strong, contender. "It offers a highly actual setting for the solidarity of black skin color, and probably also provides the American Negro with an equivalent of what all other Americans could boast about or, if they chose to, disavow: a homeland if ever so remote."

A more limited but still viable identity element is that of the "great middle class," which "will include more and more of the highly gifted and the fortunate." But, Erikson cautions, "if it does not yield to the wider identity of the Negro American it obviously creates new barriers between these few and the mass of Negroes."

There will continue to be before the black the identity choices of both *prosocial* and *antisocial action*. "Like the outcast heroes of the American frontier, some antisocial types among the Negroes are not expendable from the history of their people—not yet."

"Our genuinely humanist youth, however," he concludes,

> will continue to extend a *religious identity element* into race relations, for future overall issues of identity will include the balance within man of technological strivings and ethical and ultimate concerns. I believe (but you must not tell them for they are suspicious of such words) that the emergence of those youths who stepped from utter anonymity right into our national affairs does contain a new *religious element* embracing nothing less than the promise of a mankind freer of the attitudes of a pseudo-species: that utopia of universality proclaimed as the most worthy

goal by all world religions and yet always re-entombed in new empires of dogma which turn into or ally themselves with new pseudospecies. The churches, too, have come to the insight that earthly prejudices—fanatical or hiding in indifference—feed into that deadly combination which now makes man what Loren Eiseley calls "the lethal factor" in the universe. This factor . . . ties limitless technical ambition (including the supremacy of weapons of annihilation) and the hypocrisy of outworn moralistic dogma to the territorality of mutually exclusive identities. The counterforce, *nonviolence*, will perhaps be a compelling and creative actuality only at critical moments, and only for "the salt of the earth." But Gandhi took the first steps toward a worldwide application to politics of principles once purely religious.

CHAPTER 20

The New Century

"The problem of the twentieth century is the problem of the colorline—the relation of the darker to the lighter races of men in Asia and Africa, in America and the islands of the sea." [1]

The words may have seemed self-conscious and overly portentous when they were uttered at the turn of the century by the unknown young Du Bois, but their prophetic strength becomes more apparent with every passing year. The role of the outsider is generally painful and difficult. As sociologist Robert Park has noted, in his traditional situation the black must dwell on the margin of society, at times with a vivid sense of insignificance and denial. But in compensation, the socially marginal man—and all outsiders —often perceive social reality with a clarity denied the comfortable insider. And one of the most impressive aspects of the vision of the young Du Bois was how clearly he perceived the implications, for both black and white, of many long-range trends.

Among the social forces that have shaped this century—drastically changing the lives of every one of us and pressing upon us now more powerfully than ever—were the five discerned long ago by Marx, Max Weber, Émile Durkheim, and others: *urbanization,* or the movement from the isolation of farms to the crowded cities; *bureaucratization,* or the movement from the self-sufficiency of the small craftsman and entrepreneur to the interdependency of employees and managers in big business and big government; *industrialization,* or the movement from handcrafting and personally selling a product to mass production, mass marketing, and mass consumption (and, out of this industrialization, the explosion of technology that took us from the airplane at the turn of the century to the atom bomb in less than fifty years); and *anticolonialism,* or the worldwide movement of colonized peoples, predominantly nonwhite, out of an era of white European and American domination toward political, social, and economic independence.[2]

In his "color line" prophecy Du Bois foresaw the drive of anticolonialism, of course—the liberative thrust that has rocked our world with the emergence of India, China, and much of Asia and Africa into independence and that now rocks America with the new black drive for self-assertion and real equality.[3] But embedded in Du Bois's argument with Booker T. Washington was the beginning of his perception of how the future of the black in America would be affected by the other dominant forces of our times—and the difference in Du Bois's and Washington's viewpoints is a good demonstration of the value of social scientific sophistication. Both men were highly intelligent and had access to much the same information about the time and about blacks and whites. The less well educated Washington made this information the basis of a vision of a self-sufficient Negro farmer and craftsman who would find his own kind of dignity in these humble trades, and this vision then guided Washington in policy recommendations that were soon to seem dated and inadequate. Du Bois, however, was phenomenally well educated in the formal history, economics, and sociology of his day. A student of William James at Harvard and of the German historian Von Treischke at the University of Berlin, and himself a ranking American sociologist while still a very young man, Du Bois was superbly equipped to look beneath surfaces to discern the underlying dynamics of social reality. He was also equipped to predict the probable course of events on the basis of his learning, and thus he knew in part, and beyond knowing might infer, that Washington's vision was doomed and futile from the very beginning.[4]

The great exodus of blacks from the South was underway by 1900. Between 1890 and 1910, over 407,000 blacks streamed northward out of the economic pathology of a single-crop system and depleted soil, and out of the social pathology of brutality and segregation, to confront—and increase—a new pathology of the cities.[5] Seeing this movement beginning in his youth, aware of the worldwide trend to urbanization, and examining its ramifications empirically in his famous study of the Philadelphia Negro, Du Bois looked ahead and saw not the noble black farmer on his own precious plot, but a horde of poor, dumb folk with no marketable skills ruinously flooding the cities.

He was also equipped to foresee not the dignified though humble cobbler or hostler plying his trade in the tranquil cities of a bygone era but legions of black janitors and washerwomen shuffling through the great empty halls of bureaucracy after hours. If blacks were not educated and "equalized" by other means, Du Bois knew they would almost certainly be excluded from significant employment in the future.

The two also differed in understanding the requirements of industrialization. But here, after having been totally discredited in recent years, Washington's view may again be coming into its own. An advantage Washington had over Du Bois was a feeling for the meaning of American history from the perspective of one whom the experiment was supposed to benefit—the common man. Du Bois tended to see most blacks in America as a mass to be poked, prodded, inspired, or enticed toward greatness by a specially endowed elite, which, for its time (and perhaps for today in some parts of the world), was a practical view. But having come from among the lowly himself, Washington possibly had a deeper faith in the value, the wisdom, and the eventual triumph of the common black man.[6] There was considerably more than an attempt to accommodate Social Darwinism in his emphasis on the dignity of the common job, the importance of competence, and taking pride in doing well even the lowliest of labors. And he saw the triumph of the common man as coming not so much from what others did for him as from what every man must in the end learn to do for himself.

Thus, Washington was interested in giving to each man some skill, whether high or low, in which he could take pride, and with which he could feel competent, could cope with his environment, and as an individual push for his own advancement. This is not only very much in accord with the American Creed, but it also reflects one of the most hopeful new insights of American social science. That is, after a half-century of uncertainty, the realization seems to have dawned in psychology, sociology, economics, and political science that attempts to advance the lowly from on high—although this too is often an absolutely essential foundation—can also fail miserably if they succeed only in making a man pathologically dependent on something outside himself, whether it is a psychiatrist, a short-sighted welfare system, or a totalitarian state. Washington's view of the need to make available to the disadvantaged the tools for his own advancement is again on the rise—and in rediscovering it perhaps some experts on other subjects have begun to learn something about brotherhood.[7]

Some Presidents and a War

However much Du Bois may have personally valued the gift of prophecy, in retrospect it would seem that the blacks' greatest advantage in Washington's time was that they were not gifted with group foresight. For had they really been able to look ahead, it is doubtful that many would have kept their sanity. As it was, blindly and hauntingly hopeful, they were able to share with the whites the great general optimism that prevailed in America as 1899 gave way to 1900.

Again our Presidents provide the quickest single measure of the black hope and the white response. The great Teddy Roosevelt, whose face rightfully juts from Rushmore along with Washington, Jefferson, and Lincoln, captured black hearts and enthusiasm with his dash and bluster. Over white protests, he invited Booker T. Washington to dine at the White House, and a wave of pride and good feeling rushed through the black community in the wake of this public white-black camaraderie. Blacks were also particularly proud of the fact that many participants credited the all-black Ninth and Tenth Cavalries with saving Teddy's Rough Riders at the battle of Guasimas during the Spanish-American War. But then Roosevelt astounded them by claiming that the blacks were timid and had to be forced to fight at gunpoint and by some other ambiguous statements and dismaying acts.[8]

Roosevelt's strange about-face seems to have been the result of the old dissonance and compromise process at work again. Underlying his behavior can be seen a conflict between a strong desire to be fair and liberal and American on the one hand, and on the other an entrenched feeling for a racial hierarchy that naturally assigned the masterful Anglo-Saxon white the top slot, while blacks and all other "natives" were alloted much lower places on the bloodline scale. As Roosevelt was notably intolerant of ambiguities, and prided himself on being definite and forceful, he was undoubtedly under considerable personal pressure to resolve this mental dilemma—and so he did, unfortunately to the detriment of the blacks. His successor, William Howard Taft, also disappointed them, but not so much as Roosevelt had because they had once more learned from the pain of TR's last years to lower their expectations of white Presidents. And then Woodrow Wilson arrived amid the most enticing fanfare.

"Should I become President of the United States they may count upon me for absolute fair dealing," Wilson said of the blacks in one appealing statement of his "New Freedom" program.[9] Could this be a Democrat from Virginia speaking? When he added that he wanted to see "justice done to the colored people in every matter; and not mere grudging justice, but justice executed with liberality and cordial good feeling"[10] many began to weaken—including Du Bois. In fact, Du Bois soon gave in to the Wilson charm and from his influential post as editor of the NAACP paper *Crisis* urged the blacks to desert the Grand Old Party of Lincoln

and vote for this new Democrat. His reasons for this action—and
its reward—are particularly interesting in the light of the question
later raised as to what possible justification there could be for
Du Bois's eventual disillusionment with American democracy and
his embracing of world communism.

Du Bois urged his people to vote for Wilson on the premise that
they had nothing to lose and possibly much to gain by a major
shift in party allegiance. The Republicans, he reasoned, had come
to take the black's vote so much for granted that they no longer
bothered to do anything for him, and perhaps by switching to the
Democrats the blacks might create enough competition between
the two parties to warrant at least a few favors in exchange for
their votes. Perhaps, too, if they voted for Wilson he might actually
live up to his words.[11] The answer came soon, and the message
was clear. Shortly after their arrival in Washington, the Southern
Democratic politicians who had shaped Wilson's campaign took
over the major governmental departments. While Wilson lifted not
a finger in opposition, and in fact signed the executive orders to
effect the measures, they instituted segregation wherever they had
the power to do so—whites and blacks who had been eating together in a lunchroom in the Treasury Department for many years
were abruptly separated, and soon the familiar separate toilets and
drinking fountains began to appear throughout the nation's capital.[12]

More shocking, however, and confirming Du Bois's fears, was
the virtual exclusion of the black from government itself, which
was becoming the largest of the bureaucracies and a major source
of jobs. In 1891, 2,500 of the 23,000 federal employees in Washington were black; by 1908, the number had dropped to only
1,450, all but 300 of whom were messengers or laborers. Wilson
then delivered the *coup de grâce* in 1913 when he "dismissed all
but two of the Negroes appointed by Taft." [13]

Wilson further turned his back on the black in two incidents
that were bad enough themselves, but devastating in their symbolic impact. D. W. Griffith's *Birth of a Nation* was a first-order
advance in movie-making, and in 1916 crowds packed the streets
before theaters that were showing it, waiting to get in. But it was
more than coincidental that Griffith, a showman peculiarly sensitive
to mass passions, chose for his historic film a rabidly racist story

that portrayed the Klansmen as heroes and the blacks as a pack
of morons, rapists, and thieves. President Wilson compounded the
film's fearful impact on America by praising it as "history written
in lightning." He allowed this personal endorsement, along with
that of Chief Justice of the Supreme Court Edward White, who was
a known racist (and even, incredibly, a former Ku Klux Klan
member) to be used by the film's promoters in press releases, ad-
vertisements, and posters throughout the nation.[14] And to cap this
achievement, Wilson even had a special showing of the film in the
White House.

By now it will be apparent that Presidential actions and inactions are of interest in this context not merely as the colorful
peccadillos of the great, or to serve juvenile debunking needs, but
because of the often crucial impact national leadership has on black
advancement or retrogression. And once again it may be noted that
while it is true that the leader is often the creature of his followers
and other external social pressures—a fact to which the sociologi-
cally oriented are sensitive—there remains the choice of alternatives before him, and the margin for personal influence of social
directions.

A whole volume could be devoted to the implications of the
leader's "margin of freedom" in terms of empirical studies of group
dynamics, persuasion, risk-taking, and decision-making processes,
as well as specific leadership studies. However, to go into all this
here would be impossible, so let us fall back on Freud to make one
useful generalization. In psychoanalytic terms, the leader is not
only the ego of nationality, but the superego of morality and the
ego-ideal of aspiration. Thus it is disquieting to contemplate the
white actions toward blacks that followed Wilson's nonvicious,
generally unwitting, but nevertheless peculiarly forceful presidential endorsements of racism. The disruption and the upheaval of
World War I undoubtedly had much more to do with it, but a
sizable body of social psychology indicates that a case could be
made for associating Wilson with the almost inconceivably bloody
actions of white mobs that peaked during the "Red Summer" of
1919 and the mounting activities of the Klan.[15]

Perhaps the worst Wilson incident in terms of what it revealed
about his attitudes happened in 1914. In 1913 blacks in thirty-
eight states had petitioned Wilson to do something about the rise

of segregation in the nation's capital, and a year later the very militant black leader Monroe Trotter and a delegation arrived at the White House to ask why nothing had been done. His Cabinet members, Wilson told them, had instituted segregation because of "friction" between colored and white clerks. Then he made an astounding suggestion to the assembled blacks that was, in turn, quickly relayed to the rest of the nation through the newspapers. "Segregation," he admonished the group, "is not humiliating but a benefit, and ought to be so regarded by you gentlemen." Then he tried to silence the activists with a strange threat—which was also peculiarly revealing of Wilson's fatal belief in the power of word magic to control events: "If your organization goes out and tells the colored people of the country that it is a humiliation, they will so regard it," he suggested.

Predictably, Trotter blew up over the notion that segregation could be a "benefit" and Wilson's sneaky tactic of trying to persuade him that everything would be fine if he (Trotter) would only persuade blacks they should be happy with a subgrade status. "We cannot control the minds of the colored people and would not if we could on the segregation question," he said. And then he blurted, "Two years ago you were regarded as a second Abraham Lincoln."

"I want no personal reference," Wilson cut in.

"Sir, if you will allow me to continue you will see my intent."

"I am the one to do the interrupting, Mr. Trotter."

"We colored leaders are denounced in the colored churches as traitors to our race."

"What do you mean by traitors?"

"Because we supported the Democratic ticket in 1912."

"Gentlemen, this interview is at an end." [16]

The interview wasn't all that was ended. Also gone was the patience and the hope of many black leaders for help or understanding from either major political party—or, for that matter, from any white majority or its leadership. For most blacks were wise enough to see that it was not that Wilson was such a bad man —as far as the whites were concerned he was one of the greater American Presidents. But the horror and the sadness of it was that he was again, in answer to millions of views and pressures pro and con, expressing the dominant white consensus of the time, as well as his own bias.

World War I was an interesting gauge for sounding the depth of black disillusionment. While many whites rushed forward to battle the dirty Hun as a menace to decency and democracy, many blacks saw nothing to fight for. Wilson had undermined the faith of many in democracy; and the slaughter of several hundred black Haitians by U.S. Marines in 1915, and in 1916 incidents such as the public burning of Jesse Washington in Waco, Texas, before a "cheering mob of thousands of men, women, and children," helped shatter the faith of many in American decency.[17] The young A. Phillip Randolph, then a socialist firebrand, urged the blacks not to fight —and was sentenced to jail for two and a half years for doing so. Yet the "radical" Du Bois, fresh from the humiliation of urging everyone to vote for Wilson to no avail, again rose up like Isaiah among his people to ask them, despite everything, to continue to have faith in the nation, and to go fight for it. "Let us, while this war lasts, forget our special grievances and close our ranks shoulder to shoulder with our white citizens and the allied nations that are fighting for democracy," he urged.[18]

Forgotten now is the incredible service of the black man in World War I. One hundred thousand served overseas in World War I; the forty thousand black combat troops of the fighting 369th Infantry were "the first unit of the Allied armies to reach the Rhine. The regiment never lost a man through capture, a trench, or a foot of ground. It saw the first and longest service of any American regiment as part of a foreign army, having been in the trenches for 191 days. It won the unique distinction of being called the 'Hell Fighters' by the Germans. The entire regiment won the Croix de Guerre for its action at Maison-en-Champagne, and 171 individual officers and enlisted men were cited for the Croix de Guerre and the Legion of Honor for exceptional gallantry in action." [19]

When the war ended and the 369th returned, more than a million New Yorkers crowded along the parade route to cheer as they marched from lower Manhattan up Fifth Avenue into Harlem. But elsewhere another kind of reception committee was waiting. The danger of thousands of returning black soldiers who had had a taste of equality and self-respect while fighting overseas had not gone unperceived. To meet this threat to white supremacy, the Ku Klux Klan had been revived; within a single year it grew from only a few thousand members to a militant union of more than a hundred thousand dedicated, as they put it, to "uniting native-born white Christians for concerted action in the preservation of American institutions and the supremacy of the white race." [20]

What happened then was beyond the worst anyone could have predicted. "More than seventy Negroes were lynched during the first year of the postwar period. Ten Negro soldiers, several still in their uniforms, were lynched. Mississippi and Georgia mobs murdered three returned soldiers each; in Arkansas two were lynched; while Florida and Alabama each took the life of a Negro soldier by mob violence. Fourteen Negroes were burned publicly, eleven of whom were burned alive." [21]

Two hundred years had passed since the brutalities of colonial America, but if ever anything was needed to shatter the American delusion of the peacefulness of their land or of inevitability of progress in human affairs this should have been it. Not content with burning blacks, the Klan ranged even into the Far West to attack the Japanese. It was also soon to virtually seize the governments of Oklahoma and Texas for brief periods. And the activities of white Americans more generally were the most violent in our history. Twenty-five race riots occurred in one year. Longview, Texas, exploded. In Washington, D.C., white soldiers, sailors, and marines ran amock, killing blacks for three days. Knoxville, Tennessee, blew up. In Omaha, Nebraska, at the peak of a riot a black was shot a thousand times and hung upside down at one of the town's busiest intersections. Elaine, Arkansas, erupted. And in Chicago, thirty-eight died, more than five hundred were injured, and over a thousand were left homeless after the burning and looting of property. Of such works of man was comprised the "Red Summer" of 1919.[22]

CHAPTER **21**

Reform, Myrdal, and the American Creed

"Long after 'pragmatism' in any sense save as an application of his *Weltanschauung* shall have passed into a not unhappy oblivion, the fundamental idea of an open universe in which uncertainty, choice, hypotheses, novelties, and possibilities are naturalized will remain associated with the name of James; the more he is studied in his historic setting the more original and daring will the idea appear. . . . Such an idea is removed as far as pole from pole from the temper of an age whose occupation is acquisition, whose con-

cern is with security, and whose creed is that the established economic regime is peculiarly natural and hence immutable in principle." [1]

Thus one giant, John Dewey, summed up the impact of another,
William James, upon the sickness of his time and upon the health
to be. Actually, Dewey was speaking for more than James. In a
sense his words were a eulogy for a host of giants who at the turn
of the century created or took up a social science that was as much
of the heart as of the mind, and used it to point America more
surely toward her founding ideals.[2] In fact, considering the size of
the men and the magnitude of the task, it is as though, on some
mythic level, a divine intervention had made sure the country
would have giants at its founding, but then they departed and
things worsened over the next 125 years. In the late 1800s it became apparent that divine intervention was again called for, and
so an obliging Providence rigged the emergence of "saviors" in
several fields.

In psychology, there were William James, John Dewey, and a
large, long-forgotten, early-day figure who is now being revived by
psychologists interested in child development, J. M. Baldwin.[3]

In sociology, there were Edward Ross, Charles Cooley, and
their great precursor, Lester Ward—who, schooling himself at
night after working in the mills, took the best of Spencer, chucked
the rest, and led the attack on Spencer, Sumner, and the pack of
Social Darwinists and their industrial and governmental cohorts.
In 1906, at a meeting of the American Sociological Society, following a Social Darwinist speaker who had given a lecture on how the
unfit and dependent might be eliminated from the United States by
eugenics, Lester Ward stepped to the rostrum and ripped into the
doctrine as being "the most complete example of the oligocentric
world-view which is coming to prevail in the higher classes of
society and would center the entire attention of the whole world
upon an almost infinitesimal fraction of the human race and ignore
the rest." He wouldn't be contented, Ward said, to work in a field
that only educated and preserved a select few of the higher classes.
"I want a field that shall be broad enough to embrace the whole
human race, and I would take no interest in sociology if I did not
regard it as constituting such a field."

For a long time to come society would be compelled to assimilate a mass of crude material from the bottom, Ward continued, which might lead his opponents to conclude that "society is doomed to hopeless degeneracy." But to Ward "the only hope lies in the truth . . . that so far as the native capacity, the potential quality, the 'promise and potency' of a higher life are concerned, those swarming, spawning millions, the bottom layer of society, the proletariat, the working class, the 'hewers of wood and drawers of water,' nay, even the denizens of the slums—that all these are by nature the peers of the boasted 'aristocracy of brains' that now dominates society and looks down upon them, and the equals in all but privilege of the most enlightened teachers of eugenics." [4]

In anthropology, Franz Boas took "the writings of two generations of scientists and publicists who had squirmed under the Almighty Aryan" [5] and from them forged a mighty instrument. With the persistence of the Germanic scholar, Boas hammered away to establish the view that race could only mean a common descent for all men, and that no group of humans was more or less advanced than any other. Differences, he insisted, "appear less as differences in *value* than as differences in *kind*." Admirers of his *The Mind of Primitive Man* called it "a Magna Charta of self-respect for the 'lower races.' " [6]

In economics, a pale, tense, jobless young newspaperman in San Francisco ground out "the book of this half-century," the best-selling *Progress and Poverty*. To Henry George so much poverty in a land of such vast wealth simply could no longer be justified. And the caustic, eccentric Thorstein Veblen further shattered the faith of the public in those running a society of vast social and economic disparities with *A Theory of the Leisure Class*.[7]

In law, the incomparable Louis Brandeis used modern sociology for the first time to make a case for fitting the law to the times rather than trying to force the times to fit old laws that in all too many cases had been enacted for the privileged few.

In history, Charles Beard opened a window and let in the icy blast of irreverence to clear the room of stale theories, heroes, and deeds. Both the debunking Beard and the earlier Frederick Jackson Turner brought the new tool of economic theory to the interpretation of history.

In politics there was pre-eminently Theodore Roosevelt. To be sure, he loved to wave the big stick and seldom spoke softly, and he did little for the black. But Roosevelt was the spirit of reform in many areas, and he was the first President since Thomas Jefferson to recognize the potential of social science as an aid in the shaping of society to human ends. The first major attempt to project America's political future in terms of probable social trends, Herbert Croly's *The Promise of American Life,* was bedside reading for the old Bullmoose.[8]

In journalism there was that pack of rough-and-ready social scientists who became known as the muckrakers: Lincoln Steffens, Upton Sinclair, Ida Tarbell, and Ray Stannard Baker, who dug into and wrote a series on Negro life. Later there was the journalist-social scientist Walter Lippmann, no muckraker but a singular power, who was among the first to formalize the study of American public opinion and coined the term *stereotype.*[9]

In black studies there was preeminently Du Bois, who before the turn of the century had become Harvard's first black Ph.D., who quite early gained distinction as a sociologist and historian with *The Philadelphia Negro,* his Atlanta studies, and other works, and who became the major black polemicist and leader during the early years of the century. There was also James Weldon Johnson, whose love for black life rescued many great Negro songs for social science as well as for art.[10]

The Contribution of the New Social Science

It was a time that would beautifully support the belief that great social needs inspire the emergence of great men. It was also a time when—the visions fresh, the discoveries new, and the ranks few—a handful of farsighted men might gather fire from one another. But as the new social scientists set out to explore or effect these visions they discovered that proving a theory, like settling a territory, can be long, hard uncertain work, and sometimes quite dull. They also discovered that there was no longer time to be broad-gauged and to know and draw upon one another; if progress was to be made, each must mine his specialty.

And perhaps because they had to go their separate ways, increasingly removed from an informality that might comfortably include citizen within the scientist role, the old vision that had caught up the black along with the Jew and all non-WASPs faded. Moreover, as they moved away from the freewheeling armchair and amateur era of social science into true or hard-nosed professionalism, they came under the sway of the social and economic facts of life for professionals. That is, you earn your keep by serving specific social needs—and for most of the years since the turn of the century the needs of the black have been very far down the list in America.

Also, following the general social trend articulated by Max Weber—the progression from the charisma of founders through the routinization of followers—there spread throughout the social sciences stifling bureaucracies that have been the despair of each field's best men and best students.[11] These bureaucracies have been strongly motivated to ignore the black because blacks are disruptive to their small empires, forcing reconsideration of all the comfortable procedures that have been based on foreign or middleclass white populations. Concern for the blacks will also, they fear, inject the dangerous and contaminating element of passion into research. But precisely because the black *is* disruptive, the grip of the bureaucracies was weakened in the 1950s and 1960s, and was even shattered in a few places.

Much as World War II can be seen as the ending of one long period and the beginning of another in black-relevant history, it can also be viewed as a transitional time for black-relevant social science. Compared to the grandeur of the founders' visions and the potential of the field, the overall and direct contribution of social science to the advancement of the black by this time seems disappointing in retrospect. Yet in the face of the great external and internal pressures working against them, dedicated individuals made many remarkable contributions, and in at least eight instances this resulted in appreciable and inspiring bodies of work. Along with gaining a useful body of general knowledge, this work was to serve as the base for whatever advance time will show that social science made against the black and white sickness during "our time"—the fifties, sixties, and seventies.

Selecting any turning point is arbitrary, and the year of Kurt

Lewin's death, 1947, is as good as any. Of the work that had appeared by that time, the following seems to have had an appreciable long-term impact: a small cluster of studies of black communities; a few books by anthropologists and psychoanalysts; the important development of attitude measures by Louis L. Thurstone, Emory Bogardus, and Rensis Likert and of sociometry by Louis Moreno; the hauntingly lonely body of work by Du Bois and his black successors; the heartening attempt during the New Deal years to effect programs based to some extent on social science; the work of Kurt Lewin and his students; and Gunnar Myrdal's vast empirical study, with which this period—and the time span formally covered by this book—approximately ends.

The community studies were the most fascinating and generally forceful. The key figure in their development was Robert Park, an ex-newsman who had been a publicity man for Booker T. Washington for seven years and then became a teacher and professional sociologist at fifty. In the 1920s Park and his students at the University of Chicago explored the Chicago slums in a brilliant series of studies that touched upon black life. So did the work of Lloyd Warner, the great figure in the study of class structure in America. Perhaps the best known, however, were John Dollard's *Caste and Class in a Southern Town,* Allison Davis and Burleigh and Mary Gardner's *Deep South,* Hortense Powdermaker's *After Freedom,* a sketch of the Atlanta black community by Floyd Hunter in *Community Power Structure,* and a series sponsored by the American Council on Education that involved Davis, Dollard, Warner and black sociologists E. Franklin Frazier and Charles S. Johnson.[12]

Psychoanalyst and sociologist Dollard's book was a searching analysis of the black situation in Freudian terms. He was struck, for example, by the charm of Southern whites but increasingly found that they reminded him of paranoid patients in a mental hospital: "One has exactly the same sense of a whole society with a psychotic spot, an irrational, heavily protected sore through which all manner of venomous hatreds and irrational lusts may pour, and—you are eternally striking against this spot." [13] Anthropologist Powdermaker lived among blacks in both the Deep South and a copper-mining town in Zambia. A footnote in her superb *Stranger and Friend,* which recounts these experiences, indicates why the work of this lively and sensitive observer was almost unique within the deadly realm of formal social science in conveying black "soul" rather than pathology: "Occasionally, I wonder what would happen to the dour and grim picture of society conveyed by some social scientists, if they would really enjoy themselves, just once, at some lowbrow and perhaps bawdy party given by the economically depressed people they study." [14]

The attitude-measurement work of Louis L. Thurstone, Rensis Likert, and Emory Bogardus in the late twenties and thirties was and still is the base for much of the opinion polling that is one of social science's most consistently effective tools.[15] Polls of blacks and whites in the thirties at least managed to bridge the gulf between them by giving members of each race some insight into the real feelings of the other. (The problem was that the blacks knew without being told, and the whites paid little attention.)

Du Bois's output continued: *John Brown* in 1909, *The Negro* in 1915, *Darkwater* in 1920, *The Gift of Black Folk* in 1924, *Black Reconstruction* in 1935, *Black Folk, Then and Now* in 1939, *Dusk of Dawn* in 1940, *Color and Democracy* in 1945, *The Encylopedia of the Negro* in 1946, *An Appeal to the World, on the Status of the Negro in the U.S.A.,* presented to the United Nations in 1945, and *The World and Africa* in 1946. The black impact in social science was also strengthened by Ralph Bunche in political science (his UN post lay ahead), Robert Weaver in economics (he was to become secretary of the newly formed Department of Housing and Urban Development in 1966), Carter Woodson, Rayford Logan, Benjamin Quarles and John Hope Franklin in history (Franklin's huge, crisp *From Slavery to Freedom,* first published in 1947, is now the foremost single work spanning black history), E. Franklin Frazier in sociology (Frazier's *The Negro Family in the United States,* 1939, is the key sociological and historical study of this foundation to black life), and Kenneth Clark in psychology. Clark's *Dark Ghetto* and considerable service to the black cause lay ahead, but by 1946 he had behind him some work on the Myrdal study as a fledgling social psychologist.[16]

Also important during these years was the black-relevant work of such white social scientists as Melville Herskovitz, Clyde Kluckhohn, and Ashley Montagu in anthropology; Arnold Rose, Samuel

Stouffer, Lloyd Warner, and Talcott Parsons in sociology; Herbert Apthecker and Oscar Handlin in history; Erik Erikson, Erich Fromm, and Abram Kardiner in psychiatry; and Morton Deutsch, Ruth Horowitz, David Katz, Muzafer Sherif, Marie Jahoda, Otto Klineberg, Neal Miller, Isador Chein, E. L. Hartley, Leonard Doob, Gardner Murphy, Theodore Newcomb, and Floyd and Gordon Allport in psychology. And underway, soon to appear in beginning the Second Reconstruction, were the important black-relevant *Authoritarian Personality* studies of T. W. Adorno, Nevitt Sanford, Else Frenkel-Brunswik and Daniel Levinson; and Gordon Allport's classic *The Nature of Prejudice*.[17]

For much of this work—and for many of these social scientists, some of whom worked on the project—*An American Dilemma* was a culmination. And possibly through the condensation process of history, over centuries *Dilemma* will come to be its leading residue.

Gunnar Myrdal and the American Creed

In 1937 the Carnegie Corporation of New York invited the Swedish social economist Gunnar Myrdal to come to the United States to carry out a large-scale study of the problem of the Negro in America, which they felt was needed to guide their philanthropies. However, it turned out to be considerably more than either they or Myrdal ever expected. For the nature of the study, and of the task force of social scientists assembled for it—and, above all, the nature of this then relatively unknown Swedish scholar—expanded this work into something possibly unique in the history of sensitive and self-satisfied ruling elites. It turned out to be the master study of the workings of a huge and intricate social system from the vantage of the excluded.

The approach used was so sensible that it is a wonder it has never been tried again with America's other great problems.[18] Myrdal first informally scouted the country, much as a fresh, open-eyed visitor from Mars might have done, observing the peculiar interactions of these earthling blacks and whites and talking with a Who's Who of homegrown experts. Then a task force of seventy-three homegrown black-life experts was unleashed to take a fresh look at their special areas of interest (and "unleashed" is probably all too appropriate, for many of these men and women had gained their expertise in black life in brief bursts of sideline activity while by necessity mainly serving the dominant black-excluding culture). Anthropologists, sociologists, economists, political scientists, psychologists, educators, public administrators, jurists, and journalists examined in great depth practically everything affecting blacks in America—black and white racial beliefs, black ancestry, birth and death rates, black migration from farm to city, economic inequalities, the background of slavery, jobs and income, the political realities, the police and the courts, segregation and discrimination, caste and class status, leadership and protest, the black community and its organizations, churches, schools, and the black press.

They filed their reports with Myrdal and at this point something very rare and wonderful happened. Customarily, once the data have been gathered for large American social studies, several writers take over and produce a document which is usually a hopeless mess. Sometimes, even out of ghosts and academics, a work of some punch and clarity emerges. But then the eternal committee usually takes over and, in the name of science and the proprieties, they squeeze out whatever juice remains of style; to make sure no meanings will be dangerously clear they castrate the corpse with cautious deletions, and then they smother what is left with qualifiers. Overwhelmed at first by the shock of what he had found, Myrdal requested a committee to share his load, but fortunately the Carnegie Corporation insisted that he be the sole judge of the material, and also that he be the report's sole responsible author. The result was that the black experience in America was not filtered through the customary committee "mind," nor through the bewildering changes of style and viewpoint of many scholars, but through the single large mind and soul of a giant among living social scientists. The book that emerged was that readable rarity, *An American Dilemma.*[19]

It was quickly hailed by many critics. "One of the best political commentaries on American life that has ever been written," one noted.[20] "The most penetrating and important book on our contemporary American civilization," said another.[21] However, not everyone saw it this way. In fact, one Marxian critic, the historian Herbert Aptheker, was so enraged by the Myrdal study that he wrote a whole book attacking it. A classic in the genre of Marxian vituperation, bristling with righteousness and academic swear words and pitched to a steam-whistle level throughout, Apthecker's book concludes, "In summary, we find Myrdal's philosophy to be superficial and erroneous, his historiography demonstrably false, his ethics vicious and therefore his analysis weak, mystical, and dangerous." [22]

Why this outrage? Myrdal had relentlessly exposed all the evidence of the black and white sickness, thus confirming much of what the communists had been saying for years, but his diagnosis of the systems' overall state of health, and his hopeful prediction for the future, was anathema. Within the communist frame of reference it seemed a patently weak-kneed and even gutless sellout to the repressive moneyed interests that had financed the study.[23]

For rather than finding that the American system was on the verge of doom, which is such a comfort to many to contemplate, Myrdal found it to be basically healthy, with its self-correcting, self-healing mechanisms indeed working to advance the black, albeit far more slowly than the blacks deserved. Moreover, he predicted that after a long period of dismally insufficient progress, America was about to move with more speed. "Not since Reconstruction has there been more reason to anticipate fundamental changes in American race relations," Myrdal said in 1944, at the outset of an era that has certainly seen this prediction—bold for its time among social scientists—confirmed.[24]

It was a bitter and generally impossible pill for the Marxians to swallow, for if Myrdal's conclusions were valid their revolution had almost nothing to offer America, and the anti-American Creed might soon lose its greatest selling point. However one might try to evade it, beneath all the fine points was this compelling rationale: If this great contingent of homegrown experts, both black and white, led by this foreigner of quiet eloquence, could reveal so much horror and sickness and yet find an overriding health in the American system, reason must whisper that the case for revolt and the Marxian alternative in America was dead.

The American Creed and the Compromise Process

The basis for Myrdal's optimism has been disputed for years. Yet it is no more, in the end, than one of those insights of a calculated innocence which the expert with an investment in complexities is quick to discount but upon which all science is built. He entered a room where the life supports were being debated in weighty terms, and remarked the importance of air.

As we have seen, he had set out to gather not merely a great bag of unpleasant facts, but to try to gain some sense of the underlying social dynamics—what gave these facts form and direction, what eventually made one thing rather than another happen? Essentially, by going among the people and keeping an open mind, he found something very much at variance with the cynicism prevailing among the sophisticates of his time, who by the end of the thirties tended to believe that the whole social mess was driven solely by greed, lust, class struggle, and power drives. For what Myrdal claimed to have found was that *values* actually drove Americans, individually and collectively, as a nation. He called this set of values the American Creed, and he felt that whether the black was advanced or set back depended on the outcome of the conflict between these "higher" values and lower-order needs. To many it was as though a messenger had been sent around the corner for heroin or marijuana and had returned with a steaming apple pie.

> The American Negro problem is a problem in the heart of the American. It is there that the interracial tension has its focus. It is there that the decisive struggle goes on. This is the central viewpoint of this treatise. Though our study includes economic, social, and political race relations, at bottom our problem is the moral dilemma of the American—the conflict between his moral valuations on various levels of consciousness and generality. The American Dilemma, referred to in the title of this book, is the ever-raging conflict between, on the one hand, the valuations preserved on the general plane which we shall call the American Creed, where the American thinks, talk, and acts under the influence of high national and Christian percepts, and on the other hand, the valuations on specific planes of individual and group living, where personal and local interests; economic, social, and sexual jealousies; considerations of community prestige and conformity; group prejudice against particular persons or types of people; and all sorts of miscellaneous wants, impulses, and habits dominate his outlook.[25]

Not only was this out of step with the thinking of the sophisticated generalist, but for a social scientist to speak of values or
morality in the thirties and forties was to risk being labeled hope-
lessly unscientific, old-fashioned, and naïve. This attitude was particularly prevalent in sociology, which prided itself on its total
rejection of the old-time hogwash, and in psychology, then dominated in America by rat-runners, who finding only rudimentary
values in their little creatures assumed similar low priorities in man.
Nonetheless Myrdal bore down on this analysis, insisting that
Americans, for all their backsliding, were among the most moralistic people on earth and were driven as few others were to do good.
In the main, he felt they tended to look bad because they did have
such high ideals, and because the freedom of their press—and the
freedom of individual self-expression and the almost compulsive
national need for self-criticism—was continually exposing the gap
between the American reality and its ideal.

On the level of the psychology of the individual, this is reminiscent of the Gestalt "law" of closure—that when a person is
confronted with an open gap in a circle, he is driven to close it.
Out of this kind of thinking came, by stages (chiefly through Kurt
Lewin), ideas of how concepts under tension within the individual
mind combine to resolve the tension by forming new concepts that
in turn underlie and channel, shape, give direction to, or otherwise
guide our thoughts and actions.

As we have seen, this strain of thought has been elaborated into
the now considerable body of cognitive-dissonance theory and research, which has given us not only a good understanding of how
this process works within individuals but—through work based
upon that of Fritz Heider, Theodore Newcomb, and Charles Osgood as well as Leon Festinger—an understanding of how mental
tension-reducing mechanisms operate in small groups.[26]

It is a matter of potentially great importance that this pattern
was repeatedly found by Myrdal to be operating in our thoughts
and behavior as a nation of blacks and whites enmeshed in a great
social dilemma. "The moral struggle goes on within people and
not only between them. As people's valuations are conflicting, behavior normally becomes a moral compromise. There are no
homogeneous attitudes behind human behavior but a mesh of

struggling inclinations, interests, and ideals, some held conscious and some suppressed for long intervals but all active in bending behavior in their direction." [27]

Thus within this central American social problem, it is possible to discern a pattern to the underlying dynamics that transcends the barriers of customary social investigation, linking the individual to the small group and to society as a whole. Moreover, the pattern outlined in some detail in the chapter on Marx and the dynamics of the conflict model is clearly discernible within Myrdal's observations. That is, liberative forces versus repressive forces lead to the compromise that shapes social action. In this regard, Myrdal's key line is worth repeating: "As people's valuations are conflicting, behavior normally becomes a moral compromise."

And so the social reality and the necessity of compromise, consensus, tension-reduction, and personal and social equilibrium is clearly evident. *But so, also, is the reality and the necessity of the prelude of conflict.* And though Myrdal's recognition of this fact was quite clearly stated, this was not the general impression given by his study, which seems to be the root of the legitimate complaint about it. This also seems to be the reason it was attacked not only by Marxists and the socially cynical but also questioned by blacks and whites who, although they greatly respect the work, have been disturbed by a feeling that something very important was left out. What appears to have happened is that while compiling a mountain of physical and social evidence of the dismal results of compromise, Myrdal found only a molehill of conflict, and this was confined to the apparently harmless plane of mentality.[28]

Such matters of theory can seem far removed from reality. However, during times of great social change such as our own, they are transformed into a pressing practical question: Is violence necessary for social advancement?

The Questions of Threat and Violence

Critics of Myrdal's study have generally approached the question of violence by pointing to historical and contemporary evi-

dence that quite forcefully contradicts the idea that black advancement is solely or even mainly due to the benign workings of the
lofty American Creed.

For example, if the American Creed was so all-powerful—if
Americans were driven by such a mighty "goodness machine"—
why was there so little progress during the seventy years from 1877
to 1946, some critics asked.[29] Others, following the pioneering of
the Marxians, sought evidence of a violent revolutionary leverage
at work (rather than the quieter evolutionary machinations of the
American Creed) and uncovered the forgotten magnitude of black
revolt. Spurred by this interest, Herbert Aptheker uncovered the
250 incidents of "revolt" in colonial times noted earlier. Many
commentators have remarked the electrifying impact of John
Brown's violence in hastening the social surgery of the Civil War.
And more immediately, during the 1950s and 1960s, we have seen
that, if not violence, certainly plenty of threats have been needed
to jar loose practically every advance blacks have made. How
could such an obvious factor be overlooked, critics have asked.

The answer seems to be that for all his study's breadth and his
effort to avoid bias, on this point Myrdal was the victim of a
limited sampling over time. That is, his study, which specifically
avoided any in-depth historical probe, was nearly eighty years removed from times of the obvious influence of threats and violence
in the area of black advancement. As we have seen, this included
the abolitionists' use of moral, political, and economic threat, their
willingness to suffer violence to enlist sympathy and polarize society, the use of the violence of John Brown to gain attention and
further polarize the nation, and finally the ultimate social violence
of a full-scale war for black advancement, the Civil War.

Myrdal's study also, appearing in the early forties, immediately
preceded the eruption of evidence in our time.[30] It is, obviously,
more socially desirable to stress the negative aspects of violence as
a tactic—indeed, one hesitates to speculate openly for fear it may
incite some fool to plant another bomb. And so it must be stressed
that the evidence indicates that violence can alienate not only Right
and Middle but, in the case of any frightful act, practically all men
of decency and goodwill. Moreover, violence most certainly provokes a reaction that can set in motion not only the overreaction

of white backlash but of all the very powerful and necessary agencies of social regulation and control. For this reason, only the desperate, the unbalanced, or the damn fool resorts to frightful or terrorist acts in America.

However, what are we to make of the fact that the Supreme Court used threat in the cause of black-advancement in its 1954 school-desegregation decision—that is, the message was "submit or face a lawsuit." Or that President Dwight Eisenhower used it again at Little Rock—submit or face armed federal troops. Even the methods of nonviolence developed by Gandhi and used by Martin Luther King during the fifties and early sixties call into operation the underlying threat—give in to our peaceful entreaty or something worse may follow. Nor would any sophisticated observer deny the tactical effectiveness of overt violence in Watts, Washington, Detroit, Newark, and other rotting ghettos during the late sixties. That this violence helped accelerate backlash and regression obscures the fact that regression was already underway and that violence did call attention to black needs in practically the only way that the majority leadership finds hard to overlook or forget.

After hiding our heads and avoiding the obvious for so long, consideration of violence inevitably opens a Pandora's Box—and a promising sign at the start of the seventies is a new investment in research into this supersensitive area. There are endless questions to be answered, but in addition to our earlier attention to this issue, there are four aspects that are especially worth stressing: matters of *degree, context, interaction,* and *alternatives.*

As the earlier chapters have made plain, the methods of the abolitionists ranged in *degree* from mild threats to outright violence—and practically all of their activity remained within the threat range. The violence of John Brown was confined to two outbursts, in comparison with literally hundreds of thousands of small and large episodes within the threat range for the abolitionists. And this general effectiveness of milder methods is borne out by the psychological research discussed in Chapter 11, ranging from operant conditioning to dissonance studies.

Nevertheless, there is still evidence of the need for extreme threat and even outright violence on occasion, depending on innumerable

236 THE HEALING OF A NATION

questions of *context*. There are no simple rules—complexities of
time, place, antecedents, probable consequences, and, above all, of
persons and ethics are involved. One matter of context that seems
very important is whether the use of extreme threat or violence is
appropriate to the occasion, is widely understood, is clearly controlled, and is demonstrably socially responsible. Governmental
threat and violence, for example, is generally supported when it
conforms to such requirements, as in the case of the Supreme Court
decision on school desegregation enforced by Federal troops, or a
well-understood and clearly defensive war, or clearly responsible
riot control. Governments are notably *not* supported when they
violate such requirements, whether it be in Vietnam or Jackson
State. And by contrast, sympathy rises and support grows for the
violence of the black rioters or the North Vietnamese when this
violence, however fundamentally reprehensible, is felt to be understandable and socially responsible within a context, transcending
national boundaries, of the needs of man.

The matter of *interaction* was brought into focus by the Myrdal
study. Ever since it appeared time has been wasted in the debate
over whether black advancement in America depends on white
morality (the American Creed) or black and black-supportive
threat and violence. The answer is quite clear—*both* are necessary.
Rather than being a simple question of one or the other, it is a
question of a complex interaction of the two (and other forces) over
history. The American Creed seems to operate as a behavioral
readiness, a ready-made set of black-advancing attitudes that exert
a slight but persisting pressure on men and events. Its strength
seems to lie in a cumulative, long-term power, like the action of a
small creek that becomes a stream and finally a river as it moves
steadily toward the sea. However, quite frequently this stream has
been checked, dries up, becomes polluted, or is even dammed up
and diverted by various homegrown, *truly* anti-American, interests.
And then it has been necessary for the socially responsible to take
action in ungentle ways.

The Alternatives of History and Beyond History

As for the *alternatives,* one last capsule comparison of Marx
and Myrdal may be suggestive. Out of the Marxist and Marxian

strains over history comes an emphasis on social conflict, revolution, and the use of threat and violence to shatter a bad present system in order to raise a better one among the ashes. And out of the tradition that Myrdal dominantly expresses comes an emphasis on social compromise, evolution, and the use of nonviolent methods to improve a basically good social system.

Both history and social science suggest that not only do such views emphasize only part of the historical reality, but also, by inference, both offer only partially relevant social therapies. And perhaps the simplest way of grouping the elements that each leaves out is to note that the Marxian, with his derision of all ideas and ideals but his own as "false consciousness," is too narrow-mindedly materialist, too immersed in lower-order drives; and the tradition that Myrdal expresses, with its avoidance of the imperatives and unpleasantries of physical conflict, is too narrow-mindedly intellectual, too immersed in higher-order drives. It is basically the problem of societies and of social therapies based on irrationalist versus rationalist views of man.

But man is neither exclusively rational nor exclusively irrational. The evidence we have mustered says several obvious things: that man is *both* rational and irrational, that both cognition and emotion are powerful tools to be used for his advancement or his retrogression. And it indicates that an important mechanism driving his society is the conflict between liberatively oriented and repressively oriented men—and ideas within the minds of men, and men within groups—directed toward influencing the social-action mixture in partisan ways. The implications for the black and white sickness are equally straightforward. *To cure there must be conflict. Nothing changes on the compromise side of the equation without pushing on the conflict side.*

But to push doesn't mean a need for bombs or all-out revolution. There *is* a range of methods. And in this delicate age the intelligent revolutionary will spend time studying Gandhi rather than Lenin. For beyond all the volleying and thundering of historical, social, and academic debate—of rationality versus irrationality, of conflict versus equilibrium models, of the place of affect versus the place of cognition, of black needs versus white needs—one catches a glimpse of a people, and a nation, and a world reeling drunkenly down a darkening street that abruptly ends in the jungle.

It is a time when the drinking and the debate should long ago have been ended. By now we should have been so well armed with the knowledge of man and his society as it really is that, possessing it, unself-consciously, we could forget all these things and look upon ourselves and our world with a truly sober gaze.

Then we might see that while our books and investigations seem to open before us many alternatives, history has actually brought us to a point where the choices are rapidly narrowing each day.

CHAPTER **22**

The Sounds of Salvation

"We stand again to look America squarely in the face and call a spade a spade. We sing: This country of ours, despite all its better souls have done and dreamed, is yet a shameful land.

"It lynches. . . . It disfranchises its own citizens. . . . It encourages ignorance. . . . It steals from us. . . . It insults us.

"We return. We return from fighting. We return fighting.

"Make way for Democracy! We saved it in France, and by the Great Jehovah, we will have it in the U.S.A., or know the reason why." [1]

Thus in 1919, in his protean garb as the black Everyman, Du Bois voiced the renewed aspiration that seized the black community following World War I—as it was again to seize it after World War II. However, though the militant mood was strong, it had the entrenched strength of two centuries of intimidation to overcome. And the preying of the white mob continued. But then in 1925 an incident occurred that seems rather trivial to most whites but looms large in the black lexicon of heroism. In Detroit a white mob surrounded the home of Dr. O. H. Sweet, a black physician who had the temerity to buy a house in a white neighborhood. When the mob began to stone the house, a shot rang out from inside. One white man dropped dead, and Dr. Sweet and his brother and friends who were inside the house went on trial for murder. But the NAACP brought in Clarance Darrow for the defense—and for both predator and prey the subsequent acquittal of Dr. Sweet established an interesting new rule for black self-defense in white America.[2]

But of immeasurably greater impact was the emergence of the "fight back" spirit of that explosion of creativity known as the Harlem Renaissance. Rising in the years following World War I, it was strikingly similar to the emergence of the militant black creativity which followed World War II and Korea. James Baldwin's earlier counterpart was the black poet Claude McKay, who expressed the feelings of his time when he wrote:

> If we must die, let it not be like hogs
> Hunted and penned in an inglorious spot,
> While round us bark the mad and hungry dogs,
> Making their mock at our accursed lot.
> If we must die, O let us nobly die,
> So that our precious blood may not be shed
> In vain; then even the monsters we defy
> Shall be constrained to honor us though dead![3]

Out of this militant self-assertion—out of this lifting of aspiration and a determined fearlessness—emerged what any fair analysis must credit as one of the most meaningful outpourings of creativity in American history. Again, so characteristically, it has been flattened in white culture to a cartoon image of Fats Waller grinning over the "ivories" and Countee Cullen reciting a few quiet poems in some discrete salon—and both black and white are given a massive dose of the more acceptable flowering of New England. But for at least a decade the Harlem Renaissance worked upon the creative person in America, black and white. And though the tendency is to think that this Renaissance ended with the Depression in the thirties, some expert observers feel that it has never ended, that it has been, in fact, continuous, uninterrupted, and has yet to reach its peak.[4]

Behind today's popular black writer lies the eloquence of James Weldon Johnson, Langston Hughes, Countee Cullen, Jean Toomer, Claude McKay, and, as always, Du Bois. Those who write musicals and revues, black or white, are still in debt to the brilliant, black "Shuffle Along" in 1921, which established the genre and launched a string of similar black stage successes. Behind today's soul musicians are Duke Ellington, Louis Armstrong, Fats Waller and others, whose contribution to American music the older jazz buff sees as being greater than that of many carloads of white Ethelbert Nevins and Edward MacDowells. It is also very much to the point of the Harlem Renaissance that the greatness of Bix Beiderbecke, Frank Teschmacher, Benny Goodman, Joe Sullivan, and the other great white stars then—and of the Beatles and other rock artists of the 1960s—was and is very much a white offshoot from the black root and trunk of the Harlem Renaissance.[5]

Throughout this great outpouring one can discern the interplay of two fundamental psychological responses to stress that have a particularly well-articulated physiological base. In 1932, in his profound *The Wisdom of the Body,* physiologist Walter Cannon proposed what has been called the *flight-fight* response.[6] He had found considerable evidence to support the view that man is physiologically so arranged that when confronted with a threat to personal security the body mobilizes a vast, extremely complex defense system that can be used either to fight—to advance, grapple with, attack and demolish the threat—or for flight—to evade, avoid, to run and hide. Also in the thirties Kurt Lewin developed a similar *approach-avoidance* view of conflict and behavioral direction in psychological theory.[7]

The greatness of the Harlem Renaissance was its expression of joy—that reveling of voice, trumpet, trombone, piano, banjo,

drum, and bass, that celebration of simply being alive. But throughout its fascinating outpouring one can discern the interplay of
flight-fight responses to the continual threat to the black's status,
pride, person, and at times even his life. Claude McKay writes of
taking no more, but of fighting, of advancing on this threat and
killing if necessary—and Joe Louis becomes the living symbol of
this urge. Langston Hughes writes about—and much more so the
great jazz and soul musicians play out—the flight which is chiefly
through fantasy. Here the threat is escaped with a lighthearted
poem, a folk song, with drugs—the dope *trip*—or on a clarinet
ride, or the fast footsteps of bass and drum.

Four Kinds of Salvation

But out of the urge to flight came much more than individual or
small-group creativity. Out of it also came two powerful commentaries on the situation of the black in the twenties and thirties:
the movements of Marcus Garvey and Father Divine.

Whites laughed and many blacks cringed when Garvey's be-
spangled legions marched in their parades. What could be more
amusing than these ordinary black men—janitors, garbagemen,
and barbershop attendants in everyday life—who donned wild
uniforms festooned with phony medals, shoulder fringe and hats
with mighty plumes, and fancied themselves potentates? What
could be more ridiculous than their leader, the Jamaican immigrant
Garvey, who proclaimed himself Provisional President of the Em-
pire of Africa and who tried to convince blacks that theirs was a
noble ancient heritage, to be proud of, and that black was beautiful? And what, later, could be more ludicrous than small, fat
George Baker, who called himself Father Divine, and who bought
old hotels in the ghettos and lovely old estates in the country so
that he could establish his earthly "heavens" for black and white?

It is not too difficult to look beneath the garish surface and see
a very real measure of black desperation. Beneath Garvey's antics
was a fierce and realistic desire simply to give up the struggle, to
pull up stakes in America and go elsewhere. Raising again the old
futile dream of colonization, Garvey petitioned the League of
Nations for some plot in Africa to resettle. When this was turned

down he gave way completely to fantasy, organizing a Universal African League to "drive the white usurper out" and, as auxiliary units, a Universal Black Cross Nurses, a Universal African Motor Corps, a Black Eagle Flying Corps, and a Black Star Steamship Line. In 1923 this balloon was popped with Garvey's questionable conviction for mail fraud—but the antiwhite, black-pride vision remained, gathering steam.[8]

Behind the comic Father Divine lay something even more profound. Forgotten now is the fact that during the Depression he ran a chain of restaurants where the poor black—and the poor white —could get a good meal for only ten cents. Also almost forgotten now is the fact that his "heavens" were integrated, offering the lonely, the disturbed, and the dispossessed of all races a haven from the economic, social, and racial meatgrinder of the thirties. But Father Divine's movement, with its talk of peace and love and its direct attempt to practice its preaching, must also be seen as the first bizarre surfacing of something inconceivably meaningful in our time. It was the first mass expression in America of that integrative drive rising not out of the white, but out of the black—a desire seeking to soar above racial tension and hatred, sharpened by an antiwar vision of an oncoming disaster for all men and seeking an expression larger than the formal limits of a church and a Christianity overloaded with investments in the status quo. It was the longing for real brotherhood and peace on earth that caught up and made of Martin Luther King a great voice in our time.

The black followers of Garvey and Father Divine were mainly the equivalents of the white lower middle class, of average or below-average intelligence; among the more gifted, intellectual, middle- and upper-class blacks the urge to flight found a more congenial savior in socialism and an attractive but worrisome friend in communism. The logic of socialism was so compelling it is hard to see how the thinking black could resist it—then or now. A great many did in fact embrace it, and still do, mainly because much of what seemed radical then—the graduated income tax, for example—has by now become an organic and respectable part of our system. The appealing rationale goes like this: The main thing perpetuating racism in America is the inequal distribution of the nation's vast wealth. Reduce the economic disparity between rich and poor, black and white, and most of the race problem will disappear. (And the logical extensions of this view, which rapidly gained ground among both conservative and liberal economists in the late 1960s, were the negative income tax and guaranteed annual income plans.[9])

Communism, however, was a savior of another kind. That many smart blacks looked into it so seriously in the thirties was a measure of their alienation and desperation. For many blacks the Depression had actually begun in the twenties, for while the stock market soared in the cities, poverty and joblessness were already advancing through the farmlands. One result was the crush of wave after wave of poor, unskilled rural blacks upon the cities. This provoked a white blacklash only slightly less brutal than the bloody years immediately following World War I. Then in the thirties the whole economy collapsed and the black became very much "last to be hired and first to be fired." By 1934, 38 percent of the blacks in the United States were on relief, as opposed to 17 percent of the whites. In 1935, 65 percent of the employable blacks in Atlanta were on relief, and in Norfolk the percentage was 80 percent. Even as late as 1939, the three main sources of black income in America were farming, domestic service, and relief.[10]

It is not hard now to see why the thinking black in those days could be powerfully attracted to communism. The idea that ours was a society rotten to the core with discrimination and the privilege of birth—vast poverty existing among the born-poor masses while vast riches were held by a born-rich favored few—seemed self-evident. What was the solution? Perhaps America was indeed so rotten and doomed that it could only be finally shattered and then rebuilt along more humanitarian lines by a handful of dedicated men, as had happened originally in America, and as Russia had seemed to demonstrate in more recent times. They were also attracted by many sympathetic white communists who welcomed the blacks sincerely as brothers, and who were, in some cases, the only halfway dependable white friends they had ever known. In the end, however, most of the thinking blacks were repelled by the stupidity and the phoniness of the kind of white communist Ralph Ellison portrayed in *Invisible Man,* Brother Jack, and by the message that began to reach them of a new form of white exploitation at work, a new form of white colonialism on the rise that was trying to move in and take them over under the guise of this now questionable "brotherhood." [11]

But some very smart blacks were not repelled by communism —notably the two most gifted of their time, Paul Robeson and W. E. B. Du Bois. We will take a last glimpse into the private and public worlds of Du Bois in another chapter. As for Robeson, few Americans have cared so deeply or suffered so greatly for the American Dream. Neither black nor white understood how this could be true if he went about praising Russia and joining peace committees in the thirties and forties, and so he was literally hounded and driven from this country. Yet today, after two decades of civil rights drives have at last forced Americans to recognize the true depth and horror of their racism, and as the development and stockpiling of universal atomic death continues unchecked, Robeson no longer seems a radical. He was foolish and blind at times, but it was a small weakness in a large man. In all too many ways his only crime seems to have been that he spoke too openly and too soon of what he saw in the land—and in the world—of the very blind.[12]

"It means little when a man like me wins some success," Robeson said in 1935 to an old sportswriting friend who had known him since his All-American football days at Rutgers. "Where is the benefit when a small class of Negroes makes money and can live well. It may all be encouraging, but it has no deeper significance. I feel this way . . . because I have cousins who can neither read nor write. I have had a chance. They have not. That is the difference. And I believe that no political philosophy that does not include a chance for all of them can possibly endure. The reason I mention the Negro problem in America is to explain my feelings about Russia. In Russia the people who are 'the masses' feel they have been given their chance. They may be wrong, but that is their conviction." [13]

A New Kind of President and Another War

"I tell you frankly that it is a new and untrod path, but I tell you with equal frankness that an unprecedented condition calls for the trial of new means." [14] It was a long time coming—it had been seventy years since Lincoln's death. And it came not because blacks were troubled and starving—this was nothing new—but because troubled whites feared the ending of the great American experiment. But however the venture might be qualified, the fact remains that Franklin Roosevelt and the New Deal began to take an entire people in out of the cold.

In today's context, when questions of the extent to which government should intervene, and the extent to which social science should serve this intervention, are pressing it is important neither to overvalue nor undervalue the New Deal. This, however, is apparent: Until the emergence of Roosevelt and the large hearts and good minds he drew into government, the black had been systematically denied entry into every significant area of American life except the entertainment world, and under New Deal auspices the first systematic attempt to bring him into his rightful heritage was begun. And because it was a systematic attempt, pursued by men and women with good, tough minds—men who were relatively fearless and, like Harold Ickes, generally liked a good fight; who persisted, understanding the need for continuity of effort; and who most notably valued people more than money or procedures—much more of it worked than most men today realize or remember.

It was also, in basic philosophy and in the actual implementing of many programs, the first major attempt to apply the attitude as well as some of the findings of the social sciences to the problems of government. It marks that point in history when the American people and their elected representatives realized that, like it or not, they must forgo their traditional distrust of the "big dome" and bring the experts in. What was at stake was all too clear. The man in the street feared the end of everything, while the experts' fear was perhaps best stated by one New Deal patron saint by indirection, the great British economist John Maynard Keynes.

"You have made yourself the trustee for those in every country who seek to mend the evils of our condition by reasoned experiment within the framework of the existing social system," Keynes wrote FDR in a note with haunting overtones for our own troubled times. "If you fail, rational change will be greatly prejudiced throughout the world, leaving orthodoxy and revolution to fight it out." [15]

In they came—Adolf Berle, Rexford Tugwell, and Raymond Moley in the early years, and later Benjamin Cohen, Justice Frankfurter, Leon Henderson, James Landis, David Lilienthal, Harry Hopkins, and Harold Ickes. Few were, like the economist Henderson, social scientists formally. However, coming predominantly from Columbia or Harvard, they were brilliant generalists, and they were the first group in government to feel comfortable with economics, sociology, and the range of the social sciences—in addition to the smattering of political science many had gained through a law school grounding.

With the hiring of Dr. Clark Foreman by Harold Ickes for the Department of Interior, the building of a new kind of "black power" began in government. Foreman brought in Robert Weaver, then armed with a relatively fresh Ph.D. in economics from Harvard. Soon afterward the Commerce Department hired E. K. Jones of the Urban League, and Jones and Foreman began to work together to bring in more blacks equipped to move into positions of some power. And eventually there were enough, centering around Weaver, to constitute what came to be known as FDR's "Black Cabinet," which included the black educator Mary McLeod Bethune, Howard University Law School Dean William Hastie, historical scholar Rayford Logan, and the young black political scientist Ralph Bunche.[16]

Much was accomplished by these sophisticates (mainly white but also some black). The first relevant measure was the NIRA—the National Industrial Recovery Act; as far as the urban black was concerned, it was a dismal flop. And the first measure relevant to the rural black, the Agricultural Adjustment Act, was little better—landlords in the South had a bad habit of pocketing the crop-reduction checks meant for both black and white tenant farmers. Much like the Great Society programs of the 1960s—or like a child taking its first steps—the New Deal suffered from awkwardness and ludicrous spills and smelly accidents at first. But unlike the Great Society programs, fate gave the New Deal a few more years to roll, and once it got underway the picture radically changed.

The Farm Security Administration—which helped establish small black farming communities, loaned money to buy farms, and taught modern farm production and marketing—did so much

for the blacks that wrathful conservatives rose up in 1942 and
practically killed the agency. The National Youth Administration's
Negro affairs division, under the direction of Mary McLeod
Bethune, had an important impact on the growth of a black professional community. Thirty years after Du Bois's fear that the
black would be excluded from a future to be shaped by urbanization, industrialization, and bureaucracy, the NYA helped young
blacks gain the necessary education for entry into this new world
through a training program that reached 64,000 and through benefits that helped put many through college and even graduate
school.

Another success story was that of the Civilian Conservation
Corps. From 1933 through 1942, the CCC took two hundred
thousand jobless black boys out of the ghettos and put them to
work planting new forests and building retention dams to prevent
the soil erosion that was ruining the farm and ranchlands of the
South and Midwest. It also did what the ghetto schools had often
failed to do—it taught many of these boys to read through its
literacy programs and it tried to compensate for other lacks through
programs to combat juvenile delinquency. Perhaps the greatest
success, however, was the New Deal housing program. Several
agencies loaned blacks the money needed to pay their rent and
save their homes as well as to acquire new homes. These agencies
also saw to it that blacks had jobs on construction projects within
their jurisdiction. Most notable of all was the Federal Public
Housing Authority, which in financing low-cost public-housing
projects throughout the country gave thousands of black families
their first opportunity to live in homes with electricity, indoor
toilets, and running water.

The Public Works Authority helped build black hospitals and
colleges. And as for the WPA, which lurks in most American
memories today only as the fading stereotype of men who were
paid to stand about everywhere with a blank stare on their faces
and a motionless shovel or broom in their hands, "more than one
million Negroes owed their living to WPA in 1939," [17] and
throughout America it underwrote the efforts of the largest group
of artists and writers, black and white, who ever attempted to
capture the scope, the history, and the color of this land in paint,
song, and story.

It could have been the giant step of our time toward the ending of the sickness. "We knew what had to be done. We could have done it then, but the chance was taken from us. And now we've had thirty more years of letting our cities become sink holes, and our Negro citizens in them desperate beyond measure. And the task we face will cost billions more than it would have cost then." [18] The speaker was a former Federal Housing Administrator who became a big businessman during the fifties and a big-business statesman during the sixties—Philip Klutznick of Chicago, bitter and angry at his countrymen in 1965 after the explosion in Watts that began the cycle of riots that rocked the cities of America for three years. But just as it happened in the sixties, so it happened earlier—abruptly a war intervened, and the need for distant slaughter became a radically higher priority than the need for black salvation in the hometowns.

However, something new was moving in the land. A new sharing of fear, of suffering, of the battlefield comingling of blood, of a feeling for brotherhood, of a disgust with the social imperfections that brought on depression, war, and everything else that worked against the good life for humanity—all this again awakened the old dream of a salvation that might embrace both black and white in America. This aspiration would fire the great drive of the fifties and sixties; and then it would fade as young dreamers grew comfortable and old. But there had also emerged a more enduring concern. For by the watershed years of World War II, something had become apparent to a few practical men of power as well as to the visionairies. To men with a stake in the real estate and in the politics of cities—and in the survival of the nation and the system within an awakening and dominantly "colored" world—it had become apparent that the causes of black and white in America were inseparable.

As another man of power, morality, and practicality, Benjamin Franklin, had put it at the outset of the great experiment, "We must all hang together, or assuredly we shall all hang separately." [19] And the passage of more than 160 years since Franklin's day had enlarged the message.

PART TWO

Healing the Nation

CHAPTER 23

The Healing Urgencies

Ahead lay our times—the aftermath of World War II and the meanings that cluster to social scientists who were still children or students in the thirties, and to Martin Luther King and Malcolm X, to Harry Truman, Dwight Eisenhower, John Kennedy, Lyndon Johnson, and Richard Nixon.

There is a cycling that seems to work through both history and psychotherapy. Again by 1970 a time of great aspiration and liberative advancement was being followed by a time of apathy, of repression, and of falling back. But characteristically this falling back, while ostensibly to consolidate gains, was primarily an evasion. Once again the thrust was backward, but not to ask of the past its wisdom, for this wisdom is painful and relatively unchanging. Again the cry of the past was to be ignored by pretending that this sickness is a mystery—by calling for more research, more commissions, more committees, more time, rather than by acting on what has been learned over and over and over.

The first black slave stepped ashore in Jamestown three and a half centuries ago, in 1619. More than two centuries have passed since John Woolman lived, broadcast his phenomenal healing vision, and, in 1772, died. And after all this time—after all these hopes, all these dreams, all the suffering, the hard work, and the blood that has been spilled—we seem again to be reliving the nightmare of the post-Reconstruction era.

In Chapter 16 we outlined seven "failure indicators"—the seven areas of public life in which crucial failures of leadership on the black issue in the 1870s brought on the debacle we now seek to emerge from: failures of leadership in the political parties, in the press, in the South, in the courts, in the black community, in a social science dominated by Social Darwinism, and in the Presidency. The similarities between then and now are frightening.

In the 1870s both the Republican and the Democratic parties, weary of it all, seeking ways to rid themselves of the problem of the blacks, joined in the sellout that gave over the black to the mercy of the rednecks in the South and to indifference in the North. And in 1970, again neither party seemed to offer the black much hope. On one hand he was confronted by a Republican party dominated by men to whom his needs were an irritating minor issue. On the other he saw a Democratic party peopled with many who were highly sympathetic, but which was weak and divided in leadership, and penniless in comparison to the Republican wealth.

In the 1870s the press, after years of successful agitation, grew weary of the black issue and seized upon Social Darwinism to justify its apathy. And in 1969 the press seized, blew up, and widely disseminated the ponderings of the hapless Arthur Jensen, while coverage of black issues began to decline.

In the 1870s in the South the decent, gentlemanly leadership promised to look after the black, but it was soon replaced by

Vardamans catering to the rednecks. And in our time George Wallace is again re-elected, and Lester Maddox continued to pass out his ax handles.

In the 1870s and 1890s the Supreme Court gave death blows to Reconstruction with repressive decisions on voting rights and school desegregation. And in 1970 the nation witnessed the fiercest possible effort by the President himself to place a known racist on the highest court.

In the 1870s Booker T. Washington began to rise out of the black community to accommodate the white need for black abandonment. And in 1970, paradoxically, many particularly rabid black separatists seemed to be falling in line with much the same old white desire.

In the 1870s the weight of social science, with the best of intentions, was unwittingly given over to a radical diminishing of black freedom. Now social scientists meet and talk and write their books, but all too often little of this effort seems to have impact.

But it is in and centering around the Presidency that the similarities are most gravely disturbing. In *The Burden of Southern History* C. Vann Woodward advanced a bold new framework for comparing then and now, the idea that there have been First and Second Reconstruction Eras—and that we now await a Third.[1]

The First Reconstruction can be seen as running roughly from 1865 to 1877; the Second can either be dated from sometime during the New Deal era or from roughly 1954 through 1966, at which time Woodward feels the second great effort to end the sickness drew to a close. And the similarities that led Woodward to link the times raises a question of overwhelming transhistorical concern. The First Reconstruction was followed by seventy years of relative inaction ("Merely to mention 1877 is to conjure up the horrors of the great freeze that set in that year and lasted until the great thaw of recent times," Woodward wrote in 1967).[2] So for concerned blacks and whites alike, as the 1970s began, the question was this: is the regression that began in 1966 merely a temporary lull for resting and regrouping, or is another great freeze under way?

"It is simply inconceivable that such an appalling reversal of history could be repeated," Woodward concluded in 1967.[3] However, three years later, as the Nixon administration moved into its second year, he was by no means as certain. "The leaders of the resistance are emboldened; the Negroes feel deserted. After an era of promise, they go from disillusionment to a sense of unfulfillment to withdrawal," he noted in *Time* magazine.[4]

This was in March of 1970, after ambiguous policies and statements on school desegregation had radically strengthened the Southern resistance; after talk of a "deal" with Senator Strom Thurmond that many who were historically sensitive found uncomfortably reminiscent of the Hayes sellout; after the revelation by a top aide to the Attorney General of some thought behind the "Southern strategy" for exploiting national divisions along ethnic, regional, and generational lines; after the incredibly degrading personal attempt by the President to force the known racist Carswell onto the Supreme Court; and during the week of the Moynihan memorandum suggesting that perhaps the time had come "when the issue of race could benefit from a period of 'benign neglect.' "

Mindful of the nation's investment in gaining health out of sickness and of presidential commitments of the forties, fifties, and sixties, many were horrified by a turn of events that seemed inconceivable, and many normally discrete figures were impelled to speak out. Echoes of the warnings of the aging Wendell Phillips and the aging Garrison in the 1870s could be heard in the voices of men like Alan Pifer, president of the Carnegie Corporation, which had funded Gunnar Myrdal's great study. President Nixon had "made political gain, but he has lost moral credibility," Pifer said. He decried a policy of "being equivocal and using Vice President Agnew as a kind of stalking horse to play up to the more bigoted segments of our population" and felt that the President was "sowing the wind that will produce a whirlwind—it is such an explosive issue." [5]

Nor, incredible now, did it stop there. For by the fall of 1970 the chairman of the NAACP had been driven to formally decry the Nixon administration as antiblack and the Urban League's Whitney Young was characterizing the black mood as despair over policies that were like Jello or White Magic ("Now you see it, now you don't").[6] Nor did many find comfort even in the most extensive integration of schools in U.S. history, for the Nixon administration had so obviously moved to meet the timetable of its predecessor only after exploring all possible alternatives for evading this affront to the conservative vote. Charging there had been a "major breakdown" in enforcement, in October the U.S. Commission on Civil Rights issued the eternal warning that the country was "on a collision course" unless the President began to exercise "courageous moral leadership" in behalf of racial justice.[7] And then as 1970 gave way to 1971 came the last gasp, so shameful to the nation and the Office of the Presidency. Following the resignation of James Farmer, blacks remaining on the Nixon payroll rose up as from the dead to threaten an exodus unless things were changed.

Moreover, beyond the actions and inactions of a questionable Republican administration loomed questions concerning the black-advancing Democratic administration that had preceded it. These were not questions of caring or commitment, for Southerner Lyndon Johnson had made plain his commitment and probably did more to advance blacks than any President since Abraham Lincoln. But the enforcement failure that disturbed the Civil Rights Commission had not originated "in the current administration, nor was there any substantial period in the past when civil rights enforcement was at a uniformly high level of effectiveness." It was a failure that raised questions that went beyond men and parties to probe the nature of the Presidency itself and of our sacred political system. How, for example, in a situation that clearly calls for sustained governmental intervention, but with Presidents and vast retinues of attendant experts subject to overnight dismissal, is the vital continuity of effort to be maintained?

Here again the Reconstruction era thrusts haunting questions toward us across the years. For all their failings, both the Great Society and the Freedmen's Bureau programs were large, new, separate conceptions of some grandeur, which very definitely produced some favorable results. Most notably they were attempts to use the social science of their times and the organized skill of the expert, the professional, and the man of action—the tough-minded and the competent, whom John Gardner came to value—as opposed to relying on the willy-nilly efforts of the wandering bureaucrat, the welcome but undependable volunteer, the man of endless talk, or the so-called "pragmatists" of the Nixon administration. And the most thought-provoking transhistorical similarity is this: Aside from the New Deal effort, out of 350 years of Americans and their governments there have only been these two efforts to intervene specifically on the black's behalf—and each had essentially only *four* years to make good: the Freedmen's Bureau's effective years were from 1866 to 1870, the Great Society's from 1964 to 1968. The question rises: What might have been done with more time? And more caring? And, how *do* we maintain the needed continuity of effort?

This grim picture is relieved somewhat by several things, chief among them the fact that noting similarities is only half of the learning process and of scientific method; the other half is discerning the equally crucial *differences*. And while there are frightening *qualitative* similarities between the two eras, there are vast *quantitative* differences.

In 1865, for only a single anecdotal example, when Frederick Douglass and his black delegation left the office of Andrew Johnson, the President told those present, "Those damned sons of bitches thought they had me in a trap! I know that damned Douglass; he's just like any nigger, and he would sooner cut a white man's throat than not." [8] By contrast, in 1965 Lyndon Johnson said, "You do not take a person who for years has been hobbled by chains and liberate him, bring him up to the starting line of a race, and say, 'You are free to compete with all the others,' and still justly believe that you have been completely fair. . . . If we are to have peace at home, if we are to speak with one honest voice in the world—indeed, if our country is to live with its conscience— we must affect every dimension of the Negro's life for the better." [9]

Behind these two remarks lay vast statistical differences which cannot and must not be discounted. In Andrew Johnson's time the bulk of the blacks had no education, the job situation was chaotic, and, despite all the Constitutional amendments that had been passed guaranteeing blacks the vote, it was continually being taken away. By Lyndon Johnson's time the bulk of blacks *had* educations, *had* jobs, and not only securely *had* the vote, but they also had a growing political power in the cities that no one could ever take away. Where in the past, majority rule had worked against them in a white-dominated nation, now the power was beginning to pass to them in the black-dominated big cities.

Also in terms of then and now, in the press there was, by the fall of 1970, immeasurably greater strength than weakness, particularly in the influential national magazines and newspapers and in the black presence on television. In the South, there were, overall, far more signs of strength than of weakness, and time seems to be on the side of strength. (Indeed, walking down Peachtree Street in Atlanta in October 1970, one could thank God for so many signs of hope.) Though beginning to edge toward the right, the Supreme Court still seemed reasonably secure on the black issue. The greatest strength of all was in the black community, where the dispersed power of leadership was generally greater than in the days of Martin Luther King and Malcolm X. And despite the fact that social science continued to show few outward signs of strength in gaining specific action, behind the scenes it had personal impact, and more generally a considerable climactic impact —that is, it did serve to suggest some wise paths while acting as a constraint on the selection of poor alternatives for official action.

It was only in and around the heart to the healing effort, the Presidency, that almost unrelieved doubt remained. However much its occupants may wish to avoid this aspect of the role, the fact remains that within our peculiar American social psychology the President exists as father to his people. For most social groups the family is the prototype. Outwardly we grow out of and beyond this family of our childhood, but inwardly we cannot escape the pull of the old analogical roots that in the lift of the good times that prompt sharing, and in the fearsomeness of bad times that impels us to draw together, must make of the nation an extended family. In the household much depends on what the father does—whether the signals to the children are of caring or of not caring, of certainty or uncertainty; and by the dark fall of 1970 blacks again no longer looked for meaningful signals from the father surrogate of the Presidency.

This episode in all its disquieting detail must force anyone seeking historical parallels to go beyond the time of Hayes back to, at worst, the weasling politics and the national degradation of the Buchanan administration, or, more charitably, to the time of Hoover, when to shallow optimism and timid economic policy was added the pathos of the good intentions of the wrong men for the task and the times. But such a thought brings hope, for Buchanan preceded Lincoln, and Hoover preceded Roosevelt. And with the 1972 election in mind, by fall 1970 many were abandoning the conspiracy of hope that for a time had softened their minds and tongues toward Richard Nixon, his "team" and its policies, and were seriously beginning the old search for our traditional salvation—that dream of the Great President who, like Moses, would lead his people from this fretful new bondage to the Promised Land.

From this perspective we will now examine specifics of healing suggested by social science and the American experience through World War II. The first great healing venture of our time followed the war, and met with encouraging successes as well as cautionary failures. However, little occurred that was not foreshadowed earlier—nor did the implementation begin to live up to the earlier promise; and so it is this often-forgotten *foundation* to modern social healing that we will examine.

In some detail we will explore the works of the two men who were best qualified by genius, by training, and by experience to speak with authority on the curing of the black and white sickness, the black historian and sociologist W. E. B. Du Bois and the white experimental social psychologist Kurt Lewin. Then in two final chapters on the politics of implementation we will consider how their and other remedies may now be put to use to heal the nation.

CHAPTER 24

The Prescriptions of W. E. B. Du Bois

Very early in life W. E. B. Du Bois came upon a vision that over the centuries has shaped the lives and thoughts of many who were concerned with healing sick social bodies.

The evidence suggests Du Bois first came to grips with this vision during his undergraduate days at Fisk. During his childhood in Great Barrington, Massachusetts, he had been one of the few blacks in an almost all-white community, but at Fisk, an all-black college, he found "girls and boys of a species he had never known

left him tongue-tied and dreaming 'boastful dreams' of great remedies for the sickness of the world. For already he knew the world
was sick." Later at Harvard, while working on his master's thesis,
The Suppression of the Slave Trade, he conceived "a notion of his
mission—that 'mightier mission' of which he felt a part. He was
going to raze the barriers of race. He saw this as 'a matter of
knowledge; as a matter of scientific procedure.' " [1]

And so with the zest for battle that was to enliven all ninety-five
years of his life, while he was still a very young man he won for
himself credentials as a social scientist that no one could fault.
He first set his sights on, and gained, degrees from not just one
of the black colleges that were approved for his people, but Harvard, with William James and George Santayana. Then to go white
Harvard men one better, he attended the University of Berlin for
two years. Returning to the United States with a comfortably in-
timidating load of erudition—and the Kaiser Bill moustache and
goatee that was to project a Prussian combination of efficiency,
militancy, and threat more than sixty years before its black power
vogue—Du Bois swiftly developed the base for launching his program of full-scale therapy that was intended to end the black and
white sickness in America and possibly throughout the world.

His rationale was one that has guided perhaps 95 per cent of
the seemingly black-relevant research since his time. Social science
would be used mainly as a diagnostic tool. Through massive and
continuing surveys of every aspect of black life—economic, sociological, psychological—the old needs would be exposed not with
the easily ignored voices of simple black folk or their relatively
powerless white sympathizers, but with the Peremptory Authority
of Modern Science. White America would then take notice, Du
Bois reasoned, and the nation would begin to remedy these social
ills. In keeping with this objective, he carried out his great pioneering study *The Philadelphia Negro* in 1896, and between 1897
and 1910 (at times with as little as $250 a year to support the
whole effort!) his remarkable Atlanta studies. Du Bois's research
was almost as far-ranging as Myrdal's was to be thirty years later,
but it had little discernible impact. For research to be effective,
both researcher and consumer must really want the product. In
Du Bois's case, the researcher cared about his product—cared, in

fact, more deeply than anyone has since then, or likely ever will again—but there was nothing present to complete the cycle. Hardly anybody with any real power in America either knew of or cared about Du Bois's findings.[2]

And so Du Bois abandoned formal social science and turned to the life of the publicist, propagandist, polemicist, organizer, and promoter of the black-advancing cause. And increasingly he was driven by another, less loving vision which had begun to build within him when first he began to look more deeply into world history at the University of Berlin. There he began to see the social crime of slavery in America diminish and blur within the larger horror of an exploitation of colored by white throughout the world that ranged from the slaughter of the Aztecs and Incas by the Spanish conquistadors to the Mafia-like operations of the British in India.

Du Bois was one of the first men in this century to see a truly revolutionary kind of historical continuum that has seized and now activates many of the colored peoples of this earth but that most whites are still incapable of either seeing or assessing.[3] Inevitably the white worldview—and the view of most blacks under their domination—has been that of a glorious historical emergence of the white or Caucasian who rose out of the general savagery of early times to bring enlightened leadership and a progressive salvation to the world. Du Bois, however, saw another mighty panorama. He saw that civilization had come first to the colored races —to the brown, the yellow, and suppressed all these years but most definitely there, in the case of the pharaohs of Egypt, the black. But then these civilized colored peoples were set upon by white savages who stole their culture and began their cancerous expansion, sending out white tentacles to seize North and South America from the Indians, to seize China from the Chinese, to seize Africa from the Africans, to seize every worthwhile scrap of land and its native peoples all over the globe. He saw World War I as rising out of this movement, as the great white nations of the world fell upon each other like a pack of dogs to fight over the last scraps of colonialism. He saw the aftermath of World War I as, in the end, merely a reshuffling of white power alignments, with the colored peoples still acting as scraps for the great dogs. And bound to this vision, extending it, he came to wonder at times whether the technology of the white, resulting in the Bomb, was not the last deadly bequeathal of a race destined to ruin the earth.

This was his antiwhite vision—in language and out of an experience that remarkably prefigures the brief but stellar experience of Malcolm X in the 1960s. It is a vision that finds a distorted expression in the Black Muslim view, but also surfaces in the clearer perspective of such notable whites as Carl Jung and Jean Paul Sartre.[4] It was also, out of an experience of white racism both in America and in France, the view of Ho Chi Minh in Vietnam. It was the view of our opponents in Korea. It is the view of Mao Tse-tung in China. It gave intensity to and was part of the Japanese justification for the attack on Pearl Harbor. And generally it burns today within the whites' avowed colored enemy wherever he may reside and have any halfway certain power.[5]

But alongside this reverse-racist, antiwhite view, there still remained within Du Bois the earlier, larger vision. This, too, stemmed from his Berlin days. "Every break from books and lectures found him going to some new place. He went to the south of Germany, to Italy, France; east to Austria-Hungary, Czechoslovakia, Poland; north to Sweden, Denmark, Norway. In Holland he talked with natives of Borneo, in France with Cameroon and Algerian blacks, in England with Indians." And for Du Bois the designation "colored" came to mean "a greater, broader sense of humanity and world-fellowship." [6]

It was the sad, mighty, haunting vision that, as far as we know today, began with the half-black Egyptian pharaoh Akhenaton in 1375 B.C. A vision ranging beyond the boundaries of one's own time, place, and nationality; of the brotherhood of man, transcending all questions of racial or social difference; of the need for peace, transcending all possible rationales for war; and of respect for a universal truth that might transcend all the diversions and conventions of one's particular small milieu.[7]

Few listened when Akhenaton offered it. But time passed and Jesus, Buddha, and other great religious leaders persisted in offering it. The Quaker saint John Woolman evoked it in his time. Thomas Jefferson, Frederick Douglass, and Abraham Lincoln tried to inject it into public affairs. During the early years of our century Albert Schweitzer and Mahatma Gandhi put the vision into action. It is also what Martin Luther King and, toward the end, even Malcolm X were trying to say in the 1960s. And many felt it was what John Kennedy was trying to articulate in the American Presidency.[8]

And so there moved in Du Bois the thrust of this love and this hate, the old vision of a love that might transcend all barriers and bring peace on earth, and the new vision, rising out of the colored experience with whites, of a hate that might steel them to drive against their oppressors everywhere, and to change history from a white to a color dominance. Out of both visions, for ninety-five long years, Du Bois sought to heal his nation.

Out of his feeling for love came the stream of therapies based on a belief in man's so-called higher nature—the appeal that can, if one has this love and belief, be made to another man's rationality through conversations, speeches, letters, editorials, poems, books, and all the other devices that Du Bois used to lift aspirations, sow dissonance, and otherwise work upon the black and white cognitions of his time. Out of love, too, came all the therapies based on an appeal to the conscience one assumes in others when guided by belief in a higher nature. Thus, in speech and writing, Du Bois also worked to arouse the empathy of one human being for another, and to awaken the slumbering impulse toward brotherhood, by exposing the facts of injustice not stridently (for this particular therapy), but soberly, sadly, and persistently.

By such means, derived from the loving base, Du Bois expanded a tradition of therapy that is still continuously in use, and always at hand, for the small but important curing interventions of the commentator, the politician, the minister, and all other reformers using every possible means of communication. Martin Luther King became the great black embodiment of this healing strain, and for all its deprecation by both white and black cynics, it remains a tradition of therapy that is active every day somewhere in this land. Moreover, it contains the potential for mobilization, and with favorable leadership and circumstances, it could again be expanded beyond the isolated instance to become a forceful social movement.

But love was not enough for Du Bois—nor, unfortunately, has it ever been for anyone with a clear perception of the world's shortcomings. And out of his eventually equally deep hatred came his particular shaping of the more hard-edged social therapy of black militancy. Few would consider black militancy therapeutic, but the pressure of social need often jolts the conventional wisdom. Militant tactics can be seen as short-term shocks directed, potentially, toward long-range healing, and they were wittingly shaped by Du Bois long before most black Americans began to use them, or whites to respond to them, even unwittingly.

The first ingredient of this kind of therapy was his articulation in many writings of an open, unburdening, self-liberating hatred of the white oppressor. The second ingredient was his articulation of the love of one's own black self and one's own black kind. Out of these ingredients Du Bois then helped foster the growth of the methods whereby a black minority, through linking pride in one's self to one's group, and through black solidarity, may now advance both self and group against the threat and the pressuring indifference of the white majority. Though his efforts were laughed at and Malcolm X is credited with being militancy's chief ideologue, Du Bois's launching of the Niagara movement in 1905 and the Pan-African conferences of 1919, 1921, 1923, and 1927 were central historical events in the shaping of the paradoxical healing strategies of modern black social, political, and economic threat.

But for Du Bois and for his time neither the therapies of love nor the therapies of hate were developed enough to become effective. In the end, weary of an abnormally long exposure to racism in America, he formally turned to communism as the best solution for his dilemma. Gaining his release at last from a government that foolishly withheld both his and Paul Robeson's passports for several years, he departed for Red China and Ghana, where soon afterward he died, in 1963.

In terms of his dreams, the move made good sense. In communism the vision of world brotherhood and the revulsion of an exploiting white capitalist racism were met, love and hate seemed reconciled. And the allegiance offered the tiring old hell-raiser one other last consolation: perhaps the threat he now directly helped publicize would force America to change more rapidly. Perhaps the prospect of burgeoning communist revolutions by colored and colonial peoples, that might in the end isolate America from the rest of the world, would force white Americans more speedily to value their black brothers, if only as a matter of self-protection.

But within a larger context the defection of the ancient Du Bois made another point. It is simply that the choice seems to be upon us not of whether or not we shall use social science to cure our ills, for we probably no longer have that choice if we are to survive; but of whether we are to use it ourselves democratically, as numerous men and women acting to control our own social and personal destinies, or whether we are to have it done for us, and to us, by an authoritarian elite acting to save us from ourselves.

This was an issue to which the woefully little-known and under-valued psychologist Kurt Lewin gave a considerably shorter life-time.

CHAPTER **25**

Kurt Lewin's Remedies: I

While Du Bois despaired of the workings of democracy in America and found rule by a communist elite progressively more attractive, a spiritual kinsman was having an opposite experience. Among those who know of him at all today, Kurt Lewin is remembered as the man who had possibly the greatest influence on psychology at the mid-century point. However, Lewin had other, lesser-known sides. In addition to being a social scientist (and an ex-student of the University of Berlin), he shared with Du Bois the often suspect distinction of being a social evangelist, a talented organizer and promoter, and he was also the victim of racial and other forms of prejudice.

"Freud the clinician and Lewin the experimentalist—these are the two men whose names will stand out before all others in the history of our psychological era," the noted theorist Edward Tolman said in a rare early perception of Lewin's probable stature. "For it is their contrasting but complementary insights which first made psychology a science applicable to real human beings and to real human society."[1] Yet during his early years in Germany, when, as a lecturer at the University of Berlin, Lewin was developing an international reputation as a bold thinker and teacher, as a matter of course he was denied a professorship because he was Jewish. Moreover, after Hitler seized power and Lewin came to America, even in the land of the free he was denied the professorial posts and honors suitable to a man of his stature.[2] But this time it was not racial intolerance acting against him, but prejudice of another kind, which Du Bois also encountered—the antipathy of the academic bureaucrat for the original thinker.

Lewin's "field theory" is complex, hard to follow, often couched in seemingly eccentric mathematics. But essentially it consists of a way of viewing men and their societies in terms of a totality of forces that operate within and upon a particular individual or group, in a particular place, and at a specific point—or over a specific span—of time. Though it is impossible adequately to describe Lewin's work in this context, it is particularly fitting to end with it, for Lewin is the summary or junction point into which much of the social and psychological thought prior to his time flows, and out of whom there then emerged a new integration that, however flawed, is still unrivaled. Unknown to most of those upon whom it has worked over the years since his death, it has not only been reshaping psychology, but it has also set in motion some hopeful forces for the renewal of American life. In particular, through his development of what is known as *action research,* Lewin repeatedly demonstrated how the black and white sickness may be cured.

The foundations of action research were laid down during the mid-thirties out of Lewin's concern for his fellow Jews who were trying to escape from Germany into Palestine. They would face tremendous problems in trying to settle in the ancient homeland, Lewin knew, and he accurately forecast many of them. To help them create a new society he dreamed of founding a research institute "specially tailored to the needs of a small state" in Palestine.[3] Despite years of dedicated personal efforts, he was unable to raise funds for the project. However, the effort was the harbinger of the larger dreams he was to effect in America, and its purposes were especially revealing of Lewin's characteristic vision of social engineering. The projected goals of his institute were to "materially lessen human suffering, develop better communities, and reduce costs by millions of dollars." [4]

Over nine years, from 1935 to 1944, combining the science and the theory of his Berlin days with a growing involvement with American social problems, he laid down the practical and theoretical base for most subsequent action research. This work was done at the University of Iowa, where Lewin developed an unusual student task force patterned after the close family of students he had drawn to himself in the Berlin days. Advancing the Berlin insights, this new group carried out psychological research that was truly astounding in its productivity and long-range importance. However, Lewin became increasingly dissatisfied with most of what was then known, and is still known today, as psychological research. For despite the continuing need for greater understanding of behavior, he felt that social psychology must go considerably beyond merely explaining behavior.

"We must be equally concerned with discovering how people can change their ways so that they learn to behave better," he began to insist, to the bafflement and dismay of many academic and experimental psychologists.[5] And he made clear that this change would not be achieved by simply floundering out into society filled with idealism and some "hunches," to become bogged down in personality conflicts and social inertia, and to waste money, and become disillusioned. The key was to find out what could be done through "change experiments," where, by bringing the vast economy of theory to bear on a specific issue, one could cheaply and quickly gain a pretty good idea of what would or would not work in changing man and society.

He pointed out that "for thousands of years man's everyday experience with falling objects did not suffice to bring him a correct theory of gravity. A sequence of very unusual, man-made experiences, so-called experiments, which grew out of the systematic search for truth, was necessary to bring about a change from less adequate to more adequate concepts." [6] The old Palestine research institute dream was working in him, and it had grown considerably. Fully twenty years before the idea was to be more generally advanced, he dreamed of an institute that might be loosely affiliated with a university in or near a large city where he and his students and growing band of associates might carry out action research to find remedies for the social problems of urban and industrial life in America—problems that since his time have grown from small evils to monsters threatening our survival.

How were we to resolve the tremendous tensions of city life and the tensions between nation and nation? How were we to humanize potentially stifling factories and corporate and governmental bureaucracies? How were we to attain productivity, happiness, and self-fulfillment and group fulfillment?

Above all, having personally experienced the downfall of democracy in Germany and seen the rise of Hitler and the subsequent holocaust of racial hatred, genocide, and world war, he was concerned with how democracy might be strengthened in America. How could we, a diverse people, subject to the age-old pressures toward division and animosities based on racial, class, and caste differences, transcend or transform these pressures in keeping with the American ideal?

By giving himself over almost entirely to a grinding personal promotional effort that hastened his death, he gained his dream. By letters, visits, calls, articles, speeches, luncheons, and more letters, and more phone calls, he finally gained the funding, created the organizational structures, and got underway not one but two major action research institutes within the last two years of his life. One was the Commission on Community Interrelations (CCI) of the American Jewish Congress; the other was the Research Center for Group Dynamics at MIT. And during the last year of his life Lewin also co-founded the journal *Human Relations* and won the funding and laid the foundation for the fountainhead of leadership, group dynamics, T-group, and sensitivity training—the National Training Laboratories in Bethel, Maine.

The remedies suggested by the Lewinian whirlwind are of considerably more than historical interest, for both the methods and the findings are still generally of more use than the bulk of the

research done today. We will examine Lewin's studies by categories
—those directed to reducing prejudice, building group strength,
changing men and societies, reducing violence and aggression,
gaining control of one's own destiny, and training leadership.

Reducing Prejudice

Perhaps the most widely prevalent symptoms of the black and
white sickness are racial prejudices and stereotypes. Lewin first
attacked this problem by writing some remarkable articles on how
to combat anti-Jewish prejudice in the late thirties and antiblack
prejudice in the mid-forties. And under his guidance the Commission on Community Interrelations launched many projects relating
to this injustice.

One facet of the problem was the department store practice of
not hiring black sales clerks. "Our customers won't stand for it,"
store managers would say. In the late 1940s researchers Gerhart
Saenger and Emily Gilbert proved this wasn't true by interviewing
customers before and after they were waited on by both blacks and
whites, and they found that antiblack prejudice had little effect on
sales—a fact that when widely publicized helped to reduce em-
ployer resistance to fair-employment practices during the 1950s.[7]

A major problem in using research to spur social reform is how
to get action on the findings. Traditionally, researchers spend
months and even years documenting evils and writing their report
—and then nothing comes of it. Lewin wondered if the facts on
prejudice could be gathered in a way that would lead to action, and
to this end he and the CCI staff developed the Community Self-
Survey of Discriminatory Practices. Rather than hiring an expensive band of outside experts, under this plan the people of the
community became their own researchers, fanning out over the
city to carry out interviews and quantify their findings with an
Index of Discrimination, also developed by CCI. A pilot study in a
town of forty thousand near New York City indicated the Self-
Survey could be carried out successfully for as little as $600 a
year, and soon seventeen communities were measuring their own
"levels of discrimination" using this approach.[8]

CCI also carried out many studies of how to handle bigots at
parties, in school meetings and other semiwild encounters—finding, for example, that others in a small group will support (and,

by modeling, learn from) the person who publicly disagrees with the bigot if the disagreement is quiet, firm, and factual, but not if the disagreement is loud, irate and oratorical. The great CCI study, however, was of racially integrated and segregated housing. Both types of public housing projects were being considered and carried out at the time, and there was much speculation as to what the effects of housing desegregation would be. Would it lead to more or to less socializing? More or less happiness? More or less prejudice? More or less strife?

Planned by Lewin, the CCI study was carried out after his death by Morton Deutsch and Mary Evans Collins in the late 1940s. Over several months white and black housewives and teen-age boys and girls in four interracial housing projects in Newark and New York City were interviewed. Two of the projects were completely integrated and two were of a segregated "checkerboard" pattern—that is, whites in one building, blacks in another. The study, one of the earliest of housing integration, produced findings that obviously have still not been utilized throughout much of the land. In the segregated projects not only were prejudices toward blacks sharper and stronger than in the integrated projects, but the housewives were also generally more peevish, suspicious, and hostile toward other whites in the project. Group cohesiveness and morale were definitely higher in the integrated buildings. Moreover, the researchers found no evidence that more than 50 percent black occupancy meant trouble; in fact, the most cordial relations seemed to exist in an integrated project with 79 percent black occupancy.[9]

Building Group Strength

The controversial term Black Power gave whites of all political persuasions fits as the decade of the 1960s closed. Liberals were aghast: How could one possibly reconcile what seemed to be arrogant separatism with the goals of integration? And the Right and the Middle, while welcoming a withdrawal that seemed to cater to their prejudices, also viewed the notion as a threat of the worst order. The rise of the need to assert and believe in Black Power— or Red Power, or Brown Power, or any other minority's need for raising *group* esteem—would have held few surprises for Lewin.

"Neither an individual nor a group that is at odds with itself can live normally or live happily with other groups," he wrote in 1946. "It should be clear to the social scientist that it is hopeless to cope with this problem by providing sufficient self-esteem for members of minority groups as individuals. The discrimination which these individuals experience is not directed against them as individuals but as group members, and only by raising their self-esteem as group members to the normal level can a remedy be produced." [10]

This was no idle observation, hunch, or speculation. Implicitly, it grew out of Lewin's Jewish-based experiences and convictions as a fervent Zionist. But more directly it grew out of CCI and other studies showing that the quickest way to change an individual's attitudes and behavior was to change the attitudes and behavior of the *group* with which he chiefly identifies. It was also based on Lewin's uncanny analysis of majority-minority group relationships in field-theoretical terms.[11] Moreover, it was also linked to two other aspects of Lewinian thought—and in exploring the possible substructure to this one seemingly simple observation we will indicate something of the effectiveness of the good social scientist— that is, how he tries to build his house upon the rock of previous and related work rather than upon the sand of a well-meant speculation. By the early 1940s Lewin had become deeply concerned with numerous aspects of the blacks' problem of improving their self-image. As the individual's self-image could only be improved if the group image of blacks were improved, he stressed that it was important for blacks to value their blackness and draw together. To encourage this movement he recommended (to give only one example of a shrewd insight that foreshadowed later practice) that sacrifices on the group's behalf be made by the individual to increase the individual's stake in the group's success. Such sacrifices might range from giving time and money to risking danger and suffering for the cause—a dynamic at work among the abolitionists, as we have already observed.

An advocate of some of the tenets of the Black Muslims long before Malcolm X made them more widely known, Lewin also felt it was absolutely essential that blacks value self-help and take pride in lifting themselves by their own efforts. No doubt his feelings in this regard were to some extent based on his own experience of being Jewish. However, it is likely that his convictions in the matter were based on his students' extensive work in *level of aspiration*—the highly theoretical but extremely productive Lewin-ian exploration of the familiar phenomenon more generally known as expectancy.[12] This work was particularly far-ranging in its im-plications. (It is more than coincidental, it should be noted, that John Gardner—who has been so concerned with the quality of Americans and American life—did his doctoral dissertation on Lewin's level of aspiration. And one of the most extensive explora-tions of this theory was carried out by Lewin's student and asso-ciate Leon Festinger prior to his own development of cognitive dissonance theory.)

A basic finding is this: If a person sets himself a particular goal in advance of carrying out a task and he meets this goal, he will tend to raise his goal for the next task (or, an equivalent, if he succeeds with some task he will raise his expectation of himself). Thus, to lift oneself, one must first aspire to higher performance. But if we are to aspire as individuals, we must first see that success is possible—that is, one needs to see evidence that others in one's own group can and are making it, and thus feel the rise of group-based self-esteem. But this rise in group-based self-esteem upon which the individual feeds is, in turn, dependent upon the success of the group's aspiring individuals. And so it is important that in every possible way the black be motivated to advance himself in order to spur on this upward cycling.

And so one has a rationale for building group strength. How-ever, the other side of the level of aspiration picture has equally profound negative implications. If one sets a goal for oneself, and then *fails* to meet it, one tends to lower the goal—or lower one's expectations of oneself. Either way, the operation of level of aspiration is obviously an important factor in how we are changed for better or worse by ourselves and by our society—or, more pointedly, how a minority group may act upon itself to build per-sonal and group strength in the face of majority opposition.

Changing Men and Societies

It is hard to say which is the more impressive aspect of Lewin's approach to inducing social change—the fertility of his theorizing or the range and practicality of his methods. His great strength is the way theory and practice interact, feeding upon and reinforcing one another, which gives the Lewinian work an excitement beyond any mere checklist of worthwhile projects.

The use of force to produce social change, for example, was explored in a famous test case. Quotas placed on Jewish student enrollment by leading American colleges were a particularly galling reminder of Nazi Germany to Lewin and an affront to his dream of democracy. The quotas also enraged the leaders of the American Jewish Congress, who conferred with Lewin on what might be done. A bit of folk wisdom prevailing at the time was that old Social Darwinist gem "you can't legislate good will" (sired, no doubt, by "you can't change human nature"). Sayings of this type were widely used to justify inaction on black rights and, in this instance, on Jewish rights. Lewin, however, knew that small-group research fairly consistently contradicted this assumption—that is, the research indicated that it is easier to change attitudes by changing behavior than the reverse. And this knowledge prompted the use of a bit of force, rather than making another appeal to the college's "good nature."

As a result of their strategy sessions, the president of the American Jewish Congress filed a lawsuit against the Medical School of Columbia University for discriminatory enrollment practices. To the embarrassment and consternation of Columbia, the case became front-page news. Eventually the school was forced to open its selection records to regular inspection for evidence of bias and to publicly welcome all comers regardless of race or religion, which in turn forced a revision of discriminatory selection policies in many other leading colleges.[13]

Direct forcing, however, was an atypical approach to social change for Lewin. In some ways the most characteristic of his social experiments was the curio known as the "food habits study," which led to the extremely important concept of *group decision* to induce change. During World War II the Department of Agriculture asked anthropologist Margaret Mead to help find some quick way to change American food habits, and she called in her amiable and disarming friend, Lewin, to attack the problem. Some traditional foods were becoming scarce and expensive and the Department wanted to encourage a large-scale shift to cheaper, more plentiful, but in some cases odd or normally repellent foods, like turnips. They also wanted to increase the nutritional output of American foods by encouraging the populace not to overboil vegetables. Since this appealed to Lewin's Germanic feeling for efficiency and economy, he was soon at work "on the best psychological approaches to change, with food habits as the setting for the research," Mead recalls, "but his real interest, of course, was far wider even than how the people of the United States, or of the world for which we were also trying to plan, could learn to eat wisely and well." [14]

Of Lewin's many findings, the most important came from an experimental comparison of lecture versus discussion methods. In one experimental situation a high-prestige lecturer instructed a group of consumers on the advantages of changing food habits. In the other situation the group itself discussed possible changes and decided its own course of action. Though the lecturer was Mead herself (posing as a high-prestige expert on turnips!), group discussion with decision proved far superior to the lecture method in changing attitudes about eating turnips.

This finding hardly seems earthshaking, yet, like the legendary iceberg, there is more to it than meets the eye. The lecturer can be seen as an experimental analogue of all authoritarian figures who speak and whom the people are to follow, while the group discussion and the effectiveness of the group decision has democratic overtones. Particularly meaningful is the combination of group *decision* with discussion, rather than only a discussion that reaches no formal end—a difference that may be appreciated by anyone who has ever despaired of the imbalance between the amount of time given to bull sessions and symposia about human rights in comparison to the time given to commitment and action.

Lewin, whose talk was generally directed toward some form of action, was especially interested in decision-making as a means of inducing social change. "A process like decision-making, which takes only a few minutes, is able to effect conduct for many months to come. The decision seems to have a 'freezing' effect which is partly due to the individual's tendency to 'stick to his decision' and partly to the 'commitment to a group,' " he noted, and he predicted that group discussion *without* decision would not be nearly as effective as discussion *with* decision in changing behavior.[15] A student of his, Alex Bavelas, tested this hypothesis in an industrial setting and found it to be valid. Within the black-advancement context, the effect of such processes at work can be seen in events ranging from the dramatic liberalizing of conservative white members of the Kerner Commission Report (who, after being involved in a group investigating the 1968 riots, endorsed a large formal attack specifically on "white racism") to the gradual radicalizing of those who sign (rather than just think about signing) petitions advancing the black cause.

Underlying this approach was another aspect of the Lewinian approach to inducing change that has often been overlooked by the militant, who usually feels that applying fierce pressure to a target person or group is the only method of inducing change. While quite aware of this tactic, Lewin found its opposite, of which Gandhi was so fond, particularly inviting—that is, to concentrate on lowering the resistance of the target person or group so that change might be effected with minimal pressure.

The earliest full-scale study of this tactic was in an important pioneering experiment in industrial or organizational psychology. Alfred Marrow, a Lewin student and close associate, and later his biographer, was an officer of the Harwood Manufacturing Corporation, which operated a factory in a small Virginia farm community. Among Harwood's problems was one that afflicts many industries—a drop in the production level whenever the workers had to change manufacturing procedures for new products. Marrow brought Lewin into the picture and soon a careful analysis indicated that behind the drop in production lay a complex of resistances to changing procedures, and that behind these resistances lay another complex of personal fears and anxieties. The problem was how to quell these fears and overcome the resistance to change. For six years, from 1940 to 1946, Lewin and John French explored the problem with a series of small studies, and then they designed the following experiment, which French carried out after Lewin's death.[16]

There were three different groups, and the key element was *the degree to which the workers participated in the decision-making that centered on the job change*. The first group did not participate in any way; the workers were simply told by management what they would be doing and who they would report to when the changeover was made. The second group was asked to appoint representatives to meet with management to discuss all the prospective changes in advance of the changeover. The third group consisted of every member of the tested unit, not just their representatives, all of whom met with management and took an active part in planning the changeovers. The results were, to say the least, dramatic. With the changeover, production in group I dropped 20 percent, 9 percent of the group quit, morale fell sharply, and hostility toward supervisors was displayed in several ways. Group II, which had representatives, regained their pre-change output within two weeks, maintained a reasonably good morale, and no one quit. But in group three, which fully participated in decision-making, not only was morale high and no one quit, but the workers regained their pre-change output after only two days, and climbed steadily until they were 14 percent above their earlier average output!

French's conclusion has exceptionally wide-ranging implications in terms of practically every aspect of the black and white sickness, from the riots of ghetto blacks who are denied any sense of controlling their own fate to the rioting of black and white students who feel excluded from any decision-making process that might change a deplorable state of affairs in a wealthy nation. The dramatic surge in production and morale, French concluded, was "directly proportional to the amount of participation and . . . the rates of turnover and aggression are inversely proportional to the amount of participation." [17]

As with all of Lewin's work, this experiment was only the surface manifestation—only a cork upon a sea of theorizing that transformed the workers and managers into endless human analogues and made of the little Harwood manufacturing company a world in itself. As already noted, in the history of the black in America one finds the dynamics of liberative forces pressing against repressive forces to produce a certain social output. Out of his more general theorizing Lewin gave this interpretation of the dynamics of production at the Harwood plant: The level of production "could be viewed as a quasi-stationary process in which two types of forces are in gear: those component forces pushing production in a downward direction and those pushing production up." [18]

This dynamic is important, for such thinking led Lewin to a powerful reconciliation of the conflict and equilibrium models examined in the chapters dealing with Marx, Spencer, and Myrdal. Moreover, this reconciliation was not simply an impressive exercise in gaining an apparent understanding of social processes, *but was directly tied to social action.* As in the case of so much of Lewin's work, this again happened not too long before his death, and thus he was unable to develop the thoughts beyond a few mind-expanding statements buried within his highly personalized diagrams and formulas. However, within the thicket of one last paper, appropriately titled "Frontiers in Group Dynamics," he planted more than anyone has been able to harvest in twenty years.[19]

Though on a first reading the following paragraph may seem to say either very little or too much, it is quoted here because, like the strongest of brandies, it is a distillation of Lewin's view of social change. Moreover, for all the tartness of its abstraction, it offers both a bare-bones description of our time of turmoil and suggests an attitude for those who may wish to attempt a healing.

"Periods of social change may differ quite markedly from periods of relative social stability. Still, the conditions of these two states of affairs should be analyzed together for two reasons: (a) Change and constancy are relative concepts; group life is never without change, merely differences in the amount and type of change exist. (b) Any formula which states the conditions for change implies the conditions for no-change as limit, and the conditions of constancy can be analyzed only against a background of 'potential' change." [20]

The useful meanings of this passage can perhaps best be seen in terms of Lewin's great formulation of a three-step process to effect social change: unfreezing, moving to a new level, and refreezing. But before discussing the process, it is necessary to understand what Lewin meant by *level,* which appears throughout his thought in one guise or another. In "Frontiers of Group Dynamics" he uses the concept in terms of a *level of discrimination* against blacks that exists in a particular town. This level of discrimination is no mere oratorical construct or arguable matter subject to heated discussion and differences of opinion; it is something actual and measurable in terms that all can see and agree on.

It is determined by, on one hand, the cumulative pressures of specific black-repressing social forces, such as the various local prejudices against blacks and the desire of whites "to keep certain jobs for themselves." These forces can be visualized as, in a sense, pressing downward. Opposing them are many black-liberating social forces, such as the whites' fear of black rebellion or their recognition that discrimination is unfair and undemocratic. These forces can be visualized as pressing upward. All these forces, then, both the antiblack forces pressing downward and the problack forces pressing upward, can be measured through opinion polls and other devices. And being measurable they could either be plotted on a graph of a special kind Lewin called a "phase space" —or simply visualized and held in the mind for purposes of analysis, as we are doing here. The end result returns us to familiar territory: This opposition of liberative and repressive forces results in a temporary settling point where the forces are in balance (or a state of equilibrium, or compromise), and this line of an uneasy state of balance constitutes the *level of discrimination.*

With this fairly precise level of discrimination in Lewin's hypothetical town in mind, the goal of social action also becomes more precise. It is to *lower* the level of discrimination, which can be done through the three-step process of unfreezing, moving to a new level, and refreezing—by doing something to unsettle, or unfreeze, the prevailing level of discrimination; by actions directed toward lowering the level; and by then fixing, or refreezing, the level of discrimination at the lower point rather than allowing it to remain unstable.

One of the first moves in unfreezing is to bring about a change in the relative strengths of the liberative and repressive forces "by adding forces in the desired direction or by diminishing opposing forces." [21] In this regard, Lewin notes that in some cases unfreezing may be relatively painless, and that merely stating the more ideal level will serve to set the therapeutic dynamic in action. This is, of course, the controversial dynamic of idealism that Myrdal describes in *An American Dilemma*—the gentle working of the American Creed upon most of us over history to quietly unsettle and gradually advance the black and heal the nation. In our hypothetical town, this might be accomplished if all the ministers in town were to preach brotherhood on a particular Sunday followed in a few days by a ceremony in which the mayor and other local political figures spoke on the theme of equality, coupled with reinforcement by famous figures on national television urging more enlightened attitudes.

Such a combination of forces of idealism might serve to unfreeze the prevailing level of discrimination to some degree, but if the opposition in the town were too strongly entrenched or the liberative forces relatively shallow and insincere, nothing at all might result from this massive effort. In such cases, Lewin notes, it may be necessary to "break open the shell of complacency and self-righteousness" by deliberately bringing about "an emotional stir-up." [22] And this, equally apparent and counter to the Myrdal position, is the controversial dynamic of varying kinds and degrees of more disruptive pressures, ranging from the mild reproof to the riot, and advanced over history by men ranging from the gentle John Woolman and the abolitionists to the leaders of slave revolts and the modern black revolutionaries.

Following unfreezing by either means there is a period during which it is possible to *move to a new level*—and this time may be quite brief, like the quick breaks in the shifting and resettling of the atmosphere through which the amateur astronomer may glimpse a star. Under the formal notion of inducing and advancing personal and social change, in the Lewin work alone we have already examined the possibilities of moving to new levels by reducing prejudice, building group strength, building group-based self-esteem, group discussion, discussion with decision, and participation in decision-making. And to these small-group techniques may be added such powerful and familiar means, *all* dependent on leadership, as passing and enforcing laws to protect voting rights, implementing school and housing desegregation, improving education, instituting fair-hiring practices, and expanding and upgrading job opportunities.

In general, movement to the new levels is accomplished by everything, small or large, that works to strengthen liberative forces and weaken repressive forces—or to lower resistance to change. In the case of our hypothetical town, for example, this might be accomplished by the positive effect of a new integrated public swimming pool; those who fought for and had high hopes for the project would be strengthened and reassured, while those who opposed it and had made dire predictions would be confounded by its success.

Let us assume that there *has* been unfreezing and movement to new levels—as there surely has been within the lives of every black and white in America, and most dramatically over the two decades of the liberating and liberalizing thrust following World War II. Now we must deal with the concept of refreezing, a complex of extremely important and generally overlooked considerations. Most people and agencies pushing for social change tend to concentrate on the first two steps, and rarely consider the refreezing process. And if they do, they see it as the nefarious work of the repressive establishment, the status quo, the powers-that-be. "*Re*freeze?" they might say of such a notion. "Good god, it's all we can do to *un*freeze even one stupid regulation. The problem is to blow the lid off; don't talk to us about putting it back on."

Yet it is interesting to note that the one other figure in this century of undebatable genius in the tactics of relatively peaceful social action, Mahatma Gandhi, shared with Lewin the concern for refreezing. The central Lewinian point is that the "laws" of human nature are such that equilibrium, balance, compromise—in short, a level of new norms—must be re-established. The openness, opportunity for movement, the fluidity can exist for only a relatively short period of time, and then there must be a settling point from which the next advance is made. Thus, the wise strategist will select and state in advance the refreezing level being sought. This will prevent, on one hand, the escalation of unlimited aspirations on the part of the liberated—that urging of strong desires that cannot be immediately met that can spill over into violence (such as the urban riots in Watts, Detroit, Newark, and Washington, and the assassination of policemen). And, on the other hand, it will prevent the strengthening of resistance through the repressor's fear of the unknown and the growth of the fantasies that feed upon unknowns and fuel irrational brutality (such as the police clubbings in Chicago in 1968 and the killings of Black Panthers and students at Kent and Jackson State). This point was implicit in Lewin's theory, but explicit in Gandhi's. He set specific and reasonable goals for his campaigns, and then—resisting pressures from both sides—worked to settle with the British for neither more nor less than he had asked.[23]

Lewin stressed a second point of exceptional importance about refreezing: that "a change toward a higher level of group performance is frequently short-lived; after a 'shot in the arm,' group life soon returns to the previous level. This indicates that it does not suffice to define the objective of a planned change in group

performance as reaching a different level. Permanency of the
new level, or permanency for a desired period, should be included
in the objective." [24] One has only to consider the historical evidence of the period following Reconstruction, and the disturbing
parallels in the late 1960s and early 1970s, when after sweeping
national efforts to attain more ideal racial-relational levels, there
was a failure to refreeze at the new levels.

As C. Vann Woodward and James McPherson have so brilliantly portrayed, for a time following the great liberative pressuring of the Civil War and Reconstruction there existed an apparent
golden age of race relations in America, but the new fluidity,
ambiguity, and lack of racial-relational fixities which was the
initial strength of the period increasingly became its weakness.
For amorphous good feeling coupled with uncertain leadership
soon proved too weak to prevail against the pressure to regress
to the old levels of discrimination, to the old patterns of behavior,
the old stereotypes, the old norms. And in our time we have seen
the rise of a new time of ambivalence on both school and housing
desegregation, and a new ambiguity in racial relations where both
blacks and whites find themselves perhaps less fearful of one another but, paradoxically, even more on guard. In both instances, in
short, there is a weakening of liberative forces accompanied by a
radical strengthening of repressive forces. And to anyone truly
concerned with healing the nation it is a frightening combination,
and a profoundly disturbing warning flag.

Moreover, this is a concern that careful attention to the Lewinian
diagnosis must deepen. Although Lewin felt there was a range
within which one could backslide "safely" from the new level and
still regain it with some ease, *once past a certain point of regression
the pull of the old level begins to operate—the comfortable old
habits of hatred, indifference, or social insularity begin to pull at
us one and all.* And slowly at first, then more swiftly, gaining
momentum, attitudes and behavior gravitate toward, and may
eventually again lock into, the old levels—leaving us like Sisyphus
with his stone at the bottom of the hill, to face again the agony of
rolling it up that long and steep incline.

As Lewin warned, "for most problems of management the
width of the range in which the process has the character of a
stationary equilibrium is of prime importance. This is equally

fundamental for the prevention of major managerial catastrophes and for bringing about a desired permanent change." [25]

In other words, *the new level must be maintained for a sufficient period of time for it to become an accepted social fact of life.* We must walk and talk and think and act in the ways of the new level long enough for these new thoughts and actions to become habitual to us as individuals, and also long enough for them to become part of the social guidance mechanism of new norms, customs, and laws that governs our action as men. Hence, the fundamental distress of so many over what happened to the American drive toward health out of the black and white sickness with the arrival of the Nixon administration.

From the ending of World War II well into the 1960s there was a vast unfreezing and a vast movement to new levels. But never in any area did those behind the movement feel that sufficient time or funds had been given to reaching the sought-for levels to justify a refreezing. Thus there was hope that even if the steam was running out of the impetus toward black advancement, at least under Nixon there might be a refreezing at the most advanced levels that had been attained. But instead the new administration rapidly became the most ambiguous on the subject of black advancement in forty years, and generally avoided anything firm one way or another in the area of racial relations, except when pushed to it by massive embarrassment or by stinging personal attacks on the President himself (which became the desperation policy of the normally moderate NAACP). Though few men observing this strange performance were aware of the Lewinian terms for what was going on, the feelings and the experience, nevertheless, were there, and the conclusions about political realities grew firmer with each passing month.

CHAPTER **26**

Kurt Lewin's Remedies: II

Much of our history, both past and present, indicates that violence generally attends most large-scale efforts to unfreeze social behavior and move it to new levels. Lewin was particularly sensitive to this fact, but again his insights spring mainly from experiment and theory rather than from the customary pondering or experiencing of history itself. For the violence that attended our unfreezing, which swelled to a crescendo with the urban riots of the late sixties, lay considerably ahead of Lewin when he puzzled over the problem during the 1930s and early 1940s.

While clearly recognizing the need for force and militancy in social change, Lewin also clearly limited this recognition to *measured* applications. Force was to be used only when it was certain that other measures would not work, and it was to be used only in connection with efforts to lessen rather than increase opposition. His most telling advice in this connection was to compare the difference in tension that accompanies the strengthening of liberative forces with the tension that usually accompanies the weakening of repressive forces. To strengthen liberative forces one must do things that almost invariably increase conflict and tension, and like turning on the fire beneath a tea kettle this increase in tension can produce either hot water for a useful brew or, with repression, an explosion. However, in lowering resistance one is usually also lowering the general tension level.

"Since increase of tension above a certain degree goes parallel with greater fatigue, higher aggressiveness, higher emotionality, and lower constructiveness," Lewin concludes, "it is clear that as a rule the second method [i.e., lowering resistance] will be preferable to the high-pressure method." [1]

Throughout the idea of unfreezing and moving to new levels there runs, of course, the Lewinian view of expectancy, or, in his terms, of the level of aspiration. As blacks began their dramatic advance in gaining voting rights and school desegregation in the 1950s, jaundiced white observers noted that as soon as one demand was met three more seemed to rise in its place. Ultimately there seemed no ceiling to black demands, and when they couldn't be met violence welled up everywhere. This was no surprise to an old laborer in the Lewinian level-of-aspiration vineyard, Morton Deutsch. Social revolutions, Deutsch noted, "tend to occur only after there has been a slight improvement in the situation of oppressed groups; the improvement raises their level of aspiration, making goals which were once viewed as unattainable now perceived as realistic possibilities." [2]

The level-of-aspiration work stemmed originally from the Berlin studies years—indeed it was the young Russian, Tamara Dembo, who followed Lewin to America, who coined the phrase. Dembo's work with Lewin from the Berlin days through the 1930s in Iowa City was the pioneering experimental study of frustration and aggression, and of many findings in a series of remarkably original studies two are of exceptional importance in this context. Dembo demonstrated "that a barrier which frustrated a person's attempt to reach a goal led to anger only if the person was surrounded by an outer barrier that prevented him from leaving the field." [3] Aside from other relevant analogues, this seems a good description of the social-psychological state of the average black in America during the 1950s and 1960s. Suddenly, after years of trying to overlook or minimize the barrier that prevented him from leaving the ghetto (and its social analogue of a traveling pariahship), the average black could no longer avoid this awareness. "You are not free. You *are* surrounded by this barrier. You *cannot* leave the field," his leadership and both the white and the black press told him— and the anger rose, and when the barrier did not immediately fall, the violence rose also.

Dembo's other thought-provoking finding was of the frustration-regression effect; that is, in frustration experiments, children regressed to both earlier cognitive and general behavioral performance levels. In the experimental frustration situation a child of four and a half, for example, would begin to think on the level of a three-year-old.[4] Again, we encounter something that undoubtedly accounts to some degree for the recorded difference in black and white average IQs, which Arthur Jensen has tried to pin mainly to genes. As for aggression in the same frustrating experimental situation, when the child was confronted with a seemingly mild form of denial involving a screen between the child and some wanted toys there was a 30 percent increase in hostile actions and a 34 percent decrease in friendly approaches.

"Frustration as it operated in these experiments," Lewin, Dembo, and Roger Barker concluded, in a description that conforms remarkably to innumerable portraits of the black ghetto, "resulted in an average regression in the level of intellectual functioning, in increased unhappiness, restlessness, and destructiveness, in increased ultra-group unity, and in increased out-group aggression. The amounts of increase in negative emotionality were positively related to this strength of frustration." [5]

The general therapy here, of course, is obvious and has been repeatedly articulated—reduce frustration and you reduce aggression and violence. Give the child and the man a decent home, a decent neighborhood, a decent job, a decent future, and his need to attack, rob, or kill will be radically diminished.

Gaining Control of One's Own Destiny

One method of reducing frustration and aggression with particularly far-ranging implications deserves more attention. It emerged during the Harwood study of workers' participation versus nonparticipation in decisions affecting their lives. Among the workers who did not participate, it will be recalled, there was a sharp rise in hostility and aggression compared to those who had some voice in their fate.

Throughout Lewin's work there runs this deep recognition of man's need to have a voice in shaping his life. It infuses his psychology with a humanism akin to the old lift of William James and John Dewey, and it gave him his ultimate personal appeal to other human beings. Within himself the social scientist has the choice of two stances: He may seek to play God himself, or he may liberate the God within others. Lewin was strongly motivated in both directions, but the astounding amount of work he set in motion indicates the greater power of his desire to liberate the best in others. It is this fact that gives him his exceptional dimension as a social therapist.

In study after study his method is to use himself, the expert, mainly as a springboard for others, as a means of getting someone else underway on his own. With his students, his associates, the Harwood workers, with those who were to use the Community Self-Survey, his method was to arouse others to create their own products and to shape their own destiny. The drive can be seen in his Zionism and feeling for Palestine—his belief that the Jew, for centuries dependent on the good will of others, always in a minority, should have a place on this earth to create for himself his own destiny. It underlay his intense feeling for democracy, this precious potential for each man to pursue his own individuality.

It can also be seen in his own personal search for a resting place. Many creative fellow spirits in the social sciences recognized his genius while he still moved among them—Erik Erikson, Harold Lasswell, Robert Merton, Margaret Mead, Ruth Benedict, Max Wertheimer, Gordon Allport, Jerome Bruner, Edward Tolman, Gardner Murphy, Neal Miller, Richard Crutchfield, David Krech, Mary Henle, and Sigmund Koch.[6] But to the lesser men who controlled the bureaucracies of disciplines, schools, and professional societies he was often *persona non grata* because he played no one's game but his own. Everything he touched, including psycho-analysis, he transformed into his own suspect idiom. As he filled blackboards with his busy Jordan curves, "his restless intelligence seemed continuously to put forth pseudopods to engulf the thought of the other; but the prize once grasped was forthwith assimilated into the present body of field theory," Gordon Allport has written. "When Lewin took cognizance of the work of others, his response was an urge to reshape this thought into his own expanding system." [7]

Thus, from his years as a young Jew in Germany he learned two rules of survival that sustained him through his years as a middle-aging innovator in a middle-aging America. He learned that the price of originality—and all other positions in which one is in a minority—is that one must often work much harder than one's neighbor to gain as much recognition. And for his own protection, he learned he must rely on himself, and, in fact, while remaining an active and amiable part of a larger and often hostile world, to build his own self-sustaining system.

It was no coincidence, then, that Lewin became intensely involved with the challenge facing the black in America. Socially and psychologically there was a kinship, and out of this kinship he wrote in the mid-1940s of the need for black self-help, self-discipline, and the construction of a better self-image. In the end, in keeping with the entire thrust to his own life, Lewin believed, that others can only serve as consultants or as guides. Each man must be given the opportunity to save himself, but then he must take it and make the most of it; he cannot be saved wholly from the "outside." [8]

This is notably a position that blacks were again forced to fall back upon during the darkening years that ended the 1960s and began the 1970s. The concept of black self-help was also to be used as justification for attempts to dismantle a great deal of a general program of intervention on their behalf that had barely begun. However, the abandonment by government and, for a time, by a white majority, had positive as well as negative aspects. For in being forced back once again upon their own resources, for many blacks there was, along with the frustration and the bitterness, the pleasure of rediscovering the old survival strengths within self and within community that Lewin—out of his theory and the Jews' many centuries of experience—had stressed.

Leadership Training

The meaning of America in history, as the flowering of individualism, dictates that we see the problem of gaining control over our own destiny mainly as a challenge of personal leadership—or of ego strength, as the clinician concerned with the therapy of the individual would put it. In this regard, however, our historical record is one of small-scale successes offset by large-scale failures. For our strengths as individuals are, by the fact of our interdependence, tied not only to the success or failure of our social groups but even more so to social leadership. The solution for our plight would seem obvious, but despite this chain-linking of our fate— the individual to the group and the group to its leaders—Americans have been notably slow to train for or adequately reward great political leadership. Our leaders are supposed to emerge spontaneously, finance themselves, avoid bribes, and pretend they are interested only in service to us, never in power. They are supposed to be nothing more than just another one of us, whom luck happened to favor. But luck can run out—and suddenly we may see the horror of our dependence, but no clear solution.

Over years of sounding this theme the political scientist has been a voice crying in the wilderness in this country, and until Lewin appeared very little was done, beyond Harold Lasswell's brilliant pioneering and other psychiatric speculations, to explore the nature of political leadership in psychology.[9] As we have repeatedly seen in this survey of American history, the persistence of the black and white sickness centers chiefly on the leadership problem—the lack of a sufficient number of leaders, at all levels, who are aroused enough and capable enough consistently to push for closing the gap between the American ideal and the American reality on the black issue. Lewin stepped into the vacuum of knowledge of how to gain such leadership and brought with him a passion for democracy and the democratic form of leadership.

"Although Lewin never met John Dewey there was a community

of spirit between the German-born psychologist and the American-born philosopher," Gordon Allport once noted. "Both were deeply concerned with the workings of democracy. Both recognized that each generation must learn democracy anew; both saw the dynamic relation between democracy and social science and the importance to social science of freedom of inquiry, freedom that only a democratic environment could assure. If Dewey could be termed the outstanding philosopher of democracy, Lewin was surely the major theoretician and researcher of democracy among the psychologists." [10]

To this motivation was added—and it cannot be overstressed, because it is very relevant to the domestic turmoil of our Vietnam years—Lewin's personal knowledge of what happened when the leadership of a democracy failed. Although he hated war, he had served in the German army in World War I. He had lived through the aspirations of the Weimar Republic, and had been fired by the incredible creativity of those strange, wild years so much like our own. But out of the chaos and division and hatred that attended and followed the breakdown of democracy in Germany, he had seen the yearning for the Ultimate Authoritarian swell within Germany until it found its Hitler. And, helpless and horrified, he fled Germany to America and had been forced to witness from this distance the spread of the terror over Europe, and the sacrifice to social stability of six million Jews (including his own mother, who perished, like Freud's sisters, in a Nazi incinerator).

It is little wonder, then, that the central study of Lewin's last years in America was of the leadership styles, climates, and social and individual products of democracy versus autocracy. The study was also peculiarly Lewinian and democratic in that it is essentially the work of his students Ronald Lippitt and Ralph White, and later, to some extent, of Alex Bavelas and John French. Over several years, working with groups of eleven-year-old boys and the Harwood Manufacturing Company workers, these researchers experimentally compared the effects of three leadership styles and social climates. The main comparison was between authoritarian and democratic leadership, but they also investigated a third alternative. At the time it was mainly useful for putting the two other forms in perspective, but today it is newly relevant to the identity crisis of America in the 1970s. This third form was a rule-less, planless, freewheeling style and climate they called the laissez-faire.

In the authoritarian situation the leader would tell the boys exactly "what to do and how to do it, would dominate the group, and would make all judgments as to whether progress was being attained." In the democratic situation "goals, and means for reaching them, were left to the group to determine democratically." [11] In the laissez-faire situation the leader was completely permissive, allowing the boys to do whatever they wished and making no effort to develop rules or plans.

The results were exceptionally revealing. Lippitt and White reported that though "the groups behaved similarly at the outset, they rapidly became different, so that in the later meetings the contrast was striking. In brief, there was far more quarreling and hostility in the autocratically led group, and far more friendliness and group spirit in the one democratically led. The children in the autocratic group picked on scapegoats and showed other behavior that seemed too similar to certain contemporary dictatorships to be mere coincidence." [12]

Later they studied the effects of changing leadership styles with the same group, in effect simulating in a relatively painless way, and over a few short days within the laboratory, social revolutions that would normally require many years and lives in real life. Of only two of many startling results Lewin was moved to comment, "There have been few experiences for me as impressive as seeing the expression on children's faces during the first day under an autocratic leader. The group that had formerly been friendly, open, cooperative, and full of life, became within a short half-hour a rather apathetic-looking gathering without initiative. The change from autocracy to democracy seemed to take somewhat more time than that from democracy to autocracy. Autocracy is imposed on the individual. Democracy he has to learn!" [13]

There were numerous other indicators of positive gains for the laboratory democracy, but the negative aspects of the authoritarian and laissez-faire groups were more thought-provoking. In the laboratory autocracy the boys "were much more likely to lose initiative, to be restlessly discontented, to become aggressive and fight with each other, to damage play materials, and to function as individuals on their own with no concern for group goals or the interests of other members." In the laissez-faire situation, "there was much less work-centered behavior and discussion than under either of the other two varieties of leadership." [14] And in addition to accomplishing little, the laissez-faire group was demonstrably frustrated by the lack of rules, which eventually led to a most sinister turn of events. As with the authoritarian group, their frustrations became aggressions—and eventually they turned on the odd, the weak, or the different as scapegoats.

Spawned by the tensions of the 1930s and 1940s, by 1970 these studies were gaining a possible new relevance. Out of chaos, apathy, and the division of the country on the black and other issues, a significant minority of Americans were insisting, both implicitly and explicitly, that only be replacing democracy could the black and white sickness be cured and all other problems solved. To the young and tough-minded Far Left and to the old and tough-minded Far Right authoritarian rule by *their* elite was seen as the urgent alternative. And to the tender-minded and un-committed young, the free-floating, rulelessness of the laissez-faire style seemed the only hope. The Lewin, Lippitt, and White studies suggest the futility of looking to either alternative as a solution for our sickness or our problems.

Were America by some horrid and inconceivable fluke of fate to be placed under authoritarian rule, the Lewin, Lippitt and White studies suggest that for a time there would probably be a drop in aggression—in the internal as well as the external violence that was by 1970 the most disturbing symptom of our black and white sickness and our more general malaise. But to maintain this lower aggression level, extremely severe repressive measures would have to be instituted and maintained, which, by radically restrict-ing our freedom of movement physically, intellectually, and emo-tionally, would lead to a rise in aggression in response to this frustration. This, in turn, would require increasingly severe re-pression, and in order to provide an outlet for this "bottling up" of aggression, both internal and external scapegoats would have to be found. Our history indicates that the black, the Jew, the Indian, and the young radical would be the logical first victims domestically, and that internationally the smaller, weaker, "colored" nations would be the victims.

It is not a pretty picture, but then, surprisingly, neither is its alternative: The complete freedom that has so often been portrayed in joyous, brotherly and sisterly loving terms—of Norman Brown's living by Dionysian to the exclusion of Apollonian rule, or of Herbert Marcuse's life in Eros to the disregard of Thanatos. Were we by some seemingly appealing fluke to become a wholly open, free wheeling and planless society, the Lewin, Lippitt, and White studies suggest that, after a brief period of apparent happiness for some, there would be a rise in general unhappiness and internal aggression, and eventually—barring the development by the group of its own rules by the democratic process—there would be an authoritarian take-over to reinstitute some clear-cut goals and rules. This is almost exactly the process that William Golding envisioned in his novel *Lord of the Flies,* and it also seems to have been at work in the bands of flower children and hippies in the late 1960s who were controlled by such predators as the psychopathic Charles Manson.

We are left, then, by the Lewin studies—and by history, it would seem—with democracy as the best, as well as probably the only possible, political cure for the black and white sickness in America.[15] In comparison with the hypothetical therapy of autocracy it would seem to be more unpredictable and uncertain, and it is certainly riddled with compromises both in Lewinian field-theory terms and in "reality" terms. And in comparison with the laissez-faire therapy it is restrictive, leveling, and at times stultifying. And as for dealing with our sickness, both our past and our present experience with democracy indicates that it offers neither an easy nor a quick cure. But among other advantages, it does give us a relatively stable but still open system, *that by our own efforts can be perfected.* And to this end Lewin directed his own last great effort.

One day in 1946 he received a phone call from Frank Simpson, director of the Connecticut State Inter-Racial Commission. The Commission, Simpson explained, was badly in need of something to translate talk of improving racial relations into action and results. Could Lewin help? In terms of long-range impact, the response to this one phone call was staggering. Seeing this as a chance to bring together in one field test the thought and research of a decade, Lewin speedily mobilized his forces. Both CCI and the MIT Center would be involved; they would draw on the Iowa work and on the Harwood and other studies of group dynamics and leadership training; and jointly with the Connecticut Inter-Racial Commission staff they would develop a group leadership training experience the likes of which the world had never seen.[16]

It was billed, innocuously, as a two-week-long workshop, to which some fifty handpicked teachers, social agency workers, labor leaders, and businessmen were invited, about half of whom were blacks and Jews. The participants arrived expecting to discuss the problems of effecting social change in their particular communities, but they had no idea to what extent they were to be involved in a major "change experiment." A measure, in a sense, of the discrimination level prevailing in their communities was obtained before the workshop. Then, over the two weeks of the workshop, they were involved with the most successful methods of leadership training the Lewin groups had identified—group discussion, discussion and decision, group problem-solving, role-playing and its more involved advancement, sociodrama, and group- and self-criticism, or response feedback. Then some months afterward the participants and their communities were re-surveyed to see if anything had led to measurable improvements.

The workshop was phenomenally productive in demonstrating how to train leaders and develop techniques for effecting social change. It led to the founding of the National Training Laboratories, "an internationally recognized and powerful educational force affecting almost all of the social institutions in our society," in the estimation of Warren Bennis, a leading organizational psychologist. It also discovered the basis for the powerful new group therapy for changing attitudes and behavior known today as sensitivity or T-group training, which Carl Rogers considers "the most significant social invention of this century." "The demand for it is utterly beyond belief," Rogers has commented. "It is one of the most rapidly growing social phenomena in the United States. It has permeated industry, is coming into education, is reaching families, professionals in the helping fields, and many other individuals." [17]

In far more aspects than one might suspect, the method is peculiarly Lewinian, and of the social therapies he helped set in motion its implications for personal and social renewal seem a fitting memorial. Like the busy pages of his theoretical doodles, on the surface, sensitivity training may appear inviting, but—depending on one's viewpoint—it may also seem odd, quaint, funny, pathetic, alarming, or even suspect and dangerous. People are brought together and over time they become intimately involved with one another through talking over their problems, but they are also involved through the unavoidable intimacy of looking at and listening to one another as well as touching, feeling, clasping, or hugging one another in some forms of this method. To the uninvolved outsider the process would at times look rather weird; yet participants often emerge from these sessions speaking of a mystic sense of life-expansion and self-enlargement, and they seem to deal with problems that had previously baffled them with new energies and new vision.[18]

Beneath this observable surface of mystifying change, what actually happens during sensitivity training can be seen as a hopeful parable for our troubled times. Whatever the method, the goal is to open avenues out of ourselves into others, so that we may see through their eyes—to see their problems, see the problems that together we share, to see ourselves as they see us, and at times see into them and be seen into ourselves; to see and feel black, white, and brown, red, yellow; to recognize and value color, and to go beyond color; all parties working past exteriors to glimpse now and then the richness that generally lies behind our personal and social distortions, perversions, and denials of the gift of life. Also, given time, it lets us go beyond seeing to that experiencing of totalities that is the whole point of Lewin's field theory—beyond seeing to sense the other, oneself, and this earth of possibilities as a totality. But the purpose of all of this is not simply to bathe in some sublime understanding of ourselves, or the other, or our problems, *but through understanding to set in motion the forces that will act upon their totality for its betterment.*

And so out of (and within and during) the formality of action research and the informality of sensitivity training (or any other truth-inducing process) comes the greater understanding on the basis of which we plan and act. And there is feedback from the problem and from others. And to accommodate this feedback plans are adjusted and we act again. And there is new feedback, and new adjustments of plans, and new actions, and thus the cycling dialectic of changing and of healing is advanced.

Lewin felt that action research could "have a lasting effect on the history of this country." But it was clear to him "that this job demands from the social scientist an utmost amount of courage. It needs courage as Plato defines it: 'Wisdom concerning dangers.' It needs the best of what the best among us can give, and the help of everybody." [19]

CHAPTER 27

Social Physicians
and the Political Imperative

The lives and works of Du Bois and Lewin make many things apparent, but this above all: If one seriously wants to heal the nation of the black and white sickness, the problem is not the lack of proven measures for doing so, but the lack of healers.

As the history we have examined repeatedly demonstrates, contrary to the belief of those who see this disease as a mystery which more decades of committees and research must resolve, over the centuries we have accumulated a vast doctor's bag of understand-ings and remedies so huge that no one social physician, or even team of physicians, can begin to tap its store. But why, then, haven't all these remedies been applied with more success? Again there are many reasons, but our history suggests—and the most passionate pursuits of Du Bois and Lewin emphasize—that it is mainly for lack of good leadership.

One can say, of course, and rightfully, that leadership is dependent on economic development and social climate. But it is also true that to leadership there is generally available a margin of choice, and within this margin, leadership is sometimes free to influence economic development and to make the social climate. And within the perspective of what could and should have been done, it failed to use this margin. After being armed with all the history and the social science suggested by this sampling of 350 years, the white leadership of this nation was given, following World War II, an especially favorable margin of choice for healing the nation of this central illness. A minority of Americans, citizens and social scientists alike, made a valiant effort that everywhere excelled the official leadership, and many dramatic improvements were made. But ultimately, it was not enough. With the exception of some important court decisions and bills, some key appointments, some Federal saber-rattling, and Lyndon Johnson's well-meant but doomed gesture, the official white leadership of this nation not only failed to seize the opportunity but it also lost itself in the swamps of the greater racism of this world. Moreover, this was not just a failure of political leadership. To a considerably lesser but still relevant degree, it was also a failure of a social scientific leadership that was concerned more with its image as a science than with the crying needs of man.

Both Lewin and Du Bois foresaw this failure. For Du Bois it was the high probability of disappointment that drove him to abandon America, and given his background both as seer and sufferer, this foresight was perhaps not so surprising. But Lewin's vision was more startling. He died in 1947, long before Vietnam and the urban crisis, and he spoke out of the purblind world of whiteness and a fragmented and insular social science. Yet in one of his last papers he wrote of the danger of pursuing "the international Jim Crow policy of the colonial empires." In a rare presentiment of the explosive linkage between United States and world racism, he warned that such a pursuit would "hamper tremendously progress of inter-group relations within the United States and is likely to endanger every aspect of democracy." [1] Thus, while he remained hopeful to the end, the possibility of an American failure of leadership drove him to intensify his small efforts to save a very large nation and hastened his own death.

The pathos of these two lives—in knowing and feeling so much and having so little power to influence events—reflects, of course, the plight of all men and women of good will in troubled times. But it also reflects a more fundamental problem. For in their helplessness, Lewin and Du Bois exemplified a hard fact about life in the twentieth century that social scientists have been reluctant to face and citizens have been slow to realize. It is that for all the vaunted potential of the social sciences for healing men and nations, they are, in the end, relatively powerless to do so. For in terms of actual healing, all the bright insights, the remedies, the prescriptions, the plans, the programs, the brilliant nostrums are no better than the men, and the system which produces the men, who are to bless and implement them.

For all the hopes and postures of its practitioners, social science is, in the end, and rightfully so, a staff rather than a line function, in management terms. It can advise or deplore. It can glow with excitement or wring its hands over policy enactment. But it is powerless to decide or act. All must funnel into and through the mind, heart, body, and soul of the manager and the political leader, who by his action becomes the actual living, breathing healer of the home, the town, the city, the state, the organization, and the nation. Thus, up to this point of contact all healing measures are, in essence, just so much talk, just so many more books. *Only by passing into and through the personal being of the healing figure with the power to decide and act do they become real.* Social science proposes, leadership disposes. An alert and caring social science may present the possibilities, the alternatives, the potential for transcending history; but men and their leaders must decide and act. And history is the record of their choices.

It is only within such a perspective that something that might be called "prescriptions of the great social physicians" can have any meaning. As we have suggested, there are many remedies, many alternatives, but most of them relate to a few bodies of choices that remain pulsating before the leadership of this nation.

Some Prescriptions of the Great Social Physicians

Wallowings in symbolism and some efforts to project psycho-sexual kinks upon the indifferent backside of history have obscured the larger and simpler meanings of Sigmund Freud's vision as it may apply to social healing. At the heart of his method of indi-vidual therapy lay the workings of catharsis and insight. By dredging up the worst within himself and exposing it to the light of consciousness a man may unburden himself of the past, achiev-ing catharsis and wholeness. And weaving in and out of this proc-ess is the action of insight, or the darting of perception and thought past our defenses to gain a useful piece of truth about ourselves. "Where id was, there ego shall be," Freud said of this general thrust to his method.[2]

In the exposure and unloading of the past, and in the pustule-puncturing action of insight, can be seen an underlying rationale for the healing power of all forms of education. Commonly we think of the action of better teachers and textbooks in combating racism and advancing humanism. The new teaching of black his-tory and the new emphasis upon black studies is pointedly cathartic. Less well recognized but extremely influential is the in-formal action of our exceptionally stimulating media, both print and television. Anthony Benezet and John Dewey are the proto-typal American social physicians of education. When it is working as it should, education still remains one of the strongest therapies available to us; hence, the opposition of those who represent the sickness to most efforts to liberalize it.

The mechanism and the underlying authoritarianism of the vision of Ivan Pavlov and his successors have repelled the human-ist, and Professor Jensen's recent pronouncements demonstrate the dangers of an insular behaviorist and learning-theory tradition. But it gets results, and an equally powerful strain of social healing seems to operate according to the findings and thrust of this thought. For example, the other side to fear conditioning is conditioning *therapy,* whereby the same basic principles are used in a range of new methods to *de*condition fears and eliminate unwanted behavior. Watson cured Albert of his fear of the rabbit by replacing the repeated banging of the steel bar with a pleasurable experience: He had Albert regularly *eat* in the presence of the rabbit. Where a repetition of negative mental associations may establish the habit of fear, a repetition of positive mental associations can be employed to diminish it.[3]

An everyday analogy would be those rare blacks and whites who, in response to some fluke or social intervention, are able to live together on roughly equal terms, and in favorable circumstances, over a period of time. Generally, they lose their fears and discover many more reasons for being friends than enemies. Still more generally, the rather firm principles of conditioning or *learning* therapy can be discerned at work within the relatively loose and intuitive shaping of American social policy, in the desegregation of schools, housing, swimming pools, and all public facilities. And a fundamental point about the success of this method, both individually and socially, is the tough-minded directiveness that many find repellent. As the individual is cured by giving himself over to the benign dictatorship of the therapist, so is society shaped to healing ends in this method by the imposition of the solution from above, by executive fiat and by the passage and enforcement of laws. Again, the invariably strong opposition to such moves on the black's behalf testifies to the force of the method.

Karl Marx's prescription of revolt by the underclass is well known and discounted by most settled authorities. However, for all its apparently irrationality and futility as a large-scale measure, it has proven effective as a small-scale tool, for this is the surgical attack of the urban riot and the arming of blacks. Within the actuality of overwhelming white strength, what this, in fact, leads to is more pathetic than alarming, but the symbolism of guns and riot can be peculiarly powerful—this suggestion of what might happen, this evoking of guilt and old bugaboos, this foreshadowing of the fabled Revolution that the powers-that-be at times truly fear. It is the shame of this nation that the blacks have been forced, as was labor earlier, to riot and bloodshed to jolt the overclasses into living up to the American ideal. Though entrenched white strength should prevent use of this prescription as a full-scale measure, it will no doubt continue to be applied in small ways, producing the doubtful end product of both advance and retrogression.

Marx's other prescription of distributive justice as a healing goal (*e.g.,* the Communist Manifesto's proposal in 1848 of the graduated income tax) is another story. The goal is, of course, by no means a Marxist, or even a socialist, exclusive; but socialist pressures have forced the action. And this single prescription seems to remain the most promising healing pressure in our time. Whatever it may be called, the momentum behind the idea of taking from the haves to shore up and advance the have-nots, having gained the income tax, social security, and medicare, is now moving to lay down a more general economic flooring. The "conservative" negative income tax and the "liberal" guaranteed-income plans are met, most ironically, in that extremely important latter-day budding from the old Marxist root, the Nixon-Moynihan welfare proposal. As the seventies began, another hopeful articulation out of the tradition of distributive justice was Whitney Young's reproposal of an irrefutably logical Marshall Plan for American blacks.

Gunnar Myrdal's chief prescription at the time of *An American Dilemma*—if one can legitimately pull any one thing out of its great mass—was for more education. He believed that as Americans were better informed about the injustice suffered by blacks, and their prejudices were removed by the advance of social science, the nation would be healed. However, by 1960 his view had radically changed. Deeply disturbed by America's slowness to move against the injustice he had uncovered, and against both black and white poverty, he felt that only a vast governmental intervention on the behalf of the poor, with jobs and training and other measures, would save America from possible social and economic disaster. As work became even more scarce in the slums, about which so little was being done, the poor would be "increasingly isolated and exposed to unemployment, to underemployment, and to plain exploitation. There is an ugly smell rising from the basement of the stately American mansion." [4] Earlier Myrdal had believed that Americans were a generous people, but now, faced with urgent questions of "redistributing incomes," he saw an otherwise charitable majority as being "hardhearted and stingy." [5]

Moreover, where in the 1940s Myrdal had discounted the communist threat, now he feared that America's slowness to act on poverty would create a new underclass that might set the revolutionary class-struggle dynamic in motion. "Internally the danger is that of clamping a class structure upon the nation in blunt denial of its most cherished ideals of liberty and equality of opportunity." [6] Though these warnings of Myrdal's *Challenge to Affluence* were blunted by the Great Society programs mounted in the mid-sixties, the failure to expand or, in many cases, even to sustain this small beginning must thrust the question of large-scale governmental intervention again before the political leadership of the seventies.

Many other remedies could be summarized, but lists grow deadly, and this is quite enough in addition to those remarked throughout this book and packed into the closing Du Bois and Lewin chapters. And there is one other extremely important matter that should be examined here. Throughout the views of many of the great social physicians there runs a profoundly suggestive insight into social healing. It is the shifting view of that struggle, fundamental to life and persistently therapeutic in effect, that Freud identified as the conflict of Eros with Thanatos in *Civilization and Its Discontents*. If one looks for it, it can be found moving in an astounding number of places.

Deep within each of us as individuals, for example, the pattern seems to be at work. For Freud it was also the wish or desire that encounters repression and emerges in the compromise formation of dream, neurotic symptom, or everyday action. It has an analogue in Pavlov's theory of neural inhibition. For Marx it was the revolutionary dynamic of the proletariat versus the bourgeoisie, or more generally, the thrust of the denied against the denying class. For Woolman, it was the conflict of good and evil, or of religious love with selfishness and pride. For Lewin it was the conflict of liberative versus repressive forces.

It lies also within Maslow, the repressive forces being those of his defense needs and the liberative forces those of his growth needs. Myrdal's thinking extends the pattern from psychology into the sociology, finding within black advancement the dynamics of the liberative American Creed in conflict with the repressive needs of class and other considerations. And for Du Bois, driven by his assumption of the mantle of black suffering, it was the thrust of the long-repressed but fresh and socially needed health emergent within a new black culture, against the drained and dead perversity of the old white culture.

It is beyond the scope of this book to explore this dynamic, which has seized the imagination of many thinkers. But in general, and in its various guises, it seems to operate as an inbuilt complex of forces that act upon history to unsettle the unhealthiness of every age. And the great social therapists have discerned some of the laws governing this interaction and have learned to work with rather than against them, and have used this insight to guide successful healing interventions.

In general, this seems to be the method that Thomas Jefferson, Abraham Lincoln, Frederick Douglass, James Birney, Thaddeus Stevens and all the others who have acted in the leadership capacity—who have acted as the political agents of change—have intuitively put to use. The strategy is to do socially what every good physician does for the individual patient—to intervene on the behalf of the life forces against the killing weight of everything acting against them.

Again, all roads lead to the conclusion already expressed—that all remedies are just words until they reach the point of their choice and enactment through the mind, body, and soul of the healer.

The choices are before every one of us, but before some of us more than others. And ultimately the national yearning for health can only be fulfilled by the election of one figure to whom so much else adheres. The evidence of 350 years seems to point to this one conclusion—and it will be a bellwether for what it reveals of the people in terms of a majority sentiment as well as what it reveals of the man: The black and white sickness will not be cured until Americans elect a President willing, on this issue, to put his office on the line.

As one whose aspirations were cut short, John Kennedy, summed it up, "Only a President willing to use all the resources of his office can provide the leadership, the determination, and the direction . . . to eliminate racial and religious discrimination from American society." [7]

CHAPTER **28**

A Program for a President

It would be wrong to leave the impression that the prospect seems hopeless, or that everything rests on the Presidency. The life of John Woolman demonstrates how much can be done by one aroused individual. The lives of James Birney, Thaddeus Stevens, Charles Sumner, and Abraham Lincoln show what can be done by the aroused lawyer and the aroused legislator.[1] The millions given to black advancement by George Peabody, John Slater, John D. Rockefeller, and particularly Julius Rosenwald demonstrate what

can be done by the aroused businessman. The works of Du Bois,
Kurt Lewin, and Gunnar Myrdal demonstrate what can be done
by the aroused social scientist. The lives of Harriet Tubman, Sojourner Truth, Eleanor Roosevelt, and Du Bois's New England
schoolmarms show what can be done by the aroused woman. The
life of Frederick Douglass demonstrates what can be done by the
young, and the life of Gandhi demonstrates what can be done
by the old.

Moreover, as Charles Reich's *The Greening of America* suggests, there is reason to hope for a quiet revolution of consciousness that can remake our land. This consciousness is not new,
however, as Reich implies. It is the old loving vision that we have
come upon repeatedly, out of Akhenaton, Jesus, Du Bois, and so
many others. It is Freud's vision of the eternal renewal of Eros;
Marx's perfected society at the end of history; the self-actualizing
man of Maslow, Fromm, Erikson, and May; and the self-actualizing
group of Kurt Lewin and the prophets of the American Indian
experience [2]—it is all this expressed in terms of Reich's sensitivity
to the times and the meaning of the new youth culture. But neither
our past feeling for the mythology of individualism nor our futuris-
tic feeling for the mythology of the new tribalism should blind us
to the realities of the present. And the very grim present reality is
that for our time—now, immediately, with absolutely no reason
for faith in the goodness of the unguided social organism, and
calling once again upon the *enduring* strength and vitality of the
American heritage of reform and programmatic intervention—the
Presidency seems to be the key. So a crucial question is: What
could the right President do?

Since it would be impossible to adequately develop all the possibilities that suggest themselves, let us take a single dominant line
of thought, examine our history, consider the pressures of the
time, and bring the theory and appealing personal example of
Kurt Lewin once more into play.

Looking backward one last time, the most striking thing I observe is this: For all our current poor-mouthing, we remain the
most incredibly wealthy nation in all human history. Our fore-
fathers at Valley Forge, in tatters and with bloody feet, were
already more wealthy than their peasant counterparts in Europe.
And we are to the farmer-soldiers of Valley Forge what Croesus

was to a Lydian beggar, while in much of the world the condition of the peasant still remains unchanged.

The problem for us is no longer the old goad to gain wealth that has governed most of our history, but the growing challenge of its distribution. Thus, the central task, quite simply stated, is to shift more funds from the luxuries of the haves to the needs of the have-nots, the healing move signaled long ago by economists John Kenneth Galbraith and Gunnar Myrdal.[3] Increasingly it seems to loom as the axiomatic fact of our time and place in history, to which practically everything involved with ending the black and white sickness relates. Better education; more jobs; more psychological, social, and economic security; desegregated schools; desegregated and improved housing—all of this, and much more, depends on whether or not sufficient funds can be diverted to these ends from warfare, the second house, the third car. And although this complex and vast move is essentially economic in nature, it will take political implementation, which could benefit from the psychology of social therapy.

One might use more discreet terms, but it is a time for plain speaking: The central political strategy would be a majestic form of barter. In effect, the great President would offer the haves of America a most interesting trade. He would offer to release them from fear and to restore the domestic peace and tranquility they so devoutly desire. But in return for this gift of leadership, and in addition to turning an excess of swords into plowshares, he would be asking many to give up the second house, the third car, the pleasure-cruiser, the trip to the Riviera, the SST, the billions involved in such luxuries as raising and lowering hemlines in alternate years.[4]

It will be said that we are too self-indulgent and soft ever to accept such a move. But Hitler said this of us, and so did the Japanese, before World War II. Scared then by the prospect of annihilation, we became caught up in a cause larger than ourselves and rapidly mobilized our society to a degree unheard of before or since. Now we are again deeply frightened as a nation. All along the ideological spectrum, from Right through Middle to Left, at times the fear runs strong that we are facing the end of the American Dream. And so there is reason to believe that within a majority of Americans there may be a deep hunger to be caught

up again in something larger than ourselves and our divisions—
provided we have leadership.

To really work together—black and white, young and old, rich
and poor—to bring our society in line with its insistent potential
and with the dreams of our founding fathers would be such a
larger cause. And this is no mere dollop of rhetoric. Kurt Lewin's
ideas suggest how this goal might actually come to be realized—
and not within decades, but within a few years, and without a
revolution. With such an aim in mind, let us see what Lewin's
overall strategy of unfreezing, moving to new levels, and refreezing
might suggest for the program of the great President.

As to unfreezing, there is relatively little to be done. This will
come as a surprise to some, but not to others. As a society we are
now in the midst of a vast unfreezing process on all levels, which
is probably the fundamental cause of our fear. The alienation
caused by a lack of unfreezing has been highly evident and greatly
publicized, but more generally frightful has been the numbing
anomie that comes from too much movement. Alternately exhilarated beyond containment and fearful and unwilling, we are being
thrust into the unknown future by the vast energies and aspirations released by the unfreezing of two decades following World
War II. To this motion, as Alvin Toffler's *Future Shock* illumi-
nates, the technological explosion had added a hectic drive that
pushes us in too many directions at once.[5] Psychologically, most
of us are like Rip Van Winkle, awaking to find ourselves in the
midst of a hurricane. And so the great danger is not that we will
not unfreeze—as those who decry repression everywhere believe.
The danger is that being caught up in this vast and frightening
movement, in our panic and our ignorance we will refreeze at
short-sighted and unworthy levels—or worse yet, regress to the old
levels we have labored so hard to leave behind.

Yet this is the countering point of inconceivably greater importance: For all our fears, we are probably living during the optimum
time to finally end the sickness and peacefully advance this nation
toward its founders' goals. And it will be a social disaster of incomparable magnitude if we do not use this opportunity wisely—
for it may not come again.

Let us see how, in a sequence of carefully planned and implemented steps, the great President might accomplish the necessary reordering of national priorities and the shifting of funds.

Throughout the Lewinian remedies there appear and reappear two themes of exceptional interest. One is the intriguing picture of small groups of people meeting to discuss and decide upon matters that intimately affect their future. The other is the more wide-ranging, very intense Lewinian interest in finding new social mechanisms that might give the individual more of a voice in his own fate, more control over his own destiny—social mechanisms to strengthen participatory democracy. One of the most haunting aspects of Lewin's work was the extent to which it leapt beyond not only the social science of its time but also far beyond the technical capabilities of our society for realizing his vision. Within his lifetime, for example, the fruition of so much of his vast labor was the single two-week-long workshop in Connecticut described in Chapter 26.

However, immediately after Lewin's death—and the timing seems both pitiful and ironic—there burst upon the post-World War II scene two technologies that could have provided this giant with mechanisms to match the size of his thought. One was the explosive development of the computer with its tireless capacity for handling conceptual complexities and incredibly fast processing of huge quantities of information. The other was the equally explosive development of television and television networks, offering a new capability for the direct and instantaneous relaying of information and for instantaneously linking individuals to groups to leaders. (As politicians have rapidly discovered, beneath the glitter of its entertainments the fundamental attraction of television is that it is a truly phenomenal instrument for transcending age, sex, class, and caste barriers—for potentially catching up an entire people in one spectacular linking of hearts, hopes, and minds.[6])

Out of the inspirational milieu of the computer-television impact and the wartime brain-trusting of the RAND Corporation there has also slowly emerged an interesting new technique for obtaining consensus that has Lewinian overtones. Known as the "Delphi" method, it was originally explored by experts concerned with defense and space research but is now being applied to decision-making on crucial domestic social issues. Though it embodies many complexities, the method is essentially one of obtaining consensus on delicate issues through a sequence of carefully planned steps for gathering and then refining expert opinions.[7] One reason for current excitement over the method is that it has worked to provide wise decisions and some action where the old process of committee and commission reports has failed.

Taking these elements, then—the baseline and inspiration of Lewinian theory together with the technological tools of computer processing, television, and the Delphi approach—one might project the following plan for a great President, to begin with his candidacy and campaigning for election to office.

During his campaign, the great President would begin by attacking the many ways in which our present national ordering of expenditures and priorities is distorted by special interests, special privilege, and cultural lag. And he would promise a reordering of these expenditures and priorities that would be more clearly in keeping with both the will of the American people as a whole and with the horrendous needs not of the fictional future or the irrecoverable past, *but of our own time.*

And so let us assume that a majority of Americans feel that this promise is very much to their own personal benefit and this President is elected. Then, within only two weeks after he takes office, a very dramatic series of events occurs, all in one day: In every polling place in every city, town, and hamlet in the nation, and with provision for the overflow, registered voters meet to discuss and to *decide* upon a new, more reasonable national ordering of priorities and expenditures. The lists of priorities for discussion will have been printed in advance in the newspapers. Voter discussants would sit down together, no group larger than eight, with volunteer discussion leaders.[8] At the end of one and a half hours, the leader would begin to direct the thoughts of the group to obtaining some expression of a possible consensus on the reorderings. And at the end of two hours each discussant would use this loose consensus as a baseline for agreement or departure in rating his own priority list, one to ten or whatever, and it would go into the ballot box.

The results would then be computer-processed, like national election returns, with network television coverage, so that by the end of the day the priorities would be known not only nationally, but regionally, by city, and by all the other subdivisions of use to leaders and politicians in their crucial decision-making.[9]

It would be more efficient to do this with something like the Gallup poll, but that would be too asceptic, too remote, too non-involving. There must be this intimate, person-to-person involvement. There must be a provision for some kind of group decision as to a loose consensus preceding the individual commitment. There must be the great excitement, the vicarious involvement, the nationwide extension of these group discussions, and the new feeling for participatory democracy that national television coverage can offer. And there must be the capacity for rapid tabulation and the drama of the cumulating results, state by state, region by region, moving east to west according to the time differences, offered by the mobilizing of computer facilities that is customary in national elections.

What would such a poll show? Those representing special interests, and most of the American elites, would fear a retrogression under these circumstances—and no doubt they would, on one pretext or another, vigorously fight such a move, for this suggestion strikes the central American nerve laid bare by the historic Jefferson-Hamilton "debate." [10] It pits belief in the distrustful necessity of government *for* the people against belief in the trusting necessity of government *by* the people. But the probability is high that this vast technological ploy would show a much greater degree of acceptance by Americans of the need for major priority reorderings and fund shifts than is commonly believed not only by elites and special interests, but, more pointedly, by the leadership of both major national political parties.

This is no mere hunch. A conservative trend to national polls has been highly publicized. But a close reading of Scammon and Wattenberg's *The Real Majority* or other recent poll composites will reveal an intriguing constancy and liberality on the issues of health, education, welfare, peace, and the eradication of poverty.[11] Thus, our suggestion should provide a way for the people to record those sentiments directly, to perhaps their own amazement as well as enlightenment, rather than through the weak and filtered voice of the distant expert. Our conclusion that a more liberative reordering would result is also supported by a considerable body of recent research in experimental social psychology. Growing in part out of the Lewinian tradition, studies of what is known as the *risky-shift* phenomenon have repeatedly found that after discussing an issue, small groups will reach a consensus decision that is significantly more daring than an average of the beliefs of the individual group members *before* discussion.[12]

With the completion of this first step, three important things will have been accomplished. The voters of a nation of 200 million will have, within a single day, participated in a nationwide *group discussion with decision* on national priorities. The President will have obtained, within only a few weeks of taking office, an invaluable comprehensive reading of national sentiment. And the product of this electronic "town meeting" could represent an advancement, *in one day,* of national attitudes to a point of behavioral readiness that could take anywhere from four years to decades to reach otherwise.

The President would then take crucial steps to relate these voter priorities to the realities of resources, and gradually to freeze the results into specific national goals. His Council of Economic Advisers would meet with the director and staff members of the Office of Management and Budget and with a handful of highly respected sociologists, social psychologists, political scientists, and other experts. Within six months this group, using the priority reorderings generated by the people as the baseline but modifying them in terms of expertise, resources, and other constraints, would produce and make public a *hypothetical, nonbinding* reordering of priorities with projected expenditures in each area, possibly along with comprehensive alternate plans. At this stage there would also be made public an initial projection of some of the potential agonies, along with the benefits, that would accompany this great readjustment. Then six months later, at the traditional time for the State of the Union message, the President would report on not one, but two orderings of national priorities.

First he would describe the traditional workaday program in keeping with the customary pressures, according to which the country would be operating during the coming year (this preservation of order and allowing time for adjustment is absolutely essential). And then he would describe a second program—the inspirational product of this new process born of a social emergency. It would still be hypothetical, still nonbinding, but based on this vast attempt to transcend the slippage and leakage and inertia and expense of our customary mechanisms for carrying on democracy— in no way endangering them or superseding them, but acting as a temporary emergency measure to help our nation catch up to itself and to the times.

The President would remind everyone at this time that this special statement of national goals was based on both the clearly stated aspirations of a majority of the American people and the knowledge and experience of the nation's leading experts in the affected fields, and he would pledge himself and his administration to move toward these goals.[13] This, he would caution, would be nothing so unrealistic as an attempt to remake America overnight, *but there would be a definite broad-scale movement proceeding as fast as humanly possible within the limitation of the democratic process and executive power*. Moreover, progress would be measured, reported, and widely publicized at six-month intervals so that everyone might, as with the World Series, "keep score."

With this new-style State of the Union message, the President would have accomplished several additional things fundamental to achieving the national shift of funds and opinions. In Lewinian terms, he would have, first, dramatically raised the national level of aspiration. Moreover, the new level would be established with the highest degree of credibility, since it would be based on a direct expression of the will of the people buttressed by the prestige and power of the Office of the President. And it would be further legitimized by being presented in the traditional State of the Union message. It would have an impact, in short, immeasurably greater than the recommendations of another expert, another research study, another commission, or a partisan political platform, a bill passed by a legislature, a court decision, or of all of these put together. It would be the joint product of a people and their President using the combined power of modern technology and social science to catch up and advance the nation.

Secondly, by this move the President would begin the vital refreezing process. At present the nation boils with dissension over national means and ends that are seen by everybody as either wondrous or horrifying shapes that loom through the mists of our corporate psychic swamp. To the young, the black, the intellectual, and the lower class it seems we are moving too slowly in relation to the shape seen through the mist of a surely better future. To the old, the everyday American, and the middle class it often seems we are moving far too rapidly away from an unimaginably better past. No one has any sense of what is really wanted in specific terms, and so the gap between the aspirations of various groups seems very wide.

A move of this type to establish clear-cut national social goals *through direct participation by all the people* should greatly ease national tensions by reducing fear of the unknown among the conservatives, by forcing economic realism upon the liberals, and by narrowing the seemingly wide gap between the two to reveal that there is a much greater commonality of feeling than is generally believed. Again, this is not idle speculation, but is based on experimental studies, vastly important in quality and number, of Lewin's student Morton Deutsch, the great social psychologist Muzafer Sherif, and many others inspired by them, which have proved that sharing common goals is one of the most powerful means of conflict resolution.[14] This is also, along with an extensive observation of public affairs, part of the background to John Gardner's statements to this effect in several books and in his launching of Common Cause as an organization.

Moreover, national tensions would be further reduced by the fundamental change in the social-psychological situation of the individual American that would be brought about by this process. With the expansion everywhere of bigness and impersonality, at *all* levels of society the individual now tends to feel left out of the decision-making process. Becoming directly involved in setting national goals should give each of us not only the satisfaction of having a voice in settling our own fate, but also the lift of a great feeling of national solidarity that transcends social barriers. As we have seen in many contexts, Lewin's work clearly indicates that a change of this type in one's personal situation can result in dramatic reductions in tension, frustration, and aggression, and an increase in productivity and happiness.

By the end of the first year, the cornerstone will have been laid, but it would remain just that—another lonely monument to aspiration on a bare field—unless this is seen as only the beginning. For the major task of freezing attitudes at a high level and effecting *behavioral* change lies ahead, and much of it must be accomplished within the remaining three years of the great President's term of office (for, of course, he may not be re-elected!). There are many well-developed social mechanisms available to him for compelling rapid movement toward these vital social goals. In general, he would be guided by a strategy all good politicians use by second nature, but Lewin's insight could be used to bolster the age-old method: That is, the President would work diligently to lower resistance to the desired ends while readying and using only as much force as is clearly needed to produce measurable movement toward the selected social goals.

One powerful means for producing behavioral change is, of course, that old standby, taxation. Here the President would only need to greatly intensify trends already in motion to bring tax policy more in line with social need. Luxury purchases and production would be as rapidly and heavily taxed as practicable—the third car, the pleasure-cruiser, excessive foreign travel. Meanwhile, tax-cut incentives would be used to encourage industrial shifts into social-needs areas, to generate jobs for minorities, to encourage the move by enlightened (expert *plus* community-controlled) developers into housing and urban development, and to encourage private individual "haves" to work in areas of have-not needs such as teaching, child care, and so on.

Should President Nixon fail to gain revenue-sharing, the great President would also be wise to force through Congress economist Walter Heller's proposal, first advanced during the Kennedy years, for using the Federal tax-collection power to collect and then rebate excess revenue primarily to the desperate cities and secondarily to the states—but with strings attached. The money would be used (given, or withheld, or withdrawn) to alternately lure and force rapid movement toward the approved national goals.

The panoply offered by such methods is marvelous indeed—to the initiate, tax policy alone can be like Byzantine art in the grandeur of its frozen force and soul-searching ingenuity. However, it lifts few hearts, and specific means of this type are well known to students of government, so we will not pursue them further. There is, however, another means of lowering resistance to social change which, over the centuries, has been the inspirational core to great leadership. To this we would like to direct our final attention.

Though he is seldom given credit for the move these days, in his inaugural address President Nixon did a wise thing in calling for a national lowering of voices. He was, in effect, trying to lower a national level of aspiration and expectations that had, in many quarters, raced dangerously far ahead of the nation's capacity to realize them. Under Presidents Kennedy and Johnson the national aspiration level had sky-rocketed, while the Vietnam war, defense needs, and the space program were swiftly draining away the necessary investment of money and leadership. Thus some of President Nixon's policies seem to have been, at first, directed to the realistic objective of lowering the national aspiration level in the hope that high tension levels would also drop. But unfortunately this policy seems to have coincided with the very intense desire of the power-possessing haves to gain domestic peace at the expense of the seemingly powerless have-nots. So what may have been initiated as a wise step forward rather soon became an insular step backward, serving not the interests of the nation as a whole, but the interests of one color and one class.

It is true there was no great wave of exploding cities, as in 1968, and this can undoubtedly be attributed in part to the lowering of the aspiration level. *But a people given nothing positive or meaningful to aspire to becomes a people without hope.* And a hopeless people is a frustrated people. And as the Lewinian work demonstrates, frustration channels energy in two highly destructive directions. It can lead to regression—to apathy, infantile behavior, less sophisticated thought, to the withdrawal and turning off that seems to underlie much of the great increase in drug usage among Americans. Or it can lead to aggression—to the urge that may not presently be exploding in our cities but is most certainly expressing itself in the general rise in crime and violence out of society's "lower levels," in the polarizing of the country on all issues on society's "higher levels," and in the incredible poisoning of practically all our forums and organs of so-called free discussion.

The great President will learn from this dismal episode in our history and begin to raise the national level of aspiration. Ideally he would do this along the lines we have indicated, by directly enlisting the people in a process designed to achieve realistic and measurable progress. Additionally, he will have at his disposal another means of raising the national aspiration level that history has proven can also be used to lower resistance to change: The launching of large, well-planned, exciting interventions, both new programs and reforms that would enlist broad interests and sympathies. These programs would be of the type associated with the two periods of the greatest governmental concentration of brain power directed to domestic needs—the first two terms of Franklin Roosevelt and the aborted grandeur of the Kennedy years.

The possibilities are endless and have been proposed and reproposed—and also co-opted and debased. Building upon William James's original proposal and the success of the CCC and the Peace Corps, a National Service Corps could be launched to serve as an alternative to military service, enlisting blacks and whites, the idle old as well as the idle young, putting the skills of the haves to the needs of the have-nots (and vice versa). Or any number of other steps could be taken: Whitney Young's Marshall Plan for the black and white poor; an amplified negative income tax/ guaranteed annual income/family assistance plan, out of Milton Friedman and Patrick Moynihan; or the proposal made by that old New Dealer Rexford Tugwell for a revised Constitution, to which the Center for the Study of Democratic Institutions has given so much thought; and on and on, but with one crucial qualification. Again mindful of Kurt Lewin's liberating social psychology—and Louis Brandeis's great feeling for strengthening the small social unit—the purpose of the big Federal intervention must be to force and support the liberation of the initiative, power, and creativity of the individual and the small group. Otherwise we seem doomed to squeak our last beneath the fat foot of bureaucracy. And though it is heresy to make such a suggestion during a lackluster time when both government and scholarship serve a most repellent pudding and would have us believe that all pudding is the same, the fact remains that how the pudding tastes depends greatly on who mixes it, who cooks it, who serves it, and under what name it appears on the menu. That is, good social interventions, like good food, are a matter of *style* of preparation and presentation as well as a matter of *caring*.

There is one last observation to be made about our present divisions—and a thought to suggest the urgency of considerations such as these for the great President, wherever he may now be drawing himself together for the task of our time.

The Lewin, Lippitt, and White studies of authoritarian, democratic, and laissez-faire leadership styles and social climates may have something of importance to say about the present divisions between black and white and young and old. The studies of the authoritarian situation and of the workers without representation showed that aggression and scapegoating rose as, in both instances, the individual felt left out of the decision-making process and was thus essentially powerless. Our present situation suggests that while older Americans perceive the young as enjoying an unparalleled and dangerous freedom and abusing the privileges of an indulgent democracy, the young perceive their own situation as being radically different.

They often see themselves as living not in freedom, not in a democracy, but actually in a dictatorship. Unwanted and restricted from the labor force, expected to remain in school until at least the age of twenty-two, they must remain dependent on their parents far too long and so are frustrated by a lack of the basic power and influence associated with being respectably money-productive. Even more fundamental, they feel that power over life itself seems to have been taken from them by an arbitrary overlord: They may be drafted to die in one of the nation's most degrading wars, and most of them cannot even vote to change this. Thus they see themselves as being filled to the brim with information about democracy, but, as it affects them, living in a functional dictatorship. Moreover, this must sometimes be seen as the worst of all possible dictatorships, because the dictator is no fine flesh-and-blood Hitler one can roundly despise, but a free-floating presence that is everywhere.

These feelings are particularly intense among black youth, for to everything that affects the young is added the pain and the age-old burden of the black's historical denial. Moreover, the situation of many blacks of all ages is similar, for despite all the talk of improvement, they find themselves in the same rat-infested buildings, jobless and hopeless, preyed upon by the thief, the rapist, the killer, and the dope-pusher. They, too, must perceive themselves as living in a functional dictatorship in which the dictator (the Man, Mr. Charlie) is still everywhere.

But it does not end here, for all too often this is the perceptual world of the rest of our colored minorities—of the Indian, the Chicano, and the Puerto Rican. Nor does it end there, for this is becoming the perceptual world of many lower-middle-class and lower-class whites in America, who not only feel squeezed by the rising black but who are becoming aware of the injustice of the handicap of their *own* ethnicity in a land that is supposed to celebrate these glorious differences. And increasingly it is also the perceptual world of that segment of so much grace and denied wisdom, now everywhere fearful, our old people.

Should this increasingly *major* portion of our population be given the sense that they do indeed live in a democracy, in which they do indeed have a place, and do share in the decision-making, and do have a voice in controlling their own destiny, it seems likely that at last the soul-searing and mind-shattering tension which is the America of our time will, like a hurricane blown out, come to rest. And the more productive, powerful, and comfortable white middle class—all of us between the ages of twenty-five and sixty-five—will at last enjoy the peace and quiet and freedom from fear that we, *along with everyone else,* so passionately desire.

Acknowledgments

I was born into a white, Anglo-Saxon, Protestant family of some affluence and was blessed with more than an average share of brains. For years I felt indebted for these gifts, so often misused, and then the message came that the note was due.

I had grown up loving America. In one capacity or another I had come to know much of this land and its people, and always had found far more about it to value than to deplore. But through the exploration of our history which this book reflects, I came to see that what the whites who possessed this land have done to its black, red, brown, and yellow people is a monstrous crime.

This book, then, is to some extent an atonement for whiteness, but only very, very slightly. The guilt I feel as a white is nothing compared to the rage I feel as a human being over the inhumanity of our racism and over what men and women—mainly white, but of all colors, and certainly all ages—are now doing in their ignorance and their insensitivity to something that transcends race—to the idea and the reality of America in history, to what this great nation has represented to the aspirations of man.

I tried to suppress these feelings and, in the interest of science, to be rational and objective in writing this book, but at heart I was driven by this unbearable rage. I read the newspapers, and alternately I have wanted to weep or to do someone in. And so out of some torment—and without the benefit of a foundation grant or research assistants, using time left after a full-time job, attending school at night, and stealing time and money that would otherwise have gone to meet the needs of my family—I wrote this book to obtain some relief. And so every bit of help I received came to mean very much to me.

For reviewing portions of what was, at times, a very odd manuscript, and for their helpful suggestions, I want to thank John Hope Franklin, C. Vann Woodward, Martin Duberman, Eric Goldman, Benjamin Quarles, Philip Foner, David Brion Davis, Saunders Redding, Whitney Young, Jr., David Rosenhan, Silvan Tomkins, Robert Rosenthal, and the late Abraham Maslow. I take sole responsibility for the end product, of course.

For the necessary undergraduate and graduate education, I am grateful to Francis Gramlich, who introduced me to Freud and Marx, and to the memory of Ted Karwoski, who introduced me to experimental psychology, so many years ago now at Dartmouth, and also to Professors Feldman, Bender, Allen, and Bear in those early days; and to Molly Harrower, Mary Henle, Peter Berger, Nathan Brody, Howard Gruber, Joseph Greenbaum, Arthur Vidich, Emil Oestereicher, Earl Davis, and Nathan Kogan of the New School for Social Research, all of whom helped move an aging social dropout along toward his doctorate.

I am especially grateful to the Educational Testing Service and to Princeton, New Jersey, for providing such a pleasant home, occupationally and socially, while this book was being written. In both places more people than could be named were helpful, if only to ask how the book was coming. Of specific aid in the survey which, by field-testing many possibilities and then using the Delphi method of narrowing the choice, actually established the title, were Jane Wirsig, Orville Palmer, Winnie Proctor, Eldon Park, Rod Hartnett, John Centra, Jerry Bracey, Missy Tanaka, Walter Emmerich, Tom White, Hack Rhett, Ron Flaugher, Joe Boyd, Dinah Anastasio, Valerie Hartshorne, Nancy Beck, Holly Welke, Bill Hall, David Brodsky, and Alice Irby. Also I am grateful for readings and encouragement by Dick and Huguette Roberts, Dick Lidz, the Ritcheys, the Bannons, Orville Palmer, Plato Roussos, Chuck Stone, Suleika Conover, Elaine Kirsch, Katherine Moore, and W. M. Bollenbach III.

I am particularly indebted to Emma Epps, Henry Drewry, Sharon Campbell, Al Durrant, Bob Martin, and Clifford Moore for helping to open my eyes to the realities of black life in Princeton, which led me to seek the roots of our sickness in American history. I owe much to that small, graceful oasis, the Princeton Public Library, and to the ETS and Firestone libraries, and I am greatly indebted to Tom Hartman for field-testing the manuscript with students at Livingston College and Sarah Lawrence College. Also, I wish to thank the following members of my family and relatives who helped with encouragement and in the title survey: Mr. and Mrs. P. E. Loye, in Vermont; Mrs. C. P. Randall, in Minnesota; Mrs. Jack Seabury, in Montana; Mrs. J. H. Price and Mrs. Frank Henslee, in Oklahoma; and Mrs. D. A. Hall, in Princeton.

I am especially grateful to Ernie Anastasio for good advice, readings, and crucial early as well as continuing encouragement; to Dan Landis for good advice and taking on the incredible task of reading the whole book in manuscript; to Sam Barnett for some key suggestions and providing me with the best of all possible contacts with blackness; and, most of all, to Nat Hartshorne, who provided the kind of support unique to this writer, editor, and great human being.

I am also greatly indebted to the publishing professionals who made this into an actual book: to my agents, Martha Winston and Emilie Jacobsen of Curtis Brown, Ltd.; to editors Evan Thomas, Ned Chase, and Alfred Prettyman for early encouragement; and to my editor and publisher, George Brockway, and the remarkable Georgia Griggs, who together took it up and made something of it, working to shape it to its present form with such great good sense, good taste, and understanding.

Lastly, I am grateful to my wife, Billy, and to my children—Jenella, Kathryn, Chris, and Jonathan—for their support, encouragement, and sense of humor during a difficult time.

Reference Notes

Detailed information about the works mentioned in these notes may be found in the Bibliography. See the Bibliographical Notes for an orientation to basic references for each chapter and for areas of general interest throughout the book.

CHAPTER 1

1. Colonization references are given in the Reference Notes for Chapter 6. The sociologist who proposed colonization 150 years too late was Charles Loomis, outgoing president of the American Sociological Association in 1967. Although his remarks were not racist in intent, Loomis

was scored by Martin Luther King in an important address to the American Psychological Association later the same year for suggesting that "the valleys of the Andes mountains would be an ideal place for American Negroes to build a second Israel" and that "the United States Government should negotiate for a remote but fertile land in Ecuador, Peru or Bolivia for this relocation." See King, "The Role of the Behavioral Scientist in the Civil Rights Movement."
2. See Chapter 17.
3. See Chapters 16 and 23.
4. See Raison, ed., *Founding Fathers of Social Science*.
5. See Bibliographical Note 2.
6. See Bibliographical Note 1.

CHAPTER 2

1. Among the sources for this portrayal of a slave seizure are Silberman, *Crisis in Black and White*, pp. 82–84; Elkins, *Slavery*, pp. 27–52; and Duberman, *In White America*, p. 21.
2. This reconstruction of the mind of a part-time slave broker is based on Silberman, Elkins, Duberman, Davis, *The Problem of Slavery in Western Culture*, Jordan, *White Over Black*, and Franklin, *From Slavery to Freedom*.
3. A conclusion reached by Thomas Jefferson in 1781.
4. This important psychological matter is explored in detail by W. D. Jordan and David Brion Davis in their important studies of the roots of white attitudes toward blacks.
5. Franklin, p. 145.
6. The 250 estimate is Herbert Apthecker's, in *American Negro Slave Revolts*. W. D. Jordan, however, estimates that only a dozen could properly be called revolts (p. 113).
7. Jordan, p. 117.
8. Vecoli, *The People of New Jersey*, p. 45.
9. Jordan, p. 118.
10. From a story reporting on the 1751 Act by William M. Dwyer in the *Trenton Times Advertiser*, March 3, 1968.

CHAPTER 3

1. For a good introduction to Pavlov and behaviorism, see Miller, *Psychology*, pp. 173–212. Also see Mednick, *Learning*, and Hilgard and Marquis, *Conditioning and Learning*.
2. Watson's own account of this experiment is exceptional in the literature for its blunt and engaging clarity. See Watson and Rayner, "Conditioned Emotional Reactions."
3. Dollard and Miller, *Personality and Psychotherapy*.
4. James, *Principles of Psychology*, pp. 293–94.
5. Berger, *Invitation to Sociology*, pp. 93–110.
6. Pettigrew, *A Profile of the Negro American*, pp. 6–8.

CHAPTER 4

1. The Woolman sketch is based on Woolman's writings (Jordan, pp. 272–75); Cady, *John Woolman*; and Davis, *The Problem of Slavery in Western Culture*, which ends with Woolman's vision.

2. The Woolman quotes in this chapter are from Jordan, pp. 273–75. The classic source is *The Journal and Essays of John Woolman*, pp. 334–39.

3. Particularly telling was this passage from a speech Gardner made in December 1967 shortly before his resignation as Secretary of Health, Education, and Welfare: "We are in deep trouble as a nation. And history is not going to deal kindly with a rich nation that will not tax itself to cure its miseries."

4. See Chapter 9 for cognition; Chapters 5 and 11 for modeling; and Chapter 19 for expectancy.

5. Good accounts of both operant conditioning and programmed learning by Skinner will be found in Coopersmith, ed., *Frontiers of Psychological Research: Readings from the Scientific American*.

6. *Ibid.*, p. 357. So prolific was Benezet that Jordan calls him a "virtual one-man abolition society."

7. Vecoli, p. 49.

8. Franklin, pp. 131–35. Franklin gives the full account of Washington's dilemma, a farce of epic proportions involving Benjamin Franklin and other well-known figures.

9. Katz, *Teacher's Guide to American Negro History*, p. 59.

10. The Jefferson quotes in this chapter are from a convenient appendix to Duberman, *In White America*, pp. 88–95.

11. Franklin, p. 142.

CHAPTER 5

1. A standard source is Freud's *Complete Introductory Lectures;* also good on the broad implications of the ego ideal are Flügel's *Man, Morals, and Society* and Fromm's *Man for Himself*.

2. Their positions are articulated in Erikson's *Childhood and Society* and Fromm's *The Art of Loving*.

3. *Existentialist Psychology,* edited by Rollo May and including an article by Rogers, is the best short introduction to this view.

4. Rosenhan, "Some Origins of Concern for Others," in Mussen *et al.*, eds., *Trends and Issues in Developmental Psychology*, pp. 134–53.

5. Bryan, "Models and Helping."

6. Writing about Gestalt psychology for the general reader is rather difficult to find, except in bits and scraps in advanced texts. See Kohler, *The Task of Gestalt Psychology*, or Hilgard and Bowers, *Theories of Learning*, pp. 222–57. Two great Gestalt classics are Wertheimer's *Productive Thinking* and Kohler's *The Mentality of Apes*.

7. See Chapters 25 and 26.

8. See Bibliographical Note 9.

9. An extensive and fascinating body of research exists in communications,

one of the key names being that of the late Carl Hovland at Yale University. Offshoots from the Hovland-Yale group have made wide use of balance theories in studies of the techniques of persuasion and defense against persuasion, *e.g.*, articles by Scott, Cohen, Brehm, Rosenberg, McGuire, Abelson, and Kelman in Backman and Secord, eds., *Problems in Social Psychology*. See also Brown, *Social Psychology*.

CHAPTER 6

1. One of the most important of the early-day black leaders, Richard Allen, was the main founder.
2. Davis, *American Negro Reference Book,* p. 21.
3. Vecoli, p. 45. Jordan, p. 92, tells of the same pattern in North Carolina and Virginia.
4. Vecoli, p. 45.
5. Franklin, pp. 161–62.
6. "The Negro in New Jersey," an unsigned WPA pamphlet issued in 1938, p. 8. Also see Jordan, pp. 414–26, and Frazier, *The Negro Church in America,* which is the best single guide and lists other good sources.
8. Alexander, *A History of Colonization on the Western Coast of Africa,* p. 80. Earlier colonization moves and attitudes are covered by Jordan, pp. 546–69.
7. Franklin, pp. 162–63, and Jordan, pp. 422–23.
9. See Franklin, all texts cited in Chapter 10, and the extensive accounts in Alexander, Hageman, and Jordan.
10. Jordan, pp. 28–43, summarizes such early-American black and white sexual lore.
11. The Jefferson quotes are from Duberman, *In White America,* pp. 88–95. Also see Jefferson, *Notes on the State of Virginia,* pp. 137–43.
12. Jordan, pp. 464–68.
13. *Ibid.,* pp. 550–51.
14. Hageman, *History of Princeton and Its Institutions,* p. 328.
15. Alexander. The quotes are from the introduction.

CHAPTER 7

1. Jones, *Life and Work of Sigmund Freud,* p. 222. For general references to Freud, see Bibliographical Note 8.
2. Freud, *The Interpretation of Dreams,* preface to the first edition.
3. For Kant, see Durant's *The Story of Philosophy* or Castell's *An Introduction to Modern Philosophy;* for Pareto, see his *Sociological Writings* or Parsons *et. al.,* eds., *Theories of Society;* for Merton, see Berger's *Invitation to Sociology,* p. 40; for a brilliant presentation of all this in systems-analytical terms, see Boulding's *The Impact of the Social Sciences,* p. 60 ff.
4. For a good exploration of this debunking attitude in sociology, see Berger, pp. 38–43.
5. See Erikson's *Young Man Luther* or *Gandhi's Truth*.

6. Cleaver's *Soul on Ice,* for example, has a chapter that appears to be the mental offspring of a mating of D. H. Lawrence's abstract sexologizing with the symbolist dramaturgy of Edward Albee and possibly the sociology of C. Wright Mills.
7. Besides the extensive accounts in Grier and Cobb's *Black Rage,* black sexual disturbances are probed by Kenneth Clark in *Dark Ghetto* and by sociologist Lee Rainwater in the brilliant essay, "Crucible of Identity," in Parsons and Clark, eds., *The Negro American.*
8. Lindzey and Hall's *Theories of Personality* offers a particularly clear presentation of fixation and regression, both the theory and the supporting research.
9. Erikson, *Childhood and Society,* p. 256.
10. Rainwater, "Crucible of Identity."
11. Erikson, *Childhood and Society,* pp. 270–71.
12. *Ibid.,* pp. 241–42.

CHAPTER 8
1. St. Clair Drake in Davis ed., *The American Negro Reference Book,* p. 662.
2. *Ibid.*
3. Salk, *A Layman's Guide to Negro History,* p. 5.
4. Franklin, Chapter 8 (particularly pp. 206–7). An even better source is Franklin's *Life* magazine feature, "The Search for a Black Past." From this source: " 'The time has been,' wrote a planter in 1849, 'that a farmer could kill up and wear out one Negro to buy another, but it is not so now. Negroes are too high in proportion to the price of cotton, and it behooves those who own them to make them last as long as possible.' "
5. Collier, *Indians of the Americas,* pp. 121–30.
6. See Farb, *Man's Rise to Civilization as Shown by the Indians of North America,* pp. 250–53, for a quick general summary of Cherokee advancement; for more detail, see Chapters 5, 6, and 7 in Van Every's *Disinherited.* Most accounts are of the Eastern Cherokee; the details in our text are from obscure sources and personal research among the Western Cherokee in Tahlequah, Oklahoma.
7. Collier, p. 124.
8. Elkins, p. 18.
9. The *Narrative* is available in Signet and Collier paperbacks. The Douglass quotes in this chapter are from the Signet edition.
10. Hortense Powdermaker's remarkable *Stranger and Friend* describes the participant-observer method in the living terms of an anthropologist's study of black life in the American South and in African copper mines. An exceptionally fine exploration in philosophical terms is found in Bruyn's *The Human Perspective in Sociology.*
11. Douglass, p. 22.
12. *Ibid.,* pp. 28, 59–60, 84–85.

13. *Ibid.*, pp. 24–25, 41, 68.
14. *Ibid.*, pp. 74–75.
15. *Ibid.*, p. 23.
16. *Ibid.*, pp. 61–62.

CHAPTER 9

1. For general references on cognition, see Bibliographical Note 10.
2. The McClelland-Atkinson and Bruner experiments are recounted in Beardslee and Wertheimer, *Readings in Perception;* also see Dember, *Psychology of Perception,* and Hochberg, *Perception.*
3. The term has been largely abandoned by psychologists because of a re-search controversy over what it means. We are using it, however, be-cause no better descriptive term for the phenomenon has emerged.
4. See Bruner, "On Perceptual Readiness."
5. Brown, *Social Psychology,* p. 756. Chapter 13 of Brown's work is an advanced discussion of conformity research. Also relevant here are Chapter 11, on cognitive dissonance work, and Chapter 14, on collective behavior, which includes studies of lynching, race riots, and the Black Muslims.
6. Bartlett, *Remembering.*
7. See Brown, pp. 756–57.
8. See Kohler's *The Mentality of Apes* or Wertheimer's *Productive Thinking.*
9. See Hebb, "The American Revolution," and Razran, "Semantic Conditioning" and "The Orienting Reflex."
10. Evans, *Conversations with Carl Jung,* pp. 27–28.
11. Unfortunately, one of the best presentations of S-R research in this context is Arthur Jensen's "Social Class and Verbal Learning" (see Chapter 17). For anyone wanting to explore the ingenuity of S-R work at its best, we recommend four key papers: Razran (a summary of Soviet work) and Kendler, both in Harper; Hull, in Staats; and Osgood, in Hollander and Hunt.
12. Allport, *The Nature of Prejudice,* pp. 192, 196, 197, or Lindzey, ed., *Social Psychology Handbook,* pp. 1023–25.
13. Stagner and Karowski, *Psychology,* p. 404.
14. The original Lewin paper on this is rather hellish; more readable is the important elaboration of approach-avoidance ideas in Dollard and Miller, *Personality and Psychotherapy,* pp. 352–68.
15. See Olds, "Pleasure Centers in the Brain." Another excellent source on this type of finding is Wooldridge's *Machinery of the Brain.*
16. See Osgood and Tannenbaum, *The Measurement of Meaning,* and Os-good, "On the Nature of Meaning" and "Cognitive Dynamics in the Conduct of Human Affairs."
17. Woodward, *The Burden of Southern History,* p. 53.
18. Jordan, p. 415.
19. Elkins, p. 209.

20. This general picture is from Allport's classic "The Historical Background of Modern Social Psychology."

21. See Durkheim on solidarity in Parsons *et al.,* eds., *Theories of Society,* pp. 208–13.

22. Sherif, "On the Relevance of Social Psychology," in *The American Psychologist,* February 1970, p. 247.

23. Asch, "Opinions and Social Research," contains a particularly good account of this experiment.

24. Willis, "The Basic Response Modes of Conformity, Independence, and Anticonformity."

25. This account is based on Pettigrew, "Personality and Sociocultural factors in Intergroup Attitudes," which also describes the other studies referred to.

26. The conclusions ending this chapter are based on considerably more than the Pettigrew study, of course, and are our own, not necessarily Pettigrew's.

CHAPTER 10

1. Fladeland, *James Gillespie Birney,* p. 90. This is the basic reference for all matters on Birney in this chapter, unless otherwise noted.

2. Thomas, *Slavery Attacked,* p. 1.

3. Franklin, p. 247. Lane students "put their views into practice by going out into the community to organize groups to assist the Negro; and they instructed Negro youth and participated in the dangerous activities of the Underground Railroad."

4. Fladeland, p. 90.

5. Bernays, *Public Relations,* p. 42; also Franklin, pp. 246, 266.

6. Franklin, p. 244.

7. For two diametrically opposed evaluations of John Brown, see Foner, *Selections from the Writings of Frederick Douglass,* pp. 31–32, and Woodward, *The Burden of Southern History,* pp. 40–57.

8. Foner, *The Life and Writings of Frederick Douglass,* p. 142.

9. See Fladeland; Foner, *ibid.,* especially pp. 136–54; and Thomas, *The Liberator: William Lloyd Garrison.* Also see an exceptionally good study by Howard Zinn, "Abolitionists, Freedom-Riders, and the Tactics of Agitation," pp. 417–51, in Duberman, ed., *The Antislavery Vanguard.*

10. Foner, *ibid.,* Vol. II, p. 50.

11. Thomas, *Slavery Attacked,* p. 83.

CHAPTER 11

1. The quotes throughout this chapter are from Tomkins, "The Psychology of Commitment," in Tomkins and Izard, *Affect, Cognition, and Personality,* pp. 159, 160, 167, 168, 169, 170. This is the best source for psychologists and venturesome social scientists. A more generally available source is Duberman, ed., *The Antislavery Vanguard.*

2. See Rosenhan, "Some Origins of Concern for Others."

3. Keniston's *The Uncommitted* and *Young Radicals* are good beyond superlatives. See Bibliographical Notes 7 and 20.
4. Feuer's *Conflict of Generations* has been taken to task by some critics on this point. However one feels about its Freudian analysis, the book contains many excellent things, particularly the last chapter on the young Marx's feeling for the concept of alienation, which provides an important tie between the young black and the young white outsider today.
5. The most extensive theoretical and experimental work relevant here is that of Kurt Lewin and his students. "Leaving the field" is a familiar option in Lewinian conflict analysis (see Lewin, *A Dynamic Theory of Personality*, pp. 122–26, or the Lewin chapter in Lindzey and Hall). Among other relevant references, see Abelson, "Modes of Resolution of Belief Dilemmas"; Kelman, "The Induction of Action and Attitude Change"; and Festinger, "An Introduction to the Theory of Dissonance."
6. See B. F. Skinner's chapter in Coopersmith.
7. Essential reading in this age is Gandhi's autobiography or a good biography such as Louis Fischer's *The Life of Mahatma Gandhi*, as well as Erikson's profound study, *Gandhi's Truth*, which may probe more deeply into the question of human survival than any other work of our time.
8. For violence and nonviolence references, see Bibliographical Note 20.

CHAPTER 12
1. Quarles, *Lincoln and the Negroes*, p. 73. In general, unless otherwise noted Carl Sandburg's classic work on Lincoln is our source for background on Lincoln in this chapter.
2. Quarles, pp. 115–18.
3. *Ibid.*, p. 119.
4. *Ibid.*, p. 118.
5. Foner, *Selections from the Writings of Frederick Douglass*, p. 18.
6. *Ibid.*, p. 20.
7. *Ibid.*, p. 8.
8. Bennett's *Black Power U.S.A.*, pp. 26–33, presents the anti-Lincoln view fashionable among militant blacks of the late 1960s. An editor of *Ebony* and an excellent writer of black history, Bennett has been criticized for his ideological one-sidedness on Lincoln. White Lincoln worshipers, however, probably needed this reverse-biased jolt. Black historian Benjamin Quarles' *Lincoln and the Negroes* is a balanced account. The best perspective, pro and con, however, still seems to be that of Douglass' brilliant, moving "Oration in Memory of Abraham Lincoln," parts of which are quoted in this chapter.
9. Sandburg, *Abraham Lincoln*, p. 200.
10. See Chapter 19 for an explanation of thinking and research on expectation (or level of aspiration, in Lewinian terms).
11. Foner, *The Life and Writings of Frederick Douglass*, Vol. IV, p. 312.
12. *Ibid.*, pp. 313, 315, 318–19.
13. *Ibid.*, p. 320.

CHAPTER 13

1. For the story of Jenny and Karl Marx, see Wilson, *To the Finland Station,* pp. 205–8, 217–21, 333–34. For general references on Marx, see Bibliographical Note 14.

2. See Wilson, "Abraham Lincoln: The Union as Religious Mysticism." Of interest in this context is Wilson's report that, in addition to Darwin and Spencer, Lincoln had read Feuerbach, who greatly influenced the young Marx. Wilson also ascribes to Lincoln a Hegelian-Marxian feeling for history as a force in human affairs (p. 194). This seems to be pushing an enthusiasm a bit far.

3. Wilson, *To the Finland Station,* p. 127. This quote is the famous last thesis on Feuerbach, a short list of thoughts that, once they have been unraveled mentally, are one of Marx's most impressive productions.

4. Arendt, *On Revolution,* pp. 15–16. This is a point that many contemporary Marxians would boggle at. However, Marx's real view of the American revolution and the American social experiment holds many surprises. Much of what he had to say about the United States was gathered for purposes of propaganda as well as scholarship into *The Civil War in the United States,* which is chiefly the Marx-Engels correspondence during the incredible years when they were serving as correspondents for the *New York Herald Tribune* at five dollars per article. Readers seeking a lurid exposé of America will find that Marx actually has little with real bite to offer, for he was still mainly fascinated with the United States as "the highest form of popular government, till now realized." Later, however, he was to call it "the model country of the democratic imposture." See Wilson, *To the Finland Station,* pp. 322–26.

5. Most discussions of dialectical processes are distressingly foggy. The most solid and readable source I have found is Sorokin's *Sociological Theories of Today,* pp. 462–525, which in the end conveys what it is all about by summarizing Gurvitch, Sartre, and many other dialecticians.

6. This is most sharply conveyed by Marx's remarkable shorthand in "Theses on Feuerbach" and in parts of "The German Ideology" and "Economic and Philosophical Manuscripts," which may be found in Fromm's *Marx's Concept of Man.*

7. Although basic to Marx's view, the class-struggle dynamic seems to me only occasionally useful in interpreting American history. One problem is that Marx's view, based on another time and other settings, is too crude to fit the changing complexities of American life. Of the classical theorists, Max Weber's much more sophisticated view of class and caste complexities is more useful for grounding purposes. Also see St. Clair Drake's paper in Parsons and Clark.

8. Kaufman, *Hegel: A Reinterpretation,* p. 153.

9. Miller *et al., Plans and the Structure of Behavior.* Thanks to Miller's deft gift of expression, this is a masterpiece of communicating modern computer-oriented psychology. It takes several pages to explain TOTE, but it's worth it.

10. The Communist Manifesto makes most of these points.

11. In this connection, the life of Ho Chi Minh is instructive. Although Ho was enough of an enthusiast for the American Dream to pattern the Declaration of Independence of North Vietnam after ours, he lived in Harlem for a time during World War I and what chiefly impressed him about the American Reality were "the barbarites and ugliness of American capitalism, the Ku Klux Klan mobs, the lynching of Negroes." In 1924, out of these experiences, came his "La Race Noire" (The Black Race), which assailed racial practices in America and Europe and was given worldwide circulation by the Communists out of Moscow. See Whitman, "Ho Chi Minh."

12. Marx, *Capital,* p. 823.

13. Fanon, *The Wretched of the Earth,* pp. 73, 79, 97, 154, 313. Sartre's introduction to this work is a masterpiece, really the best statement of the antiwhite vision, discussed in Chapter 24 of this book, that I know of, by anyone, black or white. Fanon then seems disappointing. It is as though Sartre has already drained the distillate of his meaning; Fanon's insights seem like goldfish glimpsed through muddy water, and one tires of looking. His short chapter on mental disorders is compelling, however, and his very short conclusion is one of the most eloquent and moving statments of the basic humanism within revolutionary aspirations that I have read.

14. Fromm, *Marx's Concept of Man,* p. 24.

15. Durkheim, *The Rules of Sociological Method,* pp. 2, 5.

16. Inkeles' *What Is Sociology?,* pp. 37–39, gives a concise statement of these contrasting models. For general references on models and theories, see Bibliographical Note 15.

17. See Hunt, "Traditional Personality Theory in the Light of Recent Evidence," and Allport, "The Open System in Personality Theory," in Hollander and Hunt.

18. This liberative-versus-repressive-forces dynamic has been perceived working in various historical contexts by Pareto, Sartre, Arthur Schlesinger Sr. and Jr., and others.

CHAPTER 14

1. Du Bois, *Souls of Black Folk,* pp. 24–25. As indicated in the text, somewhat over half of Du Bois's great essay, "The Dawn of Freedom," is reproduced here. His classic *Black Reconstruction* should also be mentioned. Du Bois has been widely criticized for distorting the facts of Reconstruction to fit the Marxian class-struggle view. While this is certainly true, Du Bois's interpretation is, nevertheless, clearer in other respects than those presented in more respected works on the era by pre-1950 historians, and it is more readable. Particularly refreshing is Du Bois's forthright rating of his various sources in the bibliography on

their degree of prejudice. See Bibliographical Note 16 for other Reconstruction references.

2. This point is made by Staughton Lynd in his excellent collection, *Reconstruction*, which besides the full text of Du Bois's "Dawn of Freedom" includes another superb essay on Reconstruction written by Du Bois in 1910.

3. Du Bois, *Souls of Black Folk*, pp. 28–41.

CHAPTER 15

1. Parsons *et al.*, eds., *Theories of Society*, p. 141.

2. Carneiro, *The Evolution of Society*, p. 46. This is a good re-evaluation of Spencer.

3. Pareto, *Sociological Writings*, p. 104.

4. See Tomkins, "The Psychology of Knowledge," and the Mannheim selections in Parsons's *Theories of Society*.

5. Freud's speculations about the working of Eros and Thanatos will be found in *Beyond the Pleasure Principle* and *Civilization and Its Discontents*.

6. See the account in Marrow, *The Practical Theorist*, or Lindzey and Hall, pp. 240–47.

7. See Dollard *et al.*, *Frustration and Aggression*; Megargee and Hokanson, eds., *The Dynamics of Aggression*, pp. 22–31; and Berkowitz, *Aggression*, p. 48.

8. A good short account of this study is in Megargee and Hokanson, pp. 66–73. See Bibliographical Note 20. Another account is in Berkowitz, p. 58, a comprehensive compendium of frustration-aggression research by a leading authority.

CHAPTER 16

1. See Watson and Rayner, "Conditioned Emotional Reactions."

2. Woodward, *The Strange Career of Jim Crow*, p. 23.

3. Franklin, p. 326.

4. Woodward, *The Burden of Southern History*, pp. 63–64.

5. See Heilbroner's *The Worldly Philosophers*.

6. Historian James McPherson's absorbing "Many Abolitionists Fought On After the Civil War" is the source for this statement and many others in this chapter.

7. *Ibid.*, p. 14.

8. *Ibid.*, p. 15.

9. Bennett, pp. 412–15.

10. Following the pioneering work of Kurt Lewin and his students, described in Chapters 23 and 24, the study of leadership has become an important aspect of social psychology. Articles by Hollander, Bavelas, Fiedler, French, Raven, Katz, and Cartwright in Hollander and Hunt are good examples of contemporary emphases.

11. Details of these failures are from Franklin, Foner, Woodward, and, particularly, McPherson.
12. McPherson, pp. 16–18.
13. See Hunt, "Traditional Personality Theory in the Light of Recent Evidence," and Allport, "The Open System in Personality Theory," in Hollander and Hunt.
14. Woodward, *The Strange Career of Jim Crow*, pp. 97–99.
15. *Ibid.*, pp. 100, 102.
16. McPherson, p. 32.
17. Woodward, *The Strange Career of Jim Crow*, pp. 26–38.
18. *Ibid.*, p. 43.
19. *Ibid.*, p. 44.

CHAPTER 17
1. Hofstadter, *Social Darwinism in American Thought*, p. 33. Also see Bibliographical Note 17.
2. Durant, p. 356. Durant is a good source for a sympathetic view of Spencer.
3. Hofstadter, pp. 33, 128. Cooley and James were early admirers of Spencer, as were Pavlov and numerous other men of this era in their youth.
4. Goldman, *Rendezvous with Destiny*, Chapter 2.
5. Hofstadter, p. 45.
6. Psychologists who find these facts about so many of their revered forebears surprising should read very carefully pages 159–67 and 193 of Hofstadter, and also note the careful documentation in his notes. Most should, in fact, read the whole book.
7. *Ibid.*, p. 61.
8. Woodward, *The Strange Career of Jim Crow*, p. 105. Woodward also forcefully shows the connection between Social Darwinism and present-day Southern attitudes; see pp. 102–6.
9. *Ibid.*, p. 64. The Forgotten Man was also revived by FDR, who applied the term to the farmer, the black, and the down-and-out.
10. Some would contend that the eugenicists were a different breed, although Hofstadter finds the streams feeding one another and generally flowing together.
11. Jensen, "How Much Can We Boost IQ and Scholastic Achievement?"
12. Pettigrew, *A Profile of the Negro American*, p. 101.
13. Articles by Hunt, Cronbach, Bereiter *et al.* in *Harvard Educational Review*, Spring 1969.
14. Deutsch, "Happenings on the Way Back to the Forum," p. 67.
15. *Ibid.*
16. *Ibid.*, p. 68.
17. *Ibid.*, p. 69.
18. *Ibid.*, p. 81.
19. *Ibid.*, p. 92.
20. *Ibid.*

CHAPTER 18
1. Du Bois, *Souls of Black Folk*, pp. 45–46.
2. *Ibid.*, p. 46.
3. *Ibid.*, p. 47
4. *Ibid.*
5. *Ibid.*, p. 42.
6. *Ibid.*
7. Silberman, pp. 126–27.
8. *Ibid.*, p. 130.
9. Franklin, p. 444.

CHAPTER 19
1. Rosenthal and Jacobsen, *Pygmalion in the Classroom*, p. 11. Besides covering the authors' research, this book provides a good summary of past work and thinking on expectancy. For the linkage of this concept to cognitive dissonance theory, see pages 9–10. An unfortunate oversight is the authors' failure to mention the Lewinian work on level of aspiration or to relate it to expectancy.
2. *Ibid.*, p. 3.
3. See Myrdal, *An American Dilemma,* Chapter 3, section 7 ("The Theory of the Vicious Circle"), and Appendix 3.
4. Rosenthal and Jacobsen, p. 4.
5. It is fashionable to question the Rosenthal and Jacobsen findings, largely because of a very sharp critique by the prestigious E. L. Thorndike. A more recent paper by Rosenthal, "Teacher Expectation and Pupil Learning," summarizes thirteen experiments that followed the Oak School study which cumulatively seem to establish the classroom workings of expectancy beyond question. And to the work Rosenthal cites can be added the vast Lewinian work in level of aspiration over three decades.
6. Maslow, *Toward a Psychology of Being*, pp. 189, 193.
7. For those interested in more background on this group, see the summary of "self" theorists in Lindzey and Hall, pp. 467–502; Allport, *Becoming*; and Moustakas, *The Self.* Also see Bibliographical Note 7.
8. Mary Harrington Hall's interview with Maslow in *Psychology Today* is a revealing biographical source.
9. The most concise account of this search is Maslow's article in Moustakas's great selection of humanist pieces, *The Self.*
10. *Ibid.*, p. 164.
11. Maslow, Chapters 3, 4, 11.
12. Erikson, "Race and the Wider Identity," in Parsons and Clark, p. 231.
13. *Ibid.*, p. 230.
14. *Ibid.*, p. 232.
15. Erikson, *Identity: Youth and Crisis*, p. 303. The remaining Erikson quotes in this chapter are from the same source (pp. 299, 304, 315, 316, 317, 318, 318–19), although they may also be found in the Erikson chapter in Parsons and Clark.

CHAPTER 20

1. Du Bois, *Souls of Black Folk,* p. 23.
2. Stein, *The Eclipse of Community,* p. 5.
3. See Fanon, *The Wretched of the Earth;* Cleaver, *Soul on Ice;* and *Malcolm X Speaks,* particularly "Message to the Grass Roots," pp. 4–17.
4. Though not invariably reliable, Du Bois's perception of many large-scale social trends was uncanny. For example, see Broderick, *W. E. B. Du Bois,* pp. 38, 76, 77, 87, 103, 112, 113, 116, 119, 120.
5. Silberman, pp. 25–26.
6. *Ibid.,* pp. 125–31. Silberman's account of the struggle between Washington and Du Bois is particularly good from the viewpoint of an economist.
7. There are two sides to the matter of blacks becoming self-sufficient. For this reason, a clear differentiation must be made here between repressive *excluding* and liberative *including* black-self-sufficiency stances. An interesting example of both attitudes at work was Richard Nixon's carefully crafted campaign speech on black capitalism, which catered to the "bad" white desire to abandon the black as well as to the "good" black and white desire for black self-sufficiency.
8. Franklin, p. 421.
9. Link, *The Road to the White House,* p. 505.
10. Broderick, *W. E. B. Du Bois,* p. 96.
11. Redding, *Lonesome Road,* p. 203.
12. Woodward, *The Strange Career of Jim Crow,* pp. 92–93, and Silberman, pp. 106–7.
13. Silberman, p. 107.
14. Goldman, pp. 176–77.
15. The general social disruption of the war and other factors were undoubtedly of much greater importance, but the presidential-leadership link in this picture cannot be avoided. In addition to the impact of modeling processes that we have examined in Chapters 5 and 10, here is but a fraction of the relevant work in experimental social psychology: Lewin and associates on leadership processes (particularly relating leadership style to levels of aggression), effects of leader prestige and group-leader identification on opinion change, and group dynamics; Hovland and associates on source credibility, persuasion, and persuasibility in communication processes; Pettigrew on conformity; Adorno on the authoritarian personality; Buss and Berkowitz on frustration-aggression; Fiedler's contingency model of leadership; Bandura on the effects of filmed violence; and Bauer on the spongelike nature of the audience, waiting to hear and act upon what it *wants* to hear.
16. Duberman, *In White America,* pp. 66–67.
17. Franklin, p. 454.
18. *Ibid.,* p. 476.
19. *Ibid.,* pp. 462–63.
20. *Ibid.,* pp. 478–79.

21. *Ibid.,* pp. 479–80.
22. *Ibid.,* p. 481.

CHAPTER 21
1. Hofstadter, p. 123.
2. See Kelman, *A Time to Speak,* or Appendix B of Maslow.
3. Goldman, pp. 120–23.
4. Hofstadter, pp. 83, 164. Lester Ward fought the Social Darwinists and eugenicists wholeheartedly, but his disciple Edward Ross split his allegiance—and the fact reflects more than academic minutia. Although he was a leader of the liberal attack against Social Darwinist conservatism, Ross was swayed by and eventually accepted the eugenicists' arguments against blacks. Along with Woodrow Wilson, he must be assigned to the racist strain within the more generally nonracist thrust of formal white liberalism.
5. Goldman, p. 96.
6. *Ibid.,* p. 97.
7. See Heilbroner's *Worldly Philosophers* for excellent sketches of Henry George (pp. 155–63) and Veblen (pp. 181–213). Of Herbert Spencer's view of an unfit poor who should be eliminated, Henry George wrote: "Mr. Spencer is like one who might insist that each should swim for himself in crossing a river, ignoring the fact that some had been artificially provided with corks and others artificially loaded with lead."
8. Goldman, pp. 146–61.
9. *Ibid.,* pp. 134, 136. See Rossiter's *The Essential Lippmann* for a revealing view of the journalist as a great social scientist.
10. As the key compiler of Negro spirituals, NAACP secretary during the 1920s, and leader of the Harlem Renaissance, Johnson is an important figure in black history.
11. For those outside the social sciences, the extent of this stifling of creativity and social service is hard to conceive. Across the board, it has prompted innumerable cries of exasperation and outrage: in education, James Conant; in urban affairs, John Gardner; in history, Martin Duberman and Howard Zinn; in sociology, Lee Rainwater, Irving Horowitz, and Edgar Zaidenberg; in psychology, Warren Bennis, Kenneth Clark, Abraham Maslow, and Sigmund Koch; in psychiatry, Robert Coles; in economics, John Kenneth Galbraith and Robert Heilbroner; in politics, John Lindsay, Fred Harris, and many, many others.
12. Stein's *Eclipse of Community* is the best single source for summaries of these and other community studies.
13. Dollard, *Caste and Class in a Southern Town,* p. 33.
14. Powdermaker, *Stranger and Friend,* p. 177.
15. See Selltiz *et al., Research Methods in Social Relations,* for good summaries of the Thurstone, Likert, Moreno, and other techniques. Inspired by Gordon Allport, this unusual work is an invaluable compendium of black-advancing research of the 1930s and 1940s.

16. See Franklin, pp. 558–59, 573.

17. This list is not comprehensive, but represents those who surface most often in bibliographies covering this time.

18. There have been other big studies, but none to my knowledge that funneled the work of such a huge team through the final vision and style of *one* exceptional person. The advantage of the single-writer method has recently been demonstrated with the Carnegie Foundation's underwriting of Jeanne Chall's excellent investigation of the reading problems of American children (*Learning to Read—The Great Debate*) and by Charles Silberman's brilliant investigation of American education generally (*Crisis in the Classroom*).

19. May we urge anyone coming to this work for the first time to read the original. Condensations are tempting, and Arnold Rose's is good, but one loses the flavor of Myrdal's writing, which not only sustains interest but also, through asides and grace notes, adds much of importance.

20. A reviewer in the *American Political Science Review*.

21. Robert S. Lynd.

22. Aptheker, *The Negro People in America*, p. 66.

23. What could be more suspect than *Carnegie* money derived from the exploitation of his steelworkers by old Andrew?

24. Myrdal, *An American Dilemma*, p. lxi.

25. *Ibid.*, p. lxxi.

26. See references to Leon Festinger, Charles Osgood, and Robert Abelson in the Bibliography.

27. Myrdal, *An America Dilemma*, p. xxvi.

28. Out of 1,483 pages, Myrdal devotes all of three to historical protest prior to Du Bois's time (pp. 567, 736–38) and two to Du Bois versus Washington (pp. 742–43). There *are* chapters titled "The Negro Protest," "The Protest Motive and the "Negro Improvement and Protest Organizations," but reading them from today's perspective is quite instructive. According to Myrdal, Negro protest is a pathetic bubble that quickly bursts; the protest motive leads generally to frustration and personality aberration; and the NAACP is the ultimate in protest organizations. But, of course, this was the dominant opinion during the time of Myrdal's sampling. Here and there, however, there surface portents of the future, particularly in Myrdal's lines dealing with the effect of A. Philip Randolph's successful threat to march on Washington in 1941 if FDR didn't end job discrimination in government.

29. Parsons and Clark raise this question in *The Negro American*, p. xx, and Silberman speaks for many others, black and white, in concluding: "Myrdal was wrong. The tragedy of race relations in the United States is that there is no American Dilemma. White Americans are not torn and tortured by the conflict between their devotion to the American creed and their actual behavior. They are upset by the current state of race relations, to be sure. But what troubles them is not that justice is being denied but that their peace is being shattered and their business interrupted" (p. 10).

30. He sensed it coming, however. In particular, he accurately predicted the impact World War II would have in stimulating black protest (p. 756). In view of the rise of real protest beginning in the late forties, Myrdal's pages 1006–7, 1014–17, and 1022 are very much worth rereading.

CHAPTER 22

1. Franklin, pp. 478–79.
2. *Ibid.*, p. 484.
3. *Ibid.*
4. This is John Hope Franklin's conclusion.
5. Eldridge Cleaver is particularly good on this linkage. See "Convalescence" in *Soul on Ice*, particularly pages 203–4.
6. Cannon, *Wisdom of the Body*. Also Funkenstein, "The Psychology of Fear and Anger."
7. Lewin's presentation is buried in the difficult *A Dynamic Theory of Personality*. Dollard and Miller's elaboration in *Personality and Psychotherapy* is easier to follow.
8. Franklin, p. 49; Redding, p. 248; and Frazier are all good sources on Garvey and Father Divine.
9. A good source is the original, "The Alleviation of Poverty," pp. 190–95, in Friedman, *Capitalism and Freedom*.
10. Franklin, p. 496.
11. Some writers have shied away from the relation of the blacks to communism, probably for fear of adding to the files of the vicious rightists who hunger for such data, but it is an extremely important piece of the black story in America. One can obtain a fairly well-rounded view from Ellison's *Invisible Man*, Redding's *Lonesome Road*, Hoyt's *Paul Robeson*, Broderick's *W. E. B. Du Bois*, and various accounts by Richard Wright.
12. By and large, Hoyt's book on Robeson is not only the most reliable source but is also excellent on Russian-U.S. cold-war maneuvers, decolonization, and black-white confrontations of the time. Robeson's own *Here I Stand* is useful. Redding's *Lonesome Road* is good on both Robeson and Du Bois. For some sense of their spiritual importance to the thinking black militant, one has only to note how often Cleaver evokes the two throughout *Soul on Ice*.
13. Hoyt, p. 114.
14. Redding, p. 266.
15. *Ibid.*
16. Franklin, p. 536, and Schlesinger, *The Politics of Upheaval*, pp. 432–33, are especially useful for tracing the New Deal black-white interaction.
17. Franklin, pp. 547–38.
18. My recollection of a remark made to me by Klutznick when he was the chairman and I the coordinator of a symposium on "The Troubled Environment" sponsored in 1965 by *Time* magazine and Urban America to involve American business leaders in black and urban problems, and a precursor of the Urban Coalition.

19. Franklin said this at the signing of the Declaration of Independence, July 4, 1776. Before deciding to throw it all away and begin again, anyone now advocating the end of the great American experiment should be forced to read extensively of the hopes, fears, good wit, courage, and effort that went into merely assembling this one basic American document, let alone the vast aspiration and effort that has been invested in its enactment.

CHAPTER 23
1. Woodward, *The Burden of Southern History*, p. 126.
2. *Ibid.*
3. *Ibid.*
4. *Time* magazine, March 9, 1970, p. 10.
5. *Ibid.*
6. *New York Times*, August 24, 1970, p. 32.
7. *New York Times*, October 13, 1970, p. 1.
8. Duberman, *In White America*, p. 84.
9. Parsons and Clark, p. v.

CHAPTER 24
1. Redding, p. 186.
2. Broderick, pp. 28–88.
3. This is a rounding-out of views expressed by Du Bois over half a century in his *Autobiography, The World and Africa, Darkwater*, and many other works. The objective accuracy or inaccuracy of either this or the white world-view is secondary to their subjective power and social implications. We are now, worldwide, trying to emerge from the horrible consequences of the dominant white view that the white heritage is the civilized historical strain as opposed to the savagery of the nonwhites. Now, with its own distortions but with Old Testament justice, the compensatory antiwhite vision is on the rise.
4. See Jung, *Memories, Dreams, and Reflections*, pp. 247–49. This particular Jungian vision is one of his most eloquent and haunting, and also appears in *Modern Man in Search of a Soul*. Sartre's is his introduction to Fanon's *The Wretched of the Earth*. They demonstrate that this vision is not simply a peculiarity of the resenting black imagination but can also be obvious to the white.
5. In his capacity as a cross-cultural medium, Du Bois notably resonated to both Japanese and Chinese antiwhite drives (Broderick, pp. 195–96.)
6. Redding, p. 188.
7. Perhaps it should be noted that the vision of brotherhood is by no means exclusively black. Spinoza, Kant, Schweitzer—all whites, in fact, who have been impelled to think or feel for humanity as a whole—have expressed it. The significant difference in our time seems to be that the blacks *as a people* are beginning to gain and express this vision with great clarity (*e.g.*, Martin Luther King), while the whites *as a people*

have either lost it or lack the facility and the credibility for expressing it. One consequence is that the white who would express it (*e.g.,* Schweitzer) must align himself with the blacks.

8. Vision is so alien to most of us that it would be well to back up this two-vision contention with a thumbnail guide. Regarding the *brotherhood vision,* there is Martin Luther King's "I have a dream" speech; Douglass' letter from England, quoted in Chapter 13 of this book; the meaning of Gandhi ("I would not like to live in this world if it is not to be one," he said in 1947, not long before he was assassinated); the peace-seeking, internationalist tone of Lincoln's Second Inaugural Address (". . . with malice toward none, with charity for all . . ."). As for John Kennedy, his impact in this area was perhaps best stated after his death by *Transition,* the magazine for African intellectuals: "In this way was murdered the first real chance in this century for an intelligent and new leadership to the world." As for the *antiwhite vision,* see Douglass' famous Fourth of July speech ripping into white hypocrisy (Foner, *Selections from the Writings of Frederick Douglass,* p. 52); Malcolm X in "Message to the Grass Roots" in *Malcolm X Speaks;* Sartre's introduction to Fanon's *The Wretched of the Earth;* Fanon himself (". . . the colonized masses mock at these very values, insult them, and vomit them up"); the powerful antiwhite vision of Carl Jung; Cleaver's "The White Race and Its Heroes" in *Soul on Ice;* Du Bois's "Souls of *White* Folks" in *Darkwater.* Within psychology, the great root speculation concerning both visions is that of Father Sigmund himself. See *Beyond the Pleasure Principle* and *Civilization and Its Discontents* regarding the Eros-Thanatos struggle.

CHAPTER 25

1. Marrow, p. ix.
2. Quite significantly, no prestigious school in America offered Lewin a professorship in a department of psychology. His first post here was at Cornell in the Department of Home Economics, and the bulk of his years were spent at the University of Iowa in the Child Welfare Research Station. Nor was he ever offered the chairmanship or any other high post in any of psychology's professional societies. Moreover, when at a crucial point he needed to leave Iowa and was hopeful that the New School for Social Research in New York would make him the chairman of its department of psychology, he was rejected, apparently because he had departed from the purity of Gestalt psychology to go his own way. As Kuhn has documented in *The Structure of Scientific Revolutions,* in science the drive to exclude and repress difference is very powerful, and for all the talk of seeking "originality," only the strongest and most persistent can hope to retain or advance any appreciable differences in thought or procedure.
3. Marrow, p. 80.
4. *Ibid.,* p. 81.

5. *Ibid.,* p. 158.
6. *Ibid.*
7. *Ibid.,* p. 206.
8. *Ibid.,* pp. 214–16.
9. *Ibid.,* pp. 208–10.
10. Lewin, *Resolving Social Conflicts,* p. 214.
11. *Ibid.,* pp. 145–58.
12. A good discussion of level of aspiration in terms of both Lewin and Festinger may be found in Atkinson, *Introduction to Motivation.*
13. Marrow, pp. 205–6.
14. *Ibid.,* p. 129.
15. *Ibid.,* p. 144.
16. *Ibid.,* pp. 149–52.
17. *Ibid.,* p. 151.
18. *Ibid.*
19. This paper is Chapter 10 in Lewin's *Field Theory in Social Science.* It was also his first and last contribution to the journal *Human Relations,* which he co-founded in his last year.
20. *Ibid.,* p. 199.
21. *Ibid.,* p. 217.
22. *Ibid.,* p. 229.
23. See Erikson, *Gandhi's Truth.*
24. Lewin, *Field Theory in Social Science,* p. 228.
25. *Ibid.,* p. 206

CHAPTER 26
1. Lewin, *Field Theory in Social Science,* p. 218.
2. Marrow, p. 45.
3. *Ibid.,* p. 46.
4. *Ibid.,* p. 120.
5. *Ibid.,* p. 122
6. Marrow's book is an especially rich source of the observations and personal memories of such figures.
7. *Ibid.,* pp. 136–37.
8. *Ibid.,* pp. 219–21
9. See Lasswell, *Power and Personality,* and the sections on leadership studies in Hollander and Hunt and in Backman and Secord; most of these studies are by Lewin's students.
10. Marrow, p. 234.
11. *Ibid.,* p. 124.
12. *Ibid.,* p. 125
13. *Ibid.,* p. 127
14. *Ibid.,* p. 126.
15. However bad things may seem at times, if one examines America within the context of world history—and particularly in terms of value systems—it seems that nothing short of atomic disaster could produce the

social chaos necessary for the impositon of true authoritarian rule. Since these original studies, the field of leadership studies has mushroomed in social psychology. And replication of these studies in India did not produce the same results, indicating that one cannot safely generalize from the Lewin, Lippitt, and White studies beyond their own culture. A particularly sophisticated advancement in this area is Fred Fiedler's "contingency model," based on more than a hundred relevant studies, including Lewin's. This model indicates many refinements over the pioneering Lewinian data—that the democratic leadership approach may *not* be desirable in highly structured tasks or completely chaotic social situations, for example. See the articles by Fiedler in Hollander and Hunt and in Backman and Secord.

16. Marrow, p. 210, and Lewin, *Resolving Social Conflicts*, pp. 208–13.
17. *Ibid.*, p. 214.
18. Jane Howard's *Please Touch* is a revealing account of sensitivity training that would have both pleased and alarmed Lewin.
19. Lewin, *Resolving Social Conflicts*, p. 216.

CHAPTER 27
1. Lewin, *Resolving Social Conflicts*, p. 215.
2. Freud, *Complete Introductory Lectures in Psychoanalysis*, p. 544. We should also note that out of the interaction between Freudian-based psychiatrists and social problems has emerged the important new field of community psychiatry, in which Leonard Duhl, Gerald Caplan, and Erich Lindemann are innovators. Dumont's *The Absurd Healer* explains the approach.
3. An excellent summary of major therapies based on both Freud and Pavlov is "Therapy and Remediation," Chapter 15 in Rosenhan and London, eds., *Foundations of Abnormal Psychology*.
4. Myrdal, *Challenge to Affluence*, p. 52.
5. *Ibid.*, p. 49.
6. *Ibid.*, p. v.
7. Schlesinger, *A Thousand Days*, p. 929.

CHAPTER 28
1. Another qualitative similarity between the Reconstruction era and our time was the Senate's close victory over President Nixon on the Haynesworth and Carswell Supreme Court nominations in 1969 and 1970, an event somewhat reminiscent of the congressional rebellion against Andrew Johnson led by Stevens and Sumner in the 1860s.
2. For example, Vine Deloria, Jr.'s *We Talk, You Listen*, which adds to the information about the modern American Indian situation conveyed in his *Custer Died for Your Sins* a vision of how tribalism may save us from social death.
3. Galbraith in *The Affluent Society* and Myrdal in *Challenge to Affluence*.
4. This prescription of sacrifice is partly a result of Lewinian psychologic,

and partly a protection against the ambivalence of economists. Not too
many years ago they were telling us we were so affluent that we could
take care of the blacks out of our burgeoning surplus, but now they tell
us we are so poor that even the end of the Vietnam war will provide no
surge of funds to care for their needs. To be on the safe side, we prescribe sacrifice.

5. Toffler's *Future Shock* adds current detail to the visions of Max Weber
   and William Blake.

6. This is the idealistic view of the TV political potential, of course. For
   the obverse, see McGinnis's thoroughly unsettling *The Selling of a President 1968*.

7. Helmer, *Social Technology*.

8. Where do we put everybody? A little mathematics with average voter
   turnouts and school classrooms available will indicate more than enough
   room. And how do you train hundreds of thousands of discussion leaders? You don't; you rely on the same random access to a pool of skills
   that produce jury foremen and spontaneous leadership in small crises.

9. I am assured by computer scientists that this poses no insuperable
   problem.

10. Experts who assessed this plan in draft form generally centered on this
    as the key question: What if the poll *did* show retrogression rather than
    progress? We would contend that this plan, by incorporating expert
    opinion, by allowing workable time lags, and stressing no initial binding
    commitments, and by moving gradually toward defining social goals,
    takes into consideration the great practicalities of the Hamiltonian fears.
    But essentially it *is* a Jeffersonian proposal, in which I firmly believe.
    Unless we do something of this sort to tie in everybody, in not too many
    more years America may face rule not by the dictatorship of Orwell's
    1984 or Huxley's *Brave New World*, but by a managerial elite of a type
    somewhat like that projected by Michael Young in *The Rise of the
    Meritocracy* or by Kurt Vonnegut, Jr., in his flawed but socially percep-
    tive early novel, *Player Piano*. The decision to take advantage of televi-
    sion, computer technology, and social science to bring everybody into
    democracy should be made now. Obviously, it will take very great and
    courageous leadership in the Presidency. An important advantage of this
    proposal is that it could easily be pilot-tested in several representative
    communities. It is proposed, of course, as a hypothesis for testing, and
    the test of pilot study and expert discussion should reveal the need for
    many modifications of details. I'm convinced, however, that the main
    thrust of the proposal will bear up under attack.

11. Scammon and Wattenberg, *The Real Majority*. For example, see pp.
    75–76, which recounts a Harris poll in 1969 that found that alleviating
    poverty was number three in a list of national priority preferences.

12. Kogan and Wallach, "Risk Taking as a Function of the Situation, the
    Person, and the Group."

13. Senators Fred Harris, Walter Mondale, George McGovern, and others

have been pushing for several years to establish a Council of Social Advisers to the President, which would be tied to some form of national social goals (or indices) against which social progress might be measured, much as economic progress is measured by the Gross National Product. The Nixon administration's response, characteristically, has been the National Goals Research Staff, a token effort that by mid-1970 was still staffed by borrowing from other agencies, had no budget of its own, and had issued one mild report that caused no ripples. More promising were efforts in this direction outside the government by the Social Science Research Council, the Institute for the Future at Wesleyan under Olaf Helmer, and at the University of Michigan Survey Research Center.

14. The classic study is Sherif's extremely fascinating experiment with young campers at Robber's Cave State Park in Oklahoma. A good account may be found in Sherif's "Experiments in Group Conflict."

Bibliographical Notes

Following is a guide to authoritative and readable general references for the main categories of interest in this book. In each case, only a handful out of many possible references have been selected. The categories roughly follow the order in which the book deals with them, and the chapters that are primarily concerned with each category are indicated in parentheses. Additional references are listed in the reference notes to each chapter; publishers and publication dates will be found in the Bibliography.

1. *The use of social science as social therapy.* (Chapters 1, 23, 24, 25, 26, 27, 28) This theme has been expressed by many very articulate men; see,

especially, works in the Bibliography by William James, Kurt Lewin, Kenneth Boulding, Robert Heilbroner, and John Gardner. A particularly forceful expression is Chapter 6 of Harold Lasswell's *Power and Personality.*

2. *Experimental psychology.* (Chapters 1, 3, 25, 26) Donald Hebb's *A Textbook of Psychology* is an excellent expression of the experimentalist's rationale and *joie de vivre.* Better yet is *Frontiers of Psychological Research,* a collection of articles from *Scientific American,* or *Psychology Today* magazine and its publications. These two magazines are masterworks of communicating a difficult science with clarity, wit, and striking visual presentation.

3. *Black history and the black experience.* (Chapters 2, 4, 6, 8, 10, 12, 14, 16, 18, 20, 22) Of numerous excellent books, a good introductory package would include Charles Silberman's *Crisis in Black and White,* Martin Duberman's *In White America, The Autobiography of Malcolm X,* and Eldridge Cleaver's *Soul on Ice.* For a comprehensive black history, John Hope Franklin's *From Slavery to Freedom* is unrivaled. An invaluable short guide is William Katz's *Teacher's Guide to American Negro History.* Also, a wealth of good specific citations are included in the Reference Notes to the historical chapters of this book.

4. *Great psychologists and psychologies.* (Chapters 3, 5, 7, 9, 11, 19, 21, 25, 26) Few books present both the man and his psychology, which is the most effective and enjoyable way of gaining this knowledge. The standard Boring and Murphy histories of psychology are excellent but dated and too dry for the general reader. Lively and very good is George Miller's *Psychology,* which combines biographies of the giants—James, Freud, Galton, Pavlov, and others—with down-to-earth explanations of difficult basic concepts. John Dollard and Neal Miller's *Personality and Psychotherapy* is a particularly clear presentation of learning theory and Freudian theory and the combination of the two into a new psychotherapy. Gardner Lindzey and Calvin Hall's *Theories of Personality* is very clear and straightforward. Also generally very good is the Prentice-Hall series on specific psychologies and the series of interviews with great psychologists carried out by Richard Evans and *Psychology Today.*

5. *Sociology.* (Chapters 7, 9, 13, 17, 21, 27) Peter Berger's *Invitation to Sociology* and Alex Inkeles's *What Is Sociology?* are very good general introductions. Timothy Raison's *The Founding Fathers of Social Science* is an exceptionally informative collection of biographical and theoretical sketches by refreshingly literate British sociologists. *Trans-Action* is the leading new magazine for the activist in sociology.

6. *Psychological research relating to blacks.* (Chapters 3, 5, 7, 9, 11, 15, 19, 21, 25, 26) Social psychologist Thomas Pettigrew's *A Profile of the Negro American* is well written and the best single compilation; it includes 565

black-relevant studies. An earlier classic is Gordon Allport's very important, very readable *The Nature of Prejudice*. More recent, and excellent—but considerably more technical and difficult to read—is *Social Class, Race, and Psychological Development*, edited by Martin Deutsch, Irwin Katz, and Arthur Jensen, which covers some key research of the Great Society program years. (This book is also of interest in that it preceded the Deutsch-Jensen parting of the ways reported in Chapter 17 of this book.)

7. *Third-force or humanistic psychology*. (Chapters 5, 11, 19, 21) Rollo May's *Existential Psychology* and his superb introduction to *Existence* give the best possible perspective from the existentialist viewpoint. Abraham Maslow's *Toward a Psychology of Being*, Erich Fromm's great output (*Man for Himself* is a good example), and Erik Erikson's work (notably, in this instance, *Childhood and Society*) add other vast dimensions. An especially brilliant relating of the thinking of this field to youth and contemporary problems is the chapter titled "Toward a More Humane Society" in Kenneth Keniston's *The Uncommitted*. John Gardner's books, especially *Excellence* and *Self-Renewal*, relate this type of thought to our major contemporary problems of leadership and social reform.

8. *Freud and psychoanalytic theory*. (Chapters 1, 7, 19, 27) Ernest Jones's *Freud* is the great biography of a psychologist, and as such it is the best single source on Freud for the general reader. For a relatively short explanation of Freud's theory, his own *Outline of Psychoanalysis*, written shortly before his death in 1938, is largely unsurpassed for clarity as well as authority. Freud explains dreamwork and his sexual theory extensively in *Complete Introductory Lectures in Psychoanalysis*. An excellent guide is Lindzey and Hall's *Theories of Personality*.

9. *Cognitive dissonance theory*. (Chapters 5, 11, 13, 21) A good introductory piece on cognitive dissonance theory is Leon Festinger's article in *Frontiers of Psychological Research: Readings from the Scientific American*, edited by Stanley Coopersmith. Of numerous more advanced presentations, two useful articles by Festinger and Charles Osgood are included in *Current Perspectives in Social Psychology*, edited by Edwin Hollander and Raymond Hunt. Anyone wishing to explore this theory in more depth will find Roger Brown's *Social Psychology* a clear and engrossing guide. Other notable (and readable) balance theorists in social psychology are Lewin's old friend, Fritz Heider, Theodore Newcomb, and Robert Abelson. The theory's conceptual counterpart in anthropology and sociology emerges in Bronislaw Malinowski and appears in Talcott Parsons's work as imbalance in the pattern variables.

10. *Cognitive psychologies*. (Chapter 7) An excellent collection of papers on the background and current trends in cognitive studies is *The Cognitive Processes: Readings*, edited by Robert J. Harper *et al*. More advanced and

recent is the chapter entitled "Individual Variation in Cognitive Processes" by Jerome Kagan and Nathan Kogan in *Carmichael's Manual of Child Psychology.*

11. *Conformity studies.* (Chapter 9) Roger Brown's *Social Psychology* is especially good on conformity research, particularly in its relation to balance theoretical and risk-taking studies. The key pioneering figures are Muzafer Sherif and Solomon Asch, whose basic work is described in Chapter 9 of this book, and Richard Crutchfield, whose work is particularly interesting in relating creativity to *non*conformity.

12. *The abolitionists.* (Chapters 10, 11) Martin Duberman's *The Antislavery Vanguard,* John L. Thomas's *Slavery Attacked: The Abolitionist Crusade,* and biographies of Frederick Douglass, James Birney, and William Lloyd Garrison are good sources. See John Hope Franklin's *From Slavery to Freedom,* pp. 250–52, for a summary of the work of *black* abolitionists, who are often overlooked.

13. *Frederick Douglass.* (Chapters 8, 12, 18) Philip Foner's *The Life and Writings of Frederick Douglass* is a four-volume set that should be, along with the collected works of Abraham Lincoln, on more American bookshelves. Foner's biography of Douglass, which is included in this set, is exceptionally good, as is Benjamin Quarles's *Frederick Douglass.*

14. *Marx and Marxism.* (Chapters 13, 15, 21, 27) Edmund Wilson's *To the Finland Station* is a grand introduction. This study of the art of writing and making history by America's greatest living man of letters presents easily the best portrait of Marx and his times and tradition I have encountered. Another lively and excellent source is Robert Heilbroner's *Worldly Philosophers,* pp. 112–42. For Marx the humanist, see Erich Fromm's exceptional *Marx's Concept of Man,* which contains large chunks of the key early *Economic and Philosophical Manuscripts* and *The German Ideology.* For a cooler view of both Marx and Marxism, see Kenneth Boulding's *The Impact of the Social Sciences,* pp. 32–35, or Robert C. Tucker's *The Marxian Revolutionary Idea.*

15. *Social theories.* (Chapters 13, 15, 17, 21, 25, 26, 27) Alex Inkeles's chapter on theory in his *What Is Sociology?* (pp. 28–46) is a rare gem. A firm grasp of the nature and range of social scientific theory is something very difficult for both students and laymen to attain, and hard, too, for the professional and teacher to hold onto; but it is absolutely essential for maintaining any sure footing in this area. Other useful references are Talcott Parsons's vast collection, *Theories of Society;* Ernest Hilgard and Gordon Bower, *Theories of Learning;* George A. Miller *et al., Plans and Structure of Behavior;* and Alan Newell and Herbert Simon's "Models: Their Uses and

Limitations" in *Current Perspectives in Social Psychology*, edited by Hollander and Hunt.

16. Reconstruction. (Chapters 14, 15, 16, 17, 23) C. Vann Woodward's *The Burden of Southern History* and *The Strange Career of Jim Crow*, John Hope Franklin's history, James McPherson's exceptional studies, Lerone Bennett's *Black Power U.S.A.*, and W. E. B. Du Bois's essays—one of which is excerpted in Chapter 15 in this book—are good sources.

17. Social Darwinism. (Chapters 16, 7, 21) Richard Hofstadter's *Social Darwinism in American Thought* should be required reading for social scientists in America, whether established or in training. It extensively documents the danger to the nation of what William Shockley and Arthur Jensen represent—*i.e.*, a regression of scientists to earlier historical fixations, which then helps legitimize the regression of the nonexpert. Eric Goldman's *Rendezvous with Destiny* is also especially good for a perspective on Social Darwinism within the context of modern social reform.

18. W. E. B. Du Bois. (Chapters 14, 18, 20, 21, 22, 24) His last autobiography (he wrote three) is a great book, sprawling and wondrous, like Mark Twain's or like Jung's *Memories, Dreams, and Reflections*. Francis Broderick's is by far the best biography. Excellent Du Bois readers have been compiled by Meyer Weinberg and by Julius Lester; they are recommended over any single book by Du Bois himself since Du Bois's output was uneven and a good guide is helpful.

19. Kurt Lewin. (Chapters 25, 26, 28) One has to know a good deal about Lewin before his writing becomes engaging. Thus, the best first book is Alfred Marrow's *The Practical Theorist*, the essential biography that at last appeared twenty-three years after Lewin's death. The chapter on Lewin in Lindzey and Hall's *Theories of Personality* is the next logical step. Then Lewin's own writing—*Resolving Social Conflicts*, with its superb introduction by Gordon Allport, and *Field Theory in Social Science*—which is not easy reading but can be worth the effort.

20. Violence vs. nonviolence. (Chapters 10, 11, 13, 21, 24, 25, 26, 27, 28) Prompted by the urban riots and student bombings, fear of our corporate end has prompted numerous studies of violence. One of the first to receive widespread distribution was *Violence in America* by Hugh Davis Graham and Ted Robert Gurr. A more recent and invaluable collection of readings is Edwin Megargee and Jack Hokanson's *The Dynamics of Aggression*, which contains basic views and studies of Konrad Lorenz, Freud, Dollard and Miller, Bandura and Walters, Hovland and Sears, Sherif, the Lieberson-Silverman study of fifty years of race riots, and other essential bits of grounding. Kenneth Keniston's *Young Radicals*, pp. 247–56, offers remarkable insights. Particularly good on techniques of nonviolence is Staughton

Bibliographical Notes

Lynd's very fine collection, *Nonviolence in America,* which includes classics on the subject by John Woolman, Martin Luther King, and Rheinhold Niebuhr; Gandhi's *Autobiography; Gandhi's Truth* by Erik Erikson; *Resolving Social Conflicts* by Kurt Lewin; and articles by Martin Deutsch on international-conflict resolution and by Muzafer Sherif on his great Robber's Cave experiment, in *Frontiers of Psychological Research.*

21. *Post-World War II social therapy.* Though the historical span formally covered by this book ends with World War II, the perspective on healing takes into account the vast postwar therapeutic drive as well as earlier efforts. Following are a few sources relevant to this dramatic effort. Talcott Parsons and Kenneth Clark's *The Negro American* is a good collection covering the prevailing themes, leaders, hopes, projects, and statistics. A study in some depth of Great Society programs is Alfred Kahn's *Studies in Social Policy and Planning,* especially chapters 2 and 6. See also Matthew Dumont, *The Absurd Healer;* Irwin Katz and Patricia Gurin, *Race and the Social Sciences* (including James Coleman's staggering systems analytical study of social change); Urie Bronfenbrenner and J. C. Condry, *Two Worlds of Childhood;* Kenneth Clark, *Dark Ghetto;* Lilliam Smith, *Killers of the Dream;* Robert Coles, *Children of Crisis;* James Baldwin, *The Fire Next Time;* John Gardner, *The Recovery of Confidence;* Herbert Kelman, *A Time to Speak;* Jonathan Kozol, *Death at an Early Age; Malcolm X Speaks;* Gunnar Myrdal, *Challenge to Affluence; Report of the National Advisory Commission on Civil Disorders;* Charles Silberman, *Crisis in Black and White;* and Martin Luther King's haunting "The Role of the Behavioral Scientist in the Civil Rights Movement," with its tasteful accusations we so merited and its quiet pleas yet unanswered.

Bibliography

For the convenience of the general reader and the student, these references have, as much as possible, been pared to well-written and readily available introductory or basic texts. Texts have also been selected to include books with especially good bibliographies of more advanced materials for the specialist.

ABELSON, ROBERT P. "Modes of Resolution of Belief Dilemmas." In Backman and Secord, eds., *Problems in Social Psychology*. New York: McGraw-Hill, 1966.

———— *et al.*, eds. *Theories of Cognitive Consistency: A Sourcebook.* Chicago: Rand McNally, 1968.

ADORNO, T. W. *et al. The Authoritarian Personality.* New York: Norton, 1969.

ALEXANDER, ARCHIBALD. *A History of Colonization on the Western Coast of Africa.* Philadelphia: Martien, 1849.

ALLPORT, GORDON. *Becoming.* New Haven: Yale University Press, 1955.

————. "The Historical Background of Modern Social Psychology." In Lindzey, ed., *Handbook of Social Psychology.* Reading, Mass.: Addison-Wesley, 1968.

————. *The Nature of Prejudice.* Reading, Mass.: Addison-Wesley, 1954.

————. "The Open System in Personality Theory." In Hollander and Hunt, eds., *Current Perspectives in Social Psychology.* New York: Oxford University Press, 1967.

APTHECKER, HERBERT. *American Negro Slave Revolts.* New York: International, 1943.

————. *The Negro People in America: A Critique of Gunnar Myrdal's "An American Dilemma."* New York: International, 1946.

ARENDT, HANNAH. *On Revolution.* New York: Viking, 1963.

ASCH, SOLOMON. "Opinions and Social Pressures." In Coopersmith, ed., *Frontiers of Psychological Research.* San Francisco: Freeman, 1964.

ATKINSON, JOHN W. *An Introduction to Motivation.* Princeton, N.J.: Van Nostrand, 1964.

BACKMAN, CARL, and SECORD, PAUL, eds. *Problems in Social Psychology: Selected Readings.* New York: McGraw-Hill, 1966.

BALDWIN, JAMES. *The Fire Next Time.* New York: Dial, 1963.

BANDURA, ALBERT. "Psychotherapy as a Learning Process." In Staats, ed., *Human Learning.* New York: Holt, Rinehart & Winston, 1964.

BARTLETT, FREDERIC C. *Remembering: A Study in Experimental and Social Psychology.* Cambridge: Cambridge University Press, 1932.

BEARDSLEE, DAVID, and WERTHEIMER, MICHAEL. *Readings in Perception.* Princeton, N.J.: Van Nostrand, 1958.

BENNETT, LERONE. *Black Power U.S.A.: The Human Side of Reconstruction, 1867-1877.* New York: Johnson, 1967.

BERELSON, BERNARD. *The Behavioral Sciences Today.* New York: Basic Books, 1963.

———— and STEINER, GARY. *Human Behavior.* New York: Harcourt, Brace & World, 1964.

BERGER, PETER. *Invitation to Sociology: A Humanistic Perspective.* New York: Doubleday, 1968.

BERKOWITZ, LEONARD. *Aggression: A Social Psychological Analysis.* New York: McGraw-Hill, 1962.

BERNAYS, EDWARD. *Public Relations.* Norman, Okla.: University of Oklahoma Press, 1952.

BOULDING, KENNETH. *The Impact of the Social Sciences.* New Brunswick, N.J.: Rutgers University Press, 1966.

BRODERICK, FRANCIS. *W. E. B. Du Bois*. Stanford, Calif.: Stanford University Press, 1959.

BRONFENBRENNER, URIE, and CONDRY, J. C., JR. *Two Worlds of Childhood*. Russell Sage Foundation, 1970.

BROWN, ROGER. *Social Psychology*. New York: Free Press, 1965.

BRUNER, JEROME. "On Perceptual Readiness." In Harper *et al.*, eds., *The Cognitive Processes*. Englewood Cliffs, N.J.: Prentice-Hall, 1964.

BRUYN, SEVERYN. *The Human Perspective in Sociology: The Methodology of Participant Observation*. Englewood Cliffs, N.J.: Prentice-Hall, 1966.

BRYAN, JAMES. "Actions Speak Louder Than Words: Model Inconsistency and Its Effects on Self-Sacrifice." *Research Bulletin 68-16*, Educational Testing Service, Princeton, N.J.

———. "Models and Helping: Naturalistic Studies in Helping Behavior." *Journal of Personality and Social Psychology*, 1967, Vol. 6, pp. 400–7.

CADY, EDWIN. *John Woolman*. New York: Washington Square Press, 1966.

CANNON, WALTER. *The Wisdom of the Body*. New York: Norton, 1932.

CANTRIL, HADLEY. "The Human Design." In Hollander and Hunt, eds., *Current Perspectives in Social Psychology*. New York: Oxford University Press, 1967.

CARNEIRO, ROBERT, ed. *The Evolution of Society: Selections from Herbert Spencer's Principles of Sociology*. Chicago: University of Chicago Press, 1967.

CASTELL, ALBUREY. *An Introduction to Modern Philosophy*. New York: Macmillan, 1946.

CLARK, KENNETH. *Dark Ghetto*. New York: Harper & Row, 1965.

CLEAVER, ELDRIDGE. *Soul on Ice*. New York: McGraw-Hill, 1968.

COLES, ROBERT. *Children of Crisis*. Boston: Little, Brown, 1967.

COLLIER, JOHN. *Indians of the Americas*. New York: Norton, 1947.

CONANT, JAMES B. *Slums and Suburbs*. New York: McGraw-Hill, 1961.

COOPERSMITH, STANLEY, ed. *Frontiers of Psychological Research: Readings from Scientific American*. San Francisco: Freeman, 1964.

DAVIS, DAVID B. *The Problem of Slavery in Western Culture*. Ithaca, N.Y.: Cornell University Press, 1966.

DAVIS, JOHN D., ed. *The American Negro Reference Book*. Englewood Cliffs, N.J.: Prentice-Hall, 1966.

DAVIDSON, BASIL. *The Lost Cities of Africa*. Boston: Little, Brown, 1959.

DELORIA, VINE. *We Talk, You Listen*. New York: Macmillan, 1970.

DEMBER, WILLIAM. *Psychology of Perception*. New York: Holt, Rinehart & Winston, 1960.

DEUTSCH, MARTIN. "Happenings on the Way Back to the Forum." In *Science, Heritability and IQ*. Harvard Educational Review Reprint Series No. 4, 1969.

———, KATZ, IRWIN, and JENSEN, ARTHUR, eds. *Social Class, Race, and Psychological Development*. New York: Holt, Rinehart & Winston, 1968.

DOLLARD, JOHN. *Caste and Class in a Southern Town*. New York: Doubleday, 1957.

——— *et al. Frustration and Aggression.* New Haven: Yale University Press, 1939.

——— and MILLER, NEAL. *Personality and Psychotherapy.* New York: McGraw-Hill, 1950.

DOUGLASS, FREDERICK. *Narrative of the Life of Frederick Douglass, An American Slave.* New York: New American Library, 1968.

DUBERMAN, MARTIN, ed. *The Antislavery Vanguard: New Essays on the Abolitionists.* Princeton, N. J.: Princeton University Press, 1965.

———. *In White America.* New York: New American Library, 1965.

DU BOIS, W. E. B. *Autobiography: A Soliloquy on Viewing My Life from the Last Decade of Its First Century.* New York: International, 1968.

———. *Darkwater.* New York: Schocken, 1969.

———. *Souls of Black Folk.* New York: Fawcett, 1961.

———. *The World and Africa.* New York: International, 1965.

DUMONT, MATTHEW. *The Absurd Healer: Perspectives of a Community Psychiatrist.* New York: Science House, 1968.

DURANT, WILL. *The Story of Philosophy.* New York: Washington Square Press, 1952.

DURKHEIM, ÉMILE. *The Rules of Sociological Method.* New York: Free Press, 1964.

ELKINS, STANLEY. *Slavery: A Problem in American Institutional and Intellectual Life* (2nd ed.). Chicago: University of Chicago Press, 1968.

ELLISON, RALPH. *Invisible Man.* New York: Random House, 1947.

ERIKSON, ERIK. *Childhood and Society.* New York: Norton, 1963.

———. *Gandhi's Truth: On the Origins of Militant Nonviolence.* New York: Norton, 1969.

———. *Identity: Youth and Crisis.* New York: Norton, 1968.

EVANS, RICHARD. *Conversations with Carl Jung.* Princeton, N.J.: Van Nostrand, 1964.

FANON, FRANTZ. *The Wretched of the Earth.* New York: Grove, 1968.

FARB, PETER. *Man's Rise to Civilization as Shown by the Indians of North America, from Primeval Times to the Coming of the Industrial State.* New York: Dutton, 1968.

FESTINGER, LEON. "Cognitive Dissonance." In Coopersmith, ed., *Frontiers of Psychological Research.* San Francisco: Freeman, 1964.

———. "An Introduction to the Theory of Dissonance." In Hollander and Hunt, eds., *Perspectives in Social Psychology.* New York: Oxford University Press, 1967.

FEUER, LEWIS. *Conflict of Generations.* New York: Basic Books, 1969.

FISCHER, LOUIS. *The Life of Mahatma Gandhi.* New York: Harper, 1950.

FLADELAND, BETTY. *James Gillespie Birney: Slaveholder and Abolitionist.* Ithaca, N.Y.: Cornell University Press, 1955.

FLÜGEL, JOHN CARL. *Man, Morals, and Society.* New York: International Universities Press, 1945.

FONER, PHILIP, ed. *The Life and Writings of Frederick Douglass* (4 vols.). New York: International, 1964.

————. *Selections from the Writings of Frederick Douglass*. New York: International, 1964.

FRANKLIN, JOHN HOPE. *From Slavery to Freedom* (3rd ed.). New York: Knopf, 1967.

————. "The Search for a Black Past." *Life* magazine, November 22, 1968.

FRAZIER, E. FRANKLIN. *The Negro Church in America*. New York: Schocken, 1964.

FREUD, SIGMUND. *Civilization and Its Discontents*. New York: Norton, 1962.

————. *Complete Introductory Lectures in Psychoanalysis*. New York: Norton, 1966.

————. *The Interpretation of Dreams*. New York: Basic Books, 1955.

————. *An Outline of Psychoanalysis*. New York: Norton, 1949.

FRIEDMAN, MILTON. *Capitalism and Freedom*. Chicago: University of Chicago Press, 1962.

FROMM, ERICH. *The Art of Loving*. New York: Harper, 1956.

————. *Man for Himself*. New York: Holt, Rinehart & Winston, 1947.

————. *Marx's Concept of Man*. New York: Ungar, 1961.

FUNKENSTEIN, DANIEL. "The Physiology of Fear and Anger." In Coopersmith, ed., *Frontiers of Psychological Research*. San Francisco: Freeman, 1964.

GALBRAITH, JOHN KENNETH. *The Affluent Society* (2nd ed.). Boston: Houghton Mifflin, 1969.

GANDHI, MOHANDAS K. *Autobiography*. Washington, D.C.: Public Affairs Press, 1948.

GARDNER, JOHN. *Excellence*. New York: Harper, 1961.

————. *The Recovery of Confidence*. New York: Norton, 1969.

————. *Self-Renewal*. New York: Harper & Row, 1964.

GOLDMAN, ERIC. *Rendezvous with Destiny*. New York: Knopf, 1952.

GRAHAM, HUGH D., and GURR, TED R. *Violence in America: Historical and Comparative Perspectives*. New York: New American Library, 1969.

GRIER, WILLIAM, and COBBS, PRICE. *Black Rage*. New York: Basic Books, 1968.

HAGEMAN, JOHN. *History of Princeton and Its Institutions* (2 vols.). Philadelphia: Lippincott, 1879.

HALL, MARY HARRINGTON. "A Conversation with Abraham Maslow." *Psychology Today*, July 1968.

HARPER, ROBERT J. et al., eds. *The Cognitive Processes: Readings*. Englewood Cliffs, N.J.: Prentice-Hall, 1964.

HEBB, DONALD. A *Textbook of Psychology*. Philadelphia: Saunders, 1958.

HEILBRONER, ROBERT. *The Great Ascent*. New York: Harper & Row, 1963.

————. *The Worldly Philosophers* (rev. ed.). New York: Simon & Schuster, 1967.

HELMER, OLAF. *Social Technology*. New York: Basic Books, 1966.

HILGARD, ERNEST, and MARQUIS, D. G. *Conditioning and Learning* (2nd ed.), Gregory Kimble, ed. New York: Appleton, 1961.

HILGARD, ERNEST, and BOWER, GORDON. *Theories of Learning*. New York: Appleton, 1956.

HOCHBERG, JULIAN. *Perception.* Englewood Cliffs, N.J.: Prentice-Hall, 1964.

HOFSTADTER, RICHARD. *Social Darwinism in American Thought.* Boston: Beacon, 1955.

HOLLANDER, EDWIN, and HUNT, RAYMOND, eds. *Current Perspectives in Social Psychology* (2nd ed.). New York: Oxford University Press, 1967.

HOVLAND, CARL, and JANIS, IRVING, eds. *Personality and Persuasibility.* New Haven: Yale University Press, 1959.

HOVLAND, CARL, and KELLEY, HAROLD. *Communication and Persuasion.* New Haven: Yale University Press, 1953.

HOWARD, JANE. *Please Touch.* New York: McGraw-Hill, 1970.

HOYT, EDWIN. *Paul Robeson, the American Othello.* New York: World, 1967

HUGHES, H. STUART. *Consciousness and Society.* New York: Knopf, 1958.

HULL, CLARK. "Knowledge and Purpose as Habit Mechanisms." In Staats, ed., *Human Learning.* New York: Holt, Rinehart & Winston, 1964.

INKELES, ALEX. *What Is Sociology?* Englewood Cliffs, N.J.: Prentice-Hall, 1964.

JAMES, WILLIAM. *The Principles of Psychology.* New York: Dover, 1950.

JEFFERSON, THOMAS. *Notes on the State of Virginia.* William Peden, ed. Chapel Hill, N.C.: University of North Carolina Press, 1955.

JENSEN, ARTHUR. "How Much Can We Boost IQ and Scholastic Achievement?" *Harvard Educational Review,* Winter 1969. (Some responses to this article by psychologists, sociologists, biologists, educators, and other experts can be found in the Spring 1969 and Summer 1969 *Harvard Educational Review* and the Autumn 1969 *Journal of Social Issues.*)

———. "Social Class and Verbal Learning." In Deutsch, *et al.,* eds., *Social Class, Race, and Psychological Development.* New York: Holt, Rinehart & Winston, 1968.

JONES, ERNEST. *Life and Work of Sigmund Freud.* New York: Basic Books, 1961.

JORDAN, W. D. *White Over Black.* Chapel Hill, N.C.: University of North Carolina Press, 1968.

JUNG, CARL. *Memories, Dreams, and Reflections.* New York: Random House, 1961.

KAGAN, JEROME, and KOGAN, NATHAN. "Individual Variation in Cognitive Processes." In P. H. Mussen, ed., *Carmichael's Manual of Child Psychology* (3rd ed.). New York: Wiley, 1960.

KAHN, ALFRED. *Studies in Social Policy and Planning.* New York: Russell Sage Foundation, 1969.

KATZ, IRWIN, and GURIN, PATRICIA. *Race and the Social Sciences.* New York: Basic Books, 1969

KATZ, WILLIAM. *Teacher's Guide to American Negro History.* Chicago: Quadrangle, 1968.

KAUFMAN, WALTER. *Hegel: A Reinterpretation.* New York: Doubleday, 1965.

KELMAN, HERBERT. *A Time to Speak: On Human Values and Social Research.* San Francisco: Jossey-Bass, 1968.

———. "The Induction of Attitude Change." In Backman and Secord, eds., *Problems in Social Psychology*. New York: McGraw-Hill, 1966.

KENDLER, HOWARD, and KENDLER, TRACY. "Vertical and Horizontal Processes in Problem-Solving." In Harper, *et al.*, eds., *The Cognitive Processes*. Englewood Cliffs, N.J.: Prentice-Hall, 1964.

KENISTON, KENNETH. *The Uncommitted: Alienated Youth in American Society*. New York: Harcourt, Brace & World, 1965.

———. *Young Radicals*. New York: Harcourt, Brace & World, 1968.

KENNEDY, JOHN F. *Profiles in Courage*. New York: Harper & Row, 1964.

KING, MARTIN LUTHER. "The Role of the Behavioral Scientist in the Civil Rights Movement." *The American Psychologist*, March 1968.

KOCH, SIGMUND. "Psychology Cannot Be a Coherent Science." *Psychology Today*, September 1969.

KOGAN, NATHAN, and WALLACH, MICHAEL. "Risk Taking as a Function of the Situation, the Person, and the Group." In *New Directions in Psychology III*. New York: Holt, Rinehart & Winston, 1967.

KOHL, HERBERT. *Thirty-Six Children*. New York: New American Library, 1967.

KOHLER, WOLFGANG. *The Mentality of Apes*. New York: Random House, 1959.

———. *The Task of Gestalt Psychology*. Princeton, N.J.: Princeton University Press, 1969.

KOTZ, N. K. *Let Them Eat Promises: The Politics of Hunger in America*. Englewood Cliffs, N.J.: Prentice-Hall, 1970.

KOZOL, JONATHAN. *Death at an Early Age*. Boston: Houghton Mifflin, 1967.

KUHN, THOMAS. *The Structure of Scientific Revolutions*. Chicago: University of Chicago Press, 1962.

LAMBERT, WILLIAM, and LAMBERT, WALLACE. *Social Psychology*. Englewood Cliffs, N.J.: Prentice-Hall, 1964.

LASSWELL, HAROLD. *Politics: Who Gets What, When, How*. New York: World, 1958.

———. *Power and Personality*. New York: Viking, 1962.

LEWIN, KURT. *A Dynamic Theory of Personality*. New York: McGraw-Hill, 1935.

———. *Field Theory in Social Science*. New York: Harper, 1951.

———. *Resolving Social Conflicts*. New York: Harper, 1948.

LINDZEY, GARDNER, ed. *Handbook of Social Psychology* (2 vols., 2nd ed.). Reading, Mass.: Addison-Wesley, 1968.

——— and HALL, CALVIN. *Theories of Personality: Primary Sources and Research*. New York: Wiley, 1965.

LINK, ARTHUR. *The Road to the White House*. Princeton, N.J.: Princeton University Press, 1947.

LYND, STAUGHTON, ed. *Nonviolence in America: A Documentary History*. New York: Bobbs-Merrill, 1965.

———. *Reconstruction*. New York: Harper & Row, 1967.

MALCOLM X, with ALEX HALEY. *The Autobiography of Malcolm X*. New York: Grove, 1966.

————. *Malcolm X Speaks.* George Breitman, ed. New York: Grove, 1967.

MARROW, ALFRED. *The Practical Theorist: The Life and Work of Kurt Lewin.* New York: Basic Books, 1969.

MARX, KARL. *Capital.* New York: Modern Library.

———— and ENGELS, FRIEDRICH. *The Civil War in the United States.* New York: Citadel, 1961.

————. *The German Ideology.* New York: International, 1947.

MASLOW, ABRAHAM. *Toward a Psychology of Being* (2nd ed.). Princeton, N.J.: Van Nostrand, 1968.

———— and MITTELMAN, BELA. *Principles of Abnormal Psychology* (rev. ed.). New York: Harper, 1951.

MAY, ROLLO. *Man's Search for Himself.* New York: Norton, 1953.

————, ed. *Existential Psychology.* New York: Random House, 1961.

———— et al., eds. *Existence: A New Dimension in Psychiatry and Psychology.* New York: Basic Books, 1958.

McCLELLAND, DAVID. *The Achieving Society.* Princeton, N.J.: Van Nostrand, 1961.

McGINNESS, JOE. *The Selling of the President 1968.* New York: Trident, 1969.

McPHERSON, JAMES. "Many Abolitionists Fought on After the Civil War." *University: A Princeton Quarterly,* Winter 1968–69.

————. *The Struggle for Equality: Abolitionists and the Negro in the Civil War and Reconstruction.* Princeton, N.J.: Princeton University Press, 1964.

MEDNICK, SARNOFF. *Learning.* Englewood Cliffs, N.J.: Prentice-Hall, 1964.

MEGARGEE, EDWIN, and HOKANSON, JACK, eds. *The Dynamics of Aggression: Individual, Group, and International.* New York: Harper & Row, 1970.

MILLER, GEORGE A. *Psychology: The Science of Mental Life.* New York: Harper & Row, 1962.

———— et al. *Plans and the Structure of Behavior.* New York: Holt, Rinehart & Winston, 1960.

MOUSTAKAS, CLARK, ed. *The Self: Explorations in Personal Growth.* New York: Harper, 1956.

MYRDAL, GUNNAR. *An American Dilemma* (rev. ed.). New York: Harper & Row, 1962.

————. *Challenge to Affluence.* New York: Random House, 1965.

NEWELL, ALAN, and SIMON, HERBERT. "Models: Their Uses and Limitations." In Hollander and Hunt, eds., *Current Perspectives in Social Psychology* (1st ed.). New York: Oxford University Press.

OLDS, JAMES. "Pleasure Centers in the Brain." In Coopersmith, ed., *Frontiers of Psychological Research.* San Francisco: Freeman, 1964.

OSGOOD, CHARLES E. "Cognitive Dynamics in the Conduct of Human Affairs" and "On the Nature of Meaning." In Hollander and Hunt, eds., *Current Perspectives in Social Psychology.* New York: Oxford University Press, 1967.

———— and TANNENBAUM, PERCY. *The Measurement of Meaning.* Urbana, Ill.: University of Illinois Press, 1967.

PARETO, VILFRED. *Sociological Writings*. Samuel E. Finer, ed. New York: Praeger, 1966.

PARSONS, TALCOTT, *et al.*, eds. *Theories of Society*. New York: Free Press, 1965.

—— and CLARK, KENNETH, eds. *The Negro American*. Boston: Beacon, 1967.

PETTIGREW, THOMAS. *A Profile of the Negro American*. Princeton, N.J.: Van Nostrand, 1964.

——. "Personality and Sociocultural Factors in Intergroup Attitudes." In Backman and Secord, eds., *Problems in Social Psychology*. New York: McGraw-Hill, 1966.

POWDERMAKER, HORTENSE. *Stranger and Friend: The Way of an Anthropologist*. New York: Norton, 1966.

QUARLES, BENJAMIN. *Frederick Douglass*. New York: Atheneum, 1968.

——. *Lincoln and the Negro*. New York: Oxford University Press, 1962.

RAISON, TIMOTHY, ed. *The Founding Fathers of Social Science*. Baltimore: Penguin, 1969.

RAZRAN, GREGORY. "Semantic Conditioning" and "The Orienting Reflex." In Harper *et al.*, eds., *The Cognitive Processes*. Englewood Cliffs, N.J.: Prentice-Hall, 1964.

REDDING, SAUNDERS. *Lonesome Road: The Story of the Negro in America*. New York: Doubleday, 1968.

REICH, CHARLES. *The Greening of America*. New York: Random House, 1970.

Report of the National Advisory Commission on Civil Disorders. New York: Dutton, 1968.

ROBESON, PAUL. *Here I Stand*. New York: McClelland, 1958.

ROSENHAN, DAVID. "The Natural Socialization of Altruistic Autonomy." In J. Macaulay and Leonard Berkowitz, eds., *Altruism and Helping*. New York: Academic Press, 1969.

——. "Some Origins of Concern for Others." In P. H. Mussen *et al.*, eds., *Trends and Issues in Developmental Psychology*. New York: Holt, Rinehart & Winston, 1969.

—— and LONDON, PERRY, eds. *Foundations of Abnormal Psychology*. New York: Holt, Rinehart & Winston, 1968.

ROSENTHAL, ROBERT. "Teacher Expectation and Pupil Learning." A paper prepared for "The Unstudied Curriculum," sponsored by the Association for Supervision and Curriculum Development, Washington, D.C., January 8–11, 1969.

—— and JACOBSEN, LENORE. *Pygmalion in the Classroom: Teacher Expectations and Pupils' Intellectual Ability*. New York: Holt, Rinehart & Winston, 1968.

ROSSITER, CLINTON. *The American Presidency* (rev. ed.). New York: New American Library, 1960.

—— and LARE, JAMES, eds. *The Essential Lippmann*. New York: Random House, 1963.

RUCHAMES, LOUIS, ed. *The Abolitionists: A Collection of Their Writings.* New York: Putnam, 1963.

SALK, ERWIN. *A Layman's Guide to Negro History.* New York: McGraw-Hill, 1967.

SANDBURG, CARL. *Abraham Lincoln: The Prairie Years* and *The War Years* (6 vols.). New York: Harcourt, Brace & World, 1939.

SCAMMON, RICHARD, and WATTENBERG, BEN. *The Real Majority.* New York: Coward-McCann, 1970.

SCHLESINGER, ARTHUR M., JR. *The Politics of Upheaval.* Boston: Houghton Mifflin, 1960.

————. *A Thousand Days.* Boston: Houghton Mifflin, 1965.

SCHRAG, PETER. *Village School Downtown.* Boston: Beacon, 1967.

SELLTIZ, CLAIRE, *et al. Research Methods in Social Relations* (rev. ed.). New York: Holt, Rinehart & Winston, 1959.

SHERIF, MUZAFER. "On the Relevance of Social Psychology." *American Psychologist,* February 1970.

————. "Experiments in Group Conflict." In Coopersmith, ed., *Frontiers of Psychological Research.* San Francisco: Freeman, 1964.

SILBERMAN, CHARLES. *Crisis in Black and White.* New York: Random House, 1964.

SKINNER, B. F. *Walden Two.* New York: Macmillan, 1969.

————. "Teaching Machines" and "How to Teach Animals." In Coopersmith, ed., *Frontiers of Psychological Research.* San Francisco, Freeman, 1964.

SMITH, LILLIAN. *Killers of the Dream* (rev. ed.). New York, Norton, 1961.

SOROKIN, PITRIM. *Sociological Theories of Today.* New York: Harper & Row, 1966.

STAATS, ARTHUR, ed. *Human Learning: Studies Extending Conditioning Principles to Complex Behavior.* New York: Holt, Rinehart & Winston, 1964.

STAGNER, ROSS, and KARWOSKI, T. F. *Psychology.* New York: McGraw-Hill, 1952.

STEIN, MAURICE. *The Eclipse of Community: An Interpretation of American Studies.* New York: Harper & Row, 1964.

THOMAS, JOHN L. *The Liberator: William Lloyd Garrison.* Boston: Little, Brown, 1963.

————, ed. *Slavery Attacked: The Abolitionist Crusade.* Englewood Cliffs, N.J.: Prentice-Hall, 1965.

TOFFLER, ALVIN. *Future Shock.* New York: Random House, 1970.

TOMKINS, SILVAN. "The Psychology of Knowledge." In Silvan Tomkins and Carroll Izard, *Affect, Cognition, and Personality.* New York: Springer, 1965.

TUCKER, ROBERT C. *The Marxian Revolutionary Idea.* New York: Norton, 1969.

Urban America, Inc., and the Urban Coalition. *One Year Later.* New York: Praeger, 1969.

VAN EVERY, DALE. *Disinherited: The Lost Birthright of the American Indian.* New York: Morrow, 1966.

VECOLI, R. *The People of New Jersey.* Princeton, N.J.: Van Nostrand, 1965.

WATSON, JOHN. *Behaviorism.* New York: Norton, 1970.

——— and RAYNER, ROSALIE. "Conditioned Emotional Reactions." In Staats, ed., *Human Learning.* New York: Holt, Rinehart & Winston, 1964.

WEINBERG, MEYER, ed. *W. E. B. Du Bois Reader.* New York: Harper & Row, 1970.

WERTHEIMER, MAX. *Productive Thinking* (rev. ed.). New York, Harper & Row, 1970.

WHITMAN, ALDEN. "Ho Chi Minh." *New York Times,* September 4, 1969, p. 17.

WILLIS, R. H. "The Basic Response Mode of Conformity, Independence, and Anticonformity." In Hollander and Hunt, eds., *Current Perspectives in Social Psychology.* New York: Oxford University Press, 1967.

WILSON, EDMUND. "Abraham Lincoln: The Union as Religious Mysticism." In *Eight Essays.* New York: Doubleday, 1954.

———. *To the Finland Station.* New York: Doubleday, 1953.

WOODWARD, C. VANN. *The Burden of Southern History* (rev. ed.). New Orleans: Louisiana State University Press, 1968.

———. *The Strange Career of Jim Crow* (rev. ed.). New York: Oxford University Press, 1966.

WOOLDRIDGE, DEAN. *Machinery of the Brain.* New York: McGraw-Hill, 1963.

WOOLMAN, JOHN. *The Journal and Essays of John Woolman.* Amelia Gummere, ed. New York: Macmillan, 1922.

Index

369

Flight-fight response, 241
Folkways, 176
Ford, Henry, 29
Foreman, Clark, 247
Fox, John, 47
Frankfurter, Felix, 247
Franklin, Benjamin, 41–42, 58, 249
Franklin, John Hope, 103, 193, 227
Frazier, E. Franklin, 226, 227
Free African Society, 53, 56
Freedmen's Bureau, 146–53, 157, 163, 178, 257–58
  historical background of, 155
  see also Reconstruction
French, John, 278–79, 292
Frenkel-Brunswik, Else, 228
Freud, Sigmund, 45, 46, 47, 48, 63–70, 86, 88, 89, 92, 110, 114, 121, 157, 158, 175, 176, 200, 201, 202, 205, 217, 226, 269, 292, 302, 305, 308
  see also Psychology
Friedman, Milton, 319
Fromm, Erich, 45, 200, 228, 308
From Slavery to Freedom, 227
"Frontiers in Group Dynamics," 280
Frustration, aggression and, 157–60, 287–89, 294, 318
Frustration-regression effect, 288

Galbraith, John Kenneth, 309
Galton, Francis, 175–76, 179, 185
Gandhi, Mahatma, 45, 120, 121, 208, 210, 237, 264–65, 283, 308
Gandhi's Truth, 121
Gardner, Burleigh, 226
Gardner, John, 36, 257, 275, 316
Gardner, Mary, 226
Garrett, Henry, 179
Garrison, Wendell Phillips, 167
Garrison, William Lloyd, 105, 106–7, 111–12, 116–19, 124, 125, 126, 165, 193, 256
Garvey, Marcus, 242–43
George, Henry, 223
Gestalt psychology, *see* Psychology
Ghettos, 159–60
Gift of Black Folk, The, 227
Gilbert, Emily, 272

Golding, William, 295
Goldstein, Kurt, 200
Goodman, Benny, 241
Grant, Ulysses S., 169
Great Society, 146, 147, 155, 157, 247, 257–58, 305
Greeley, Horace, 127, 167
Greening of America, The, 308
Grier, William, 68
Griffith, D. W., 216–17
Group
  decision, 289, 320
  dynamics, 276–80
  strength, 273–75, 282
Guasimas, battle of, 215
Guevara, Che, 138

Haiti, 57, 189, 219
Hall, G. Stanley, 176
Hamilton, Alexander, 41, 313
Handlin, Oscar, 228
Harlem Renaissance, 240–42
Harpers Ferry, 106, 107, 192, 193
Harper's Weekly, 167, 168
Hartley, E. L., 228
Harvard Educational Review, 179, 180, 181
"Harvard Test of Inflected Acquisition," 197
Hayes, Rutherford B., 13, 166–67, 170, 256, 259
Head Start programs, 37, 178, 182–83
Hebb, Donald, 31, 142
Hegel, Georg Friedrich, 37, 134, 188
Heider, Fritz, 48, 232
Heller, Walter, 317
Hemmings, Sally, 60
Henderson, Leon, 247
Henle, Mary, 289
Herskovitz, Melville, 227
Higginson, Thomas Wentworth, 170–71
Hill, James J., 175
"Historical Background of Modern Social Psychology, The," 93
History, 12, 13, 14–15, 16–17, 110, 188, 223
  conflict v. consensus theory of, 141–42

380

INDEX

(Social science, con't.)
  Myrdal and the American Creed, 228–38
  bureaucratization in, effects of, 225
  conflict and compromise models of social processes, 141–44, 155–56, 233
    Marxist and Spencerian strains compared, 156–57
  equilibrium, social tendency toward, 156, 233
  motivation through ideas and, 49
  New Deal programs and, 246–47
  organism, society as (Spencer), 156
  Social Darwinism and, 174, 178–79
  specialization and professionalism in, 224–25
  Spencer's contribution to, 174
  at turn of the century, 221–25
  see also individual concepts and sciences
Society, *see* Social science
Society for the Psychological Study of Social Issues, 184
Sociology, 45, 65, 67, 77, 92, 110, 132, 176, 222, 232
Solidarity, 92, 93, 94
"Some Considerations on the Keeping of Negroes," 35
Sorokin, Pitrim, 45, 92
Souls of Black Folk, The, 192
"Southern strategy," 13, 256
Spanish-American War, 215
Spencer, Herbert, 142, 155–56, 157, 173–74, 181, 191, 222, 280
  see also Darwinism, Social
Spinoza, Baruch, 12, 65
Springfield (Ill.), 1908 riot in, 193–94
Stalin, Joseph, 45
Steffens, Lincoln, 224
Stevens, Thaddeus, 127, 162, 163, 164, 167, 306, 307
Stewart, T. McCants, 171
Stimulus deprivation, 31
Stockton, Robert, 61
Stouffer, Samuel, 227–28
Stowe, Harriet Beecher, 105, 127

Strange Career of Jim Crow, The, 170, 171
Stranger and Friend, 226–27
Structuralism, 47, 48
Suggestibility, 92
Sullivan, Joe, 241
Sumner, Charles, 127, 162, 163, 164, 167, 307
Sumner, William Graham, 176–77, 222
Suppression of the Slave Trade, The, 262
Supreme Court, U.S., 166, 235, 236, 255, 256, 259
  and Reconstruction civil rights legislation, 169
Sweet, O. H., 240
Systems, theory of, 199

Taft, William Howard, 215, 216
Tarbell, Ida, 224
Tarde, Gabriel, 92
Teaching, "discovery" method of, 85
Teschmacher, Frank, 241
Then and Now, 227
Theory of the Leisure Class, 223
Thinking, process of, 83, 87–91
  Osgood's studies in, 89–90
Thoreau, Henry David, 105
Thorndike, Edward, 28, 29, 170
Thurmond, Strom, 166, 256
Thurstone, Louis L., 226, 227
Tilden, Samuel, 166
Tolman, Edward, 269, 289
Tomkins, Silvan, 46, 110–12, 114–19, 120, 121, 135
Toomer, Jean, 241
Totalism, 207, 209
Treischke, Heinrich von, 213
Trotter, Monroe, 218
Truman, Harry S., 169, 253
Truth, Sojourner, 308
Tubman, Harriet, 308
Tugwell, Rexford, 247, 319
Turner, Frederick Jackson, 223
Turner, Nat, 105, 189, 190, 207

Uncle Tom's Cabin, 105
Underground Railroad, 103, 192
United States v. *Cruickshank,* 169
United States v. *Reese,* 169